T0146256

American Civil-Military Relations

American Civil-Military Relations

The Soldier and the State in a New Era

Edited by
Suzanne C. Nielsen
and
Don M. Snider

The Johns Hopkins University Press
Baltimore

The Johns Hopkins University Press
2715 North Charles Street
Baltimore, Maryland 21218-4363
www.press.jhu.edu

Library of Congress Cataloging-in-Publication Data

Nielsen, Suzanne C.
   American civil-military relations : the soldier and the state
in a new era / Suzanne C. Nielsen, Don M. Snider.
      p. cm.
   Includes bibliographical references and index.
   ISBN-13: 978-0-8018-9287-5 (hardcover : alk. paper)
   ISBN-10: 0-8018-9287-2 (hardcover : alk. paper)
   ISBN-13: 978-0-8018-9288-2 (pbk. : alk. paper)
   ISBN-10: 0-8018-9288-0 (pbk. : alk. paper)
1. Civil-military relations—United States. 2. Civil supremacy
over the military—United States. 3. Militarism—United States.
I. Snider, Don M., 1940– II. Title.
   UA23.N5495 2009
   322'.50973—dc22   2008042211

A catalog record for this book is available from the British Library.

Special discounts are available for bulk purchases of this book.
For more information, please contact Special Sales at 410-516-6936
or specialsales@press.jhu.edu.

The Johns Hopkins University Press uses environmentally friendly
book materials, including recycled text paper that is composed of at
least 30 percent post-consumer waste, whenever possible. All of our
book papers are acid-free, and our jackets and covers are printed on
paper with recycled content.

In memory of Samuel P. Huntington,
April 18, 1927 to December 24, 2008,
for his immense contribution
to the study and practice of
American civil-military relations

Contents

Foreword

Just a few hours ago, my father, retired Army Major General Robert C. Marshall, died peacefully at home with his children surrounding him. I find myself thinking of his guidance over the years, and, as I sit to write this foreword, one of our conversations seems particularly apt. I had telephoned just to see how dad and mom were doing. Before I could ask or say anything of substance, dad started the following exchange:

> "I hear you're running for Congress."
> "Yes, sir."
> "Democrat?"
> "Yes, sir."
> "You're going to have to lie a lot."
> "And I wouldn't if I were a Republican?"

That last question prompted a brief pause from dad. Then he asked, "Why are you doing this?" I replied, "Well sir, it's very much about duty, honor, —" He cut me off. "Don't you use those words with reference to politics. Politics is the furthest thing from anything that is honorable."

Now it was my turn to pause before replying, but then I teed off: "Dad, you know I left Princeton to enlist for Vietnam; you know what I did in Vietnam. You also know I've been the mayor of Macon for four years now. So let me tell you something. For a guy like you or me, what I've done for the last four years is a hell of a lot harder than anything I did in the military. You and I have no problem charging a machine gun. Death before dishonor. Isn't that right, dad? Well politics is the art of the possible, the art of compromise. How do you know, how does anyone know, which compromises are principled efforts to advance a greater good, a good within the realm of the possible, and which compromises merely advance a party agenda or a political career? So politicians are often disdained. But politics is also the substitute for war. What happens if honorable people abandon it?"

After my outburst, dad and I changed the subject, but our exchange reminds me now of the words of John Adams to Thomas Jefferson, who had been his bitter political rival. Long after each had left political life, Adams wrote: "You and I ought not to die before we have explained ourselves to each other."[1] Those of us who have experienced both sides of the civil-military relationship see a wide gulf of misunderstanding, dislike, and distrust, evidenced by my father's words. Had we continued our conversation, dad and I might have compared and contrasted military and political service. That conversation could have led to a discussion of the roles of the military and politicians during war, preparing for war, and avoiding war. Eventually we would have agreed that a great deal is at stake in having better "explained ourselves to each other." The gap between the civil and military cultures must be narrowed or closed if America is to position itself properly to address current and future threats to our security.

Some twenty years ago, Francis Fukuyama famously contended that we had reached "the end of history," a state of global equilibrium courtesy of liberal democracy and free-market capitalism.[2] He asserted that insular nation-states would soon be relegated to the dustbins, overwhelmed by global economic interdependence. The march of liberal democracy was unstoppable, he argued, because no other form of government was its equal in assuring personal freedoms and efficiently generating material wealth. He suggested that profit-seeking mercantilists worldwide would dominate liberal, representative governments, removing trade and travel barriers and assuring peace because profit was less certain without it.

What Fukuyama did not foresee or sufficiently appreciate were the potential threats and turbulence posed by poorly integrated and ungoverned global interdependence. Billions of people worldwide survive on less than two dollars a day, and because of modern communications and transportation, they are daily reminded of their poverty. Billions of people worldwide want to be like us: they yearn for modern, well-capitalized, free-market economies that enable and entice consumption well beyond subsistence needs, at levels of consumption today's world could not possibly sustain. Severe economic disruptions are inevitable, and greater global interdependence means that many such disruptions will be global in reach and could literally be deadly for thousands, even millions. Add to this the threats of global pandemics, climate change, terror networks, resurgent nationalism, and religious xenophobia, and we can only hope the end of history has not yet arrived, because if it has, it holds constant conflict. The lethality of hatred is geometrically expanding: chemical, biological, or nuclear, the technology of death and mayhem has become readily available, portable, and well within the reach of angry individuals throughout the globe. America's enemies will use both traditional and asymmetric strategies and tactics to achieve their goals.[3]

Our civilian and military leaders must collaborate to address the challenges of holistic threats and holistic warfare. Major change is needed, made challenging by diminishing resources. Pay-me-now or maybe-pay-me-later decisions must be made by both military and civilian leaders. Routines must be altered and turf ceded in a wholesale reorganization, at multiple levels, of the military and civilian components of our government.

None of this would be easy under the best of circumstances, and, as *American Civil-Military Relations* quite clearly shows, the success of this effort will depend largely upon the interactions between our military and the society and government it serves. Poor civil-military relations, often played out between the executive and congressional branches of our government, have failed to produce the most effective national security capabilities—military and civilian—and have failed to produce the best policies and strategies to govern their use. Witness, for example, the mismatches among the needs of postconflict stability operations in Afghanistan and Iraq, the size and types of military forces available, and the pitiful scarcity of capability in the civilian branches of our government to effect nation-building efforts, as well as our utter incompetence as a government in strategic communications.

Fortunately, serious scholarship on this issue is coming from the U. S. Military Academy at West Point. Let me highlight two conclusions from the research found in this volume, spelled out in the concluding chapter. Suzanne Nielsen and Don Snider point out that the development of future leaders for both sides of the civil-military relationship—those who bring both technical expertise and the ability to engender and maintain mutual relationships of comity and trust—has "been more talked about in recent decades than fulfilled." To this I must say that few members of Congress understand very much about the use of military force, which greatly hampers their ability to make decisions about military matters or any subject that might be influenced by the availability of military capabilities. Few of my colleagues in Congress fully appreciate how much our forces conducting counterinsurgency operations depend upon the support of the indigenous population and indigenous security forces. Few of my colleagues appreciate how effective highly motivated indigenous forces can be, even if meagerly equipped and trained, whether they are working for or against U.S. interests.

Let me also reinforce another conclusion articulated in chapter 14, which has to do with the vital role of Congress in creating and maintaining effective civil-military relations. I do so by offering an example. During the colonial era, French and British foreign legions openly incorporated, as part of their military strategy, management of the "political rear." America's military does not do so in any organized way. Yet in many asymmetric engagements, our enemies focus upon America's "political rear"—our homeland and the will of the American people—as a primary strategic target. In selecting the military tactics and strategies to be employed in any asymmetric engagement, American leaders must more effectively take into account the likely impact their choices will have on the political rear. This can happen efficiently only with a much closer, more effective set of civil-military relationships. Congress and the military must address this issue, with Congress taking the lead.

Having served for many years on each side of the U.S. civil-military relationship, I am certain that few topics are of more relevance today to the students and practitioners for whom this volume has been prepared. We face significant domestic challenges—education, health care, an aging population, immigration, and other issues—that we will be unable to address without the freedom and security provided by our armed forces. As the research in this volume so cogently tells us, the quality and character of the relations between our military and the society they serve remains both vexing and critical to that freedom and security.

Jim Marshall
Member, U.S. House of Representatives
for the Eighth District of Georgia
Washington, D.C.

Marshall is a member of the House Armed Services Committee, Subcommittee on Terrorism and Unconventional Threats. He is also a member of the West Point Board of Visitors and Professor of Law at Mercer University School of Law. He served in 1969 and 1970 as Platoon Sergeant, C and E Recon, 1/52nd, 198th Light Infantry Brigade, Americal Division, Quang Ngai Province, Vietnam. He was awarded the Combat Infantry Badge, the Purple Heart, and the Bronze Star with V Device and 1st Oak Leaf Cluster. He is a member of the U. S. Army Ranger Hall of Fame.

Foreword

In the early twenty-first century, the troubled quality of American civil-military relations continues to have enormous and important implications for the United States. Given the uniquely coercive capabilities of the U.S. armed forces as well as their large claim on national resources, it is vitally important that military professionals loyally serve the country's elected leaders in the executive branch and support the legislative intent expressed by Congress, and that they do so in a manner that reflects America's democratic principles. The senior military leadership must be objective, expert, and determinedly nonpartisan.

As this volume indicates, what behaviors are effective and appropriate for both civilian and military partners to civil-military relationships are once again being vigorously debated. Many Americans believe that the military instrument of power is currently playing a disproportionately large role in U.S. foreign and security policy. In addition, the initial disastrous years of the U.S. military intervention in Iraq—during the stewardship of Secretary of Defense Donald Rumsfeld and his senior military leaders—have demonstrated the need for a candid and sweeping review of the relationships and procedures of national security policy-making at the highest level.

For these reasons, this important book is coming at the right time, from the right people, and from an appropriate place. To assess the current state of civil-military relations, Don Snider and Suzanne Nielsen have brought together some of the very best scholars in America in the fields of political science, history, policy studies, and sociology. Working in a collaborative fashion over the course of a year, these scholars have brilliantly used concepts from Samuel P. Huntington's *The Soldier and the State*—written more than fifty years ago but still a classic—as touchstones for their assessments. The result is a volume that is rich with insights of value to both scholars and practitioners.

This book also benefited from the annual Senior Conference organized by the Department of Social Sciences at the U.S. Military Academy at West Point. Over the past half century, many topics have been the focus of this informal gathering of national security professionals, but none has been more timely or cogent than this review of U.S. civil-military relations. The issues this work addresses go to the heart of our form of democratic governance. To provide for their security, how different and how separate will the American people allow their military to be? How do we expect the Republic's military professions, members of society at large, and government leaders to interact?

I have had the opportunity to learn at first hand lessons relevant to U.S. civil-military relations during a lengthy career of military service, starting in combat as a rifle platoon leader in Vietnam and continuing through division command during Operation Desert Storm in 1990. I have also served as the strategic planner for the U.S. Army; the strategic planner for the Joint Chiefs of Staff (JCS); the special assistant to the Chairman, JCS, for interagency coordination; a joint theater commander; and a presidential cabinet officer with national security responsibilities for drug-related issues.

From my time in uniform, I have come to recognize that—from the perspective of the military services—the issues of civil-military relations are largely situational. They vary in salience according to rank, assigned scope of responsibility, and position. In lectures to military audiences, I sometimes say, provocatively, that as a battalion or brigade commander in combat, I would pay attention only to my intelligence and operations staff officers; as a division or corps commander, I would pay attention only to my logistics and communications staff officers; as a joint theater commander, however, I would listen only to my legal officer, my public affairs officer, and my State Department political advisor. The reality is that, in most military positions, civil-military relations mean nothing more than obedience to the Constitution, moral courage, personal honor, and professional excellence. However, in the Washington interagency process—and at many military ranks and positions—civil-military relations get murky very quickly.

Experience in both realms, as a general officer and a senior civilian cabinet officer, suggests some fundamental guidelines for senior military officers serving in the political-military arena. First, senior military leaders must adamantly manifest nonpartisan behavior and attitudes while on active service. The nation selects by election the commander in chief and the members of Congress who are assigned by the Constitution critical roles for our national security. They, in turn, appoint senior civilian leaders. Senior uniformed leaders, however, must be viewed by the public and senior civilian leaders as politically neutral and blind to partisan considerations.

Second, senior military leaders must be utterly transparent and honest when dealing with their constitutional masters in the Congress; with the president and the president's officers; and, where appropriate by law and regulation, with the media who are the watchful guardians of the national security process. Senior uniformed leaders must speak frankly and objectively where their professional judgments are asked for and not reflect a loyalty to hierarchy that leaves the policy process adrift.

Finally, we must broadly develop selected officers for service at senior levels and convey to them their responsibility to be expert at their assigned political-military roles. From battalion through division command in the Army—and at equivalent levels of responsibility in the Army's sister services—U.S. military leaders are the best in the world. We invest fifteen to twenty-five years to create these magnificent officers who are the masters of their professional universes. However, many of our senior flag officers who encountered the arrogance, disingenuous behavior, and misjudgments of Secretary of Defense Donald Rumsfeld during the initial years of Operation Iraqi Freedom were ill-prepared to respond effectively. Although these uniformed leaders came to senior military positions with enormous accumulated experience, technical skills, and integrity, some lacked the confidence that could have been derived from an earlier and broader set of experiences, such as graduate education and other assignments outside their services, to give them an essential sense of history, the law, languages, and other cultures, and how our constitutional form of government really works. They simply were not prepared to take the initiative to shape the political-military dialogue responsibly. It is not enough to say that a senior military leader has only the options of obedience to the Republic or principled resignation. The nation needs senior military flag officers who are respectful of civilian authority, principled in their behavior, deeply experienced in their understanding of strategy and the international environment, and masters of the history of U.S. national security and governance.

Through firsthand and sometimes grueling experiences in over thirty-seven years of federal service, military and civilian, I have become convinced that getting U.S. civil-military relations right is critical to the quality of our democracy as well as to the success of our national security policy. In this spirit, I commend the chapters that follow to the reader's careful consideration. Effective civil-military relationships that are fully consistent with our Constitution and the powerful role the United States will continue to play in the international arena are essential for the future security and welfare of all Americans.

Barry R. McCaffrey
General, United States Army, Retired
West Point, New York

McCaffrey is president of BR McCaffrey Associates LLC in Alexandria, Virginia, a national security consulting firm. He formerly served as the Allen Bradley Distinguished Professor of National Security Studies at West Point, 2001–5.

Acknowledgments

When we started this research project almost two years ago, our primary aim was to enhance the teaching of American civil-military relations at West Point, where we were both on the faculty, and at other educational institutions interested in this fascinating interdisciplinary field. Specifically, we sought to create a book that would amplify for this twenty-first-century generation of students, both graduate and undergraduate, the remarkable contribution that Samuel P. Huntington's *The Soldier and the State* (1957) has made, and continues to make, to the study of civil-military relations. We therefore used Huntington's work as a touchstone for an examination of issues in civil-military relations today. Seeking to advance the theoretical literature as well as to address important policy concerns, we sought to follow the trail blazed by Huntington in his original work. In the process, we have produced a volume that will, we hope, be useful to educators such as ourselves and also be of value to readers who are broadly interested in military issues, American politics, and national security policy.

The completion of this volume did not proceed exactly as we originally had planned—more evidence for a proposition we often teach, that no plan survives initial execution. Suzanne Nielsen unexpectedly spent five months of the project serving in Iraq on General David Petraeus's staff; before the end of the project, Don Snider departed West Point at the conclusion of fifty years of public service. We are confident, nonetheless, that our intention has been achieved. This fortunate outcome was the result of many factors, the most important of which was a marvelous team of professional colleagues, all like-minded in their pursuit of teaching excellence in this critical field, who pulled together through two conferences, many discussions, and seemingly endless rewrites to produce this volume.

Thus, our first and most profound acknowledgment is to our fellow researchers and chapter authors. The extraordinary men and women who agreed to participate in this project are tremendous scholars who share a deep dedication to the education and development of the next generation of America's civilian and military leaders. Without their incisive comments, encouraging support, and unfailing good humor throughout, this project could not have succeeded. Any opportunity we have in the future to work again with these scholars, who are now also our friends, we would gladly take.

Our second acknowledgment must go to the Department of Social Sciences at West Point. Scholars need a certain type of environment in which to flourish, and we are both very fortunate that at West Point, and particularly within the Department of Social Sciences, a positive and open environment has long been the norm. The distinguished, productive tradition of Senior Conferences, hosted every year since 1963 by the superintendent and run by the "Sosh" Department, made available a venue where our own ideas and those of our chapter authors could be vetted by a uniquely seasoned assembly of scholars and practitioners of civil-military relations. We particularly thank the department's leadership, Colonel Mike Meese and Colonel Cindy Jebb, for their support, and our colleague Major Jason Dempsey who, in mid-2006, first suggested using the fiftieth anniversary of Huntington's work to inform the 2007 Senior Conference theme.

Third, we gratefully acknowledge the financial and human resources that made this project possible. We appreciate the generous financial support of the United States Military Academy Association of Graduates, the North Atlantic Treaty Organization, and a private foundation that has chosen to remain anonymous. And we offer a huge "thank you" to the staff and faculty in "Sosh"; without them, this project would never have come to fruition. Specifically, we acknowledge the tireless work of the Senior Conference executive secretary, Major David Dudas; his deputy, Major Scott Taylor; the conference coordinator, Joy Pasquazi; and the many other talented faculty members who contributed in a variety of ways to making Senior Conference 2007 a success.

Our fourth acknowledgment must go to our editorial consultant, Teresa Lawson, for all she did to bring this volume to print. Having joined us in the latter stages of the project, her talent and thoroughness helped us make this a better unified and teachable chorus of interdependent ideas about American civil-military relations. Within these pages lie concepts and issues that our future national leaders will need to grapple with—and resolve—if we are to have both capable military forces and sound policies for their use.

Finally, for each of us, loved ones paid a dear price so that we could pursue this project. For their understanding and forbearance, we are deeply grateful.

American Civil-Military Relations

CHAPTER ONE

Introduction

Suzanne C. Nielsen and Don M. Snider

Samuel Huntington published, in 1957, a seminal study of civil-military relations titled *The Soldier and the State*. Because he believed that field had suffered from "too little theorizing," his central purpose was to develop a theoretical
framework that would support critical examination of its crucial issues.[1] However, he was also driven by a weighty policy concern: Would the United States be
able to sustain the large professional military establishment it would need to succeed in the Cold War? Would it be able to preserve a military that was democratically appropriate, fulfilling what he called the societal imperative, and was at the
same time militarily effective, fulfilling what he called the functional imperative?
By exploring the tension between these two imperatives within liberal democratic states, Huntington created an influential classic that has remained a touchstone over the past fifty years for those who think about, research, write about,
and practice American civil-military relations.

Huntington's work retains tremendous value in the present day. In an era in
which the military instrument of power plays a central role in U.S. national security policy, democratically appropriate civil-military relations that also produce
effective military forces and the policies and strategies for their utilization are

vital. Several developments since the attacks of September 11, 2001, however, indicate that a broad consensus does not exist on many important aspects of these critical relations. Controversies have arisen over such issues as the soundness of U.S. strategic decisions and the decision-making processes that produced them, interpersonal relations at the nexus of defense policymaking, the quality of military advice rendered to civilian leaders, and the appropriateness of public dissent by retired general officers. The December 2006 Iraq Study Group articulated particular concern over several of these issues: "The U.S. military has a long tradition of strong partnership between the civilian leadership of the Department of Defense and the uniformed services. Both have long benefited from a relationship in which the civilian leadership exercises control with the advantage of fully candid professional advice, and the military serves loyally with the understanding that its advice has been heard and valued. That tradition has been frayed, and civil-military relations need to be repaired."[2]

A central premise of this book is that Huntington's work remains a useful starting point for an urgently needed review of the realities and challenges facing American civil-military relations. Seeking to advance the theoretical literature as well as to address pressing policy concerns relating to both partners in the civil-military relationship, this book follows the trail that Huntington blazed.

Civil-Military Relations in Perspective

Civil-military relations, as Huntington wrote in *The Soldier and the State,* "should be studied as a system composed of interdependent elements." Particular incidents can best be understood within a larger context.[3] Like most other processes within the U.S. government, civil-military relationships are both institutional and personal. They are affected by different institutional responsibilities, varying organizational cultures and perspectives, and even personal style and approach. Five important sets of relationships, detailed in this section, compose this system of interdependent elements. Unless each of these sets of relationships is kept in view, understanding of U.S. civil-military relations might be distorted by the often narrow focus of the mass media. Rumors of disagreements within the Pentagon, or between the Pentagon and the White House or the Congress, are too often presented as if they were the whole substance of civil-military relations. Focus on controversies that make headlines may result in neglect of other dynamics that are more significant or that have long-term ramifications for the democratic appropriateness and the strategic effectiveness of U.S. civil-military interactions.

These five sets of interdependent relationships are those of civilian elites with military leaders, of military institutions with American society, of military leaders with their professions, among civilian elites, and of civilian elites with American society.

Civilian Elites and Military Leaders

Leaders within the military professions work directly with elected and appointed civilian leaders at the federal level—the executive and Congress—as well as state and local levels of government to create and execute U.S. national and homeland security policies. Civilian elites who play a role in this relationship (a relationship we sometimes refer to as the civil-military nexus) also include university researchers and faculty, business leaders, and members of the media.

Military Institutions and American Society

The U.S. military consists of armed forces, comprising distinct ground, air, and maritime military professions.[4] Members who volunteer for service come from the larger American society, retaining most of their rights and obligations as citizens. Salient issues include whether the U.S. armed forces are able to attract and recruit sufficient volunteers; whether those serving in the military are representative of the society they serve; whether military professionals view themselves, or are viewed, as so different or so separate from society that an undesirable civil-military "gap" exists; and whether, within the military professions, civilian values sufficiently infuse the military ethics under which U.S. forces are deployed and employed.

Military Leaders and Their Professions

Relationships within the military professions, mainly between the strategic leaders and the more junior professionals, affect the professions' ethos and expertise as they evolve over time. This evolution shapes institutional capabilities and the expertise and perspectives of the military partner in civil-military interactions at the highest levels.

Civilian Elite Interactions

Relations between the executive and the Congress shape the manner in which they manage their shared constitutional responsibilities for military affairs. Important factors include the relationship between the country's two major political parties; whether the same party controls the executive and legislative branches of government; the intensity of partisanship, especially over national security policies; and relationships between government officials and members of the news media.

Influential Civilian Elites and American Society

Political officials and other civilian opinion leaders have their own sets of relationships with the American public. Through these relationships civilian elites help inform the views of the public about national security policy and about the instruments of power used to execute it.

The Contributions of *The Soldier and the State*

Using *The Soldier and the State* as a touchstone, and keeping in mind these sets of relationships—Huntington's "system composed of interdependent elements"— the chapters in this volume provide a comprehensive review of just where the theory and practice of American civil-military relations stand and where they are going. As context, therefore, we offer here a brief review of the central elements and concepts that are Huntington's legacy.

In *The Soldier and the State,* Huntington's starting point was to argue that the objective of a nation's civil-military relations is to "maximize military security at the least sacrifice of other social values."[5] In developing his analytical approach, Huntington made conceptual contributions in three main areas on which scholars doing subsequent research in the field have repeatedly relied to inform their own work. These concepts relate to the sources of influence on the nature of military organizations, patterns of civilian control of the military, and the description of the military's officer corps as a profession.

Influences on Military Institutions

Huntington argued that both functional and societal imperatives shape a country's armed forces and military institutions. The functional imperative, flowing from the need to defend the state and its way of life, focuses on external threats and the need for effectiveness when the state calls on its armed forces to perform military functions. These are the influences that make martial institutions martial; they establish a rationale for the value that militaries place on such traits as discipline and obedience. The functional imperative requires militaries to focus on issues such as exploiting or managing a state's balance of technological capabilities relative to its adversaries and devising doctrines to guide the development and organization of military capabilities.

The societal imperative causes militaries to be shaped by the social forces, ideologies, and institutions that are dominant in the society they protect. An example of issues raised by the societal imperative is whether the military's professional ethic is compatible with, and subordinate to, the prevailing ideology in the society. Another is whether the resources consumed by the military, and the political influence the military possesses, are compatible with a nation's other values.

Huntington considered the interaction of these two influential imperatives—the functional and the societal—to be "the nub of the problem of civil-military relations."[6] A society that cannot balance these two imperatives might thus be incapable of providing for its own security. As he wrote in 1957, this was Huntington's fear: he viewed American liberalism as so hostile to the military function that the United States might be unable to develop and sustain the effective military institutions necessary to guarantee U.S. security in the extended struggle of the Cold War.

Patterns of Civilian Control of the Military

A second concept of Huntington's legacy relates to patterns of civilian control of the military. In Huntington's view, there are only two main patterns: subjective control and objective control. Under the former, control of the military reflects the competition among the state's civilian factions. Groups distinguished by characteristics such as social class, branch of government, or partisan identification each seek to control the military by getting the officer corps to conform to its own views and serve its particular interests. Huntington argued that, under subjective control, the societal imperative dominates the functional imperative. Thus, it has a negative impact on military effectiveness, and the state's security may be threatened as competing civilian groups constantly struggle for control over the military. He viewed this as the inevitable pattern in the absence of a professional officer corps.[7]

Under objective civilian control, the officer corps agrees implicitly to serve the state and thus to serve whatever civilian group attains legitimate authority within the state. This system minimizes the political influence of the military because it becomes, voluntarily, politically neutral. Huntington argued that professional officers will seek a pattern of objective control because it is most compatible with the ethos of their profession. Although the military possesses minimal political power, it is granted significant autonomy within its own sphere and is better able to function according to the demands of its professional status. The societal imperative and the functional imperative are balanced. Huntington concluded that objective control is best for two main reasons: civilian control is more secure because the military is politically neutral, and the state is more secure because the military's professionalism, and hence its effectiveness, are maximized.

The Officer Corps as a Profession

The third concept from *The Soldier and the State* that has been fruitful for subsequent research and analysis is the idea of the officer corps as a profession, which is a special type of vocation. Huntington argued that the military shares three characteristics with other professions in Western societies: expertise, responsibility, and corporateness. The specific expertise of the officer, developed by prolonged education and experience, is in the "management of violence."[8] This includes organizing and equipping the force, planning for its use, and the direction of the force in and out of combat.

The performance of this function is accompanied by a particular responsibility: officers must exercise their expertise only for the benefit of society. This social, and thus moral, responsibility to develop expert knowledge and expertise, and to use them only on behalf of a client otherwise incapable of self-defense, distinguishes the professional officer from other experts with only intellectual knowledge of military affairs.

The concept of corporateness refers to Huntington's argument that members of a profession develop, over time, a unity and consciousness of themselves as a group apart from the society they serve. This collective sense originates in long years of study and service together and the sharing of a common social responsibility, and it manifests itself in objective standards of competence applied and enforced by the members themselves.[9]

To the extent that an officer is a professional driven by the functional imperative, the officer will, wrote Huntington, hold a particular professional military ethic, that of conservative realism; Huntington described this world view as the "military mind." Its elements include a belief in the fallibility of man and the permanence of conflict in human affairs, an appreciation for history, a belief in historical cycles rather than progress, an emphasis on the primacy of the group over the individual, a focus on the state as the fundamental unit of political organization and on the centrality of power in international relations, an emphasis on the immediacy of the threat and worst-case analyses, bias toward strong forces-in-being and skepticism of alliances, a desire to avoid initiating conflict unless victory is assured, and hostility toward military adventurism. "The military ethic is thus pessimistic, collectivist, historically inclined, power-oriented, nationalistic, militaristic, pacifist, and instrumentalist in its view of the military profession," Huntington wrote; it is "both realistic and conservative."[10]

Huntington's policy prescriptions flowed from these major elements of his analytic framework. For the United States to succeed in the Cold War, he argued, it would have to develop policies and practices for civil-military relations consistent with his conception of objective control. This approach would best safeguard liberal democracy in the United States by enabling the country to develop and maintain the immense armed forces, professionally led, that it would need to succeed in an extended armed confrontation with the Soviet Union. Further, he argued, U.S. national security would be better served if America were to shift rightward ideologically, to a conservative ideology more compatible with the military's functional imperative as he saw it.

Outline of This Project

Fifty years after the publication of *The Soldier and the State*, in June 2007, the interdisciplinary group of scholars researching and writing for this project met at West Point to have their manuscripts reviewed by a selected audience of academics and practitioners of American civil-military relations—both civilian and military, actively serving and retired.[11] Drawing on the rich literature in U.S. and comparative civil-military relations, as well as their own considerable research, they reviewed, tested, and critiqued many of Huntington's original concepts and added their own prescriptions. The remainder of this chapter outlines their work, which can be divided in to four thematic groups. Conclusions from the research project are presented in the final chapter.

In the first section of this volume, three chapters provide contrasting perspectives of American civil-military relations from different vantage points within the five decades that Huntington's ideas have framed the analysis. In chapter 2, Richard Betts assesses the state of civil-military relations in America after 9/11 and several years into the Iraq war. He cautions against the tendency to see crises in civil-military relations where they may not exist. In chapter 3, Matthew Moten offers a detailed account of an incident that many viewed as a crisis: the rejection by Secretary of Defense Donald Rumsfeld in 2002 of the advice of the Army Chief of Staff General Eric Shinseki on the number of troops required for a successful intervention in Iraq. In chapter 4, Peter Feaver and Erika Seeler assess the influence of Huntington's ideas on a half century of development of the study of civil-military relations. Reviewing the literature both before and after Huntington's work, they argue that it deserves its status as a classic because it marked a critical advance not just in substance but in the methodological approach to scholarly investigations of civil-military relations.

The second section of this volume addresses more directly Huntington's conception of the societal and functional imperatives and their influences on American civil-military relations. With respect to the societal imperative, in chapter 5 Michael Desch explores the origins of Huntington's concern over the clash between the American liberal tradition (tracing it to Louis Hartz) and the inherent conservatism of the military. He documents the reemergence of this clash again after the end of the Cold War and argues that it explains the troubles of the administration of President George W. Bush in the area of civil-military relations and the ineffectiveness of policy and strategy produced through them. He concludes with a strong defense of objective control.

Chapters 6 and 7 then turn to the functional imperative. In chapter 6, Nadia Schadlow and Richard Lacquement argue that Huntington's conception of the role of the professional officer as "the manager of violence" is, in the post–Cold War era, far too narrow. In Huntington's conception, officers and the military professions they lead focus primarily on conventional, kinetic warfare; this is "a military that focuses on battles, not wars." Winning wars in the sense of achieving political objectives through the use of force now requires more expertise in irregular warfare and stability operations, as made evident in the recent U.S. experiences in Iraq and Afghanistan. Looking inside the military professions and how they educate their members, Williamson Murray argues in chapter 7 for reform of professional military education; he calls on U.S. military organizations to rejuvenate the emphasis they once placed on education as critical to the development of today's military professionals.

The third section of the volume addresses issues associated with the military partner in U.S. civil-military relations. In chapter 8, James Burk critically examines Huntington's concept of "loyalty and obedience as the cardinal military virtues" by offering a nuanced analysis of the difference between blind and responsible obedience. He argues persuasively that an officer's professional and moral responsibility extends to the correct use of expert knowledge: "Military professionals require autonomy, including moral autonomy," he writes, "to be competent actors who can be held responsible for what they do."

The conservative-realist world view attributed to the officer corps is taken up in chapter 9 by Darrell Driver. His research challenges Huntington's "military mind" construct, which attributes the formation of a common set of mostly conservative public beliefs to the military function. Driver's data indicate a surprising heterogeneity of views among the military officers sampled; what is shared is a belief in public service. Chapter 10, by David Segal and Karin De Angelis, traces evolving conceptions about the military profession in light of the sociology of professions. They give particular attention to the ideas of the other major theorist of civil-military relations, Morris Janowitz at the University of Chicago, who argued for greater fusion of the military with the broader American society rather than the voluntary separation advocated by Huntington.

The final section of this volume is focused on the current state of civil-military relations at the nexus: those direct interpersonal relations between senior military and civilian leaders, and the norms and practices that should guide them. In chapter 11, Risa Brooks offers a critical look at the risks and costs of military leaders' participation in domestic politics and the various rules that have been advanced to guide their doing so. She concludes with a cautious norm for such practices.

The last two chapters address the issue of how, and how well, the military relates to the Congress and to the executive. In Chapter 12, Chris Gibson offers what he calls a Madisonian approach as an alternative to either objective or subjective control. He gives particular attention to the ways in which the military should render advice during national security policy formulation and execution. In his model, "the national security experts within the Department of Defense — civilian and military—would develop competing plans [and] . . . would critique each other's ideas and concepts. . . . [S]eparate and even competing proposals for executive deliberation would be encouraged." In Chapter 13, historian Richard Kohn examines the element of personalities in civil-military relations. He proposes a set of behavioral norms for both sides of the civil-military nexus to foster cooperative relationships that would result in improved civilian control as well as wise policymaking informed by military expertise.

The final chapter of the book offers an assessment of the major lessons of this collective research project and thoughts on the way ahead for civil-military relations in the United States.

Conclusion

The United States will continue to rely on the military instrument of power to safeguard national interests and values. The character of its civil-military relations will make critical contributions to success or failure when it does employ force. How well will the executive branch, Congress, and uniformed leaders work together to create, develop, and equip the U.S. armed forces appropriately for the Republic's future needs? How well will political and military leaders craft and implement strategic and operational plans to ensure that a particular use of force meets national purposes? Although political leaders have the ultimate authority and responsibility in these areas, the effectiveness with which they interact with the leaders of the military professions across the entire range of civil-military relationships will be vital to success.

CHAPTER TWO

Are Civil-Military Relations Still a Problem?

Richard K. Betts

Democracy and powerful professional military organizations do not rest easily with each other. This is the premise of Huntington's *Soldier and the State*. Many who ponder civil-military relations do not share his formulation of the problem and its solutions, but most share the premise that the relationship between the two camps is a significant continuing problem. Some believe that the problem reached the proportions of a "crisis" even in recent times.[1]

Is this true? The underlying potential for serious political conflict over the role of military professionals in foreign policy seemed apparent in the 1950s. In the half century since, however, the potential has not been realized, despite harsh experiences in war and sharp political divisions within American society. The state of civil-military relations is indeed a problem worth concern, but politics and government are full of problems. Struggles for influence and control among political and bureaucratic constituencies pervade our national life. But contrary to the fears of many in the twentieth century, civil-military relations are not an outsized problem as conflicts in a democracy go.

How has the problem been kept manageable? Not by clear and consistent adoption of either of Huntington's ideal types of "objective" or "subjective" civilian control: neither has ever been officially proclaimed as the norm. This is natural given the difference between an ideal type and actual practice. In practice, the balance has been kept through a dynamic equilibrium, as political players tack back and forth in tacit emphasis on the two approaches.

Either emphasis revealed problems. Academic critics tend to focus on the deficiencies of objective control. Critics within the military tend to oppose subjective control. Critics in the political arena have gone in all directions at different times. As with most competing ideal types, practical solutions in real cases tend toward compromise. In practice, objective control should never extend to absolute division of labor and removal of civilian prerogatives to direct military operations. On balance, though, given the record since he wrote, Huntington's opposition to subjective control remains persuasive in the twenty-first century. It remains persuasive because the critics of objective control have focused on the risks that professional soldiers may make the wrong *military* choices and have neglected the risks that go with politicization of the military—which objective control is designed to avoid.

This chapter outlines the terms of reference for assessing the state of civilian control and the main enduring sources of tension between military and civilian leaders; explores how big changes in the political environments, international and domestic, affected the evolution of civil-military relations, and why the effects of those changes were not more decisive; and argues that the civilian control problem became a modest and manageable one after the early 1960s. Finally, it makes the case for tilting in favor of Huntington's model of objective control.

The Two Faces of Military Policy

The concern behind *The Soldier and the State* was that the Cold War posed a demand unique in American history: prolonged peacetime mobilization. No longer could the nation rely on the militia system and the tradition of the citizen-soldier who would provide armed force for only as long as necessary to fight a war. In the Cold War, the professional military would have to perform a major role in national life indefinitely rather than episodically. This novel challenge existed only because the United States was engaged in containment and deterrence of a superpower with staying power.

So why did the American defense establishment not return to its historic role and status after the end of the Cold War and the unprecedented prolonged mobilization of 1940–90? Why has uncertainty persisted about the proper degree of professional military involvement in policy and strategy, despite two hundred years of experience and experiments to get it right, and a half century of concentrated concern with military affairs? Do the answers lie in external developments in national security over this period, in the internal development of domestic politics and government institutions, or in something else?

Huntington's second book, *The Common Defense,* covers the broader political canvas on which civil-military relations play out. It opens by focusing on the interaction between the external and internal realms of American policy:

> The most distinctive, the most fascinating, and the most troublesome aspect of military policy is its Janus-like quality. Indeed, military policy not only faces in two directions, it exists in two worlds. One is international politics, the world of the balance of power, wars and alliances, the subtle and the brutal uses of force and diplomacy. The principal currency of this world is actual or potential military strength: battalions, weapons, and warships. The other world is domestic politics, the world of interest groups, political parties, social classes, with their conflicting interests and goals. The currency here is the resources of society: men, money, material. Any major decision in military policy influences and is influenced by both worlds. A decision made in terms of one currency is always payable in the other. The rate of exchange, however, is usually in doubt.[2]

The Janus faces of military policy overlay the two imperatives Huntington posed at the outset of *The Soldier and the State* for understanding the more specific challenge of civil-military relations: the functional imperative (effectiveness in war making and deterrence) and the societal imperative (conformity of the professional military with the liberal American social and ideological order). The problem motivating Huntington was the concern that, on one hand, "it may be impossible to contain within society military institutions shaped by purely functional imperatives" but, on the other hand, the Cold War had made the functional imperative ascendant. Historically, Americans could handle the problem of civil-military relations by suppressing military professionalism, but the threats of the mid-twentieth century made it too risky to continue to do so: "Previously the primary question was: what pattern of civil-military relations is most compatible with American liberal democratic values? Now this has been supplanted by the more important issue: what pattern of civil-military relations will best maintain the security of the American nation?"[3]

Although the priority of the two imperatives had changed, the interaction between them remained the central issue for Huntington. Neither imperative could be ignored; the model by which they could be reconciled was the issue. Critics who were unhappy with the course of civil-military relations in subsequent years, or who rejected Huntington's preferred model of objective control, did not all recognize this. Many focused entirely on the problems in one side of the equation alone. Some did not like objective control because it appeared to contribute to the social "gap" between the military community and the rest of society, but these critics did not apply equal attention to the impact of alternatives to objective control on military effectiveness, the functional imperative. Others did not like objective control because it appeared to deprive the civilians of leverage over military operations and strategy, but these critics did not argue forthrightly in favor of subjective control. Part of the problem with debates about objective control is that they have not engaged the two faces of military policy, or the two imperatives of civil-military relations, with equal attention.

Two recurrent sources of friction between military and civilian leaders since the middle of the twentieth century stand out. One is about strategy and operations: the tendency for military professionals to oppose undertaking combat actions without a commitment to application of "overwhelming force," in frequent contrast to politicians' interest in waging low-profile war, intervention on the cheap, or economically efficient operations. Another is about management and control: the question of where to draw the line between military expertise and political authority, and whether military leaders have too much influence or not enough.

The preference for overwhelming force is a long military tradition because it is associated with *decisive* action as opposed to piecemeal and ineffectual pressure. The preference is rooted in sensitivity to the unpredictability of combat, the pervasiveness of Clausewitzian "friction," and the unanticipated resilience of many enemies. Safer to crush an opponent, it is assumed, than to poke him. (This does not mean that soldiers prefer total war, only that they prefer erring on the side of more force than seems necessary to compel submission to whatever American demands are at issue.)

Conservative politicians often share this disposition. What became known as the Powell Doctrine in the 1990s, after all, was no more than the Weinberger Doctrine of the previous decade.[4] Liberal and neoconservative politicians (in contrast to paleocons or leftists) often see recommendations in this vein as obstructionist, exaggerated caution and a disingenuous attempt to put down a marker to ensure that any failure is blamed on civilian authorities.[5] Civilians are often more interested in using small doses of force to accomplish good deeds, such as peacekeeping or discipline of odious regimes abroad, or they wish to show that force can be used economically, without wasteful overkill. Soldiers tend to see these urges as naive or feckless. Joint Chiefs of Staff Chairman Colin Powell complained to a journalist, "As soon as they tell me it's limited, it means they do not care whether you achieve a result or not."[6] Tension over the scale on which combat power should be applied bubbled up in the 1960s, particularly in regard to deliberations about intervention in Laos, the Cuban missile crisis, and the air war against North Vietnam; again in the 1990s, when the military resisted pressure to use force hesitantly in the Balkans; and in the 2002 run-up to war against Iraq as recounted by Matthew Moten in chapter 3 in this volume.[7]

The question of where to draw the line between the legitimate spheres of authority of civilian policymakers and professional soldiers arose in the past in the context of the management of budgets and procurement programs and of interference by civilian managers in choices of tactics in combat operations. In the political arena, these disputes were most intense in the 1960s and in 2001–6. Among academic analysts, two contrasting lines of argument have been prominent. One, in opposition to the Huntington model, was that civilians should play a much more active role, intervening deeper in the hierarchy of the military establishment than allowed by the division of labor envisioned for objective control. The other, implicitly more sympathetic to the principle of division of labor, was that precisely that sort of civilian interference produced bad functional results: irresponsible strategies and corruption of military plans and operations by naive or dishonest politicians.

Examples of the first genre are the works of Graham Allison, Barry Posen, and Eliot Cohen.[8] They represent attempts to enforce the essential Clausewitzian notion that policy and operations must be integrated rather than separated if war (or preparation for it) is to be rational. Allison's "organizational process" model of decision making emphasized the danger that parochialism and goal displacement by complex organizations such as the military could produce dysfunctional implementation of policy, unanticipated consequences, and accidental escalation.[9] To avoid bureaucratic slips between cup and lip, in this view, top policymakers needed to burrow into tactical details and interfere in the military chain of command to ensure that standard operating procedures did not refract the president's intent when force was used. Posen argued that militaries could not be counted on to adapt doctrines or to procure forces appropriate to changing strategic circumstances and that civilian leaders should "audit" programs and cooperate with minorities in the officer corps who offered sensibly novel solutions. Cohen argued that the mark of a great civilian war leader was the inspiration and willingness to question military advice on operational matters and to impose alternatives to military preferences when their judgment conflicted. Cohen's was the one work that directly attacked Huntington's model of objective control, citing it as the "normal theory" of civil-military relations.[10] (It is really normal only among professional officers; there is no consensus against subjective control among civilian politicians or lay observers.) Cohen looked to examples of civilian war leaders whose military judgment appeared better than that of the military.

The opposite critique of civil-military relations, popular among professional soldiers, is represented by H. R. McMaster's *Dereliction of Duty*.[11] The greatest sin leading to the biggest national security policy disaster of the past half century, in this view, was the imposition by Lyndon Johnson and Robert McNamara of a no-win strategy for waging war in Vietnam, against the expert advice of military leaders. The second greatest sin—the one behind the book's title—was the willingness of the Joint Chiefs of Staff (JCS) to go along with the misguided plan, keeping quiet in the face of alleged administration duplicity about it, rather than resign or speak frankly to Congress. That is, the sin of JCS Chairman Earle Wheeler and company was to do as Cohen prescribed: disagree with their superiors and then shut up once those superiors made their decision, irresponsible as it may have seemed.[12]

The knowledge on which all of these arguments about civil-military relations were based came from the Cold War or earlier. Huntington's arguments were about the American political system as it was organized in the 1950s. Since then, the strategic environment of American national security, and the domestic environment of American politics, have both changed substantially. Have those big changes altered the logic of Huntington's theory, or of the criticisms of it?

The New Face of Foreign Threats

In 1957 a reader contemplating the hypothetical end of the Cold War might well have expected that if it occurred as it ultimately did, with the virtual unconditional surrender of the adversary, the societal imperative of containing the military domestically would trump the functional imperative again. The change in external threats after 1989 was as profound as the changes in the 1940s that brought the United States to center stage in world politics, but in the opposite direction, bringing it far greater relative power and security. So why is the United

States allocating three times more of its economy to defense than it did in 1939, the last year before readiness for war against a great power was the norm, when 1.4 percent of GNP was spent on defense?[13] There is no threat to American security remotely comparable to the old Soviet Union's 175 divisions and 40,000 nuclear weapons. (Al Qaeda looks hefty only by default, because it is the only threat in town.) In the heady days of the early 1990s, some observers steeped in realpolitik expected that the United States might move "forward to the past"—that is, stand down from a long but aberrant period of high peacetime preparedness and activism abroad to adopt a more relaxed foreign policy oriented primarily to economic interaction, watchfulness about the rise of other great powers, and abstemious resort to force. This did not happen. Keeping a large standing force in peacetime, in contrast to the historic norm of demobilizing after victory, eased civil-military relations because the military did not have to contract radically. Continued U.S. foreign policy activism, however, abraded civil-military relations because it opened up disagreements between realpolitik-minded soldiers and idealist-minded civilians.

Despite defeating the epochal challenges of fascism and communism, American activism abroad did not wane; it accelerated. The United States elected to wage twice as many hot wars (and about as many small-scale interventions) in the fifteen years after the implosion of the Soviet bloc as it did during the Cold War, in a span of time one-third as long. The baseline U.S. military budget alone, exclusive of costs for actually using it in war, rose to more than half a *trillion* dollars by 2008, about as much as the military spending of the whole rest of the world, and more than five times the spending of all potential enemy countries combined. Spending on this scale is not explained by the war against Al Qaeda, which primarily relies on intelligence collection and special operations forces that account for a modest portion of the defense budget. The burdens suggested by these numbers are lower than during the Cold War—the four wars (Iraq 1991, Kosovo 1999, Afghanistan since 2001, Iraq since 2003) have all been much smaller than the wars in Korea and Vietnam. The 4+ percent of gross domestic product allocated to the armed forces is lower than most of the earlier period, when it was 6–9 percent, but it remains far higher than the norm before the mid-twentieth century.

Current activism was spurred by the shock of September 11, 2001, but even before then the United States was not moving forward to the past. Although forces and budgets had declined markedly during the 1990s, and reductions were huge by Cold War standards, what remained was a peacetime military establishment that was still gargantuan by pre-1940 standards. Over the course of fifty years of World War in Europe and Asia and Cold War on virtually every continent, Americans had developed the habit of empire. The Soviet collapse made it easier to indulge this impulse: to take on the mission of providing world order at a cost that appeared relatively low because the standard of comparison was the baseline that Americans knew during their own lifetimes, rather than the republic's first 150 years. By the time the Cold War ended, no one below retirement age had even a youthful memory of an America without large armed forces.

The current Cold War–size defense budget is due in part to the growth in cost per unit for maintaining a military establishment as utilization of new technologies expands and as personnel require greater inducements to volunteer and to reenlist. Weapon system costs accelerate far beyond the rate of inflation, and costs of health care, incentive pay and bonuses, and other human-resource investments are far above the burden of manning the conscript force of the first half of the Cold War. Corporate interests that live off military expenditures have also become more adept at spreading subcontracts across congressional districts and stoking pork-barrel politics. These differences, however, do not explain away the huge baseline defense budget. If the United States were designing military forces simply to *defend* American territory and vital interests, in a world presently without great-power enemies, the quantity and quality of forces necessary would not be those we find necessary for trying to depose objectionable regimes, spread American values such as democracy, and regulate world order.

In the hiatus between the opening of the Berlin Wall and the Al Qaeda attacks of September 11, foreign-policy objectives became matters of choice rather than necessity more than at any time since the 1930s. U.S. policy did not have to worry about the balance of power because there was no balance, only American hegemony. After the splendid and easy success of the 1991 war against Iraq, the main issue was how much of the responsibility for world order to take on, and how to exert American leadership and control over small conflicts without paying much blood or treasure. Debate revolved around when and where to become involved in humanitarian intervention, peacekeeping, and peace enforcement. Decisions about commitment to combat were about small wars such as Bosnia and Kosovo and about forcing unstable states or fractious societies to organize themselves according to civilized Western standards.

These choices created mild civil-military tensions. The neo-Wilsonian impulses of President Bill Clinton and, after September 11, President George W. Bush meant that the civilian leadership's idea of war was closer to what it had been in the early twentieth century, flowing from experience in pacifying the western frontier. As Morris Janowitz described it, war "was essentially a punitive action . . . to bring people who lived outside the rules of law and order within the orbit of civilization. . . . There was little concern with the philosophy of the use of organized violence to achieve a specific political settlement or a new balance of power. Military action was designed to facilitate total political incorporation, or merely to 'punish' the lawless."[14]

For military professionals, this way of thinking created anxiety. They had long since forgotten the frontier experience and the policing of the Caribbean region and instead were oriented to modern conventional warfare against militarily worthy opponents. Their self-image was dominated by what the armed forces accomplished in Europe and the Pacific in the 1940s and in forty-five years of preparation for World War III on NATO's Central Front, and not least because the Vietnam experience confirmed their distaste for unconventional warfare. "Rogue" states with big armies replaced the Soviet colossus as the object of the armed forces' strategic planning.

Not until after 2003 was this orientation effectively challenged, as it had been in the 1960s. September 11 and its aftermath highlighted the importance of unconventional special operations, but most military professionals still saw it as an additional important mission, not the most important one. The failure of victory in the conventional opening phase of war against Iraq to produce final victory was a deeper blow to the ethos of the professionals. The descent into inconclusive counterinsurgency aggravated tensions in civil-military relations, although not as much as the war in Vietnam had done (there the main conflicts were over the air war against North Vietnam, which has no analogue in Iraq).

After Vietnam, friction between the two camps was mild compared to the 1950s and 1960s. The Air Force resisted civilian pressures, begun under President John Kennedy and Secretary of Defense Robert McNamara and revived by President Richard Nixon and Secretary of Defense James Schlesinger, to develop a menu of options for limited nuclear war, until President Jimmy Carter finally made the directives stick. Otherwise, the services were content to be as recalcitrant as any large bureaucracies usually are, to lick their wounds from Vietnam, and to retreat to their preferred mission: conventional deterrence and preparation for World War III against the Soviet Union. Civilian leaders did not counter the military's desire to forget Vietnam and did not insist that it preserve counterinsurgency capability as a hedge against the future—a terrible mistake that came home to roost in Iraq in 2003.

The options of falling back on a European mission and ignoring unconventional warfare do not exist in the twenty-first century. A worthy great-power opponent or coalition may emerge in coming years: a full-grown China, or an alliance of China and a recovered Russia. Until balance-of-power politics comes back, however, the main issues will be how to fight a global counterinsurgency war against Al Qaeda and its allies and whether to elect missions using American power for charitable purposes (humanitarian intervention) and grand ambitions (regulation of world order). The regular military is a secondary instrument for the counterterrorism mission, and the elective missions remain potential sources of contention between military realists and idealist politicians. Enthusiasts for using force to promote justice and democracy—liberals in the 1990s, neoconservatives afterward—believed the mission could be accomplished cheaply. Military pessimists will continue to demand commitment to overwhelming force if they are to support the habit of empire.

The New Face of Government

Changes in political processes, institutional constraints, and partisan tendencies have accumulated over fifty years. The one most often cited as worrisome, the "Republicanization" of the officer corps, is actually not a terribly threatening development (I say this as a Democrat)—*unless* the principle of objective control is abandoned.[15] The change that has had the biggest negative effect is one scarcely noted in debates about civilian control: the reorganization of the Army in the 1970s to require mobilization of reserve forces for any significant contingency.

Consider some milestones in the evolution of government and politics:

- The year after *The Soldier and the State* was published, the 1958 legislative reorganization of the defense establishment codified the system of unified and specified commands (later renamed "combatant commands" by Secretary of Defense Donald Rumsfeld); these evolved into major centers of regional politico-military coordination, with unusually influential diplomatic roles for the four-stars in charge of them.
- In subsequent years, staffs of the military services, commands, and JCS; the civilian secretariat of the Defense Department; the National Security Council (NSC); and congressional committees and agencies such as the Congressional Budget Office all expanded, creating more complex interactions and mechanisms for leverage.

- Heavy-handed civilian management of Pentagon business came and went in the 1960s and came back again after 2000.
- Legislative oversight of foreign relations, defense, and intelligence activities increased significantly, and budget committees were established in Congress.
- Congress asserted its constitutional prerogatives through the 1973 War Powers Resolution but then consistently failed to enforce it in contests with the executive.
- The federal budget became top-heavy with obligations of domestic entitlement programs, while the share of national resources spent on defense declined.
- The Joint Chiefs of Staff was strengthened by the 1986 Goldwater-Nichols legislation but was removed from the chain of command.[16]
- Conscription ended, and the portion of the American population with experience of military service steadily declined. Political elites and Congress in particular, in which veterans had traditionally been overrepresented, came to underrepresent them, as the percentage of members of Congress with military-service experience became smaller than the percentage of the population at large.[17]
- Many traditionally military support functions were privatized by shifting them to civilian firms such as Halliburton, KBR, DynCorp, and so on.
- The two national political parties became more polarized, and the partisan identification of military officers became more pronounced and concentrated in one party.

One change whose significance is little appreciated has been the relaxation of resource constraints. This is quite ironic, considering how stretched budgets seem today to those inside the military, and how little the recent growth in military spending has increased the quantity of deployable military power, compared with increases in earlier times. In the early 1960s, with a 13 percent real increase in defense spending, "the number of army combat divisions went up from eleven to sixteen and air force tactical wings from sixteen to twenty-one. Marine Corps manpower increased from 175,000 to 190,000 and army manpower by 100,000."[18] The large increases in the defense budget since the late 1990s—an average of 6 percent a year for a whole decade, a record unmatched in any previous decade since World War II—bought far smaller increases in deployable armed forces. The president's FY 2009 request for total national defense spending, including war costs, came to well over $700 billion, almost 40 percent greater in real terms than the 1968 budget at the height of the Vietnam War, where there were three times as many American military personnel deployed in the theater of combat, as well as the large deterrent force then stationed in Germany.

The current situation would seem less anomalous if there were not a post–September 11 strategy-structure mismatch. The pre–September 11 goal of "transformation" and the "revolution in military affairs" focused on conventional warfare and relied on maximizing the quality of forces. Imperial policing, unconventional warfare, and the need for "boots on the ground" in multiple places simultaneously, however, require manpower in quantity and get only a minimal boost from expensive high-technology advantages in naval and air power. Maintaining personnel levels in the ground forces under the strain of prolonged deployments and combat, and without the cushion of conscription, costs progressively more in bonuses and other expenses that did not enter the equation in the era of mass conscript forces.

Nevertheless, money for the military in recent peacetime has been less pinched than it ever was before the era of confrontation with great powers. In the early Cold War, in fact, military budgets were often determined by criteria having little to do with the functional imperative. In the Truman and Eisenhower administrations, seriousness about budget balancing meant that military expenditures were decided by the "remainder method": the amount left over after subtracting spending for domestic programs, debt interest, and foreign aid from revenues was the amount available for national security spending.[19]

This changed with the Kennedy administration, which declared in principle that the United States would spend whatever was needed for strategic purposes. In practice, however, budget ceilings were actually applied to the military, so the principle created more friction. Now unable to throw up their hands and say simply that there was not enough money available, the civilian managers could reject military recommendations for what programs were needed only by saying that the managers' judgment of what was militarily necessary was better than that of the professional soldiers. The shift away from Truman's and Eisenhower's arbitrary caps on spending crippled a prime means of civilian control, the ability to divide and conquer, exploiting interservice rivalry by requiring the military professionals to make trade-offs among programs. Given the official fiction that spending would be determined by the functional imperative, the services could present a united front, endorsing each other's programs.[20]

Consider the glaring difference between the slugfest in the B-36-versus-super-carrier controversy of the late 1940s and the utter lack of struggle between the Navy and Air Force in the 1990s over which means of projecting firepower—B-2 bombers or aircraft carrier battle groups—should be favored. Comparison with the investment and operating costs of a carrier task force was the one and only thing that could make the B-2 look cheap, yet the Air Force did not try to argue in public or in Congress that it offered the more cost-effective option for strategic airpower. The Air Force put other programs higher on its list of priorities and assumed it could get more B-2s only if the president and Congress provided a bigger total defense budget. In the earlier years when more trade-offs within a set total budget were worked out through logrolling in the JCS, the service might have tried to wrest a bigger share of the pie from the Navy. The shift in later years to giving more of the responsibility for program trade-offs to civilian managers and politicians may be wise in the end, but it raises the price of civilian control: the attempt to impose economic efficiency worked against tranquillity in civil-military relations by shifting the arena of conflict from intramilitary bargaining over how to divide a given pie to competition between professional and political judgments about how big the pie should be.[21]

Nevertheless, between the Democratic Party's urge to shed its post-Vietnam image of weakness on national security and the Republicans' gradual abandonment of genuine insistence on budget balancing—beginning with Richard Nixon's famous 1971 statement that "we are all Keynesians now" and proceeding through Ronald Reagan's and George W. Bush's priority on tax cuts over expenditure cuts—the defense budget became comparatively unbound. This eased civil-military relations when political appointees managed programs with a light hand, which was most of the time apart from the tenures of McNamara and Rumsfeld. Intramural peace was purchased by a modicum of objective control, restraining the intrusive civilian monitoring endorsed by critics such as Allison, Posen, and Cohen.

Unconcealed partisanship of military professionals is one of the bigger changes since Huntington wrote. Its implications are badly misunderstood, however, if it is seen as a reason for subjective control. Ruling the armed forces by choosing military leaders from among those identified politically with the civilian administration would turn an unfortunate but manageable problem into a destructive one.

The stances of the two American parties have evolved, nearly crossing over each other, in the past forty years. Once upon a time, the Democrats were labeled by Republicans as "the war party," responsible for World Wars I and II and the Korean War. Democrats also regularly favored more defense spending than Republicans did during the first phase of the Cold War.[22] In the 1970s Democrats became identified with opposition to military spending and to the use of force. They were repeatedly burned by the electorate for the shift and, after the 1980s, tended to leave the military's priorities nearly intact. Between 1994 and 1999, the Clinton administration spent more on defense than the preceding Bush administration had projected for that period. In the 2000 election, even before September 11 and even with Russia crippled and in decline, Al Gore promised to increase defense spending by $80 billion over the following decade, and George W. Bush promised to add $20 billion per year. Bill Bradley was the only major candidate that year to oppose more increases in defense.[23] In 2004 neither candidate recommended cutting defense spending, and, as of mid-2008, no major candidate for nomination had done so.

The Republican Party nevertheless succeeded in capturing the mantle of nationalism in the decades after the Johnson administration, and the Democrats' image of strategic fecklessness became rooted in public opinion.[24] Straws in the wind—Senator James Webb's defection from the Republicans and return to the party of his youth, the Democrats' effort to recruit other former military officers as congressional candidates, and the pro-military rhetoric adopted by Democrats in their attacks on George W. Bush's Iraq policy—suggest that the tide of Republican advantage on national security may have crested. Professional officers, however, have always been conservative in ideology, in line with Huntington's model of the military mind. They became overtly Republican after the 1960s because realignments concentrated conservatism unambiguously in that party. (The fact that a fair number used to think of themselves as Democrats before the 1960s was due mostly to sociology—the old affiliation of southerners with the party and the World War II cohort of other officers whose social origins were in the New Deal coalition and who did not retire until the Vietnam period.) So it is still not likely that officers' party identification will change much.

But so what? Officers' Republican affinity did not compromise civilian control when Democrats took power. Although some critics were alarmed at reported episodes of disrespect for Clinton, those incidents appeared motivated less by partisanship than by anger at Clinton's perceived personal record of antimilitary sentiment and behavior. Apart from the military resistance that forced a compromise on the plan to admit homosexuals to the armed forces (a plan that aborted because civilian political leadership was also divided), Clinton had no trouble of consequence from the military. It is true that he did not challenge many military preferences, but this was because of his vulnerability to public opinion at large on national security issues, not because he feared military insubordination.

Although officers overwhelmingly prefer the Republican Party, this is rarely a big part of their sense of identity, and it is not the biggest problem of politicization of professions.[25] The weak salience of officers' party identification allows Democrats like Clinton to maintain businesslike relations with their military subordinates. Paradoxically, however, that would change if real subjective control of the military became the norm. If Democratic administrations looked for officers who were Democrats, promotions and assignments would become politicized, and military careers would involve explicit choices of which party to bet on for personal advancement. Ironically, therefore, military partisanship is less problematic when the functioning concept of civil-military relations is some form of objective control.

One change that links the functional imperative (military effectiveness) and the societal imperative (conformity with ideological values) is the de-democratization of war. The era in which American defense policy was absorbed in the challenge of fighting World War II and then preparing for World War III, both of which entailed significant mobilization of society, ended long ago. Yet many remain reluctant to lose the social effects of the mass military. Several decades of conscription and draft-induced officer accessions after 1940 replaced the long tradition of social distance between the military and society with the ethos of the nation in arms. The norm of readiness for major war allowed many Americans to believe that civilian control would be enhanced by the mass military, which ensured that the ranks represented all of society, not just a self-recruited professional elite.[26] Reemergence of a "gap" between the military and society in recent years has alarmed some critics.[27] This reflects in part fear that an unrepresentative military is dangerous, in part nostalgia for the Jacksonian ethos of reliance on militias and citizen-soldiers and desire for subjective control of the military establishment from the bottom up, and in part egalitarian resentment at the vanishing involvement of social elites in responsibility for national defense.[28] Whether it matters or not, there is little that can be done about the gap as long as the military is small and self-selected, but also little reason for concern that the change will damage the system of political control. Given modern communications, the gap will never become huge.

Interest in keeping social bonds between the armed forces and society at large has been almost as great in some sectors of the military itself, especially the Army. In one sense, this is now a forlorn hope, irrespective of whatever efforts may be made to make temporary military service appealing. It is mathematically impossible to have a society where service is the norm and where, at the same time, the standing military force is small. Moreover, the civilianization of the military that characterized the Cold War era has been reversed, as more support functions have been taken over by contractors, leaving a larger proportion of those in uniform remilitarized.[29] In another sense, it is not hard at all to keep the armed forces linked with society because modern communications make the day-to-day connections of military personnel with people and institutions elsewhere easy. (Consider the revolutionary novelty of soldiers in combat able to telephone home or converse by e-mail.)

Whatever the desirability of social representativeness of military personnel might be, there is scant evidence that it matters much for civilian control. If purchased at the price of long-service professionalism, it also limits military effectiveness. The notion that conscription and mass forces are safeguards against professional military usurpation or misconduct is sentimentally satisfying and played a more central role in many other countries with a problematic tradition of civil-military relations, such as France. In reality, however, it is an unreliable restraint apart from the expectation that enlisted soldiers and junior officers would refuse to obey illegal orders by rebellious senior officers. Conscript forces did not prevent coups or military revolts in French Algeria, Greece, Turkey, Argentina, or elsewhere. If the idea is that nonprofessionals would exert a leavening effect on military politics in general, there is no reason to believe this. Participation at the policy level is always limited to career officers far above the ranks at which citizen-soldiers are found.

A Problem without a Crisis

Neither perfect amity between military and civilians nor obsequiously unquestioning obedience by the military is the proper measure of good civil-military relations. There is a problem not only if the military has excessive influence but also if it does not have enough—that is, if civilian control is exerted irresponsibly. The former possibility is what concerns most civilians. But has it been more of a threat to good political order than the latter? The record since 1957 is mixed.

For at least three reasons, civil-military relations should be of more concern than relations between the political leadership and other professional and bureaucratic groups within government. First, the military has the hypothetical capability to impose its political will by force; second, mistakes in communication or in understanding between the two camps about policy objectives or operational actions risk inadvertent escalation and disaster in crises; and, third, lack of integration of policy and operations can produce strategic incoherence that wastes blood and treasure in uses of force even when they prove successful. Even critics who worry mightily concede that the first of these, the risk of a coup d'état, is not an issue in the United States. The second risk was extremely important during the Cold War, when mistakes could hypothetically trigger World War III. The third risk is constant.

When Huntington wrote, the potential for significant civil-military conflict seemed greater than it does now. In 1957 the protogarrison state born in World War II was barely fifteen years old, and the National Security Act and the Department of Defense were only ten. The military had eclipsed the State Department in the policymaking process during World War II; General George Marshall had run both the State and Defense departments in the years following; and General Dwight Eisenhower became the most powerful political leader in the Western world. More to the point, the Truman-MacArthur controversy, involving clear insubordination by a top commander who had more prestige in public opinion than the president, was only a half-dozen years in the past; today it is more distant in time than the Spanish-American War was then. Today, the United States has lived with a large military establishment for almost seventy years. There have been episodic military challenges to civilian authority since 1957, but they pale in comparison to that posed by MacArthur.

Tensions simmered closest to the boiling point in the early 1960s, when a youthful president, a technocratic secretary of defense, and a brashly confident clique of defense intellectuals came to manage a military establishment led by officers who had already been generals in World War II. The worst moments were in the Cuban missile crisis, when Chief of Naval Operations George Anderson tangled angrily with Secretary of Defense Robert McNamara, and the other chiefs grumbled that the civilian leaders were irresolute. The military leadership was certainly restive but not as rebellious as legend has suggested. For example, the sources on which Graham Allison relied in the original edition of *Essence of Decision* claimed that the Navy failed to implement the president's orders to draw the blockade line closer to Cuba—orders intended to allow Khrushchev more time to decide to halt the Soviet ships—and that Admiral Anderson resisted explaining to McNamara what procedures the Navy would use when intercepting the first ship to approach the line. Others claimed that civilian leaders were not aware that U.S. antisubmarine warfare operations were using depth charges to force Soviet submarines to surface, raising the risk of inadvertent war.[30] Subsequent research indicated that these stories were incorrect. Indeed, as Joseph

Bouchard shows, McNamara actually ordered antisubmarine warfare procedures that were *more* aggressive than the ones standard in peacetime. Harried civilian leaders may not have fully comprehended the implications of all these technical measures, or may later have had second thoughts, but the relevant procedures and initiatives did not escape their review and approval.[31]

The Kennedy administration, only a few years after Huntington wrote, was a turning point. It was then, in crisis discussions over intervention in Laos, Cuba, and Vietnam, that the rift between civilians and military over limited versus decisive use of force emerged again. Limited war in Korea had been controversial, but military leadership then was divided and, if anything, more in favor of limitation (for fear of diverting resources that would be needed if war broke out in Europe). With Kennedy and later presidents, civilian initiatives to make war in small doses usually provoked united military recommendations for overwhelming force. This then inhibited the civilians' interest in using force or frustrated the military when intervention proceeded with less force than they recommended.

The gap in mutual understanding, respect, and trust between soldiers and statesmen in the early 1960s was greater than in decades before or since. In the 1950s President Eisenhower had directed military personnel to participate in educating the public about the danger of communism, an initiative that led to formal collaboration between military institutions and right-wing organizations.[32] Such official links did not occur in later decades. With the start of the new administration in the early 1960s, it was a harsh jolt for the leaders of the military's World War II generation to move overnight from answering to five-star General Eisenhower to taking orders from Lieutenant Kennedy. The "whiz kids" in McNamara's Office of the Secretary of Defense were seen as usurpers, and McNamara's insistence on assessing programs in terms of their comparative advantage for combat missions rather than the service requesting them struck at the traditional essence of military organization. Visibly contemptuous chiefs such as LeMay and Anderson came close to kicking over the traces, but their rebellions were successfully contained, and none of the men who followed as service chiefs or field commanders in later years made as much trouble for their civilian masters. Ones who might have were simply not selected by the politicians or avoided appointment when it seemed clear that they were being set up to be co-opted or ignored. For example, Army General John Vessey was passed over for Army chief of staff after an interview in the Carter administration when he said that he disagreed with the policy of withdrawing U.S. ground forces from Korea (although he was later appointed JCS chairman by President Reagan). More recently, Marine Corps Commandant James Jones declined to be considered for the chairmanship of the JCS under Secretary of Defense Rumsfeld.[33]

After the 1962 missile crisis, the military posed no significant obstacle to presidents' preferences on policy toward the Soviet Union, the main issue of consistent importance through the remainder of the Cold War. In strategic arms control negotiations, the Joint Chiefs of Staff bargained for offsetting programs but supported the treaties that resulted.[34] On the most important issue concerning the use of force, the Vietnam War, military leaders remained equally compliant, despite strong reservations about the limitations imposed by the Johnson administration. They grumbled mightily sub rosa, and there is an unconfirmed legend that the Joint Chiefs of Staff aborted a plan to resign en masse in 1967.[35] The fact remains that the chiefs did not resign or otherwise protest in public. Their compliance, in fact, was what enraged critics like McMaster.

Neither Johnson nor his successors ever faced a McClellan or MacArthur. Since Huntington wrote, no general or admiral has ever flirted blatantly with running for president while on active duty, as MacArthur did in 1944, or has gone directly from uniformed service to political candidacy against the party in power, as Eisenhower did in 1952. Westmoreland did venture into politics but not to oppose national policymakers, and with results that made any threat of a "man on horseback" look pathetic: years after leaving Vietnam and the position of Army chief of staff, he lost the Republican primary for governor of South Carolina to a right-wing dentist. The few flag officers who have ventured into high-level electoral politics have fared no better, and their attempts do more to mock the threat of a man on horseback than to warn of it: Major General Edwin Walker finished sixth and last in the Texas gubernatorial primary in 1962 after being relieved of his command by the Kennedy administration; General Curtis LeMay ran as the vice presidential nominee of George Wallace's losing American Independent Party in 1968; Admiral Elmo Zumwalt lost in his bid as the Democratic candidate for the Senate from Virginia in 1976; Vice Admiral James Stockdale humiliated himself in debate as Ross Perot's running mate in 1992; and General Wesley Clark finished several notches down in the Democratic primaries for president in 2004. John McCain's candidacy for president counts as a prominent success for a professional officer. He gained nomination only after a quarter-century political career following retirement from the Navy, however, and he left the service before attaining flag rank. McCain is a lonely example of political capitalization on military prestige.

Every president except Clinton in the six decades after World War II was a veteran, but almost all of the citizen-soldier type. The only professional officer (meaning one with a regular as opposed to reserve commission) to run success-fully for president since Ulysses S. Grant, apart from Dwight Eisenhower, was Jimmy Carter, and he had left the Navy as a young lieutenant. In any case, Carter hardly symbolized militarism to anyone. The one general who had a good chance of unseating a president, Colin Powell, decided not to try in 1996. Of the thirty-four presidents who had served when Huntington wrote, military heroes totaled one-third, and of those, six were career professional officers.[36] (Huntington does not count Washington as a professional. If we do, a full one-fifth of presidents by 1957 had been professional generals.) Of the nine presidents who have followed in the past half century, however, only Kennedy and George H. W. Bush might possibly be counted as military heroes, and not a single one has been a general or an admiral. In modern times, a military takeover via "One Day in November" ap-pears no more a threat than the fictional *Seven Days in May.*[37]

In the wars since Vietnam, military leaders have been no harder to handle than they were then. There was much muttering and tearing of hair behind the scenes on Bosnia, Kosovo, and during the initial planning for the second war against Iraq, but in each case the generals fell into line, their objections unheard outside the Washington Beltway, and posed no significant political problems for presidents. They did inhibit the intervention enthusiasts in the Reagan and Clin-ton administrations, prompting, for example, Secretary of State Madeleine Al-bright's irritated question to JCS Chairman Colin Powell: "What's the point of having this superb military you're always talking about if we can't use it?"[38] Clin-tonites, in particular, were cowed because the men in uniform were a constant reproach to their own strategic amateurism and privileged absence from service in their generation's war.[39] And, if military leaders constrained decisions by the substance of their intramural arguments, this was in no way an illegitimate wield-ing of influence. They did not block presidents who finally decided that they wanted to use force, as in Bosnia by 1995 or Kosovo four years later. Civil-mili-tary relations in the Clinton administration were not good, but they were not dangerous. The imbalance in the equation was due primarily to self-inflicted deficiencies in the sociology of the administration's leadership. (The one and only legal affirmative-action category that the administration failed abysmally to honor in hiring for Schedule C appointments was that of Vietnam-era veter-ans, who would have been three times as numerous among Clinton personnel if they had been appointed in proportion to their percentage of the American pop-ulation.)[40]

In arguing strenuously for using force decisively and without ambivalence, or not at all, Powell did more to constrain Clinton than the JCS of the mid-1960s did Johnson. Was this a blow to civilian control, or a good thing resulting from healthy debate within the government? Powell was not shy about pushing his strategic preferences with political skill. Critics made much of his 1992 *New York Times* op-ed article discussing reasons to avoid limited intervention in the Balkans ("Why Generals Get Nervous"), as if it represented subversion of civilian leadership.[41] The article, however, was approved in advance by both the secretary of defense and the NSC staff.[42] The argument that it was improper rests primarily on the fact that it appeared during an election campaign in which the out-party candidate was hinting at the desire to intervene. Perhaps this discredits Powell's publication, but if so, it is hard to see justification in any instance for a career government official to publish an opinion on how a hypothetical policy initiative could raise operational problems that might call the policy into question.

In the 2002 run-up to the assault on Iraq, when the military acted more like Wheeler and Westmoreland than like Powell, was this a progressive return to good norms, or a tragic failure of the sort mourned by McMaster? The lack of publicly audible protest when Rumsfeld steadily whittled down the size of the 2003 invasion force was a deafening silence to observers who knew anything about the preferences of the Army and the Marine Corps. Not only did the generals not resist: they were induced to make the formal decisions themselves, so that Rumsfeld could later say disingenuously, but without literally lying, that his generals had not asked for more.[43]

If Powell was criticized for publicly opposing a policy favored by out-of-office Democrats, the main comparable controversy involved the September 2007 report to Congress of General David Petraeus. In making the case for the strategy he was applying in Iraq, he was charged by war opponents with acting as a military shill for the Bush administration. Indeed, there is no question that Petraeus's stance put him on the side of the president and against Democratic critics. But what is a military commander to do if not to make the case for his own strategy? If he does not believe in the strategy, he should ask the president to relieve him and appoint someone who can pursue the plan with a clear conscience. If the president insists on having him remain despite his opposition—a hypothetical but hardly plausible possibility—then the commander could legitimately refuse to testify in favor of the strategy because the testimony would be false. But obviously Petraeus and Bush were aligned on the question, as is to be expected in war except in unhealthy or outright destructive situations like the Truman-MacArthur controversy. Those on the left who would have been happy to see Petraeus oppose the president while remaining in command would have to say that Mac-Arthur, too, had been within his rights, which of course none of them would believe. So what else could a field commander have done that would have been more proper for civil-military relations? (Again, I say this as a Democrat, and as a strong critic of the war in Iraq.)

This situation was complicated, again in a manner somewhat reminiscent of the Korean War, because Petraeus's views were not entirely shared by the military leadership in Washington. Some, such as Army Chief of Staff George Casey, reportedly feared the drain and damage to other military missions imposed by the burden of maximizing effort in Iraq and favored larger and faster withdrawals than did Petraeus.[44] This raises other questions, such as how far Congress should go in demanding that military leaders publicly voice their disagreements with their commander in chief, but it does not provide grounds for charging Petraeus with crossing a line into political behavior that should be forbidden.

With few exceptions, overt challenges to civilian supremacy in the past half century have been limited to promptly disciplined minor incidents involving officers below the top level, such as Major General Edwin Walker's attempt to indoctrinate his division on matters of domestic politics in 1961, and Major General John Singlaub's public disagreement with Carter administration plans to withdraw U.S. troops from Korea. More troublesome, because they reflected widespread animosity within the ranks, were scattered incidents of speech disrespectful to President Clinton early in his administration.[45] These were understandable, given Clinton's record—not simply the first of ten presidents since World War II never to have served in uniform, but one who had actively evaded the draft and had made common cause with antimilitary activists. But these incidents were effectively suppressed. They were worrisome in terms of ideal notions of harmony and good order in civil-military relations, but not when considered from the perspective of realistic expectations about interactions between chief executives and civilian institutions of the permanent government.

There were three recognized exceptions to the inconsequential nature of such infractions during the past half century. One was General John Lavelle's conduct of unauthorized bombing raids on North Vietnam in the early 1970s, under the cover of phony "protective reaction" strikes that the rules of engagement permitted if U.S. aircraft were attacked. Lavelle was fired and retired at lower rank, but not prosecuted, and his insubordination was not definitively established. A congressional investigation exonerated him, and the president's right-hand man, John Ehrlichman, later claimed that Nixon had circumvented Secretary of Defense Laird secretly and directed the raids (although JCS Chairman Thomas Moorer denied this).[46] The second exception was the role of two officers detailed to the National Security Council staff in the Reagan administration, Vice Admiral John Poindexter and Lieutenant Colonel Oliver North, in executing the plot to divert funds illegally from sale of arms to Iran to support of the Contra rebels in Nicaragua. These actions were the most blatant betrayals of the Constitution by military officers in many decades, but Poindexter and North were not serving in military positions, asserting military demands, acting as military officers in any way, or resisting presidential authority when they committed their crimes. Indeed, they were promoting the policy objectives of the civilian administration they served, even if Reagan did not direct the illegal actions. The third exception was resistance of the military leadership to President Clinton's plan to allow homosexuals to serve in the armed forces. On this, the generals simply made known their opposition, which had enough support in the other branch of government (Congress) to force the chief executive to compromise, in an example of the bareknuckled form of what Huntington called "the lobbying functions of Congress."[47] None of these exceptions were trivial, but none posed a major challenge to civilian political control. Top civilian officials did not even consider the Lavelle and Singlaub incidents important enough to mention in their memoirs.

The main initiative of the past half century that inhibited civilian political control may be one not usually recognized in that light, and which turned out to have unanticipated consequences. It was also one in which, ironically, the professional military tried to align itself with the societal imperative. This was the reorganization of the Army in the 1970s under Chief of Staff Creighton Abrams that integrated reserve and National Guard units with active forces in war plans, to create the Total Force.[48] According to folklore, Abrams's aim was to avert a repetition of the Vietnam experience, in which few reserve units were ever mobilized, allowing the political leadership to avoid demanding the national commitment to war that a call-up of reserves would have symbolized. There is no clear evidence that the Army undertook the reorganization deliberately to subvert civilian control: indeed, it was prompted first by Secretary of Defense Laird and was designed primarily to get more forces out of limited resources. The effect of the change, nevertheless, was to constrain the options of the commander in chief. "The military sought to fix the incentives," as Secretary of Defense Schlesinger put it, "so that the civilians would act appropriately."[49] General John Vessey, then on the Army staff, often heard Abrams say, "They're not taking us to war again without calling up the reserves."[50] This constraint did not prove to be a problem, however, until more than two decades later, because the only war of consequence was the one against Iraq in 1991, a short and popular one.

Rigging the system in this manner did not lead to trouble until the prolonged peacekeeping deployments in the Balkans and then, especially, the second war against Iraq. In the planning stage for the latter, Rumsfeld steadily browbeat the leadership of the ground forces into chopping down the size of the invasion force for Iraq and deranged the Time Phased Force Deployment List.[51] As a result, the conventional phase of the war ended with no government functioning in Iraq and barely 150,000 American troops covering an area with 25 million people. If three times as many American forces had been available after the fall of Baghdad to impose "shock and awe" not just in the invasion but in the occupation of Iraq as well, history might or might not have been different, but that alternative was the only one with a chance of avoiding the anarchy that gave would-be insurgents a green light. Rumsfeld's concerns, however, had been motivated in part by desire to fight the war with reduced reserve mobilization. In this way, his micromanagement was the counter to the thirty-year-old scheme that would have forced civilian leaders to confront the full implications of war.

As it turned out, the requirements of the long counterinsurgency campaign after 2003 made unprecedented demands on the reserves and National Guard—prolonged and repeated tours of active duty in a combat zone—but without energizing society on behalf of the war effort. This revealed the downside of any military plot there may have been in the 1970s to manipulate the weekend-warrior system as a political forcing mechanism. Those who saw the Abrams reorganization as such a mechanism did not quite grasp that the bigger measure of a nation's commitment is willingness to send conscripts to fight its wars, which comes into play only with reliance on a large active force. Thus, the Bush administration never had to face the intensity of domestic political opposition that the Vietnam draft caused for Johnson and Nixon. Reliance on reserves has not proved to be as potent a forcing mechanism as Cold War conscription was. Indeed, inhumane as it proved for the civilians who joined the reserves, the system allowed other American families to avoid any material stake in the war. The war became highly unpopular in public opinion polls but provoked nothing like the mass demonstrations and unruly active opposition of the Vietnam antiwar movement. In contrast to the 1960s, the Bush administration demanded no sacrifice whatever—not even war taxes—from those civilians who did not elect to join the military in any of its forms. If there was any Abrams plot, it backfired. The integrated active-reserve organization did limit the president's options but in a way that allowed him to fight an unpopular war and failed to prevent him from doing so with underwhelming force.

Equal Dialogue and Unequal Authority

Civil-military relations have been a problem, but less than might have been anticipated in the shadow of MacArthur, and not a severe one as problems in politics and government go. How do recent frictions between political leaders and professional soldiers compare in severity with protests from professionals in the Environmental Protection Agency about distorted editing of scientific reports on global warming by nonexpert political appointees of the Bush administration, or with administration concerns that professionals in the Central Intelligence Agency were trying to subvert Bush policies on Iraq, or with administration attempts to discipline liberal bias among National Public Radio personnel? Those who worry more about the civil-military problem would say that comparisons to other areas of public policy, such as public broadcasting, set the standard too low, because the stakes in military affairs are higher. Examples from conflict between politicos and professionals over crucial issues such as global warming and intelligence warnings about Iraq, however, refute that argument. Yet no coherent literature of concern on professional-political relations on other vital matters rivals the amount of analytical handwringing about civil-military relations.

Conflict between technical specialists and political generalists is natural in democratic government. Experts risk undermining policy objectives by narrow application of professional formulas that ramify in the policy realm with unanticipated negative consequences; politicians risk deranging operations by imposing requirements meant to safeguard higher concerns but whose implementation creates dangers of which only specialists would be aware. Conflict between the camps can be constructive if it is well managed, destructive if either denies the purview of the other. The principle of objective control still accords the military profession less autonomy than most others—certainly less than lawyers, doctors, or professors.

Civilian leaders have often gotten less support or enthusiasm from the generals and admirals than they would have liked, and military preferences have sometimes been wrong and difficult for civilians to handle. But contradictory civilian preferences have sometimes been wrong too, yet have carried the day because civilian authority is, when the last word is said, unchallenged. Presidents always get their way unless another civilian branch of government—Congress—supports the military's preferences. When this happens, we are just witnessing good old checks and balances, the essence of constitutional constraint on executive power, and civilian control of a sort, just not one of executive supremacy. To observers who are horrified to find that presidents and civilian managers in the Pentagon sometimes bend to bureaucratic resistance, or compromise with conflicting preferences of other constituencies, one can only say, *Welcome to the U.S. government!*

This leaves us with two main overlapping questions for judging Huntington's two models of civilian control: first, whether a line should be drawn between the legitimate spheres of authority of military professionals and of political leadership and, if so, where it should be; and, second, whether either the professionals or the politicos have tended to have too much influence in the equation.

One could make the case that for ideal integration of objectives, strategy, and operations, civilians and military should be equally conversant in each others' terms of reference and should participate equally at all stages. In the end, however, few would deny that there is some level of high politics at which soldiers should be silent, and some level of tactical specificity or micromanagement where civilians should keep their hands off. Huntington himself was not as explicit as he might have been about where exactly the lines should be drawn. At one point, he cited Hitler's intervention in the chain of command to direct battalion-level operations as clearly beyond the line.[52] If this were the standard for objective control, at least in wartime, would many oppose it? Similarly, at the other end of the range, one can surmise that Huntington would endorse Roosevelt's overruling Army Chief of Staff Marshall in order to send American weapons to Britain before U.S. entry in the war.

Even the extreme tactical limit suggested earlier might have exceptions. For near-war crisis management, to avoid 1914-type escalation, civilian monitoring of standard operating procedures like the execution of the 1962 blockade of Cuba may be valid. This is risky, because there can be negative unintended consequences from civilian interference, just as from unthinking military application of drill-book procedures. For example, in the Cuban missile crisis, civilian monitors were oblivious to the way their attempts to keep abreast of all relevant details in the military operation wound up clogging naval communication channels and delaying transmission of important messages down the chain of command. (In this light, efforts of Admiral Anderson and Admiral Robert L. Dennison, head of the Atlantic Command, to keep civilians at arm's length from the command and control system become more understandable, even if still unjustified.)[53] The vital importance of avoiding accidental war in the nuclear age is a topic *The Soldier and the State* did not really engage, and this issue gives grounds for more fusion of military and political judgment than the objective control model implies.

In wartime, when crisis management is less of a concern, the case becomes stronger for bowing to the military norm of overwhelming force. At the beginning of *On War,* Clausewitz said that "the mistakes which come from kindness are the very worst."[54] (This norm should not be confused with indiscriminate force that is indifferent to collateral damage.) Clausewitz also notes the danger of half measures when he says, "A short jump is certainly easier than a long one: but no one wanting to get across a wide ditch would begin by jumping half-way."[55] The norm of overwhelming force can be wasteful, as military estimates of requirements may sometimes prove excessive. But that mistake is better than the reverse, undertaking combat with a level of effort that proves indecisive and that squanders blood and treasure to no purpose. Would we have been worse off if the invasion of Iraq in 2003 had immediately installed an occupation force of several hundred thousand, as Army Chief of Staff Eric Shinseki had advised, or if in 1993 Secretary of Defense Les Aspin had authorized the requested dispatch of tanks to Somalia before the "Blackhawk Down" incident, or if the Air Force's 94 Target Plan—the only scheme for bombing that the service claimed would be effective—had been implemented against North Vietnam in 1965, rather than in gradual increments over the succeeding years?

More overwhelming force in these cases might not have succeeded. Cohen rightly points out that criticism of civilian leadership on Vietnam "would be infinitely stronger if one could adduce evidence that Johnson's professional military advisers had a better idea of how to fight the war," but he also concedes that the gradualist rationale for the air war, which the JCS did firmly oppose, proved "calamitously false."[56] On Vietnam, neither camp had a recipe for success, and the worst mistake of the JCS was its unwillingness to see withdrawal from the war as preferable to acceptance of the civilians' fatal strategy for stalemate. If the overwhelming-force alternative for the air war had been tried, though, at least the fact and price of failure would have been evident sooner and the choices for policymakers clearer, diminishing the temptation to forge ahead with continued slow bleeding.[57]

The contrast between the results of the first and second American wars against Iraq makes McMaster's concerns more salient than Cohen's. McMaster's portrait of criminal prevarication by Johnson and McNamara is exaggerated, and his lack of empathy for the Joint Chiefs may reflect lack of high-level experience in the Washington arena. His important point, however, was that because the chiefs adhered to the silence outside the confines of the Pentagon and White House that Cohen would insist upon, professional military opposition to the Johnson administration's planned strategy for Vietnam was unknown to the public. This in turn reduced the constraints on Johnson, made it easier for him to avoid the choice between the extremes of withdrawal and overwhelming force, and facilitated the descent into disaster that did not end until a decade later, at a price far higher than a choice of either of the extremes in 1965 would have cost.

It is quite true, as Cohen suggests, that at the outset of wars, especially ones different from recent experience, professional soldiers cannot claim superior expertise about which uses of force will work to achieve political objectives. Westmoreland, Wheeler, and company were clearly not fonts of strategic wisdom. There were also very powerful reasons that Johnson had to avoid risky escalation and that compelled him to follow a middle course. The point is simply that the luxury of hindsight shows civilian political leaders to be no wiser in the end than the soldiers.

Cohen's portrait of four civilian war leaders whose intervention in military planning and operations turned out well points to a different verdict. He does not demonstrate, however, that these four were a representative sample of intrusive hands-on political managers, rather than just four he came to know and admire. (In academic jargon, this is "selecting on the dependent variable.") He does not compare the lessons of their cases with ones in which the civilian impulse to meddle deep in the chain of command produced bad military results, such as Hitler's armchair commands in World War II, and he does not indicate how one should decide whether the effects of such meddling are more often good than bad. (Nor does he indicate whether he approves of the records of activist secretaries of defense like McNamara and Rumsfeld in managing peacetime programs, the supreme examples of the demanding management style he endorses in chief executives in wartime.) It is possible that a systematic survey would show that political leaders are usually wiser than their uniformed subordinates about operational-level matters, but it is no less possible that military advisors would prove more prescient about the deficiencies of strategy than their civilian masters. Military autonomy often leads to bad results, but so does civilian meddling. With this reality, muddier than the intellectually clean ideal types of objective and subjective control, practical solutions will not embrace either one unequivocally, but they should tilt toward Huntington's old preference.

Critics of objective control sometimes skirt the question of why subjective control should be preferable. They might argue against the polarity Huntington poses, denying that subjective control need be the alternative. If it is not the alternative—if presidents do not concede military leaders any autonomy but also do not try to ensure that those leaders share the administration's views—the only plausible third alternative is one in which the professional military has no influence at all: where its advice is so unimportant that civilians do not care who gives it. This would not be an unequal dialogue but a superfluous one. Otherwise, opposition to objective control must imply some measure of preference for what Huntington calls fusion, in which military leaders are politicized in the mold of their masters, lest the soldiers resort to political maneuvering against civilian preferences.

Subjective control does not mean civilianizing the military in the sense that Morris Janowitz saw happening ineluctably in the postwar period as the military adapted to modernity. Janowitz described civilianization as a process of bureaucratization, assimilation of noncombat functions, ascendancy of a managerial rather than heroic ethos, and reduced physical isolation from the rest of society.[58] Huntington's concept of fusion involves more direct politicization of the military. For example, the replacement of the commanding general of the Army by a chief of staff, under the reforms of Secretary of War Elihu Root in the early twentieth century (as close in time to *The Soldier and the State* as that book is to us today), made the military leader's term coextensive with the president's. "Under this system, the Chief of Staff became a part of the administration in power. He was not simply the spokesman for permanent military interests. He was also political. . . . His position was, in effect, that of an undersecretary in an executive department."[59] Had this system endured, defense policy would probably have witnessed increasingly explicit partisan activity by ambitious officers. Which set of problems would be more worrisome: tension between the professional military elite and political leaders, or competition among Republican and Democratic officers for appointments and advancement?

The main critique of objective control barely mentions this, the alternative that Huntington poses, and does not fully engage what Huntington meant. For example, Cohen quotes Huntington's line that in World War II, "So far as the major decisions in policy and strategy were concerned, the military ran the war," but Cohen then says, mistakenly, "And a good thing too, he seems to add." In fact, on the page in *The Soldier and the State* where the quoted line appears, it is followed by Huntington's lament that the military accomplished this dominance through fusion, "only by sacrificing their military outlook" and becoming one with the liberal society, with bad effects on the peace that followed the war.[60]

How should the dialogue be made equal? Clausewitz recommended that the top commander be in the cabinet, to ensure that policymakers understood the limitations of military options and the ramifications of their choices at each point.[61] U.S. practice does not go that far; the chairman of the Joint Chiefs of Staff is a statutory advisor, but not an official member, of the National Security Council. This is good enough, as long as he and the chiefs are as free as the regular members to discuss their views. It is also only realistic to expect presidents to pay some attention to whether top military appointees have views that are at least minimally compatible with their own aims. Having Curtis LeMay as a member of the JCS under Kennedy and Johnson served no one's interests. But this outcome does not suggest that it would be best to look for clones. It may mean exerting close control of military appointments at the four-star or occasionally the three-star level, but not vetting all general officer promotions, as critics believe Rumsfeld did.

A better way to balance the equation is desirable but probably not achievable. The principle endorsed by Cohen—the "unequal dialogue"—is not literally apt. Inequality of authority between civilian and military executives is as it should be, and if checks on executive authority are a problem, blame the Founders. But the proper inequality of authority makes it all the more important for the dialogue between the camps to be equal. Subjective control that keeps bruising dialogue limited to the bureaucratic level within the Defense Department by appointing accommodating officers at the top has not served the functional imperative. Equality in strategic discussion does not compromise the civilians' ultimate primacy. Presidents have the right to be wrong in the end, but generals should have every chance to prevent error before that end.

In *The Soldier and the State*, Huntington posed two stark ideal types of civilian control and endorses one. In *The Common Defense*, which covered a much broader set of problems, he presented a more complex and richer set of ways to understand military policy. That book made clear that the genius of the American system was not its consistent adherence to planned courses of action but its robust ways of muddling through, thereby implying how civil-military relations might work satisfactorily without always embodying the pure form of objective control. He ends *The Common Defense* by describing Fisher Ames's 1795 address in the House of Representatives:

> A monarchy or despotism, Ames suggested, is like a full-rigged sailing ship. It moves swiftly and efficiently. It is beautiful to behold. It responds sharply to the

helm. But in troubled waters, when it strikes a rock, its shell is pierced, and it quickly sinks to the bottom. A republic, however, is like a raft: slow, ungainly, impossible to steer, no place from which to control events, and yet endurable and safe. It will not sink, but one's feet are always wet.[62]

In American civil-military relations the water never gets chin-deep. In the worst of times, it splashes up toward knee level. Our feet are always wet, but the water rarely gets above our ankles.

CHAPTER THREE

A Broken Dialogue

Rumsfeld, Shinseki, and Civil-Military Tension

Matthew Moten

In the weeks before the start of Operation Iraqi Freedom, Senator Carl Levin had serious doubts about the war plan. Ranking Democrat on the Senate Armed Services Committee, Levin was one of his party's most respected experts on national security issues. At a February 2003 committee hearing, therefore, less than a month before the invasion, Levin asked Army Chief of Staff General Eric K. Shinseki how many troops would be required to secure Iraq after a successful offensive. Shinseki had his own reservations about the plan, reservations that he had aired with his superiors at the Pentagon and at a meeting with President Bush. When Levin asked, however, he demurred; he preferred, he said, to leave such an estimate to the combatant commander. Levin, one of Congress's most tenacious and effective interrogators, persisted: "How about a range?" Finally, drawing on his experience as Allied commander in the Balkans and historical analysis that his staff had provided, Shinseki answered that, given the geographic expanse of Iraq and its ethnic tensions, "something on the order of several hundred thousand soldiers" might be necessary to administer the country after a cessation of hostilities.[1]

The next day, although Shinseki's estimate squared with Central Command's own internal figures, Deputy Secretary of Defense Paul Wolfowitz, testifying before the House Armed Services Committee, called Shinseki's projection "wildly off the mark." At a press conference, Secretary of Defense Donald H. Rumsfeld likewise told reporters, "The idea that it would take several hundred thousand U.S. forces I think is far off the mark." Vice President Dick Cheney echoed those comments to NBC's Tim Russert on *Meet the Press*, and predicted that American forces would be "greeted as liberators."

These official and public repudiations of a sitting service chief indicated a widening gulf between the nation's civilian and military leaders and between the Office of the Secretary of Defense (OSD) and the Army.[2] Along with other episodes during the overlapping tenures of Army Chief of Staff Shinseki and Secretary of Defense Rumsfeld, it displayed politico-military tensions at the highest levels and in particularly challenging times.

This chapter examines this and other episodes of major conflict between Rumsfeld and Shinseki, and then explores what each might have done differently. In a broad examination of the roles and duties of service chiefs, the chapter offers a guide to normative behaviors and competencies for officers at the politico-military nexus and suggests alternative models that could improve on Huntington's model of objective control.

Civil-Military Tensions: A Clash of Cultures and Loyalties

Civil-military tensions are natural and, to the extent that they foster informed decision making, can be productive. Yet frequently since World War II, American civil-military relations have been so strained that both policy and strategy have suffered. Some of the causes of tension are structural, codified in the Constitution or in legislation governing the Department of Defense. However, over recent decades the principal causes have stemmed from alterations in security conditions. The United States gained a preeminent role in world affairs after the Allied victory in the Second World War. The combination of growing nuclear capabilities and a superpower rivalry with the Soviet Union brought an age of limited war. Nevertheless, the need to maintain a nuclear arsenal and ready surface forces led to rapid growth in the power of the U.S. military establishment and in the size of the defense budget, both absolutely and as a proportion of federal spending. Growing budgets spurred bureaucratic and political efforts to gain control of all that spending. Each of these developments magnified the importance of defense and security issues. As military leaders took on more prominent roles in national affairs, political leaders began to demand tighter control of national security. Apart from the superpower rivalry, these conditions are likely to persist well into the future, and heightened civil-military tensions are therefore likely to persist as well.

Managing these tensions should be a high priority among all concerned, but participants on both sides of the relationship are handicapped. Most civilian policymakers have little acquaintance with the military and with warfare. If they have any experience, it was usually gained briefly and at an early stage, before a long career in politics and government. Thus, they may be politically astute and militarily naive. Senior officers have at least a quarter century of military experience in progressively more responsible positions, yet their experience in the political arena is usually recent and short. They are militarily expert but often politically naive. Thus, in this most important of relationships, the stage is set for a clash of cultures.

In *The Soldier and the State,* Huntington proposed an ideal model for the management of those tensions. Writing in the first decade of the Cold War, he posited a form of civil-military relations called "objective civilian control." As Huntington defined it, objective civilian control maximizes military professionalism, and hence national security, by divorcing the military from political life in exchange for professional autonomy within its own sphere. It "furnishes a single concrete standard of civilian control which is politically neutral and which all social groups can recognize."[3] Objective control attempts to erect a wall between overarching policy and the strategy by which to implement it that neither general nor politician should breach.

Seen as an ideal theoretical type, objective control has much to recommend it. In an ideal world, professional soldiers would remain unequivocally subordinate to their political masters, who would, in turn, develop clear, unambiguous policy goals before a forthright declaration of war. Then, soldiers would prosecute war to its successful conclusion unfettered by political interference. Upon the outbreak of peace, civilians would resume their supremacy.[4]

The problem with Huntington's model is that it is incompatible with human reality and the U.S. Constitution. Clausewitz's fundamental theoretical insight is that "war is merely the continuation of policy by other means." The two activities may have different grammars, but they do not have different logic. "Nor indeed is it sensible to summon soldiers, as many governments do when they are planning a war, and ask them for *purely military advice.*"[5] There is no such thing as "purely military advice." In the real world of civil-military relations, soldiers sometimes enter the realm of policymaking, while civilian leaders can and do involve themselves in professional military matters, including operational planning and even battlefield decisions. In practice, no Huntingtonian wall of objective control separates political and military matters.[6]

Huntington contrasts his ideal model with another type, which he calls subjective civilian control, in which civilian groups maximize their power over the military. He argues that subjective control has historically been achieved where certain government institutions or social classes monopolize control of the military, generally at the expense of competing civilian groups. He asserts that subjective control actually decreases military security in the state because it compromises military professionalism. "Subjective civilian control achieves its end by civilianizing the military, making them the mirror of the state." In Huntington's view, since the advent of military professionalism, subjective control, regardless of the form it takes, is the worst possible outcome for national security, except, perhaps, no control at all.[7]

Yet in the United States, as the controversy surrounding Shinseki's 2003 Senate testimony illustrates, the Constitution divides civilian control of the military between the executive and legislative branches, creating a constant tension among the military and its two civilian masters. Huntington himself describes at length how the separation of powers and the allocation of authority subverts objective civilian control.[8]

Congress controls the purse, raises and supports armies, writes military laws and authorizing legislation, and declares war. The president is commander in chief of the armed forces and appoints the civilian and military officers of the armed forces, subject to the advice and consent of the Senate. Thus, while the president and secretary of defense are at the top of the military chain of command, officers owe fealty to the legislative branch as well.[9] Senators in confirmation hearings over the past several years have required appointees to four-star billets to answer some form of the following question: "If confirmed, do you pledge to return to this committee and other congressional committees when asked and to render your best professional military judgment regardless of administration policies?"[10] Candidates must answer in the affirmative if they hope to be confirmed.

A service chief's roles are further complicated by multiple responsibilities. The Army chief of staff, for example, works directly for the secretary of the Army as head of the service. As a member of the Joint Chiefs, however, the Army chief of staff has responsibilities to that body, is subordinate to the chairman of the Joint Chiefs, and through that officer advises the secretary of defense and the president. When a service chief disagrees with the chairman or the consensus of the Joint Chiefs, he can, according to law, exercise the option to offer a differing opinion, through the chairman, to the president. Thus, wearing multiple hats and serving several masters just within the executive branch, a service chief may easily come into conflict with one or another of those who, by law and the Constitution, are supposed to exercise "control" over him.

It is reasonable to ask whether, contra Huntington, it is possible to sustain a healthy military profession under such conditions. Manifestly, the answer is yes; for most of the past two centuries, military professionalism has grown and flourished in the United States, although at some times more fully than at others.

Another complication is that relationships among generals and civilian leaders are always personal and political, as well as professional. Interpersonal relationships between people with great responsibility can become stormy, and the problems inherent in these relationships demand exploration. How does the military professional navigate among competing professional military responsibilities and political responsibilities to the executive and legislative branches? What should generals do when their superiors' decisions appear to threaten damage to the military institution or to national security? Is it possible to structure civil-military relationships to ensure both effective policymaking and successful strategic planning and execution?

Shinseki Becomes Chief of Staff

In the 1990s the Army found itself stretched in many directions. After the end of the Cold War, the global stability imposed by the superpower rivalry had given way to a series of regional conflicts. The United States was freer to intervene and did so more often, deploying the Army into Panama, the Persian Gulf, Haiti, Somalia, Bosnia, Kosovo, and many smaller contingencies. At the same time, the active Army was reduced in size from 785,000 soldiers to 480,000, and its budget reduced more than one-third in real terms. Thus, even as the Army was busier and deploying more than in the Cold War, it had fewer soldiers and less funding. Little modernization of Army equipment had taken place in the decade since 1989. The service missed its enlisted recruiting target in 1999 for the first time in years. A series of scandals—involving generals in some cases and drill sergeants in others—had damaged morale in the force. Midgrade officers were resigning at an increasing pace, often citing a lack of trust in their leaders.[11] The service's readiness was in question; the Army needed renewal.

General Shinseki became Army chief of staff in 1999. With three-and-a-half decades of service, including two combat tours in Vietnam—both of which ended with grievous wounds—several command and staff positions in Europe, and five stints in the Pentagon, Shinseki was a veteran officer with a thorough understanding of the Army and the Department of Defense. Trim, reserved, and unassuming, he was well respected in the Army for his integrity and his toughness, although some outside the service opined that he might be too traditional, a "dinosaur."[12]

Nevertheless, he came into office with a charter to shake his service loose from its Cold War moorings and move it into the twenty-first century. Secretary of Defense William Cohen had selected Shinseki and charged him with modernizing the service to make it more rapidly responsive and deployable to trouble spots around the globe. Recognizing the magnitude of the task, Shinseki commenced his tenure with a four-year campaign plan that soon became known as "Transformation."[13]

He aimed to transform the Army into a twenty-first-century force through substantial institutional change. Before he took office, Shinseki brought together a transition team and charged it with a broad assessment of the Army. After interviewing hundreds of people inside the service and out, the team distilled a short list of priority issues for the new chief's attention. Shinseki refined this list further, writing a tight statement of his intent as chief of staff to focus on three major areas: people, readiness, and transformation. The Army had to refocus on recruitment, training, retention, and well-being of its members; it had to maintain its current war-fighting ability in a time of tight budgets and high operating tempo; and it needed to modernize for the future. These tasks would not be simple or easy. Although Cohen had given Shinseki a charter to change the Army, the secretary had committed no additional resources for the task. The Army would have to transform within its current budget or convince Congress to support the concept with additional funds. Shinseki opted for a little of both, rearranging some internal priorities as well as presenting his plan to congressional committees and meeting with individual members to sell them on it. His efforts paid off. In the final year of the Clinton administration and Shinseki's first year as chief, Congress registered its support, adding $3.5 billion to the president's defense budget request, specifically targeted at beginning the transformation of the Army.[14]

The New Administration and Rumsfeld's Department of Defense

During the 2000 presidential election campaign, both Governor George W. Bush and Vice President Al Gore had pledged to increase defense spending, and both spoke in terms that Shinseki himself had been using to describe the Army's modernization efforts, calling for the armed forces to be leaner, more deployable, more responsive, and more agile.[15] It seemed that, regardless of the election outcome, the new administration would be supportive of the Army's ongoing transformation efforts. When George W. Bush was finally declared winner, the Army looked forward to good working relations with his new defense team. It was not to be. As the Bush administration took office, the Army was embroiled in a public relations fiasco surrounding what should have been a relatively trivial issue.

The Black Beret

In October 2000 General Shinseki had announced that the Army would soon adopt a black beret as part of the uniform. Intended as a symbol of the "transformation" that would encompass the entire Army, the beret decision came as an unwelcome surprise to many inside and outside the service. For twenty-odd years, the Army's Ranger Regiment had worn a black beret, which many saw as a badge of its unique contribution to special operations warfare. Before long, various Ranger alumni groups were protesting the decision. Two former Rangers staged a march from Fort Benning, Georgia, to Washington. An Internet and media campaign flared when news broke that some of the new berets were to be manufactured in the People's Republic of China. The House Government Reform and Small Business Committees both became interested in the issue.[16]

Reaction inside the Army was not much better. Many soldiers wrote letters to the editor of the *Army Times* protesting the change. The active-duty Ranger Regiment remained mostly quiet, but the regimental commander nonetheless felt compelled to issue a gag order to his soldiers. Shinseki was almost alone among Army senior leaders in defending the decision, although it had vocal support from Jack Tilley, sergeant major of the Army (the Army's senior enlisted member), and Thomas White, the new Army secretary. A Vietnam-era photo of Tom White as an armored cavalry lieutenant wearing a black beret was published in *Soldiers* magazine, both as a sign of the secretary's support and a visual refutation of the argument that the headgear was a unique and ancient Ranger emblem. Still, the controversy continued for most of a year, boding ill for the future of Army transformation. If the Army was so resistant to a minor uniform change, many wondered, how could it possibly muster the unity to undertake major institutional reform?

This flap was the backdrop for the Bush administration's introduction to the Army and its leadership. Although the furor died down after a congressional hearing in May 2001, the beret controversy provided an inauspicious beginning for the Army's relationship with the new administration and for Shinseki's dialogue with the new secretary of defense.

The 2001 Quadrennial Defense Review

In 2001 the new leadership in the Office of the Secretary of Defense (OSD) led the service staffs through the Quadrennial Defense Review (QDR), an extensive exercise in defining strategic roles and missions and determining the apportionment of resources for the long-term future. Mandated by law, the QDR has become an all-important event for the services and an opportunity for each administration to put its stamp on defense policy. It was apparent that Secretary Rumsfeld intended to do just that. He had definite ideas about the future of warfare. He had voiced his commitment to "transformation," a term Shinseki had coined, but for Rumsfeld it connoted a high-tech, network-centric approach to war, emphasizing precision-strike weaponry, information-age intelligence, and ballistic missile defense. The Army would have only a limited role in Rumsfeld's vision of the future.[17] When it became apparent that Rumsfeld might seek to cut as many as four Army divisions from the force structure, Shinseki and his staff insisted on an opportunity to refute the arguments with evidence of the need for a larger rather than a smaller army.[18] The debate took place out of the public eye and, inasmuch as no divisions were cut, the Army's view prevailed in the final report to the president and Congress, but the victory was Pyrrhic.[19] Rumsfeld and others in OSD were furious at losing what they saw as an important opportunity to transform the Army. They developed the opinion that the Army was resistant to change; this came as bitter irony to Shinseki, who was fighting within the service to transform the Army into a more mobile, agile, and deployable force, just not a smaller one. His ideas about how to accomplish transformation strongly clashed with those of his superiors in OSD. The episode badly tarnished his relationship with Rumsfeld.[20]

Rumsfeld's Goals as Secretary

Like Shinseki, Rumsfeld had entered office with a mandate for change. President Bush had campaigned on a platform of defense transformation. Rumsfeld believed that, in order to transform the Defense Department, he would first have to assert authority over the Pentagon. Having served before as defense secretary under President Gerald Ford, Rumsfeld had personal experience with the Pentagon bureaucracy and knew how difficult it could be to cause change in such a large institution. Moreover, the new team in OSD believed that the Clinton administration had allowed civilian control of the military to weaken.[21] They saw Shinseki's dissent during the QDR as resistance to necessary institutional change and a sign that the military that had gone too long unbridled. Rumsfeld aimed to restore order and discipline.[22]

On another level, differences of personality had effects. Shinseki was by nature courtly, polite, and respectful. Rumsfeld was by turns ebullient, abrasive, charming, and confrontational. The news media began to report on Rumsfeld's ego and personal style and how they would affect the department and Washington itself; the word "arrogant" was frequently used. Yet Rumsfeld was renowned as a seasoned political infighter, having served in Congress, in several positions in the Nixon administration, and as White House chief of staff for President Ford before his first tenure as secretary of defense. Notoriously impatient and disdainful of bureaucratic processes, Rumsfeld soon began sending memos throughout the Pentagon demanding quick answers to all manner of questions; these "snowflakes" upset time-honored procedures. He affected a hectoring style in press conferences and meetings with senior officers. A January 2003 Rumsfeld press conference provides a flavor of that style. Responding to a question citing a frequently heard complaint, "that you tend to ride roughshod over your military leadership," Rumsfeld said:

> I have received on occasion from people, military and civilian, work that I was not impressed with. . . . And there have been times when I've sent things back six, seven times. Why? Well, because it strikes me that it's terribly important that we do things well and we do them right. . . . And I will keep right on doing it. Now, it's no fun for somebody to have their work sent back four or five times, six times, seven times. . . . And if that disturbs people and their sensitivities are such that it bothers them, I'm sorry. But that's life, because this stuff we're doing is important. . . . The Constitution calls for civilian control of this department. And I'm a civilian. . . . This place is accomplishing enormous things. . . . And it doesn't happen by standing around with your finger in your ear hoping everyone thinks that that's nice.[23]

At one meeting he upbraided Shinseki in front of several junior officers, waving his hand and saying, "Are you getting this yet? Are you getting this yet?" Shinseki, incapable of boorishness himself, seemed genuinely stumped as to how to improve the relationship.[24]

9/11 and Afghanistan

The 9/11 attacks and the nation's response to them set the agenda for the second half of Shinseki's four-year tenure as chief of staff. In September 2001 President Bush ordered an offensive into Afghanistan to retaliate against Al Qaeda and the Taliban regime. General Tommy Franks, commander of Central Command (CENTCOM), presented a plan for a robust package of joint forces that would have taken months to assemble and deploy. Rumsfeld rejected such traditional thinking and insisted on forces that were lighter and fewer and that would arrive faster.

When the relatively light force that Franks deployed, comprising special operations forces and air power in support of allied Afghan fighters, succeeded quickly in defeating the enemy and placing Hamid Karzai in power, Rumsfeld and his staff felt vindicated, not just in Afghanistan, but in their view of transformation: ponderous, heavy land forces were obsolete, and precision-strike weapons, special operations forces, and effects-based operations were the wave of the future. Shinseki, an advocate for overwhelming superiority of combat power in operational planning, was seen as a hopeless traditionalist.[25]

In April 2002, when Shinseki's term still had some fourteen months remaining, the *Washington Post* reported that Secretary Rumsfeld had decided to nominate Army Vice Chief of Staff John Keane to succeed Shinseki. This leak by a "senior defense official" of a successor's name so far in advance further diminished Shinseki's standing; indeed, it seemed calculated to do so. As it turned out, Keane did not succeed Shinseki, so the story was erroneous, but the damage had been done. Shinseki began to joke about being a lame duck, but would remind audiences that plenty of work remained in the rest of his tour of duty. Despite Shinseki's stoicism, however, relations between the Army and OSD, and especially with Rumsfeld, seemed only to get worse.[26]

The Crusader Episode

The Army's Crusader artillery program, on the drawing board for more than a decade and about to go into production, had drawn critical comments from Governor Bush during the presidential campaign as an example of a weapons system that did not fit into his plans for military reform. For his part, General Shinseki had cast a critical eye on Crusader early in his tenure, demanding that its designers drastically reduce the weapon's weight to make it more deployable or risk cancellation of the entire program. Before long, the hundred-ton behemoth had become a relatively svelte forty tons. An accurate and rapid-firing system, the Crusader represented a technological leap ahead of its Vietnam-era predecessor.[27] Shinseki thought that the program was on the right track.

The president included Crusader in his budget proposal to Congress in February 2002, but rumors persisted that the administration might cancel the program. In late April, Deputy Defense Secretary Paul Wolfowitz told Army Secretary Thomas White to review the program and to offer recommendations. It was clear that OSD was now actively considering cancellation. Yet, believing that the Army had been given an opportunity to make its best case, White told his legislative affairs office to rally Crusader's congressional supporters.[28] Following a coordination meeting the next day, an Army officer drafted a memo to guide that effort, offering arguments in defense of the program. Full of provocative language, the "talking points" memo was meant only for internal Army use. Nevertheless, a senior Army civilian official released the memo on Capitol Hill, and within hours a copy found its way to Secretary Rumsfeld.[29]

While the writing of the memo and the release of it were ham-fisted, they were not illegal. All of the services had long-established legislative affairs offices to handle communications with Congress. Secretary White had simply directed his legislative office to continue to argue in support of a program that was still in the president's budget request.

Yet Rumsfeld, furious at what he viewed as insubordination, ordered an investigation into the "leak." OSD public affairs spokeswoman Victoria Clarke warned that "anyone who may be responsible for inappropriate behavior will be held accountable" and refused to confirm that Secretary Rumsfeld retained confidence in Secretary White. Her office launched a month-long campaign to dispute the Crusader "talking points." Rumsfeld, using characteristic congressional jargon, said that he had "a minimum of high regard for that kind of behavior," referring to the leaking of the talking points. Following the investigation, the official who released the memo resigned. Rumsfeld ordered both the major general in charge of Army Legislative Liaison and the lieutenant colonel who wrote the memo reassigned. Rumsfeld required Secretary White to attend the press conference at which Wolfowitz announced the administration's decision to cancel the Crusader program. White's official review of the program was moot. As Rumsfeld saw it, he was moving decisively to reassert civilian control of the military and, more specifically, Defense Department control over the Army.[30]

Many members of Congress saw matters differently. The armed services committees, then in the midst of "marking up" the president's budget proposal, viewed the decision to cancel Crusader as a "process foul": OSD had not played according to the rules of the game, killing a program for which it had expressed its official support in the budget submission to Congress. Senator Levin, then chairman of the Senate Armed Services Committee, moved quickly to call a hearing on the Crusader program, which set up a public showdown between Rumsfeld and Wolfowitz on the one hand and White and Shinseki on the other.[31]

General Shinseki was thus caught between executive and legislative branches contending for control of a policy question. He had publicly and repeatedly voiced his support for Crusader in speeches and congressional testimony, asserting its importance to the transforming Army. Yet, as chief of staff, he was now obligated to support an administration funding decision. As far as he was concerned, the spectacle of a Senate hearing would only serve to highlight differences that should have been shelved following his superiors' decision. Nevertheless, Levin insisted on holding a hearing to explore the issues between OSD and Congress, as well as the merits of the Crusader system itself.

On May 16, the day of the Senate hearing, Rumsfeld starred in an elaborately choreographed media blitz to shore up support for his decision. He published an opinion piece in the *Washington Post* and appeared on Rush Limbaugh's radio talk show. During the hearing, the secretary's presentations lasted until the evening television news programs had begun to air, ensuring that Shinseki's views would be presented too late to get much media attention.[32]

Shinseki found a way to remain true to his previous position and yet uphold the principle of obedience to civilian authority. He attempted to downplay the sense of discord between OSD and the Army, saying that descriptions of the matter "as a pitched battle are not helpful." He testified that the Army still required the novel indirect-fire capabilities that Crusader would have brought to the battlefield. Not having those capabilities would increase operational risk to the force. However, if it were possible to gain those capabilities in another way, perhaps in the new Future Combat System, the Crusader program itself was not essential. His testimony reiterated that the Army would obey: "The Army has its order, and we are executing it."[33]

Despite Shinseki's acquiescence in the decision, Rumsfeld's victory in the policy dispute, and the clear assertion of civilian primacy, the poisoned relationship between the two men had become an embarrassingly public spectacle. The Crusader controversy and the conflict between Rumsfeld and Shinseki had offered fodder to the media for over a month. The June cover of *Armed Forces Journal* showed a photo montage of Rumsfeld and the Crusader, emblazoned with the caption "Does He Really Hate the Army?"[34] Many inside the service felt besieged by a hostile Defense Department. The retired general officer community, which was more vocal than its active-duty counterpart, began to grumble about Rumsfeld's high-handedness, his treatment of Shinseki, and his perceived disdain for the professional military. The episode also damaged the secretary's already contentious relations with Congress. It haunted all subsequent interactions between Shinseki and Rumsfeld.

The Iraq War Plans

The administration began to shift its attention from Afghanistan to a confrontation with Iraq; by the summer of 2002, planning for an invasion was underway. Bush, Rumsfeld, and Franks were working together to develop a plan of operations—although they equivocated about the existence of such efforts when asked.[35] As in the Afghanistan planning sequence, Franks argued for a relatively large offensive force, but Rumsfeld repeatedly pressed him to reduce troop numbers, resting his argument on the success in Afghanistan. These negotiations, which Franks later euphemistically described as an "iterative process," went on with little input from anyone outside OSD and CENTCOM.[36] Nonetheless, Franks seemed to revel in his independence from all but Rumsfeld and the president. Close coordination among these three principals diminished the statutory role of the Joint Chiefs of Staff. Franks understood the service chiefs' role as force providers to his command but not as military advisors to the president and secretary of defense. He reluctantly and infrequently briefed the Joint Chiefs, disdained their questions and advice, and even collected all briefing copies at the end of their meetings.[37] At one point, Franks employed a vulgar expletive with two of the service chiefs to express his disdain for their statutory responsibilities under Title 10 of the U.S. Code.[38]

The chiefs were understandably uncomfortable with the plans they saw but had little opportunity to affect them. Franks's secrecy and exclusivity prevented the services from assisting the planning with their expertise on force provision and sustainment. Moreover, Rumsfeld's insistence on controlling every detail exacerbated their concerns. Having demanded a minimalist operational plan, Rumsfeld then tweaked logistical details to pare the force even further. The services ordinarily coordinate overseas deployments with a complex database called the Time-Phased Force Deployment List (TPFDL, pronounced tip-fiddle), which is meant to synchronize the logistical demands of deploying units with the operational needs of commanders on the ground. Military staffs study and compose TPFDLs years in advance for many possible contingencies, to ensure that soldiers and their equipment arrive at seaports at the right times to avoid bottlenecks, that fuel trucks are on hand before tanks have to move, that ammunition resupplies and medical support are in place before the battle starts, and so on. Shinseki and the Army Staff were appalled when Rumsfeld delayed signing deployment orders, essentially invalidating the timing of the TPFDL, and refused to deploy some logistical units.[39] They were concerned that chaos might ensue and that deployed soldiers would go unsupported.

In January 2003 President Bush held a meeting in the White House Cabinet Room with Vice President Dick Cheney, Rumsfeld, Wolfowitz, the Joint Chiefs, and the combatant commanders. The purpose was to review the war plan and to determine whether the services and combatant commands could support it. The president began asking the assembled flag officers for their views, starting with the Army chief of staff. Calmly, Shinseki specified seven concerns about the plan, focusing on the strength of invading forces and the logistical capability to sustain them for the fight. The gist of his comments was not that the Army was incapable of providing enough forces to support the plan; indeed, he was offering to provide more. To one observer, the president seemed unsure of what to do after Shinseki spoke; he asked no questions. None of the nation's other senior civilian and military leaders spoke up to address the general's reservations. Finally, President Bush quietly thanked General Shinseki for his comments. Continuing around the room, every senior officer spoke, but no one else raised serious concerns about the war plan. The moment had passed. The meeting adjourned.[40]

Secretary Rumsfeld and others, enamored of his particular view of "transformation" and seeing heavy ground forces as vestiges of the industrial age, intended to win the war with high-tech precision weapons and minimal land power and to prove the efficacy of such an approach to warfare. Shinseki, however, continued to have serious misgivings. He worried that the administration was sending his soldiers into war without a decisive capability to defeat Iraqi forces and to control the defeated country afterward, even though the Army possessed that capability and stood ready to provide.

Senator Levin, sharing Shinseki's concerns, once again placed him publicly in a precarious position between executive and legislative branches engaged in a conflict over national security policy. When Shinseki testified before the Armed Services Committee a few weeks later, on February 25, 2003, Levin pressed Shinseki to make his concerns explicit. Although Shinseki had every right and duty as a service chief to share his unvarnished professional judgment with the Congress in an open committee hearing, he repeatedly tried to avoid embarrassing the administration by articulating his dissenting assessment. Instead, he provided a numerically vague answer, that "several hundred thousand troops" would be required for the occupation of Iraq. In response, Rumsfeld, Wolfowitz, and Cheney could have let his testimony pass without comment, or could have offered a bland "reasonable minds can differ" response, but instead the three administration leaders chose to treat him publicly as if he were a political rival rather than a military subordinate. They questioned Shinseki's professional judgment, each using more or less the same phrases, in three public venues. Shinseki himself refused further public comment on the matter.

The relationship between Shinseki and the administration was broken. Rumsfeld leaned on Secretary White to distance himself publicly from Shinseki's testimony. White refused, both out of loyalty to his counterpart and because, as a former Army brigadier general, he shared the chief's professional opinion. Shortly thereafter, Rumsfeld forced White to resign.

In March 2003 U.S. and coalition forces invaded Iraq from Kuwait and fought their way north toward Baghdad. A week later, tougher than expected enemy resistance, a sandstorm, and the logistical shortages that had worried Shinseki forced a halt for several days.[41] Still, within a few weeks, the U.S. coalition had overrun the Iraqi army, seized the capital, and continued north. On the first of May, President Bush landed on the USS *Abraham Lincoln* and, standing before a banner proclaiming "Mission Accomplished," declared that "Major combat operations in Iraq have ended. In the battle of Iraq, the United States and our allies have prevailed."[42] Half a decade later, around 157,000 American troops, 10,000 allied soldiers, and 163,000 contractors—a total of 330,000—remained in Iraq in the midst of an ongoing insurgency and civil war.[43]

Shinseki's Legacy

In June 2003 Shinseki retired from the Army and stepped down as Army chief of staff. Contrary to subsequent mythology, he was not relieved and his term was not foreshortened: it ended almost precisely four years after he took office, the norm for service chiefs. His successor was not named in advance.

The farewell ceremony at Fort Myer was a grand send-off, with a full-dress review by the Army's 3rd Infantry Regiment, "The Old Guard," to the strains of martial music from the Army's premier military band, "Pershing's Own." Several members of Congress were in the audience. A constellation of flag officers, including members of the Joint Chiefs and dozens of Army generals and foreign military attachés, contributed to the pageantry. Yet the relationship between the Army and OSD had so deteriorated that no administration representative attended, save the acting secretary of the Army, Les Brownlee, and his staff. Contrary to custom, no high-level OSD or White House official was invited, and none attended. Rumsfeld was traveling in Europe.

In his valedictory address, Shinseki bade farewell to his service and offered a brief discourse on the differences between command and leadership. Fond of describing the Army's process of "growing leaders," he discussed how his mentors had developed him as an officer and how, in the wake of a divisive war in Vietnam, they had "worked to reestablish that most important of virtues in our Army: trust." He singled out for praise his old boss, former Army secretary Tom White:

> We, in The Army, have been blessed with tremendous civilian leadership, most notably the service of Secretary Tom White. . . . Leadership is not an exclusive function of uniformed service. So when some suggest that we in The Army don't understand the importance of civilian control of the military, well that's just not helpful, and it isn't true. The Army has always understood the primacy of civilian control. . . . To muddy the waters when important issues are at stake, issues of life and death, is a disservice to all of those in and out of uniform who serve and lead so well.[44]

Implicit was Shinseki's understanding that his dysfunctional relationship with Rumsfeld was unhealthy for the Army as a profession. As in his Crusader testimony, he asserted the Army's obedience to civilian authority, but such obedience, he said, was not passive. It was his duty as a service chief to offer his professional advice whenever he thought it appropriate, not just when others found it welcome. He reminded his audience that he had begun his service four decades earlier in Vietnam, and that he had, in a sense, come full circle by ending his career in the midst of another war. He noted the importance of drawing lessons from such experience and from history. Yet, he warned,

> We must beware the tendency some may have to draw the wrong conclusions, the wrong lessons from recent operations. . . . We must always maintain our focus on readiness. We must ensure The Army has the capabilities to match the strategic environment in which we operate, a force sized correctly to meet the strategy set forth in the documents that guide us—our National Security

and National Military Strategies. Beware the twelve-division strategy for a ten-division Army.[45]

Following that admonition with a farewell to his beloved Army, Eric Shinseki left the stage and concluded his thirty-eight years of military service.

Shinseki had begun his tour of duty with a stated intent to focus on the Army's people and its readiness and to transform it for the future. With intense effort, the Army had turned around its recruiting shortfall in a single year. The Army had addressed its readiness problems with a focus on bringing deployable units up to full strength and enhancing their training. Shinseki had introduced seven major programs that focused on the well-being of soldiers and families.[46] When called upon to go to war, Army units performed admirably in both Afghanistan and Iraq. Shinseki's program for transformation, a process acknowledged to be the work of more than a decade, likewise began to bear fruit. By the end of his tenure, six new Stryker brigades were being fielded, many of them later deployed to Iraq where they proved their mettle in combat. The new Future Combat System, revamped to include the novel indirect-fire capabilities of the canceled Crusader, was in development, although the demands of two simultaneous wars later slowed its progress. By the measure of his own intentions, Shinseki achieved remarkable success during his tenure as chief of staff.

The issue of the problematic civil-military relationship, however, remains. Was there anything Shinseki could have done to improve his relations with Rumsfeld and the administration? What did he do that he should not have done? What did he fail to do that he should have done? What can we learn from the overlapping tenures of Rumsfeld and Shinseki to improve civil-military relations in the future, particularly at the politico-military nexus?

In retrospect, it is difficult to find anything General Shinseki might have done to improve his dialogue with Secretary Rumsfeld. The duties of a service chief, broadly defined, are to lead his service as its chief professional, to ensure that his service is prepared for any foreseeable contingency—which includes advocating for resources with the executive and legislative branches—and to serve as a member of the president's body of senior military advisors, the Joint Chiefs of Staff. Shinseki ran afoul of Rumsfeld in the latter two roles because of honest differences of judgment. During the 2001 QDR, Shinseki argued within the Defense Department that the Army should not be reduced in its number of divisions and personnel strength. Likewise, during the Crusader controversy he sought to modernize the Army's decades-old indirect-fire capabilities. He made the case for

Crusader publicly when it aligned with administration policy and dropped his advocacy for the program when the policy changed. In his role as a member of the Joint Chiefs, he sought within closed-door councils of the Defense Department to make the forces deployed for the invasion of Iraq more robust, more operationally capable, and better sustained logistically. Alone among his colleagues, he took the opportunity to repeat his arguments to the president. When he failed to persuade, he did not publicly break ranks with administration policy; instead, he offered a vaguely worded contrary assessment of the need for more forces, and did so only when pressed in an open congressional hearing. Rumsfeld honestly disagreed with Shinseki on each of those issues.

Given his worsening relationship with Rumsfeld, Shinseki might have chosen to stifle his disagreements. He could have done so at any time, but to do so would have been a dereliction of duty. If he felt that his superiors' judgments were harmful or incorrect, he had a professional responsibility to question their arguments. According to military tradition, soldiers have a duty to offer forthright opinions and even dissent, until their superiors decide, and then their duty is to salute and support those decisions. Those principles—both of loyal dissent and of subsequent obedience—hold in the military's relations with civilian superiors as well. Shinseki offered his best professional judgment on issues of great importance to the Army and to national security. After his superiors made decisions contrary to his advice, he loyally supported administration policies.[47]

It is worthwhile to note what Shinseki chose not to do. For example, having raised serious concerns about the war plan with the president, Shinseki had the right to speak clearly and forthrightly to Congress about his reservations. Senator Levin gave him ample opportunity to speak. Although his comment about the requirement for "several hundred thousand soldiers" brought forth vehement rebuttals from his civilian superiors, it was a rather understated characterization of the concerns he had already expressed to President Bush. Consistent with the pledge he had made at his confirmation hearing almost four years earlier, Shinseki owed his best professional judgment to the Senate Armed Services Committee, even if it differed with administration views. He might have described more clearly and more forcefully his view that the invasion force was too small, that it lacked adequate logistical support, and that it would likely be unable to secure the country after a successful invasion. The constitutional separation of powers gave him the right—members of Congress might argue it was a duty—to make his stated reservations explicit. He chose not to do so. One can only speculate at the nature of his superiors' responses had he made such comments.

Second, rather than engaging in public and open dissent, Shinseki might have chosen to subvert his OSD superiors. In a time-honored Washington fashion, he might have cultivated back-channel political alliances at the White House, in other Cabinet departments, and on Capitol Hill. The State Department, with former military officers in top positions, would have been a natural ally in some of the four controversies just described, especially in the Iraq war plan debate.[48] Shinseki had numerous close relationships with influential members of Congress. Yet there is no evidence that Shinseki sought to make use of these contacts for assistance. It appears that he performed his duties entirely within the established chain of command.

Shinseki might, alternatively, have retired early. He might have done so quietly, or he might have gone in protest, making his disagreements public. Resigning in protest, or in public acceptance of blame for a policy failure, is an inherently political gesture common to parliamentary government. In American governance, the tradition is much weaker; there is almost no precedent for resignation in protest in the American military.[49] That such a tradition does not exist is a mark of the historical good health of civil-military relations in the United States. For a general to resign in protest of strategy or policy would be a political act by a military professional. Shinseki, if he ever considered such a course—and there is no evidence that he did so—chose not to establish such a precedent. Instead, Shinseki repeatedly said publicly that he still had much work to do as chief of staff, indicating that he believed he could still be effective in the job despite his disagreements with his superiors.

In brief, then, General Shinseki set a textbook example of a professional soldier at the politico-military nexus. He led his service, worked to keep it ready to fight, and offered his best judgment as a member of the Joint Chiefs. In each of the major disputes with Rumsfeld—the 2001 QDR, the Crusader cancellation, and the Iraq war plan— Shinseki consistently argued for gaining or maintaining Army capabilities in order to meet known operational risks. He carried out his duty to illuminate those risks, to eliminate or alleviate them if possible and, if he could not, to make sure that his superiors knew and accepted those risks with a clear understanding and a sense of responsibility for the likely consequences of their decisions. He offered his advice, welcomed or not, until decisions were made, and thereafter he supported the policies of his civilian superiors. Likewise, he remained subservient to the principle of civilian control of the military, even in the face of official public criticism by his civilian superiors and personally embarrassing leaks to the press. He never returned such slights, never differed with administration policy publicly, and aired differences between his assessments and those of OSD only when required to do so in congressional testimony. He was forthright, loyal, and obedient. He could have done little more to uphold both the principle of civilian control and the responsibility to provide his best professional judgment to the executive and the legislative branches.

Rumsfeld's Civil-Military Legacy

What of Rumsfeld's legacy for civil-military relations? Rumsfeld had conflicts with many senior military and civilian officials, not just Shinseki. He was renowned for his intellect, but also for his impatience, his imperiousness, and his unwillingness to accept responsibility. His micromanagement of war planning and troop deployments provides an example. Having pared down the operational force for the invasion of Iraq, having delayed the TPFDL timetables, and having reduced the numbers of support troops, Rumsfeld disavowed his involvement in the planning. "I keep getting credit for it in the press—but the truth is I would be happy to take credit for it, but I can't. It was not my plan. It was General Franks's plan, and it was a plan that evolved over a sustained period of time, which I am convinced is an excellent plan." Further, having done his best to wall off input from other quarters, Rumsfeld insisted that Franks had "worked through" the Joint Chiefs, the combatant commanders, and the National Security Council to develop the plan.[50] The kindest interpretation of these remarks is that they represent a faulty memory on Rumsfeld's part. Having largely left the Joint Chiefs out of the planning process, Rumsfeld was now suggesting that any misgivings on the chiefs' part were unfair as they had had plenty of opportunity to shape the strategy. Moreover, if they wished to set the record straight, the chiefs would have to contradict the secretary in public, which they would be loath to do. Such gambits were not uncommon for Rumsfeld, and they served to create an atmosphere of distrust within the Pentagon and throughout the defense establishment.

The differences between Shinseki and Rumsfeld were partly a matter of personality—a clash of style, values, and world view—but, like most people, even generals are not able to choose their bosses. Moreover, the two men had honest differences of opinion; the Crusader controversy is a case in point. Both had a duty to make decisions about the program. Shinseki felt that Crusader was important to the Army's future; Rumsfeld concluded that it was a relic of unimaginative Cold War thinking. Regardless of how he did it, canceling the program was well within Rumsfeld's authority. His subsequent agreement to transfer the advanced capabilities of Crusader into the Army's prospective Future Combat System represented a constructive compromise. Perhaps Rumsfeld's view of the Army as an institution and the form of military power it constitutes, combined with his combative personal style, would have made it impossible for the relationship to have prospered, no matter what Shinseki did.

So what might Rumsfeld have done differently in the relationship? One course would have been to relieve General Shinseki as Army chief of staff. If Rumsfeld had lost confidence in Shinseki's abilities or his willingness to support administration decisions, this might have been an appropriate step. Yet the perception in Washington today is that relieving a high-level general is politically risky: firing a general is a tacit admission of failure on some level, and the civilian leader who makes that decision likewise must take political responsibility for remedying the problem that lies behind it.[51] Instead, Rumsfeld subjected Shinseki to multiple embarrassments, from letting a senior defense official leak a potential successor's name more than a year before his term was up, to the public repudiation of Shinseki's Senate testimony that several hundred thousand soldiers would be needed to secure Iraq. Rumsfeld clearly had reservations about Shinseki's judgment at that point, and he said so publicly. The forthright course would have been to ask Shinseki to step down but, perhaps unwilling to sack a service chief on the eve of war or to offer a political opening to congressional critics of the war plan, Rumsfeld chose instead to impugn Shinseki's judgment and dispute his testimony. Ironically, Rumsfeld's actions, both undermining the credibility of a senior military officer and politicizing that relationship, further damaged his standing with Congress and his influence with the military. Senior officers were now on notice that professional candor and honest debate were unwelcome. Indeed, the OSD's treatment of Shinseki gave strong incentive to those who might be inclined toward the kind of back-channel political subversion that Shinseki abjured.

Since the creation of the Department of Defense in 1947, the track record of success for its secretaries is discouraging. The title of a 2006 study, *SECDEF: The Nearly Impossible Job of Secretary of Defense*,[52] clearly describes the author's views of the position. Perhaps the myriad responsibilities—managing a huge bureaucracy, balancing budgets for four services, advising the president, dealing with Congress, and overseeing the actions of millions of soldiers, sailors, airmen, and marines around the globe—are too much for one person. Attempting to reform such a complex organization makes the task that much more difficult. Yet Rumsfeld seemed to handicap himself from the beginning with a management style that cast his subordinates as adversaries and seemed almost calculated to foster their mistrust. His successor, Robert M. Gates, provides a striking contrast.

Equally capable, Gates gained a reputation for honest consultation and listening to military leaders. He has not always accepted their advice, but he has not denigrated it either publicly or privately. Ironically, he proved far more willing to discipline his subordinates than Rumsfeld, firing a service secretary, relieving general officers, and accepting the retirement of a combatant commander, but that has done nothing to diminish his good reputation with the uniformed military, who respect leaders who maintain clear and consistent standards.

Lessons for Civil-Military Relations: Navigating through the Storm

The Rumsfeld-Shinseki dialogue was contentious, but the vicissitudes of one relationship are not enough to illuminate the future of civil-military relations. How should military professionals at the politico-military nexus navigate among the competing political demands of the executive and legislative branches and their professional responsibilities? What should generals do when they judge that their superiors' decisions are potentially damaging to the military institution or to national security? How can we address each side of the relationship constructively? Is it possible to structure civil-military relationships, particularly at the nexus, to ensure effective policy and strategic outcomes?

Duties of a Chief

Among the myriad responsibilities of a service chief, most fall into three broad categories: leading the service as its chief professional; ensuring that the service is prepared for any foreseeable contingency, which includes advocating for resources with the executive and legislative branches; and serving as a member of the president's body of senior military advisors, the Joint Chiefs of Staff. Many of these authorities are, quite appropriately, delegated to subordinate commanders and staff officers, so this discussion of the role of the service chief at the politico-military nexus may be useful to other senior officers as well.

As the military professional who leads the service, the chief assists the service secretary, the civilian who legally commands the institution and who, with the secretary, gives it vision and direction. Yet the service chief's role as senior military professional is unique. He is the public face of the uniformed service: its chief professional, the head of its professional guild, and the keeper of its institutional values and heritage.[53] One part head coach, one part chief operating officer, and one part archbishop of Canterbury, the chief represents the service to the administration, to Congress, to the other services and combatant commands, and to the public. He sets the tone in public relations. He develops the skills and guides the careers of subordinates, especially among the general officer corps, and has a significant influence in the selection of the service's future senior leaders. He is ultimately responsible for both the profession's expert knowledge and its expert practice. In this role, his focus is on a distant horizon, at least a decade beyond his tenure.

His second role—that of preparation—also focuses on the long term. Under Title 10 of the U.S. Code, the military services provide forces to the combatant commands, such as the joint operations in Afghanistan and Iraq. The chief of staff does not command those forces; rather it is his responsibility to recruit, train, and equip his service for employment in any contingency that the national command authority (the civilian leadership) deems appropriate. These duties include determining force size and structure, maintaining the readiness of the force, sustaining the force, overseeing military training and professional education, setting personnel policies, and developing and procuring future weapons platforms and other equipment. In an ideal world, from the chief's point of view, after he determined requirements, he would ask his civilian superiors to supply the necessary resources, and they would fulfill his requests. In the real world, however, budgets and manpower are finite, and there are many other claimants on those resources, not least all of the other services. The administration and the Congress almost never see completely eye-to-eye on the requirements of national security. Thus, the chief must become an advocate for his service. He must build consensus within the service and then persuade his colleagues on the Joint Chiefs of Staff and his civilian superiors in the Department of Defense, the Office of Management and Budget, and sometimes the White House. Having gained the president's approval of a budget, the chief must then make his case to Congress, particularly in the House and Senate Armed Services and Appropriations committees. Those arguments may focus on anticipated threats to national security, a broad range of capabilities to meet a spectrum of threats, or some combination of the two. However he makes his determinations, his arguments must be well articulated and persuasive.

In the third role, that of providing professional military advice to his civilian superiors as a chief of staff, the service chief wears the hat of a member of the Joint Chiefs rather than that of the head of his service. This role, which gets the most attention from students of civil-military relations, entails advising on the uses of force to achieve national security objectives, judging what force capabilities will be required, and assessing strategic and operational risk. As a member of the Joint Chiefs, he can and should be called upon to evaluate plans developed by the Joint Staff or by the combatant commands. In consultation with the other chiefs, he advises the secretary of defense, the National Security Council, and the president. When called upon, he also testifies before congressional committees, rendering his best professional judgments to them as well. As an advisor, his focus is usually on the medium to short term.

Political-Cultural Expertise

The performance of these duties requires, among the other kinds of expertise and leadership capabilities that one would expect of long-serving professionals, competency in civil-military relations. Such knowledge, attributes, and skills can broadly be described as political-cultural expertise. Its essence is the ability to represent the profession to people and institutions outside the service, including other agencies of government and other countries and their institutions.[54]

First, the most successful service chief will be a highly educated officer or at least a disciplined and conscientious lifelong learner. Many charismatic tacticians may find themselves out of their depth as general officers because a lack of intellectual curiosity has prevented them from expanding their horizons into the strategic and political realms. A service chief should have a thorough understanding of history, current threats, and global trends. He should be a critical thinker who can handle complexity and ambiguity. As two of his three main roles require focus on the long-term future, he should be visionary but also sufficiently grounded to understand that the future gets hazier as the horizon becomes more distant.

Beyond being a voracious learner, the service chief must possess the attributes that enable him to establish trust and interdependent relationships with other senior officials. He should have well-honed interpersonal skills—as most senior officers do—especially those of negotiation, persuasion, and consensus building. He should have the ability to see issues from other perspectives and the empathy to understand people from other cultures. These attributes confer cross-cultural savvy, allowing senior leaders to interact effectively with their civilian superiors, other service leaders, foreign counterparts, other government agencies, and members of Congress and their staffs. A chief of staff must understand the art of politics. Although *in* the political arena, he is not *of* it. Thus, while he is not and should not be a politician and should be scrupulously nonpartisan, he should understand what makes politicians tick, such as the give-and-take, the rhythms of political life, and the art of compromise. A chief of staff must be able to communicate: to speak and write fluently and eloquently. Many new service chiefs are surprised at how much more public speaking they have to do in their new positions. While the chief will have speechwriting assistants, the words, when spoken, will be his, and he must own them.

Because of the control that military professions have over the education and training of officers, developing senior leaders for service at the politico-military nexus is relatively simple—it just requires concerted effort. As the service structures its personnel policies for professional development, it must find ways to guide officers from tactical leadership to operational and strategic leadership. Too often, Army policies seem shaped mainly by tactical proficiency; this is a necessary but not a sufficient condition for senior leadership. Professional development for senior leadership requires rigorous education at midcareer to expand intellectual horizons and foster political-cultural expertise. The Army has a robust program for educating officers at civilian graduate programs, with subsequent assignments such as a faculty appointment at West Point, but far too many anti-intellectual commanders discourage their best and brightest officers from enrolling. Overseas assignments and language training, especially when it results in fluency, can also foster cross-cultural savvy. The Army should encourage and reward such developmental assignments. It can assign field-grade officers to the Pentagon, combatant commands, and interagency positions in order to expose them to professional cultures outside the military. Congressional and White House fellowships also pay tremendous dividends. The Army should recognize that it cannot produce strategic leaders simply by moving excellent officers from one tactical assignment to another over a long career.

Having developed these skills, attributes, and knowledge, what should a chief of staff do? First and perhaps most important, a service chief needs to have a firm understanding of the professional and personal values and principles that will guide his actions. This requires a thorough self-awareness: a clear-eyed understanding of his own strengths, weaknesses, habits, and predilections. Early in his tenure, he should find quiet, uninterrupted time to determine for himself what is negotiable and what is not, what lines he will not cross, what standards he will not violate. Likewise, after establishing what transgressions he will not tolerate in others, especially his subordinates, he should be consistent in applying those principles and be true to himself and others.

He needs a system for gathering information and making decisions that suits his own style. Processes exist in the Pentagon, but the chief should not become captive to them but instead tailor them as he sees fit. Next, he should find means of gaining advice from a wide range of counselors, especially those outside the service: former officers, politicians, trusted friends, businessmen, and academics. They should be people who owe the chief nothing (and are owed nothing by him), so as to be free to speak their minds. He need not take their advice, but it will be useful for the chief to get perspectives from outside his organization. Within the service, the chief should find ways to foster debate and critical thinking on professional topics. The chief's personal attention and imprimatur can help such opportunities and venues, such as the annual service association convention or conferences at service academies and war colleges, to flourish. The chief should foster healthy relations with the media, setting the example himself by granting interviews and asking his subordinates to do so as well. A reputation with the media for integrity and openness will pay big dividends when crises come, as they surely will.

The chief should work assiduously to develop strong relations both upward, with his boss, the service secretary, and downward, with his immediate subordinate, the vice chief. The former commands the service and the latter runs it on a daily basis. A relationship of trust and interdependence among these three, as well as the service undersecretary, is important, and unfortunately uncommon. The chief should develop strong relationships with the Joint Chiefs, the secretary of defense, and the senior members of the latter's staff and secretariat. Sometimes it will be possible to build trust, sometimes—as in the case of Rumsfeld and his secretariat—it will not, but the chief should take the first step, attempting to build the relationship and educating his client-superiors about the profession and the capabilities of his service. These relationships will be critical in all three of the service chief's roles.

Not least important, the service chief must build associations with members of Congress and insist that his vice chief, his deputies, and subordinate commanders do so as well. The chief will be required to testify several times a year before the armed services committees and the defense appropriations subcommittees in each chamber. Members of these panels are enormously influential in determining the future of the service, so getting to know them well in advance of hearings is most beneficial. Meeting privately with them, understanding their concerns, explaining the service's requirements, and respecting their constitutional role in providing for the common defense can be most helpful to the service; failing to do so can bring big trouble. Maintaining the appearance and reality of evenhanded nonpartisanship in these associations is essential.

The greatest complexity of a service chief's professional life is the multiplicity of his bosses. Members of an administration will frequently see members of Congress as political rivals, yet the service chief owes loyalty to both branches of government. A service chief must determine early on how he will render his best professional military advice to both. Will he choose to be as forthcoming with the chairman of the Senate Armed Services Committee as he is with the secretary of defense? Will he express the same reservations in open committee hearings that he raises with the president, the Joint Chiefs, and the combatant commanders? As this chapter shows, answering these questions is not a mere academic exercise. It is important for the chief of staff to establish for himself, early on, in quiet moments that he controls, the principles that will guide him as he makes these decisions. Then, he should explain these principles to his superiors in the Department of Defense well before the crisis arrives.

In the event that the chief of staff disagrees with his superiors' judgments, he should argue his case until a decision is made, then carry out his orders to the best of his ability. That much is simple. But what of the extreme case, in which he judges that those decisions are damaging to his institution or to national security? In all cases, he should make his arguments in terms of risk: the risk of mission failure and the operational risk to units and their soldiers. He should insist that his superiors acknowledge his concerns and that they accept responsibility for their decisions should they choose to ignore his advice. Putting one's concerns in writing is an effective way to achieve such accountability.[55]

If a chief's advice is overridden, he should still carry out orders, leaving to the competence of civilian officials the questions of damage to national security or military institutions. Only in the extreme case, when he judges that he is being asked to carry out orders that are illegal, immoral, or unethical, should an officer consider another action, such as resignation. Such cases are exceedingly rare.[56]

When a chief has been overridden on a matter of national import, he must decide how he will treat the matter with members of Congress. Again, thinking about these matters before the crisis and determining one's principles is invaluable. Obviously, he should refuse to lie or equivocate. He might explicitly reserve the right to decline to support publicly a decision that he has expressly opposed in closed-door meetings and may attempt to avoid situations, such as congressional hearings, where questions about such decisions might be asked. In the extreme case, a chief might ask his civilian superiors for permission to have private meetings with members of Congress to explain his views, in order to avoid a public confrontation that would place him and his service in the political crossfire.

Answering a generic question about what to do in such cases is difficult, which is why principles are so important.

The single greatest asset that General Shinseki possessed was his reputation for integrity. Although he was never able to establish a relationship of trust with Secretary Rumsfeld and his lieutenants, Shinseki offered them his best advice and his honest professional judgments. He did the same with members of Congress and its committees. He chose in February 2003 to be less forthcoming with Senator Levin than he had been with President Bush, offering less detail on his reservations about administration assessments. But he spoke the truth to both centers of power.

Structuring Civil-Military Relationships: Trust

What can be done to the structure of civil-military relations to foster effective policy and strategy outcomes? Can Huntington's model, or indeed any model, govern relationships at the civil-military nexus?

Huntington's notion of objective civilian control is an ideal type at odds with human reality. Implicit in it is the notion of a wall between strategy and policy: between the soldier's and the statesman's roles and duties. Try as each party might, however, maintaining that wall is impossible, given the nature of warfare, the seamlessness of policy and strategy, the Clausewitzian idea that war is an extension of policy by other means, and the constitutional separation of war powers. The essential flaw in Huntington's theoretical wall is that it splits the responsibility for policy from the responsibility for strategy. This bifurcation demands too little both of military professionals and of their civilian superiors. "At the highest level," as Clausewitz wrote, "the art of war turns into policy,"[57] and the boundary between the two is porous: both soldiers and civilians can and should maintain a shared responsibility for sound policy and strategy and for their interaction. The U.S. Constitution requires this; daily reality demands it. Officers swear an oath to defend the Constitution; so do civilian officials, and the Constitution makes them accountable to the electorate to provide for the common defense. Thus, both civilians and officers have the responsibility to do so. Contrary to Huntington's assertion, admitting that this responsibility is shared does no violence to military professionalism.

Huntington's model also neglects the complexity caused by the dual control of the military—control by both the executive and the legislative branches. Civil-military relations at the politico-military nexus are never as simple as a dialogue between a general and his civilian superior in the Pentagon. They are always complicated by the various allegiances, interests, and constituencies of competing politicians from both parties, both houses of Congress, and the White House—in other words, by democracy. Absent the development of political-cultural expertise, no officer can hope to navigate the storm.

To redress the shortcomings of Huntington's model, Eliot Cohen developed a more nuanced view of the civil-military relationship that he termed "the unequal dialogue," a continuous conversation between military and civilian leaders. In a vigorous and candid give-and-take, civilians must always emerge preeminent.[58] Military professionals today readily accede to the principle of civilian control of the military, as General Shinseki demonstrated. Cohen's model requires that they also accept the uncomfortable idea that civilian and military leaders share overlapping areas of competence and jurisdiction. Military leaders make operational decisions with political ramifications, just as civilians make policy that affects strategic and operational matters. Still, the idea that civil authority must dominate, even in matters of operational detail if civilians so choose, may be difficult for some officers to accept, for it demands a high level of professional maturity— self-abnegation, a tolerance for ambiguity, and a willingness to accept compromise between important but competing values. Yet it is the very essence of civilian control.

Cohen's "unequal dialogue" has its own shortcomings. Civilian and military leaders who engage conscientiously in the unequal dialogue might not necessarily arrive at successful policy decisions; even in the best of cases, human beings may lack complete information or fail to discern what is most relevant. They might misinterpret historical precedent, fail to build public support, or underestimate their enemies. There is never a guarantee of success in the realm of policymaking.[59]

Moreover, no model can provide the sine qua non of successful civil-military relations: mutual trust between the soldier and the statesman. Certainly trust is the moral basis of any healthy human relationship. It is the bulwark of any effective organization. However, trust is never a given between human beings; it is granted, if at all, by mutual consent. When one or the other party does not consent, as in the case of Rumsfeld and Shinseki, trust cannot exist.

In the final analysis, no model can completely portray the civil-military relationship. We can train and educate our senior officers. We can, as a body politic, hold our leaders accountable for their decisions. We can uphold the checks and balances inherent in assigning the civilian control of the military to both the executive and legislative branches. We can attempt to promote an understanding of the intermeshing of strategy and policy that Clausewitz articulated. We can value personal qualities in our military and civilian leaders—such as integrity, self-awareness, and humility—that foster trustworthiness. But no model of such a process—political at its core—can prescribe and ensure adherence to any ideal form of civil-military relations, because such a prescription is foreign to American governance, unnecessarily constraining to both professional judgment and political action, and contrary to human nature.

Epilogue

After his retirement, General Shinseki was remarkably quiet. As the war in Iraq remained America's central national security challenge, Shinseki gave few interviews, made few speeches, and did not appear on television to offer his critique of ongoing operations, even as many of his retired colleagues did so. Notably, he did not join the group of retired generals who called for the resignation of Secretary Rumsfeld in the spring of 2006.[60]

Shinseki's February 2003 testimony and farewell speech became, however, touchstones for critics of the Bush administration's conduct of the war. Numerous opinion and analysis pieces referred to his warnings. Senators and generals and presidential candidates cited his prescience in calling for more robust forces at the beginning of the invasion of Iraq. On November 15, 2006, in testimony before Congress, CENTCOM Commanding General John Abizaid affirmed that General Shinseki's prediction of the level of forces necessary for the occupation had proved correct. The administration changed course in January 2007, calling for more troops to secure Baghdad in what came to be known as the "surge" strategy, a shift that some saw as long overdue, or as too little, too late. Five years after President Bush declared victory, the outcome of the war in Iraq remained in doubt. There is no doubt, however, that American policy and strategy could have benefited from a more mutually trustful dialogue between Secretary Rumsfeld and General Shinseki.[61]

CHAPTER FOUR

Before and After Huntington

The Methodological Maturing of Civil-Military Studies

Peter D. Feaver and Erika Seeler

Huntington's substantive argument in *The Soldier and the State* has been criticized for decades, yet the work remains an influential benchmark for all civil-military studies. Part of the reason for this longevity, we argue, is that it made important advances in the methodological development of security studies generally, but especially the study of civil-military relations; it shifted the field's terrain of inquiry from one previously dominated by descriptive historical and biographical sketches to one increasingly guided by standard social-science reasoning.

The postwar debates about epistemology and methodology that shaped all of the social sciences had particular influence on civil-military studies through the work of Huntington. Three hallmarks of Huntington's approach stand out: that more rigor would enrich our understanding of civil-military relations, that methodological eclecticism was needed, and that method must be the servant and not the master. These insights continue to be relevant and appropriate for scholarship today. *The Soldier and the State* changed the way those of us who study civil-military relations think and, whether or not we concur with all of its theoretical propositions or empirical details, we cannot avoid having our own analyses shaped and stimulated by them. Huntington's themes of military professionalism, conservative versus liberal societal imperatives, the shifting nature of external threats, and subjective versus objective civilian control remain influential, not because subsequent scholars have accepted Huntington's argument in toto—most have not—but because it is almost impossible to think or write about civil-military relations without engaging Huntington.

One of the distinguishing attributes of science is its aim to establish organized bodies of knowledge and models of reality based upon systematic method; method, therefore, is central to scientific progress. Our ideas, predictions, and prescriptions in any field of inquiry are shaped by the methodological lens through which we study: if this lens changes, then our thinking also changes. Our focus here, therefore, is on *The Soldier and the State* from this methodological point of view.

To do this, first, we offer a brief description of changes after World War II both in social science as a whole and in the newly maturing subdiscipline of civil-military relations. We then point out the innovations of *The Soldier and the State*, with particular attention to the ways in which Huntington's emphasis on methodological rigor contributed to subsequent literatures in American civil-military relations. We close with a brief sketch of recent theoretical developments in the field and note, by way of conclusion, the value of Huntington's approach for future development in civil-military studies.

The Development of the Social Sciences

From the nineteenth-century birth of the social sciences until World War II, disciplinary identity building and methodological development proceeded only slowly. The "Chicago school" in political science (including Harold D. Lasswell, among others) was famous for its early emphasis on empiricism, quantification, and psychological and sociological interpretations of politics, but it was not the norm.[1] Before World War II, there was no consensus on standards of scientific excellence for evaluating research, apart from modern historical method, which was gradually evolving to emphasize external and internal criticism and scientific method and problem-solving capabilities rather than simply recounting events.[2] Scholarship sometimes incorporated emerging qualitative and quantitative techniques, but these were still rudimentary and were applied with little attention to theory building or knowledge cumulation. Although the separate fields were beginning to mark out disciplinary territory, many social scientists were largely indistinguishable from traditional historians telling the narrative of important events or from lawyers analyzing particular problems of public administration (e.g., whether to consolidate bureaus in the Navy Department).

During and after World War II, especially in the United States and the developed countries of the West, the social sciences underwent deepening and accelerating innovation. The needs of the war, particularly in the United States, strengthened the institutional and financial basis for research and created a high demand for social scientists in military and civilian sectors.[3] After the war, social scientists combined their wartime training in survey research and experimental methods to transform their disciplines. Determined to use the means and modes of science to address the world's problems laid bare by two devastating world wars—dictatorships, industrial- age warfare, atomic weapons, the Cold War, and the difficulties faced by newly industrializing and democratizing countries—social scientists in many countries and disciplines embarked on vast problem-solving campaigns.[4] This expansion came with professionalization and the spread of meritocratically recruited departments, professional societies, specialist associations, working groups, conferences, and refereed journals.[5]

The growth in institutional foundations and specialists was complemented by increased interest in research methods and methodology (the study of methods), which became a recognized subfield in most disciplines. Much of the postwar work drew upon modernism, empiricism, formalism, rationalism, positivism, and what collectively became known as the behavioral revolution: a focus on precisely describing social behaviors as they actually occur (rather than as we might wish them to be) and explaining causal relationships among the various behaviors. These approaches share a commitment to science, guided by rules of evidence and inference, to make knowledge cumulation possible.[6] With some exceptions, a positivist-modernist consensus remained dominant throughout the postwar era, with most researchers pursuing science as "systematic enquiry, building toward an ever more highly-differentiated set of ordered propositions about the empirical world."[7]

Flowing out of this prevailing epistemology was an emphasis on research design, a topic to which many new publications were exclusively devoted.[8] These were arranged around what we might call "the twin pillars" of research design: theory and evidence. Postwar social scientists stressed the goal of making descriptive and causal inferences about the social world through theory building and hypothesis testing. The goal for some was grand theorizing and paradigm building in the tradition of Thomas S. Kuhn, but most pursued minor-level hypothesizing and middle-range theorizing.[9] The objective was to explain relationships among specified phenomena (operationalized as x and y, or independent and dependent variables) by making falsifiable theoretical assertions that generated observable implications and were susceptible to real-world tests.[10]

Theorizing in this manner gradually became synonymous with rigor in postwar research. In treating theory building as part of research design, social scientists recognized that the very approach of theorizing involved both inductive and deductive processes: the content of any theory was not the same as the methods used for testing it; the process of reasoning scientifically and nomothetically—that is, aimed at developing a system of generalizable principles or patterns, as distinct from ideographically, which focused on the particulars of the case under study—was integral to, and inseparable from, methods.

The second pillar of research design—evidence—was directly connected to the first in that systematically collected data were needed to test theory. Innovation and broader use of empirical methods thus complemented theorizing. A range of qualitative and quantitative techniques were refined: statistics, case studies, experiments and quasi experiments, survey research, face-to-face interviews, focus groups, participant observation, documentary analysis, input-output studies, computerized simulation models, systems analysis, and more. Debates on appropriate procedures for applying such methods flourished, involving such topics as conceptualization and operationalization, index and scale construction, sampling methods, questionnaire formatting, and the like. Quantitative investigation developed, using tabular demonstrations; graphic presentations; measures of variability, ratio, and rates; correlational analysis; factor analysis; binomial or multinomial and linear or nonlinear regression; time-series and cross-sectional analysis; simultaneous equation models; and Bayesian statistics. Confidence in empiricism spread, and standards of validity, reliability, replicability, efficiency, parsimony, and avoidance of bias were applied to both quantitative and qualitative analyses.

Interest grew in macromethodological approach, or grand theorizing (in contrast to micromethodology, or using methodology as a technical instrument for specific qualitative or quantitative applications). Macromethodology studied systematic ways of doing or approaching something; it sought general patterns in knowledge seeking and tended toward grand theorizing or paradigm building. Major examples included behavioralism (or behaviorism in psychology); structuralism and its subtypes, such as systems analysis, functionalism, institutionalism, and organizational analysis; the rational choice approach; and sociocultural and ideational approaches. While often categorized as theoretical movements, they were also integral to the refinement of methods and affected considerations of research design.

In short, the postwar era was a time of flourishing innovation in the social sciences, with worldwide growth, disciplinary consolidation, increasing specialization and diversification, and methodological developments. Before World War II, the social sciences had lacked coherent vision and strong qualitative and quantitative tools; social science methods strongly resembled traditional historical or legalistic (applied public administration law) approaches. After World War II, at the level of micromethodology, qualitative and quantitative tools multiplied and became progressively more sophisticated, while in terms of macromethodology, social scientists became increasingly rigorous and theoretical in their approach. No longer was social science a purely descriptive endeavor; explanation and prediction became paramount.

Civil-Military Studies and Methodology before Huntington

Trends in civil-military studies mirrored wider social science trends. One indication is institutional. While important civil-military works were written before World War II, civil-military relations did not become a widely recognized field of study until after the war.[11] Before the twentieth century, the United States had enjoyed a fairly insular and isolationist history, freed by the luxuries of geoposition and comparatively stable domestic conditions to neglect the study of global war and leadership. World War II necessitated a complete rethinking of security, especially civil-military relations.[12] Scholars and policymakers alike saw the challenge: how could they preserve civilian control under the new circumstances? How could they ensure military capacity to meet major and long-term external threats without undoing the very liberal constitutional values they sought to protect? These questions, which identified a particular type of problem in civil-military relations, became known as the liberal-democratic strand of the field that focused on the traditional "civil-military problematique": how to have a military that would be strong enough to protect the polity from outside threats but that would conduct its own affairs so as not to destroy the polity, its liberal virtues, resources, and way of life.[13]

This was not the only possible normative conception of civil-military relations, but this issue dominated early postwar thinking on civil-military affairs.[14] Also of great concern were the various sociological questions—such as how to recruit and train and motivate civilians to serve effectively as soldiers—raised by the total mobilization for war that the major combatants in World War II underwent. These questions came to constitute the research agenda of Huntington's great sociological contemporary and rival, Morris Janowitz, and his examination of the citizen-soldier ideal—what came to be known as the civic-republican approach to civil-military relations.[15] Most subsequent research in civil-military relations can be traced to one or both of these two intellectual bloodlines, Huntingtonian and Janowitzean.

Other issues that received attention from civil-military researchers in the postwar period included:

- The congressional appropriations process as a means of popular control over the military[16]
- Historical case studies of civil-military conflict in the war in the Philippines and in World War I[17]
- Military influence in foreign policymaking and the ties between diplomacy and strategy (and therefore between diplomats and military officials)[18]
- Military management and the organizational structure of the national military establishment[19]
- Sweeping historical accounts of American military history and the disappearing antimilitarist tradition in the United States[20]
- The nature and interactions of the power elite, including the military, in America at midcentury[21]

This dramatic expansion of scholarly activity led civil-military specialists to form a new subdiscipline, generating papers and books, symposia, funding, cross-disciplinary projects, new programs at major universities, and bibliographies.[22]

With regard to methodological developments, the new subdiscipline of civil-military relations echoed the trends evident in the social sciences generally. There was some increase in methodological sophistication before *The Soldier and the State*, but changes were gradual and irregular. Traditional legalistic, historical, and philosophical approaches coexisted with the increasing push for empirical methods and testing. The generalizing norm began to spread slowly, although descriptive accounts were still common. Exceptions before the war included landmark work by Lasswell and Alfred Vagts.[23] Most work in civil-military studies came after the war and followed the mixed transitional pattern of methodological development found throughout the social sciences at the time.

Civil-military research reflected theoretical concerns that foreshadowed both

Huntington and Janowitz. Works that foreshadowed Janowitz's concerns touched on such issues as the military family, race and the military, and military social structure and personality.[24] These showed varying complexity and used empirical techniques ranging from descriptive-historical and personal retrospective accounts to systematic quantitative analyses of survey research and government-compiled data. Most rigorous was *The American Soldier,* edited by Samuel A. Stouffer, a model of modern behavioral, empirical, and large-scale quantitative research.[25] Concern for proper measurements, controls, replication, and temporal effects demonstrated the growing desire to arrive at empirically grounded results. Simultaneously, technical empirics began to meld with theory, evident in rising, if uneven, concern for explicit statements of assumptions, variables, and hypotheses.

Most early postwar works were liberal-democratic in that they focused on the protection of democratic values from external threat and also from internal abuse—specifically, the need for a strong military that could ward off external threats without simultaneously constituting an internal threat to the polity. These works anticipated Huntington's concerns about how best to delegate power to the military and ensure military effectiveness while also retaining civilian supremacy over the military.[26] The works evidenced a range of micromethods, but few used highly sophisticated quantitative techniques or even particularly advanced qualitative techniques. Because the field was in an early state, no overarching theory had yet been developed for testing.

Most important, these early postwar works marked a growing shift from the search for specific facts to the search for general patterns and principles, that is, from contingent, specific knowledge-seeking (idiographic) to generalizing and theorizing (nomothetic) methods of research. A number of writers touched on the central concerns of the civil-military problematique, but did not specify the conditions under which it operated or propositions for its resolution. For example, Louis Smith's groundbreaking work on the administration of civilian control in the United States gave many insights into the nature and institutions of American civil-military relations but did not provide a cohesive approach to analyzing the problematique in terms of variables, hypotheses, and predictions.[27] Ekirch provided a clear narrative of the ebb and flow of American militarism but never fully discussed implications or responses.[28] These works inched toward a mature theoretical approach, and recognized real and pressing policy problems, but did not ground their analyses in a broader deductive approach that framed deductively grounded questions in terms of empirically testable hypotheses. With few exceptions, no one before Huntington did so.

One who did was Lasswell in his work on the garrison state.[29] The others were the "fusionist" (to use Huntington's term) scholars, such as Hensel and Hoopes, who sought to solve civil-military problems by denying the necessity of functional specialization or differentiation between military and civilian roles and expertise.[30] Each specified theories addressing the civil-military problematique, although neither theory was entirely satisfactory. The paradigm Lasswell used was too deterministic, yielding warnings (high threat inexorably leads to a loss of civil liberties) that were only marginally helpful for guiding policy. Lasswell also exhibited a number of misconceptions about military values, the possibility of militarization in a liberal society, and relationships between patterns of military relations and forms of state, as Huntington noted.[31] Huntington likewise criticized the fusionist approach because, he said, it would result in subjective civilian control and in unacceptable patterns of civil-military relations.[32] Fusionism, he argued, confused an overlap between civilian and military functions with a merger of the two spheres. The civilian and military spheres were, however, analytically and practically distinct, as even the fusionists repeatedly had to concede.[33]

In sum, just before Huntington wrote *The Soldier and the State*, the newly founded modern civil-military studies field mirrored broader social science trends in institutional and methodological development. Implicitly, the subdiscipline was dominated by two visions of democratic civil-military relations: liberal-democratic and civic-republican. These early works did not speak to each other because they were parts of largely separate debates: the liberal-democratic discussion was focused on protecting democratic values from external threat and internal abuse, whereas the civic-republican debate was focused on sustaining and promoting democratic values through active civic engagement by citizens within the military establishment. In the Cold War security environment of the early postwar period, liberalism was ascendant. Both of these two most systematic early postwar theories of control over the military had internal weaknesses. What was needed was a synthesis of technical method with analytic rigor, and a stronger generalizing approach, a development that came with Huntington's *The Soldier and the State*.

The Soldier and the State: Advances in Methodology

The Soldier and the State was the most self-consciously rigorous nomothetic work of early postwar civil-military studies. Huntington's work marked an important step forward in the methodological development of the study of civil-military relations, revolutionizing ways of thinking and providing an exemplar for how it could be conducted. It became, in other words, a classic. The time was ripe for classics in political science, and scholars still read contemporaneous works by Gabriel Almond, Robert A. Dahl, David Easton, Morton Kaplan, Charles E. Lindblom, Seymour Martin Lipset, V. O. Key Jr., Richard N. Rosecrance, Thomas Schelling, Kenneth Waltz, and others. Yet few works have dominated the subsequent development of a subfield as thoroughly as has Huntington's *The Soldier and the State*. A key to this dominance, we argue, lies in its approach to method.

The single most important methodological advance of Huntington's work was his approach to macromethods: Huntington identified the key purpose of his research not as "an historical description of civil-military relations in general nor of any specific aspect of civil-military relations in particular." Instead, he sought to "develop a way of looking at and thinking about civil-military relations, in short, a theoretical framework."[34] The critical feature missing from earlier works on civil-military relations was, as Huntington recognized, the lack of encompassing theory.

Thus, Huntington sought to create a general theory of the American civil-military problematique from which he could derive prescriptions for addressing it in the new Cold War environment. Although he did not use these terms himself, his theory can be presented by simple propositions laid out in X-Y format, that is, exogenous and endogenous variables, or independent and dependent variables. His model also resembles those of path analysis or structural equation modeling, which allow researchers to examine multiple direct and indirect causes of a given dependent variable (although Huntington does not use these labels).

In Huntington's theory, there were two independent variables, one intermediary variable, and one dependent variable. The first independent variable, or X_1, Huntington labeled "functional imperatives." Functional imperatives were threats to society's security.[35] The second independent or X_2 variable comprised societal imperatives: social forces, ideologies, and institutions dominant within society, such as ideology (liberal antimilitary, conservative pro-military, fascist pro-military, or Marxist antimilitary) and structure (the legal-institutional framework, such as the Constitution).[36]

The intermediary variable, Y_1, encompassed patterns of civilian control. These, he argued, could be objective or subjective. Objective civilian control sought maximization of military professionalism and effectiveness. It implied military autonomy—an independent military sphere of action where civilians did not meddle or interfere—and military political neutrality and subordination (which weakened the military politically but not militarily).[37] In subjective civilian control, each element of the civilian elite identified civilian control over the military as synonymous or coterminous with its own control over the military. In the U.S. case, that might be Congress equating civilian control with congressional control, while the president equated civilian control with presidential control, and the secretary of defense equated civilian control with secretarial control, and so on. In the communist system, it would involve party control over the military. Subjective control maximized the power of civilian institutions over the military, but it would result in what Huntington called "transmutation": the civilian authority would seek to refashion military institutions along liberal lines and, as a result, they would lose their distinctly military characteristics.[38] The dependent variable, or Y2, was military security, or military preparedness and national security in the classic sense: the ability of the military to meet outside threats and ensure the polity's physical protection.

Huntington treated his variables essentially as dichotomous variables.[39] Huntington saw the two societal imperatives of X2—ideology and structure—as constant throughout U.S. history.[40] Thus, according to his logic, it must be changes in the functional imperative (X1)—threats—that explained changes in patterns of civilian control and levels of military armament. In Huntington's model, when the external threat was low, liberal ideology caused virtual elimination of military forces; when the external threat was high, liberal ideology resulted in transmutation of military institutions along liberal instead of specialized military lines. Because neither result would give the United States the capability of meeting a sustained Soviet threat, Huntington concluded that the United States must change its traditional antimilitary liberal ideology, adopting instead a pro-military conservatism: conservative realism was required in order to preserve democracy and to generate satisfactory fighting forces. (The other two ideologies, pro-military fascism or antimilitary Marxism, would not have solved the problem, because they would not preserve democratic values.) Pro-military conservatism brought with it objective civilian control and military professionalism—as measured by expertise, responsibility, and corporateness—which in turn would maximize military security to create a stable and workable equilibrium in the Cold War.[41] Rejecting liberalism would, paradoxically, succeed in preserving the liberal-democratic value of civilian control over the military.

Huntington thus offered a textbook example of clear, concise, and concrete theorizing. Specifying a few key variables and associated propositions about their relationships, Huntington was able to sketch a causal pathway to a distinct dependent variable while taking into account direct and indirect causal effects. In examining this causal pathway so laid out, Huntington was able to isolate unique equilibria with the desired outcomes. Implicitly if not explicitly, Huntington had applied the logic of statistics and formal theory all in one.

It was not Huntington's theory per se that made Huntington's work a classic. Over the years, numerous critics landed heavy blows on the content of Huntington's theory. One well-known critique is that the role professionalism played in his theory was tautological—maximizing the professionalism of the military will ensure civilian control because professional militaries are by definition subordinate; he looked to military professionalism as a source of voluntary subordination, but it was also an inherent attribute of professionalism as he defined it.[42] The logical fallacy of definition was compounded by empirical problems: subsequent scholars claimed that his theories were not substantiated by examinations of civil-military relations in other cultures.[43] Another problem was difficulty in operationalizing and testing Huntington's crucial variable of civilian control patterns: levels of civilian interference and perceptions of external conflict varied during the Cold War, but Huntington's concepts and measures were not formulated in such a way that they could capture such dynamics. His categories could not account for patterns in which, for example, civilians violated military autonomy on operational issues yet did not destroy professionalism, even measured with Huntington's own criteria of expertise, responsibility, and corporateness.[44] This reflected the problematic presumption of a sharp civil-military division, which was analytically useful but empirically inaccurate. The value change to conservative realism that Huntington's theory required did not take place, and yet this did not produce the negative outcomes his theory predicted.[45] Huntington's theory relied too much on the nation-state as the locus of civil-military interaction; this assumption was reasonable at midcentury but has become less realistic since, as changes in the nature of world politics and of security problems increase the salience of transnational and international actors in civil-military relations. Huntington's theory also ignored different normative desiderata; it addressed only liberal-democratic concerns in civil-military relations (what we call the civil-military problematique) and did not engage with other potential democratic concerns, civic republican or otherwise, such as the extent to which the military conformed to key social values of the society.[46]

Our summary of these critiques of Huntington's content is not meant to imply that content is trivial. Huntington's theory was full of content, but what was most valuable (and enduring) was his initial framing of the empirical sphere. The categories and concepts he created had lasting value for the question of civilian control, because they could be reworked and repositioned by others to yield further insights. Our point is that his deliberately theorizing (nomothetic) approach did as much for the development of civil-military relations as did the particular content of his theory. As Mattei Dogan has noted, methods often have a much longer life than the theories they go with.[47] What the field needed was theorizing, and this is what Huntington provided.

While the foremost methodological contribution of Huntington's work was its example of theoretical rigor, a second contribution was its methodological ecumenism. Huntington used a variety of tools rather than limiting himself to a narrow set of methods. Especially at the epistemological and macromethodological level, Huntington made use of an array of disciplinary subcurrents. Huntington was acutely aware of the dangers posed by the domestic as well as the international state of affairs, but he nevertheless endorsed a moderately positivist or modernist view of scientific possibility (if not, his endeavor would have been meaningless). Huntington could be positioned among the "new conservatives" and academic realists, such as Reinhold Niebuhr and Louis Hartz, whose work he discussed in the final chapter of his book.[48] Such thinkers recognized that protecting liberal virtues such as life, liberty, and property required recognizing inevitable human and worldly limits. Huntington's conservative sensibility and dislike for naive "solutionism" anticipated some of the postmodern and post-positivist normative critics of the social sciences of the 1970s.

At the macromethodological level, Huntington avoided identification with any particular ideological camp. While Huntington's policy prescriptions were ultimately cultural-ideational, in that he called for changes in values, his work as a whole was structuralist, systemic, institutionalist, and culturalist. His approach—framing civil-military patterns within repetitive social, economic, political, and cultural patterns—was structuralist. He was systemic, both in recognizing the influence of the international system on domestic politics (and vice versa)[49] and in relating his posited structure through multiple interdependencies evidencing patterns of equilibrium and disequilibrium. He was institutionalist, in recognizing the importance of the legal institutional framework for shaping actor roles and behavior. Cultural and ideational issues informed his descriptions of military professionalism and societal-ideological milieus. Although Huntington did not apply the assumptions or techniques of rational choice theory, his logical rigor was consistent with the systematic values at the heart of that approach. In common with the postbehavioral synthesis that emerged a decade later, Huntington accepted the broad goals of empirical science, without affirming the insistence of maximalist behavioralists on quantification and actor analysis.

Huntington's macromethodological approach was thus manifestly eclectic. However, it was ordered eclecticism: he did not utilize compound approaches simply to replicate all the variability and detail of the real world. He used different approaches with a constant reference to theory; the result was an elegant and parsimonious whole that credited the complexities of the social world without being merely a descriptive account or an entirely unfalsifiable and worthless theory that, attempting to explain everything, explained nothing.

Third, Huntington's work embodied the virtue of pragmatism. In *The Soldier and the State*, method was the servant and not the master. This is true of the book's micromethods[50] and of its macromethods. Methods were chosen and applied with regard for their theoretical utility and practical value, not simply created out of methodological expediency with post hoc theorizing. Huntington was an early example of the social scientist as "methodological opportunist," employing whatever methods could best address real-world problems. Huntington's theory utilized a blueprint of formal theoretic and statistical logic, although not explicitly: such methods can clarify problems but, at the stage of theory development, are not essential to systematic thought.

Thus, Huntington's work foreshadowed methodological agreements that were not yet popular during that stage of the behavioral revolution: that "a method can be used by anyone, with or without imagination";[51] that empiricism was valuable but not enough in itself; that studies reliant on more than one particular methodological device had potential for greater resilience; and that researchers could benefit from being conversant with many micro- and macromethodological traditions, using each as the occasion required.

Huntington's method was not beyond reproach. By modern standards, the theory in the book is not clearly presented, and the research design is implicit rather than explicit. As noted earlier, some of the key variables such as "objective control" and "subjective control" are hard to operationalize, and Huntington offered insufficient guidance on how to operationalize them. The historical chapters are thinly referenced, and the comparative chapters looking at Germany and Japan are impressionistic rather than authoritative.

Yet, at a prolific time in the social sciences as a whole, *The Soldier and the State* marked an important advance in the subdisciplinary development of civil-military studies. Huntington applied rigor to considerations of research design. He demonstrated the influence of several macromethodological approaches but sidestepped the permanent fissures and Manichaean struggles that separated maximalist followers of the various camps, adopting instead a pragmatic and ecumenical posture that allowed him to transcend methodological debates and make real progress toward theoretical and practical understanding. While Huntington's liberal-democratic normative orientation meant that he addressed only a confined area of civil-military concerns—civilian control—his insights in this area had far broader impact.

Civil-Military Studies after Huntington

After *The Soldier and the State*, civil-military studies continued to mirror wider social science trends, in becoming more institutionalized and more interdisciplinary. Micromethods also advanced considerably. The interdisciplinary nature of the subfield was reflected in Morris Janowitz's founding in 1960 of the Inter-University Seminar on Armed Forces and Society, which includes political scientists, sociologists, psychologists, economists, historians, anthropologists, and, indeed, representatives from most disciplines in the social sciences and humanities —and the subsequent founding of that society's journal, *Armed Forces and Society*, in 1974.[52] Substantively, research followed two main tracks: a sociologically oriented examination of the military in the civic-republican tradition, and an institutionally oriented examination of civil-military relations in postcolonial and developing societies.[53]

In the sociological strand, the landmark study was Morris Janowitz's 1960 book, *The Professional Soldier*. It examined the evolution of professional life, organizational setting, and leadership in the American military during the first half of the twentieth century. Janowitz's disciplinary paradigm, a radically different vision from Huntington's, became the major alternative for much of the postwar era. Whereas Huntington prescribed a division of labor that would respect both military professionalism and objective civilian control, Janowitz rejected objective control on the basis of his civic-republican concerns for a closer fit between civilian and military values. Although Janowitz drew from some of Huntington's insights, he sought different answers; the divergence between the two was a matter of differences in their underlying democratic visions and could not be resolved without normative debate.[54] Despite its limitations, *The Professional Soldier* was a theoretical and methodological classic that spawned hundreds of studies in the civic-republican tradition: topics addressed included military personality and culture; military education; military family life; substance abuse; race, gender, and minorities in the military; and issues of manpower policy such as military recruitment, training, and retention.[55]

A second, more institutionally oriented line of research investigated civil-military relations outside the developed West. This strand was more closely associated with Huntington, and he made important original contributions to it.[56] Researchers addressed topics such as postcolonial adjustment, coups, and the military's role in modernization and governance, reflecting general social science trends in using sophisticated, diverse, and combined micromethods. The most compelling works also utilized multiple macromethods. For example, Huntington's book *Political Order in Changing Societies* examined large structural forces, immediate political institutional context, and societal and agency factors to understand the problem of political order and military interventions. Despite the rich empirical and theoretical work done in this area, however, its relevance for mature Western democracies was less certain. This was underscored by Huntington's conclusion that, in underdeveloped nations, "military explanations do not explain military interventions"[57]—specifically, military coups cannot be explained by factors inherent in the military institution. Civil-military relations operated under quite different societal and institutional circumstances in the developing world, even under democratic regimes, and varied between countries. Thus, Huntington's theory had some influence on non-Western civil-military research, but that research did not have significant reciprocal influence on the study of American civil-military relations.[58]

Besides these two strands of research, there were also notable empirical studies on topics Huntington introduced, some by his former students, but these did not purport to be rival theories. Examples include *Soldiers, Statesmen, and Cold War Crises* by Richard K. Betts in 1977; the 1973 volume edited by Bruce Russett and Alfred Stepan, *Military Force and American Society*; Bruce Russett's 1990 book, *Controlling the Sword*; Eliot A. Cohen's 1985 book *Citizens and Soldiers*; and Adam Yarmolinsky's 1971 edited volume on the military establishment.[59] These works varied in methodology and empirical contributions: some were descriptive and exploratory, others were methodologically sophisticated.[60] Some were empirically rich and theoretically important at a middle level of theorizing. Betts's counterintuitive conclusions about the preferences of civilians and military on the use of force, for example, inspired much subsequent research on civilian and military attitudes.[61] Each owed an intellectual debt to Huntington (even if paid only in that most sincere scholastic fashion—by criticizing him), but none sought to provide a comprehensive theoretical reformulation that could supplant *The Soldier and the State*.

In the post–Cold War era, civil-military studies enjoyed a renaissance. The urgency of policy debates surrounding gays in the military, the downsizing of the Cold War force, the emergence of new humanitarian missions, the frictions between President Clinton and senior military officers, an alleged growing gap between the military and American society—all of these made civil-military relations prominent in the media and in the public consciousness.[62] In the academic world, this vigor was matched by new and revived debates that were triggered by an expansion of survey methods beyond traditional issues of morale and welfare, and by systematic attention to the nomothetic standard, aiming to bring research beyond middle-range theorizing to reengage the core normative concerns of the subfield, especially Huntington's focus on the civil-military problematique.

The use of surveys to explore political issues at the heart of civil-military relations was most prominently seen in the flurry of studies that sought to measure and examine the purported civil-military gap.[63] Later survey research more systematically investigated military attitudes toward post–Cold War missions and identified the conditions under which the military is likely to accept nontraditional missions.[64]

The revival of grand theorizing in civil-military studies is perhaps best seen in the efforts by theorists to explain the friction in post–Cold War American civil-military relations. In so doing, they developed new theories that challenged Huntington's, seeking to provide more explanatory value than Huntington's model without losing parsimony. Michael Desch revived the international systemic structural strand in Huntington's theory and argued that "external threat" was the key factor driving civil-military relations.[65] Deborah Avant and Peter Feaver separately pursued different forms of neo-institutionalist theories, drawing on the principal-agent framework developed in economics and, in Feaver's case, developing a game-theoretic model that sought to subsume Huntington's argument in a larger theory.[66]

Other theoretically grounded arguments were advanced. Risa Brooks drew on both system theory and principal-agent insights to engage explicitly the other part of the Huntington problematique: what determines different levels of military effectiveness.[67] Drawing from communication studies, Cori Dauber interpreted civil-military relations as a contest in which standards of argumentation dominated policymaking.[68] Douglas Bland revived the fusionist line of civil-military relations that Huntington had challenged by arguing that responsibility for control must be shared between civilian and military elites, but that the manner of sharing was conditioned by a civil-military regime particular to each nation, which could evolve further depending on values, issues, interests, personalities, threat assessments, and other factors.[69] Don Snider and others argued that the concept of the military as a profession—a quintessentially Huntingtonian notion—should be reimagined on the basis of new theories of professions.[70]

What all these neo-Huntingtonian (and neo-anti-Huntingtonian) theories shared was their commitment to rigor, pragmatism, and ecumenism. They used deductive inquiry to outline key assumptions about actor preferences, strategy, and the environment to specify conditions under which different equilibria obtained. In civil-military relations research before these works, explanatory variables had proliferated, with few systematic attempts to compare them or specify the conditions under which one set of factors had more explanatory leverage than another. In contrast, formal theoretic approaches generated conditional and comparative statements of variable influence and limited numbers of variables. These approaches were also pragmatic: formal theory clarified the conceptual terrain and restored empirical accuracy to theoretical descriptions. This adjustment made civil-military studies more relevant to the policymaker or practitioner, remedying one weakness of Huntington's approach, its neglect of behavior and decisions, or the normal strategic interactions of everyday politics. The formal theoretic approach also allowed for refinement and profitable engagement with other methods. For example, while Feaver's initial two-person model was criticized for oversimplification of bargaining dynamics, recent research has extended the approach to the multiple-actor environment.[71] Likewise, as games become more complex (incorporating more actors, assumptions, stages) and as indeterminacy (multiple equilibria) becomes more of a problem, scholars can use cultural, societal, and ideational information to help explain and predict equilibrium. Pragmatism also characterized the search for generalizability, a focus of most of these approaches even when the United States was the principal case under study. The approaches were ecumenical and eclectic: they borrowed from economics, from sociology, and from communications studies. Some explicitly recognized the norm of ecumenism. Desch, for example, recognized that some threat environments are structurally indeterminate, making other variables such as culture more important. These diverse macromethodological and micromethodological approaches showed how ecumenism could provide multiple alternative insights into the social world, which could then be tested and compared.

The Janowitzean tradition also experienced important theoretical renewal. For instance, Charles Moskos, David Segal, John Allen Williams, and others argued that the evolution of military professionalism had reached a new era, the era of a "post-modern military."[72] James Burk's work merged sociohistorical insight with theories of military and societal change, to investigate the loosening of the citizen-soldier linkage in modern times and its consequences for civil-military relations. Similarly, Rebecca Schiff's proposed "concordance theory" posited that domestic intervention in military affairs was forestalled when the political leadership, the military, and the citizenry agreed on four issues: the social composition of the officer corps, the political decision-making process, recruitment method, and military style.[73]

Thus, the post–Cold War research in civil-military studies experienced a surge of growth and development, spurred by real-world events and new methodological developments and inspired, implicitly or explicitly, by Huntington's methodological advances. The most important new tool was self-conscious and rigorous theorizing; ecumenism and pragmatism were also important.

Conclusion

The story of modern civil-military studies is rich and varied. We chose to highlight the methodological development of the subdiscipline and the ways in which Huntington's landmark *The Soldier and the State* set a pattern and a standard for much of the subsequent work in civil-military relations. Methodologically, Huntington's work espoused norms of rigor, ecumenism, and pragmatism, reflected in the most influential works that followed. Civil-military studies as a whole progressed as researchers addressed pressing new policy issues; the most lasting work followed Huntington's pattern in articulating rigorous theoretical frameworks and combining the contributions and insights of multiple macro- and micromethodological approaches.

Huntington's methodological approach offers guidance for the future, as well. Civil-military relations at the beginning of the twenty-first century are complex: in the vast and dynamic empirical domain of civil-military relations are complex bargaining, political maneuvering, bureaucratic politics, and legislative haggling of civilian and military elites; the relations between ordinary people, institutions, and the military; the communicative struggles, collegial and sometimes conflictual interactions, and raw power plays of military versus civilian actors; and the rise and decline of governing regimes. All are proper subjects for civil-military studies. None of these topics can be studied without attention to multiple, interactive, and fluid contexts: transnational, international, domestic, regional, developmental, historical, cultural, ideational, and more. Key actors, structures, and variables are continually evolving, as are the dynamics within military professions, the changing domestic scene, and the changing nature of warfare.

Many questions will emerge. What is the scope of civil-military relations? How generalizable are its patterns? What are the influences of new actors, issues, and relationships? How well will old ideas fit new contexts? What are the proper normative bases of the subdiscipline? Can there be a unified democratic theory for civil-military relations?[74] What would its internal trade-offs be? How do we debate and determine normative questions about the meaning and purpose of democracy and the nature of civilian control? Where do we ground practical policy concerns in theoretical debates?

Huntington's insights into the need for methodological rigor will—ironically perhaps—long outlive his original theory. Rigor will always be needed, whether one is working from a liberal-democratic, civic-republican, federalist, or other mode of democratic thinking. Rigor will always enhance prescription, whether one is working on topics of defense policymaking, congressional appropriations, manpower supply, or democratic transition.

Ecumenism likewise will always be essential, both for individual research and for collective endeavors. Every method has strengths and weaknesses. Some methods can be integrated with other approaches to compensate for weaknesses and enhance strengths. The best work of the future in civil-military studies will be synthesized or ecumenical, in an orderly way, utilizing a variety of micro- and macromethodological approaches. Civil-military theorists should not think simply in terms of agency versus structure, or interests versus institutions, or ideas versus interests as driving forces; explanations will be a judicious blend of all. Nor will it be a matter of wide-ranging cross-national comparisons versus single case studies, or detailed historical work versus finely honed statistical instruments.[75] Civil-military theorists will benefit from the added insight brought by a spirit of ecumenism.

Pragmatism, too, will be important. Methods must be the servant, not the master. Empiricism, for example, will always be valuable, but massive empiricism without balancing vision does not accumulate knowledge or result in wisdom. The gathering of data and the formulation of theories should work together: theory to help avoid the collection of irrelevant facts, and facts to help avoid the construction of misleading theories. Methods should be used to solve real-world problems, not just serve as instruments for cloistered debates in academia.

Unlike most academic work with a short shelf life, Huntington's *The Soldier and the State* has stood for fifty years. For the future too, its appeal will endure, we argue, because of its methodological approach: its rigor, its ecumenism, and its pragmatism.

CHAPTER FIVE

Hartz, Huntington, and the Liberal Tradition in America

The Clash with Military Realism

Michael C. Desch

One of the most unanticipated developments of George W. Bush's administration was the marked deterioration in the relationship between civilians and the senior military leadership. Indeed, many had expected the 2000 election of Bush to usher in a new age of amity and cooperation after the period of fractious civil-military relations during the Clinton administration. Bill Clinton suffered under twin handicaps: he represented a Democratic Party that had, since George McGovern, been perceived as antimilitary.[1] Moreover, he carried some personal baggage that freighted his relationship with his subordinates in uniform. This baggage was pithily summarized by one Air Force general who ridiculed his "pot-smoking, draft-dodging, skirt-chasing Commander-in-Chief" in an after-dinner talk in Europe.[2]

Bush had campaigned for military votes in 2000 with the promise that "help is on the way" after eight years of supposed neglect under the Clinton administration.[3] Accepting his party's nomination in August 2000, the Republican hopeful warned that "our military is low on parts, pay, and morale. If called by the commander-in-chief today, two entire divisions of the Army would have to report . . . *not ready for duty.* This administration had its moment. They had their chance. They have not led. We will."[4] Unlike Clinton, Bush had at least served in the military during the Vietnam era and he seemed much more comfortable with military traditions and culture. An administration that included two former secretaries of defense—Vice President Dick Cheney and Secretary of Defense Donald Rumsfeld—and had as secretary of state a former chairman of the Joint Chiefs of Staff, General Colin Powell, ought to have had excellent relations with the senior military leadership. Yet civil-military relations under the Bush administration may have been even worse than they were under Clinton.

Almost immediately after taking office, Bush's appointee as secretary of defense, Donald Rumsfeld, alienated senior officers with his abrupt and dismissive style as he pushed a revolutionary military transformation agenda.[5] Civil-military conflict intensified during the run-up to the Iraq war, as Rumsfeld and his deputy, Paul Wolfowitz, sought to reduce the number of troops sent to topple Saddam Hussein and to accelerate the timetable for their deployment.[6] As the disastrous consequences of this civilian interference in war planning became clear in Iraq by the spring of 2006, a number of recently retired generals began to speak out, demanding Rumsfeld's resignation and criticizing the Bush administration's conduct of the war.[7] The breach between Bush and the generals had become so wide that the bipartisan Iraq Study Group explicitly recommended that "the new Secretary of Defense should make every effort to build healthy civil-military relations, by creating an environment in which the senior military feel free to offer independent advice not only to the civilian leadership in the Pentagon but also to the president and the National Security Council."[8] In addition to this anecdotal data, there is more systematic evidence that civil-military relations frayed badly under the second Bush administration. According to a 2006 *Military Times* poll, almost 60 percent of service men and women did not believe that civilians in the Pentagon had their "best interests at heart."[9]

This civil-military strain is indeed a puzzling development. In order to understand it, I propose that we think of both Clinton and Bush as part of what the late Harvard government professor Louis Hartz characterized as America's "Liberal Tradition."[10] Building upon Hartz, his junior colleague Samuel Huntington famously argued in *The Soldier and the State* that the core of the problem of American civil-military relations was the ongoing tension between America's Liberal civilian society and the conservative Realism of the U.S. military officer corps. The key to managing this ongoing tension and to balancing military effectiveness with civilian supremacy, Huntington argued, was to adopt the right framework for civilian control of the military.[11] In my view, Huntington's Hartzian argument sheds important light on the Bush administration's civil-military woes, although I argue that this culture clash actually became a problem as early as the end of the Cold War, which returned the conflict between civilian Liberalism and military Realism to the forefront. I also endorse Huntington's claim that the system he called "objective control" could best reconcile military effectiveness with civilian oversight, a position that Bush and his neoconservative advisors explicitly rejected.[12]

To make the case that "Huntington's Hartz" can help us to understand the puzzling deterioration in relations between the Bush administration and the senior military leadership, I begin by outlining the Liberal tradition argument. Next, I show how the Bush administration and the neoconservative intellectuals inside and outside of it were fully part of this tradition. I then identify the links between the Liberal tradition and the recent problems in U.S. civil-military relations. I conclude by showing how Huntington's objective-control framework still represents the best approach for resolving the tension between America's Liberal culture and the conservative Realist ethos of the military profession in the post–Cold War world.

The Liberal Tradition in America

The word *Liberalism* is much freighted in American political discourse and so it is important to be clear what I mean by it.[13] The term *liberal* or *liberalism*, with a small "l," usually refers to those on the left of the American political spectrum, such as members of Americans for Democratic Action or the American Civil Liberties Union, or political figures such as former Massachusetts governor and Democratic presidential candidate Mike Dukakis or Massachusetts Democratic senator Ted Kennedy. But what I am referring to is "big L" Liberalism, or what Hartz called "Lockeanism," after British philosopher John Locke.[14] This was Hartz's shorthand for a political system or set of political values based on a combination of individual freedom, equality of opportunity, free markets, and political representativeness.[15] Historian Arthur Schlesinger famously called this the "vital center" of American politics.[16]

There are other Liberal regimes around the world, such as Britain since the nineteenth century, but what made America unique, in Hartz's view, was its lack of a feudal past. Unlike most other Liberal regimes, America was born democratic and never really had to reconcile its Liberalism with other political ideologies or to define its Liberalism in opposition to other ideologies. This was made possible by America's favorable geographical position far from powerful adversaries in Europe.[17] American Liberalism thus embraced a number of unique premises: that political and economic development are easy; that "all good things go together" (e.g., that our moral and ideological commitment to spreading democracy would also serve our national interests by making the world more peaceful); that radicalism and revolution are bad; and that political democracy is more important than political order.[18] In and of themselves, of course, these beliefs seem benign; taken together, however, they can be the source of illiberalism.

The problem with America's Liberal tradition, according to Hartz, is that at its core it contains a "deep and unwritten tyrannical compulsion" that "hampers creative action abroad by identifying the alien [i.e., the non-Liberal] with the unintelligible, and it inspires hysteria at home by generating the anxiety that unintelligible things produce."[19] Hartz referred to this as the problem of "Lockean absolutism." As scholar Eric McKittrick put it, "With nothing to push against it, [Liberalism] thinks in absolutes; the occasional shadows which cross its path quickly lengthen into monsters; every enemy is painted in satanic terms, and it has no idea how it would behave if the enemy were either bigger or different."[20] Robert Packenham explained that "the first two Liberal premises make the United States excessively optimistic or utopian; the third Liberal premise often makes us counterrevolutionary or reactionary; and the fourth assumption inclines us toward a special kind of pretentiousness or arrogance."[21] Today, it is widely recognized that Liberalism can have such illiberal consequences. Ira Katznelson, for example, observes that "liberalism's ordinary functioning can . . . advance and thus bond with nonliberal and illiberal impulses of various kinds."[22]

America's Liberal absolutism has had pernicious consequences both abroad and at home. Externally, this absolutism fosters a desire among many Americans to spread Liberalism everywhere. One way it does so is by suggesting that virtue and self-interest can be reconciled in Liberal imperialism.[23] The virtuous side of Liberal imperialism can be found in the idea of a "benign hegemony" that brings the benefits of progress to benighted regions of the world.[24] The self-interested side of Liberal imperialism is reflected in the premise that Liberalism cannot survive in a non-Liberal world. American Liberalism has now fully internalized this notion. For example, in a 1974 lecture, Senator Daniel Patrick Moynihan argued that "democracy in one country was not enough simply because it would not last." Or, as Nathan Glazer put it, "For us the world is a safer and more congenial place with such [democratic] societies in it and would be a more dangerous and depressing place without them."[25]

But it was the Liberal tradition's domestic consequences that primarily concerned Hartz when he wrote in the 1950s. He feared that American Liberalism was bound to try to expunge non-Liberal currents from U.S. society. The "red scare" after the First World War and McCarthyism during the early Cold War were the most obvious manifestations of that impulse. For Hartz, the paradox of American Liberalism was its intolerance, verging on hysteria, in the face of non-Liberal ideas and institutions.[26] The wellspring of this Liberal absolutism, in Hartz's view, is its presumption that "its norms are self-evident."[27] Given that premise, there is no legitimate reason not to accept them, and so, if someone does dissent from Liberalism, it can only be evidence of a moral defect or malign intent. To quote H. L. Mencken from a slightly different context, the Liberal's "distinguishing mark is the fact that he always attacks his opponents, not only with arms, but also with snorts and objurgations—that he is always filled with moral indignation—that he is incapable of imagining honor in an antagonist."[28]

The Liberal tradition is so deeply ingrained in American political culture that it is now bipartisan. Political figures as seemingly diverse as Theodore Roosevelt, Woodrow Wilson, Franklin Roosevelt, John F. Kennedy, and Ronald Reagan all fit under its umbrella.[29] Indeed, non-Liberal politicians and thinkers such as Richard Nixon and Henry Kissinger are the exception rather than the rule in America. As neoconservative pundit Robert Kagan rightly notes, "Americans have never accepted the principles of Europe's old order, never embraced the Machiavellian perspective. The United States is a liberal, progressive society through and through, and to the extent that Americans believe in power, they believe it must be a means of advancing the principles of a liberal civilization and a liberal world order."[30]

Bush, Neoconservativism, and the Liberal Tradition

President George W. Bush and the neoconservatives who have been so influential in shaping his foreign policy embraced significant parts of America's Liberal tradition.[31] Many saw continuity between Bush and earlier Liberal political figures as Woodrow Wilson. "Bush is becoming," wrote Lawrence Kaplan, "the most Wilsonian President since Wilson himself," a view supported by some historians.[32] Even Bush's fundamentalist Protestant faith, seemingly at odds with Liberalism in some respects, was compatible with what Hartz called American "hebraism" (the notion that "we are a chosen people"), which is another prominent feature of America's Liberal tradition.[33] Indeed, the messianic fervor of American evangelicalism further reinforced the crusading impulses of American Liberalism.[34]

The link between Liberalism and the neoconservative movement in contemporary America also had much deeper roots than acknowledged in Irving Kristol's famous quip that he and his colleagues were simply "Liberals who got mugged!" As Ronald Steele concluded, "Liberals and neoconservatives may both be correct in considering themselves to be Wilsonians. In truth, they are more alike than they admit in their ideological ambitions and their moral justifications. . . . In practice the difference between interventionist Liberals and the interventionist neoconservatives is more a matter of degree than of principle."[35] When one looks closely at the content of neoconservativism, one can see that it has much in common with Liberalism.[36]

As table 5.1 shows, while neoconservatives are not identical with Liberals, there is substantial overlap in their attitudes on various issues relevant to American foreign policy. In particular, neoconservatives and Liberals can find enough common ground on six of the eight issues (all but "individual vs. group" and the role of international institutions) to make them allies in the fight to promote an activist U.S. role in the world. The most important difference between them, however, concerns the role of international institutions: neoconservatives are far more unilateralist than Liberals, who believe that the United States ought to conduct its foreign policy in a multilateral framework under the auspices of international institutions.[37] This essentially tactical difference aside, there is still enough commonality among neoconservatives and Liberals to justify placing the former squarely within America's Liberal tradition.[38]

Table 5.1.   Comparison of Conservatives, Liberals, and Neoconservatives by Issue

Issue	Conservatives	Liberals	Neocons
Individual vs. group	Group	Individual	Group
Natural condition of man	Conflict	Cooperation	Cooperation
Human rationality	Little	Much	Mixed
Human nature	Unchangeable, bad	Changeable	Changeable
Society improvable	No	Yes, from below	Yes, from above
Norms vs. power	Power	Norms	Norms and power
Role of international institutions	Negligible	Central	Negligible
Role of military	Protect national security	Promote ideals and protect human rights	Promote ideals and protect human rights

The most compelling evidence that the second Bush administration was part of the ongoing Liberal tradition in America was that the administration fully embraced four key premises of the Liberal tradition: that political and economic development are not difficult, that America can simultaneously advance both its interests and its principles, that radicalism must be checked, and that democracy is more important than political order.

Consider first the Liberal tradition's belief that development is a relatively smooth process. The notion that economic development was something that most of the world could enjoy was a staple of the liberal development economists of the late 1950s and early 1960s.[39] The Bush administration shared this optimism about the prospects for economic development, though it preferred to rely more on markets and global economic incentives than state guidance and foreign aid to foster it. The 2002 *National Security Strategy* struck a sanguine note on this score: "Economic growth supported by free trade and free markets creates new jobs and higher incomes. It allows people to lift their lives out of poverty, spurs economic and legal reform, and the fight against corruption, and it reinforces the habits of liberty. . . . The lessons of history are clear: market economies, not command-and-control economies with the heavy hand of government, are the best way to promote prosperity and reduce poverty."[40]

Like previous presidents, Bush was also confident that political development—particularly the spread and consolidation of democracy—could take place nearly anywhere. "Do not bet against freedom," he advised.[41] And on this, he put the country's money where his mouth was, against long odds: "There was a time when many said that the cultures of Japan and Germany were incapable of sustaining democratic values," Bush said in February 2003. "Well, they were wrong. Some say the same of Iraq today. They were mistaken. The nation of Iraq—with its proud heritage, abundant resources and skilled and educated people—is fully capable of moving toward democracy and living in freedom."[42]

The vice president boasted in 2005 that

the fact of the matter is, the town [Washington, D.C.] has got a lot of people in it who are armchair quarterbacks, or who like to comment on the passing scene. But those who have predicted the demise of our efforts since 9/11, as we fought the war on terror, as we've liberated 50 million people in Iraq and Afghanistan, did not know what they were talking about. And I would submit to you today that we'll succeed in Iraq just like we did in Afghanistan. We'll stand up a new government under an Iraqi draft constitution; we'll defeat the insurgency. And in fact, it will be an enormous success story that will have a huge impact, not just in Iraq but throughout the region.[43]

On the related Liberal premise that "all good things go together," the Bush administration again seemed squarely within America's Liberal tradition. In the late 1950s and 1960s, Liberals were optimistic that, as Third World countries became more economically developed, they would also become more politically stable.[44] More recently, the Bush administration argued that "America's vital interests and our deepest beliefs are now one."[45] President Bush told Bob Woodward: "I believe the United States is *the* beacon for freedom in the world. And I believe we have a responsibility to promote freedom that is as solemn as the responsibility is to protecting the American people, because the two go hand-in-hand."[46] Bush has pointed to his administration's efforts to democratize Iraq as a prime example of how two good things—democracy and U.S. security—go together: "A free, democratic, peaceful Iraq will not threaten America or our friends with illegal weapons. A free Iraq will not be a training ground for terrorists, or a funnel of money to terrorists, or provide weapons to terrorists who would be willing to use them to strike our country or allies. A free Iraq will not destabilize the Middle East. A free Iraq can set a hopeful example to the entire region and lead other nations to choose freedom. And as the pursuits of freedom replace hatred and resentment and terror in the Middle East, the American people will be more secure."[47] Similarly, Paul Wolfowitz said, "Democracy is a universal idea," but in addition, "letting people rule themselves happens to be something that serves Americans and America's interest."[48]

Another key premise in the Liberal tradition is the belief that the United States must actively oppose radicalism and revolution. A prime illustration of this was Woodrow Wilson's speech in March 1913 in the midst of the Mexican Revolution, explaining his decision not to work with the revolutionary government of Francisco I. Madero: "Cooperation is possible only when supported at every turn by the orderly processes of just government based upon law, not upon arbitrary or irregular force. We hold . . . that there can be no freedom without order based upon law and upon the public conscience and approval."[49]

The Bush administration took the view that the "the gravest danger to freedom lies at the perilous crossroads of radicalism and technology."[50] As Bush's 2002 *National Security Strategy* asserted, "Traditional concepts of deterrence will not work against a terrorist enemy whose avowed tactics are wanton destruction and the targeting of innocents; whose so-called soldiers seek martyrdom in death and whose most potent protection is statelessness."[51] Secretary of Defense Donald Rumsfeld viewed the root of America's problem with the Islamic world as being its increasing radicalism. Rather than the United States changing its policies in the region or finding some accommodation with Islamic fundamentalism, he maintained that "the Muslim world needs to take back its religion—it's been hijacked by a small minority."[52]

The Liberal tradition's final premise is that fostering democracy is more important than maintaining stability. It was this belief that led President Jimmy Carter to press authoritarian U.S. allies for more respect for human rights and to hold elections during the Cold War, even when this would undermine their continued hold on power.[53] This same thinking was apparent in the Bush administration's handling of events in post-Saddam Iraq. Nothing better captured its belief that democracy is more important than order than Rumsfeld's cavalier dismissal of the widespread looting and disorder in Iraq after the fall of Baghdad to U.S. forces in April 2003: "Freedom's untidy, and free people are free to make mistakes and commit crimes and do bad things. They're also free to live their lives and do wonderful things."[54] Later, in a speech at the Council on Foreign Relations, he would compare the anarchy in Baghdad to the disorder in the United States after its revolution.[55] Two of the most ill-advised and consequential decisions made by the Coalition Provisional Authority were to disband the Iraqi army and to undertake a large-scale purge of Iraq's civilian government; these, too, were motivated by the belief that democracy was more important than order.[56] Indeed, had the Bush administration cared only about establishing a pro-American regime in Iraq, it would have been content to replace Saddam Hussein with a friendly dictator rather than pushing for an elected government, with all the turmoil that effort caused. But Wolfowitz said plainly before the war that "we're not interested in replacing one dictator with another."[57]

President Bush applied the same rationale to other areas of the world. He maintained in 2002, for example, that democracy is more important than stability in the Occupied Palestinian Territories.[58] His secretary of state, Condoleezza Rice, believed that this yardstick should apply to the whole of the Middle East:

> For too long the West, and indeed the United States, assumed that it could turn a blind eye to what Arab intellectuals called the freedom deficit in the Middle East and that that would be all right. We did that for 60 years. And we were doing it in the name of stability, but of course we got neither stability nor democratic change; . . . it is our belief that we instead got a kind of malignancy

underneath which produced al-Qaida and the extremist philosophies, and that the only way to fight those extremist ideologies is to spread freedom.[59]

Bush and Rice were so committed to the notion that democracy is more important than stability that they were unwilling to call for cancellation of the Palestinian Authority elections in the spring of 2006 even after it became clear that the Islamic fundamentalist party Hamas was likely to win them and thus to pose a serious threat to stability both inside and outside the Occupied Territories.[60] Late in the summer of 2006, Rice dismissed the border war between democratic Israel and democratic Lebanon as merely "birth pangs of the new Middle East."[61] *Washington Post* defense correspondent Tom Ricks described the stark contrast between the cautious realism concerning regional transformation of major figures in the first Bush administration and the radicalism of the second Bush administration: "'Stability' wasn't their goal, it was their *target*. They saw it as synonymous with stagnation. They wanted radical change in the Mideast. They were determined to drain the swamp—that is, to alter the political climate of the region so that it would no longer be so hospitable to the terrorists inhabiting it." In Ricks's view, the second Bush administration was "willing, a bit like [1960s radical] Jerry Rubin, to take a chance and then groove on the ensuing rubble."[62]

In sum, the Bush administration and its neoconservative allies were clearly part of the Liberal tradition; like many American liberals, they fully embraced its four core premises.

Links between the Liberal Tradition and Current Civil-Military Conflict in America

Drawing on Hartz, Huntington found the mainspring of the tension in American civil-military relations in the clash of two very different mind-sets: military Realism and civilian Liberalism:

> The military institutions of any society are shaped by two competing forces: a functional imperative stemming from the threats to a state's security and a societal imperative arising from the social forces, ideologies, and institutions dominant within the society. Military institutions which reflect only social values may be incapable of performing effectively their military function. On the other hand, it may be impossible to contain within society military institutions shaped purely by functional imperatives. The interaction of these two forces is the nub of the problem of civil-military relations.[63]

Military Realism, which Huntington attributed to a "functional imperative" flowing naturally from the anarchic nature of international politics, embraced a number of distinct tenets: the conviction that violence is a permanent feature of international relations; the assumption of the primacy of the state in international relations; a discounting of intangible factors such as intentions and ideology in favor of a focus upon tangible things such as material capabilities; and reluctance to commit military force and to wage war in all save the most pressing circumstances, but then a willingness to do so without limitation of the means employed.[64]

Huntington's intellectual debt to Hartz was greatest in his discussion of the particular societal imperative in the United States. Drawing implicitly upon *The Liberal Tradition in America*, Huntington argued that America's civilian political culture is thoroughly Liberal, with five distinct elements that conflict with military Realism. First, it is largely indifferent to international affairs. Second, when American Liberalism occasionally looks abroad, it seeks to spread its own domestic institutions to resolve international problems. Third, American Liberalism manifests an absolutist stance: it seeks either to withdraw from the non-Liberal world or to convert it, never to compromise with it. Fourth, American Liberalism is quite ambivalent about war, either eschewing it altogether or fighting numerous wars-to-end-all-wars. Finally, American Liberalism is wary of, and distrustful toward, the professional military institution.[65]

Huntington employed Hartz's analysis of the Liberal tradition to explain recurrent civil-military tension in America as the result of efforts by civilian leaders to liberalize the conservative Realism of the American military's officer corps.[66] This societal imperative, in Hartz's account, was largely constant throughout American history. The analytical problem arises because, as Huntington admits, American civil-military relations have in fact varied. At some times, they have been relatively harmonious, at others quite fractious. Because one cannot explain a variable (civil-military relations) with a constant (Liberalism), we need to find a variable explaining when Liberalism mattered and when it did not. Building upon Huntington's argument about the functional imperative, I argued in my book *Civilian Control of the Military* that the key variable explaining different patterns of civil-military relations in the United States and other countries has been the threat environment the state faced. In my view, environments of high external threat have tended to make civilian leaders more likely to embrace objective control of the military and hence to reduce civil-military conflict. This would explain why, during the Cold War, U.S. civil-military relations were for the most part harmonious.

Conversely, less challenging international threat environments such as the post–Cold War era and even the Global War on Terrorism (far fewer Americans have been killed in the latter struggle than in any previous American war, by an order of magnitude)[67] are more prone to civil-military conflict, in part because civilians reassert themselves and try to impose Liberalism upon the military institution. America's Liberal tradition explains, in my view, both Clinton's and Bush's poor relationships with the U.S. military.

The continuity between these two administrations is shown by the fact that both Clinton and Bush shared many of the Liberal tradition's core premises. To begin with, the Liberal tradition was primarily concerned with domestic politics, and Clinton and Bush shared this focus. The members of Clinton's team, for example, famously reminded themselves of the importance of their domestic focus during the 1992 campaign with the motto "it's the economy, stupid."[68] The same lack of attention to international politics was true of candidate George W. Bush, who admitted in 1997 to Saudi Arabia's Ambassador, Prince Bandar, "I don't have the foggiest idea about what I think about international, foreign policy."[69] Bush's foreign policy advisors, including Colin Powell, Condoleezza Rice, Dick Cheney, Paul Wolfowitz, and Richard Armitage, played a huge role in shaping his agenda; most of the story of his administration's foreign policy can be told through the struggles among members of this group to shape the president's thinking.[70]

The Liberal tradition also seeks to externalize our domestic political system to solve America's problems abroad. Evidence of this in both the Clinton and Bush administrations was their embrace of the Liberal theory of the "democratic peace" as their rationale for believing that the spread of democracy would bolster U.S. security. Clinton's 1996 *National Security Strategy* stated explicitly that "the more that democracy and political and economic liberalization take hold in the world . . . the safer our nation is likely to be and the more our people are likely to prosper."[71] President Bush's 2004 State of the Union Address similarly declared that "our aim is a democratic peace."[72] National Security Advisor Rice subsequently claimed: "President Bush's foreign policy is a bold new vision that draws inspiration from the ideas that have guided American foreign policy at its best: That democracies must never lack the will or the means to meet and defeat freedom's enemies, that America's power and purpose must be used to defend freedom, and that the spread of democracy leads to lasting peace."[73]

Both Clinton and Bush were uncompromising Idealists who rejected what they saw as the cynical and limiting approach of Realism to world politics. President Clinton argued that in the post–Cold War world, "where freedom, not tyranny, is on the march, the cynical calculus of pure power politics simply does not compute."[74] As candidate, Bush tried to recast his Idealism as Realism:

> Our realism must make a place for the human spirit. . . . Some have tried to pose a choice between American ideals and American interests—between who we are and how we act. But the choice is false. America, by decision and destiny, promotes political freedom—and gains the most when democracy advances. America believes in free markets and free trade—and benefits most when markets are opened. America is a peaceful power—and gains the greatest dividend from democratic stability. Precisely because we have no territorial objectives, our gains are not measured in the losses of others. They are counted in the conflicts we avert, the prosperity we share and the peace we extend.[75]

As president, Bush dropped any pretense of blending Idealism and Realism; he and senior members of his administration became outspoken critics of Realism.[76] To be sure, Clinton and Bush took distinctly different approaches to achieving their idealistic objectives, with Clinton more inclined toward multilateralism, while Bush sought to remake the world unilaterally. But these are differences in ways and means, not ends.

The Liberal tradition abhors the fact that war is a regular feature of international politics. Liberals either want to eschew military force entirely or, paradoxically, to use it extensively to reengineer the international system. Bill Clinton, for instance, was not much of a fan of the military but ended up using it quite often for "operations other than war," such as in Somalia, Haiti, Bosnia, and Kosovo.[77] George Bush criticized the Clinton administration's frequent use of the military in his presidential campaign debates with candidate and Vice President Al Gore, noting that "one of the problems we have in the military is we're in a lot of places around the world."[78] By 2002, however, he was saying, "As we think through Iraq, we may or may not attack. I have no idea. But it will be for the objective of making the world peaceful."[79] Nothing better reflects Liberal tradition thinking than this. The roots of civil-military conflict in both administrations were civilian efforts, animated by Liberal tradition motives, to push a reluctant military to engage in operations it did not embrace wholeheartedly.[80]

As Huntington pointed out, American Liberalism is deeply ambivalent about the military institution, and both Clinton and Bush manifested this same wariness. Clinton famously acknowledged that during his younger years he had "loathed" the military. Apparently something of that view was shared by one of his transition staffers, who reportedly told General Barry McCaffrey that she "did not talk to the military."[81] Clinton's continuing discomfort with those in uniform was painfully obvious throughout his tenure as commander in chief.[82]

Despite the overtly pro-military rhetoric of the Bush campaign in 2000, it soon became evident that senior officials in his administration had little respect for the professional expertise of those in uniform. Shortly after taking office as secretary of defense, Donald Rumsfeld made it clear that he regarded military leaders as dull and lacking vision, and he often treated them with contempt and disdain.[83] Rumsfeld dismissed concerns about his abrupt manner in remarks to the Pentagon press corps in January 2003 by claiming, "if that disturbs people and their sensitivities are such that it bothers them, I'm sorry. But that's life, because this stuff we're doing is important. We're going to get it done well. We're going to get it done right. The Constitution calls for civilian control of this department. And I'm a civilian. And believe me, this place is accomplishing enormous things. We have done so much in the last two years. And it doesn't happen by standing around with your finger in your ear hoping everyone thinks that that's nice."[84]

While not every civilian policymaker treated those in uniform as cavalierly as Rumsfeld did, the prevailing ethos in the Bush administration was clearly not to defer to those in uniform, even on tactical and military operational issues usually requiring professional military expertise or specialization.

Huntington argues that Liberals seek to "extirpate" military Realism by imposing Liberal values upon the institution. This approach was reflected in Bill Clinton's efforts to transfer America's civilian mores to the military by ending its exclusionary policies about homosexuals and about women in combat.[85] In the supposedly more pro-military Bush administration, there were also constant efforts to infuse the military with civilian values, in this instance those of the corporate world. Rumsfeld, who had spent a considerable portion of his career in the private sector, was a firm believer in the superiority of the business management model.[86] "In for-profit institutions," he declared, one must innovate: "You simply cannot do it any other way. . . . There's a penalty if you don't. You die. It ends. It's over. That really focuses the mind. That doesn't exist here [in the Pentagon]. Therefore, there isn't anything that focuses the mind. Therefore it's a job that's never over."[87]

In sum, the views of both the Clinton administration and the Bush administration about the American military institution embraced significant aspects of the Liberal tradition. This, I argue, explains why both administrations experienced significant civil-military tension. Further, as I explained earlier, neoconservatism, the guiding intellectual force behind the Bush administration's strategy in the Global War on Terrorism, draws heavily upon America's Liberal tradition. It is precisely this Liberal philosophy that led to many of its key mistakes in Iraq and elsewhere. As Tom Ricks put it,

> The idealist view is key in this—in shaping the war plan, because it gives you your strategic assumptions. If you think that you will be greeted as liberators, then you don't need as big a force to occupy. If you think you really can wipe your hands of this pretty quickly, then you don't plan for a long-term operation; then you don't have to plan for "Geez, what do we have to do if we have to have two or three or four rotations of troops through Iraq?" . . . They thought they could win by decapitating the regime, and then they basically would put a new head on the regime and that was it. And what happens is they cut the head off the chicken, and the chicken started running around, and they never really caught it.[88]

It was clear from early on that Realists in the U.S. military questioned the wisdom of attacking Iraq after 9/11. Hearing increasing calls from neoconservatives in the Office of the Secretary of Defense and the White House, Secretary of State Colin Powell reportedly chided General Hugh Shelton, his successor as chairman of the Joint Chiefs of Staff: "Can't you get these guys back in the box?"[89] Once it became clear that the "victory" Bush declared in the spring of 2003 had turned into a quagmire, finger-pointing and mutual recriminations between recently retired generals and civilian leaders in the Bush administration exposed the persistent fault lines in American civil-military relations. Former Joint Staff director Lieutenant General Greg Newbold wrote sharply of his "sincere view . . . that the commitment of our forces to this fight was done with a casualness and swagger that are the special province of those who have never had to execute these missions—or bury the results."[90] Newbold later joined five other recently retired generals—including former Central Command (CENTCOM) commander General Anthony Zinni, former head of the Iraqi training mission Major General Paul Eaton, Army Transformation Task Force chief Major General John Riggs, and former Iraq war division commanders Major General Charles Swannack and Major General John Batiste—in calling publicly for Rumsfeld's resignation.[91] In 2006 the single largest group (42 percent) of the troops polled by *Military Times* disapproved of the president's handling of the war in Iraq.[92]

Rumsfeld's skepticism about the senior military leadership, combined with his faith in civilian strategic wisdom, led him to micromanage the military. Former secretary of the Army Thomas White later characterized Rumsfeld's style:

Well, the secretary by nature likes to get into the details of things. And a view that he always held was that we were sloppy with manpower, that we deploy too many people, we would deploy them before they were really needed and so on and so on and so forth. . . . He decided to micro manage every one of the deployment incremental packages by itself, and it drove everybody just about to the point of distraction. And his argument was he was trying to save us from ourselves. And our argument was, "if you'd just get out of the way, we'll get the force generated, and we'll go conduct this operation." But it caused great pain for everybody. . . . In some specific cases, the sequence got all screwed up, and extraordinary measures had to be taken to fix it.[93]

The root of the Bush administration's willingness to ignore professional military advice in planning for Iraq was its belief that civilians better understood the potential of high technology and new modes of organization to revolutionize warfare.[94] In a September 1999 speech on military transformation, candidate Bush had promised that he intended to "force new thinking and hard choices" upon the military to ensure that it did not miss the "opportunity . . . created by a revolution in the technology of war."[95] In the first few months of the new administration, Rumsfeld's efforts to transform the U.S. military in what he and other civilians anticipated would be a "revolution in military affairs" (RMA) led to friction with the services (and their allies on Capitol Hill), who had deep reservations about both the new secretary's style and the substance of those efforts. To be sure, some military visionaries, including Admiral William Owens and Admiral Arthur Cebrowski, hopped aboard the RMA bandwagon.[96] But Rumsfeld did not trust the uniformed services to implement transformation, believing it would take place only if there were close civilian prodding and guidance. As a result, Rumsfeld's relations with the senior military and with the congressional leadership could not have been much worse by the fall of 2001. Indeed, many predicted that he would be the first departure from the Bush cabinet.[97] His public performance after the 9/11 attack temporarily elevated Rumsfeld from goat to hero, and the quick apparent victory over the Taliban in Afghanistan seemed to vindicate the neoconservatives' view that technology and new modes of organization could now substitute for numbers in warfare.[98]

In the final analysis, however, the Liberal tradition tenets identified by Huntington produced in Bush, Cheney, Rumsfeld, Wolfowitz, civilians in the Office of the Secretary of Defense, and their neoconservative allies elsewhere in and out of government a naive optimism that explains the abysmal state of civil-military relations as well as the disaster in Iraq. Indeed, the assumptions that the war was necessary in the first place and that it would be easy to win were directly attributable to the Liberal tradition's view of the world. The Liberal tradition reinforced the neoconservatives' claim that regime change in the Middle East was the key to advancing U.S. interests in the region and that the overthrow of Saddam could be the first step in regional transformation. The Liberal tradition also led civilians in the Bush administration to believe that the war in Iraq would be a "cakewalk," as Kenneth Adelman predicted, because U.S. forces would be greeted as liberators, a democratic Iraqi government would quickly come to power after the war, Iraq's great oil wealth would soon pay for reconstruction, and democracy in Iraq would prevent the emergence of ethnic conflict.[99] All of those Liberal assumptions proved wrong.

Perhaps the most consequential strategic mistake made by Rumsfeld, Wolfowitz, and other civilians in the Office of the Secretary of Defense was to underestimate the number of troops necessary for Phase IV in Iraq, the postwar stabilization and reconstruction phase. Because it was "convinced it would win quickly, the [Bush] administration decided to pull some punches."[100] Indeed, Rumsfeld and Wolfowitz argued that the U.S. Army was overestimating the number of troops necessary for these operations. "Rumsfeld was always of the view," former Army secretary White recalls, "that the military was excessive in its manpower demands and that they would ask for three or four times more people than they really needed just to give them an enormous measure of assurance . . . and that his role in life, therefore, was to save them from themselves and to discipline the process by convincing them that they could do a lot more with a lot less."[101] Exasperated with what he saw as the overly conservative assumptions of U.S. Central Command war planning, Rumsfeld at one point echoed Lincoln's frustration with General George McClellan during the Civil War, accusing his generals of having "the slows."[102] On at least six separate occasions, Rumsfeld insisted on reducing the number of troops slated for the operation.[103] He also inserted himself deeply into the tactical aspects of the war plans. Not only did he want to limit the overall numbers of troops deployed, but he also wanted to reshape the Time-Phased Force Deployment List (TPFDL), the annex to the war plan that scheduled when and how the troops would flow into the theater.[104] The net result of Rumsfeld's interventions was to leave the United States with too few troops for Phase IV operations and to make it harder to employ those troops who were in the theater in a fully effective way, because they were deployed ad hoc rather than according to a carefully worked-out timetable. It is, of course, by no means clear that more troops deployed in a timely fashion could have preempted the immediate post-war chaos and nascent insurgency. But it is certain that civilian interventions made these problems inevitable.

Managing the Enduring Tension between Liberalism and Realism

Given the functional imperative of military Realism and the political constant of civilian Liberalism in the United States, Huntington thought that managing civil-military relations would be a continuing challenge. The enduring influence of *The Soldier and the State* suggests that this diagnosis still resonates widely with scholars and policymakers.

In addition to a compelling explanation of the source of recurrent civil-military conflict, Huntington offered two possible ways to manage it. One solution he considered was that there could be an ideological convergence between civilians and the military institution. This convergence might occur around Realism because, during times of acute threat, civilians might gravitate toward the military view of the world.[105] This has indeed happened a few times in U.S. history, but Huntington worried that it has been only a temporary expedient, because American civilian leaders are more inclined toward promoting a convergence on Liberalism by "extirpating" military Realism.[106] The problem with the latter form of convergence, in Huntington's estimation, is that it is likely to undermine military effectiveness and thus to compromise the security of the state.

These problems with ideological convergence led Huntington to focus on a second approach to managing this enduring tension: the method of civilian control. In *The Soldier and the State*, Huntington identified two distinct approaches. "Subjective control" aims to make the military more like the dominant group in civilian society by infusing it with that group's particular values. "Objective control" recognizes an "autonomous military professionalism" and a separate sphere of military expertise.[107] Huntington endorsed this as the optimal way to balance military expertise with overall civilian political supremacy. To maintain this balance, civilian leaders cede substantial autonomy to military professionals in the tactical and operational realms in return for the military's complete and unquestioning subordination to civilian political control. While not always reflected in practice, this system of civilian control has shaped U.S. thinking for fifty years about how civilians ought to exercise their oversight of the military and has generally been conducive to good civil-military relations.

It was precisely this form of civilian control that the Bush administration and its neoconservative allies rejected. Key figures in Bush's civilian national security team believed that the Clinton administration had failed to "keep a tight rein" on the military.[108] Rumsfeld, Wolfowitz, and other senior national security officials in the Bush administration came into office believing that, in order to overcome service parochialism and bureaucratic inertia and to transform the U.S. military, they would have to adopt a more intrusive form of civilian control. Tellingly, the first of Rumsfeld's famous rules identified civilian control of the military as the secretary of defense's primary responsibility. Another is to "reserve the right to get into anything and exercise it."[109] After 9/11, civilian proponents of a war of regime change in Iraq quickly realized that a key obstacle to their goal of quickly launching such a war and waging it with minimal forces would be the senior leadership of the U.S. Army. Given the conservative tenets of military Realism, civilians in the Bush administration concluded that they would have to fight hard to overcome widespread military skepticism about the imperative of regime change in Baghdad, as well as bureaucratic inertia that shaped how the services thought about the appropriate size and force mix necessary to accomplish such a mission.

Civilians in the Bush administration were determined to reassert civilian control, and they were willing to do so by immersing themselves in operational issues such as war planning, force sizing, and even details of deployment scheduling. Rumsfeld was determined to "show everybody in the structure that he was in charge and that he was going to manage things perhaps in more detail than previous secretaries of defense, and he was going to involve himself in operational details."[110] Such an intrusive form of civilian oversight was bound to lead to friction with the military because traditionally, as Major General Eaton points out, "tactics are the domain of the soldier on the ground."[111]

The Bush administration sought to impose a fundamentally different form of civilian control from what it perceived had come before. Without aggressive and relentless civilian probing of military policies and decisions at every level, administration officials worried, they would not be able to accomplish their objectives of radically transforming the military and using it in the Global War on Terror in fundamentally unprecedented ways. Eliot Cohen, a member of the Defense Policy Board under Bush, provided the intellectual rationale for this more intrusive regime of civilian control.[112] His book *Supreme Command* was read widely by members of the senior Bush national security team, reportedly even landing on the president's bedside table in Crawford, Texas.[113] Cohen's thesis was that civilian intervention, not only at the strategic but also at the tactical and operational levels, was essential for military success. His rationale was twofold. Following Clausewitz's famous dictum that "war is the continuation of politics," Cohen rightly questioned the "notion that politicians [should] step aside" during war as "empirically untrue and theoretically undesirable."[114] But more controversially, Cohen denigrated the military's claim to superior expertise with the argument that most military officers do not in fact have much more experience in waging war than do their civilian counterparts.[115] Endorsing a radical interpretation of French premier Clemenceau's famous dictum that "war is too important to be left to the generals," Cohen asserted that "there is no evidence that generals as a class make wiser national security policymakers than civilians."[116] In order to overcome military resistance or incompetence, Cohen argued, civilian leaders must be willing to "probe" deeply into military matters. He called this "the unequal dialogue," which involved "politicians engaged in very intense and sometimes unpleasant interaction with their senior military leaders. It is in the course of that unequal dialogue," said Cohen, "that you get much better strategy than you do any other way."[117] Cohen lauded Rumsfeld as "a very active secretary of defense, rather along the lines essential for a good civil-military dialogue," and he continued to defend Rumsfeld's approach publicly as late as April 2006.[118]

As if taking cues from Cohen, Rumsfeld and Wolfowitz showed little compunction about meddling even in such issues as the number of troops required and the phasing of their deployments for Operation Iraqi Freedom.[119] There is no clearer evidence of civilian willingness to challenge the professional military on tactical and operational matters than Wolfowitz's cavalier dismissal as "wildly off the mark" of Army Chief of Staff General Eric Shinseki's prewar estimates that the United States would need in excess of "several hundred thousand troops" for postwar stability operations. Wolfowitz's public rebuke of Shinseki during congressional testimony had a chilling effect on other Army officers.[120] The fact that Wolfowitz, rather than Shinseki, prevailed in the debate about force size for the war was evidence of the Bush administration's success in imposing its preferred framework for civilian control of the military.

Former secretary of the Army White summarized the Bush and Rumsfeld legacy by noting that "the last secretary of defense we had that was a war fighter was probably George Marshall. By definition, they [secretaries of defense] are civilians. Some of them might have had experiences in their younger years in the military, but their job, among other things, is to take the wise advice offered them by the military and think that over and give it some credence and then make a decision. The question is, have we lost the balance of that. I think they went too far."[121] Given the parlous situation in Iraq that resulted from willful civilian disregard for military advice, it would have been far better for our country if President Bush had read Huntington's book *The Soldier and the State* during his summer vacation in 2002 rather than Cohen's *Supreme Command*. Had he done so, I suspect he would have been reluctant to allow his underlings to overrule military advice on such critical tactical issues as the number of troops necessary for Phase IV operations in Iraq. Given the concern of senior Bush administration national security officials with reestablishing civilian control of the military after the Clinton era, it would be ironic if their legacy were to be, instead, the discrediting of the whole notion.

CHAPTER SIX

Winning Wars, Not Just Battles

Expanding the Military Profession to Incorporate
Stability Operations

Nadia Schadlow and Richard A. Lacquement Jr.

In *The Soldier and the State,* Huntington described the military profession as set apart from other professions by its focus on "the management of violence." Huntington's definition of the military's professional expertise was focused: "The direction, operation, and control of a human organization whose primary function is the application of violence," he wrote, "is the peculiar skill of the officer."[1] Although clear, such a definition is too restrictive. It does not extend to include essential military tasks, the stability operations associated with the restoration of political and economic order.

Stability operations encompass "various military missions, tasks, and activities conducted outside the United States in coordination with other instruments of national power to maintain or reestablish a safe and secure environment, [and to] provide essential governmental services, emergency infrastructure reconstruction, and humanitarian relief."[2] They comprise the political and economic tasks necessary for the restoration of political order and stability and for "winning the peace."

This chapter evaluates the key challenge to Huntington's narrow interpretation of the military profession that is raised by stability operations by examining

American efforts in this regard since the end of the Cold War. A reassessment is important because Huntington's arguments[3] have "colored the military's self-perception for an entire generation."[4] The nature of war requires, we argue, a broader, more inclusive definition of the profession, one that places stability operations squarely within the military's required area of expertise.

American military operations are conducted by joint forces and led by joint headquarters that include officers from all of the American military services. The effectiveness of American military operations is therefore a function of professional judgment and leadership drawn from all of the military services. However, the burden and responsibility for stability operations is mostly borne by ground forces. The Army, in particular, along with the Marine Corps, is and will be responsible for providing the land power to set the conditions for enduring peace and for sustaining those conditions as long as needed to achieve policy aims.[5] The Army and Marine Corps have extensive historical experiences that provide a positive foundation and make them best suited to take the lead in fostering improvements in the military's preparedness for stability operations. These improvements, we argue, can be adopted by the U.S. military as a whole.

The Military Profession and Its Expertise

Huntington's description of the military profession as a relatively narrow area of expertise illuminated two key premises. First, his view of the military as an organization that is focused on the management of violence reflected the American military's—and especially the Army's—own conception of itself as it evolved after World War I. Following that war, the Army deemphasized its past as a constabulary force, when it had spent a tremendous proportion of its time and energy on policing the frontier and providing much of what passed for local authority.[6] Instead, it focused on the apparent lessons of World War I: that modern armies would fight heavy adversaries, using vast quantities of munitions.[7] This view emphasized the kinetic nature of war; defeating the enemy's combat forces was seen as the primary mission of the American military. This emphasis continued during and even after World War II: the relatively successful occupations in Germany, Japan, and Italy consolidated the combat victories achieved in these countries, but the American military made few changes to its active force to incorporate preparation for stability operations.

Second, Huntington's delineation of a distinct military profession was meant to address the long-standing American concern about the need of a democratic, liberal state to keep a large standing military in check. To preserve civilian over-sight of the military, he developed a theory of civil-military relations that sought to specify distinct realms for civil and military judgment. The emphasis on "mili-tarizing the military" relied on extensive military professional autonomy over a clear jurisdiction of professional practice.[8] This provided what Huntington termed "objective control."

Huntington's description of the military profession was derived from his pri-mary concern: how to maintain democratic, civilian control while simultane-ously allowing the maintenance of large and effective military institutions. This tension shaped his description of the military profession, which neglected many of the actual tasks undertaken by the armed forces during times of war on behalf of American security interests.

His prescription is for a military that focuses on battles, not wars. In war, po-litical, strategic, and operational concerns intersect, and the conceptual clarity of objective control clashes with reality. Objective control as a concept is inadequate to the strategic and operational dimensions of war, which require integration of civilian and military judgment. Huntington's reliance on an abstract construct that removes political judgment from the realm of military professionalism un-duly narrows the focus of military leaders to operations and tactics. Huntington's construct would direct the military's attention away from strategy and the con-cepts of victory that link military actions to overarching national policy aims.

Nowhere are the deficiencies of such an approach more evident than with re-spect to stability operations. Effective stability operations require complex pro-fessional judgments in realms of activity not easily separable into military and civilian compartments. Examples of this overlap include the need to restore po-litical order in towns and cities, which often arises simultaneously with ongoing military operations; the need to develop political strategies to restore the legiti-macy of political actors who are left in place; targeting decisions about infrastruc-ture (such as electricity and water systems), which can affect both enemy military operations and the needs of the local population; decisions about the character and duration of martial law; and the allocation of key local resources (food, fuel, shel-ter, infrastructure), which has profound effects on empowering political actors.

In his survey of post–Civil War U.S. military history, Huntington noted the difficulty the Army had in focusing on purely military tasks during its participa-tion in the reconstruction of the South after the Civil War, its constabulary duties on the western frontier during the Indian wars, its occupation of Cuba and the Philippines at the turn of the twentieth century, and its postwar governance duties in Germany and Japan. Huntington expressed concern that such duties compromised professional military perspective. In performing these tasks, Huntington said, the Army was acting as the "government's obedient handyman performing without question or hesitation the jobs assigned to it."[9] He believed that the Army had followed such orders like a "machine" and had therefore tried to divest itself of all political responsibility and controversy, "despite the political nature of the tasks it was frequently called upon to perform."[10]

Rather than accepting the postwar occupations as central to America's consolidation of victory in World War II, Huntington interpreted the military's role in these governance operations as an undesirable expansion of the military's activities. He observed disapprovingly that during the postwar occupations, the military "dealt more and more openly with political questions."[11] The difference between the American and British approach to the conduct of war, as he saw it, was that American military chiefs were forced to "adopt a broadly political viewpoint," whereas their British counterparts could "adhere to a professional military outlook."[12]

The Soldier and the State treated tasks associated with the restoration of political and economic order—essential elements of stability operations—as extraneous to war itself. Its view of war is thus a narrow one: stability operations fall outside "the management of violence." Huntington's book suggests that war (by which he meant combat, as we have argued) could be separated from inherently political tasks such as occupation and reconstruction. Within Huntington's framework, stability operations would be excluded from the military profession.

Over the years, Huntington's view of the military profession provided the military with an elegant rationale for its persistent tendency, despite its considerable history of involvement in stability operations, to exclude them from its version of war and its concepts of military security. Huntington's circumscribed view offered support for the U.S. military's intellectual "blind spot" regarding the full spectrum of activities that are integral to war. As Williamson Murray in chapter 7 of this volume explains, the profession of arms in American strategic culture has, for the most part, developed around a stark dichotomy between the idea of peace on one side and the idea of war on the other.[13] Huntington's view of war reflected this cultural and historical split.[14] The subsequent popularity of his book also strongly reinforced and shaped it.[15]

Particularly since the end of the Vietnam War, U.S. military leaders have emphasized the narrower operational characterization of their responsibilities that reflects Huntington's view. They have placed a particular focus on conventional warfare. This reflected the heightened emphasis on the Soviet Union as a conventional threat, as well as the military's desire to leave behind the complexities and relevance of its experiences in Vietnam. A significant manifestation was the development of AirLand Battle doctrine in the 1970s, which reinforced the military's focus on heavy combat.[16] Its emphasis on battles against similarly structured armed forces of other states emphasized force-against-force conventional operations to disrupt Soviet ground attacks throughout the depth of the battlefield. This concept of war provided the intellectual underpinnings of joint doctrine that persists down to the present. It was reinforced by the Weinberger Doctrine of the 1980s.[17] Widely embraced in military circles, the doctrine was an attempt to shape civil-military discourse on the appropriate uses of the American armed forces in ways that favored the military's preferred conception.[18] The doctrine's principles are, however, a poor guide for professional military advice.[19] They are particularly ill suited for addressing stability operations.

Huntington had a real and immediate challenge in mind as he developed his theory of civil-military relations. The Cold War dominated the national security context, and Huntington gave explicit attention to the military requirements of addressing the Soviet threat. He cast a critical eye on World War II, when the Cold War originated, criticizing both military and civilian leaders for a lack of appropriate attention to broader national security threats and arguing that this compromised American national security in relation to the Soviet Union. He believed that too much attention was given to military victory over Germany and Japan and too little to the possible contours of military security in the postwar world.[20]

Huntington's view reinforced the military's traditional view of war, which emphasized the centrality of battle rather than the achievement of broader strategic outcomes. This approach essentially focused on "defeating an adversary tactically" rather than approaching war with a "holistic view of conflict, one that extends from prewar condition-setting to the final accomplishment of national strategic objectives."[21] The American way of war since World War I has predominantly emphasized strategies of annihilation and attrition.[22] This narrow approach failed to accord much attention to the military's role in helping to integrate combat and stability operations to achieve strategic victory in war. Military involvement in political planning processes and in tasks related to consolidating "peace" were dismissed by Huntington as examples of excessive military involvement in nonmilitary matters.

The requirement for armed forces to be masters of organized, disciplined violence on behalf of the state is still central, because the capacity for effective armed combat is important for deterring and, if necessary, defeating other armed adversaries.[23] However, we argue that stability operations, too, fall squarely within the military profession's expertise, for two primary reasons. First, military forces are a key instrument in achieving the effective integration of combat and stability operations, which is essential to the achievement of the desired policy aims of a war. Wars are fought for political purposes; stability operations are fundamental instruments necessary to the achievement of the political objective in war; they are a consistent and regular feature of war. Strategic success requires attention not just to confronting the challenges of combat against enemy armed forces but also the challenges of the state of peace, for which military operations are merely instrumental. As Liddell Hart said, "The object in war is to attain a better peace—even if only from your own point of view. Hence it is essential to *conduct war with constant regard to the peace you desire.* This is the truth underlying Clausewitz's definition of 'war as a continuation of policy by other means'—the *prolongation of that policy through the war into the subsequent peace* must always be borne in mind."[24]

Strategic success requires leaders and organizations to take the operational steps necessary for restoring basic security and shaping the political environment in a manner favorable to U.S. interests. As an inherent feature of the landscape of war, stability operations shape decisions about combat such as rules of engagement, and efforts to influence different segments of the local population, such as local factions or groups with varying degrees of comity, enmity, or neutrality toward the armed opponents. The success of stability operations can affect the duration of the U.S. presence in a country or region because a failure to restore political stability is likely to make it more politically difficult for U.S. troops to depart. This kind of tension is apparent in Iraq today, as well as Afghanistan, where the failure to restore political stability in both countries is generating serious debates about the implications of a U.S. withdrawal of forces. Leaving a country more vulnerable to renewed violence would call into question the original rationale for the intervention of U.S. forces.

Second, stability operations are part of the spectrum of war because, for a considerable period of time, the military must retain control over instruments of violence so it can restore order and establish conditions that will meet policy aims and permit the reduction or complete departure of armed forces from a state or territory in which they are deployed. Thus, even a strict adherence to Huntington's narrow view of the profession would place stability operations within the military's domain. Moreover, international law requires armed forces to assume responsibility for the protection and well-being of the local populations in areas they come to control as part of combat.[25] Area security—establishing freedom of action in a territory to allow for the safe movement of troops and people—is a fundamental element of stability operations. It is the level of security necessary to ensure that enemy forces do not attack U.S. troops; it is also the security required to allow local people to leave their homes safely and go about the business of daily life. As one Army special forces officer observed in Iraq, "I considered security the top priority: for me, the function of security and governance were inseparable."[26] The absence of area security is more noticeable than a successful operation; without area security, as developments in Iraq and Afghanistan have shown, enemies are able to secure a foothold and use violence to begin a chain of destabilizing activities.[27]

At the turn of the twentieth century, area security was considered to be a crucial part of military missions and a task that only the military could adequately fulfill. In the early 1900s, officials at the War Department argued that the department was the only agency capable of restoring order on the ground in the event of "disturbances" and that there had been numerous occasions in the past when, because of "unforeseen contingencies," it had been "suddenly called upon to exercise civil control in occupied or disturbed areas."[28] Examples included activities on the frontiers of North America as the United States expanded; occupation and reconstruction in the American South following the Civil War; domestic support to the U.S. government during uprisings, riots, and strikes; and operations in Cuba, Puerto Rico, and the Philippines during and after the Spanish-American War.

Security and reconstruction, as well as combat and the political end state of war, are linked: stability operations are thus a central and necessary area of expertise for the military. This aspect of stability operations provides the rationale for military leadership of such operations. Although we agree that overall political direction of the war—and of stability operations—should be guided by civilians, there is a period of time after major combat ends in which the military must take charge of these necessary operations.

Post–Cold War and Post-9/11 Military Operations

In the early 1990s, following the Soviet Union's collapse, the U.S. military shifted from preparing to face the Soviet threat to preparing for two major theater wars or major regional contingencies. A conventional, state-centered conception of major national security threats was still dominant. However, as the contours of the post–Cold War world emerged, the missions that the U.S. military actually had to undertake did not bear much resemblance to the missions for which U.S. forces had systematically prepared and that they considered appropriate.[29] Contingencies in Somalia, Haiti, Bosnia, and Kosovo, among others, exposed the mismatch between the emerging national security challenges facing the United States and the military's preparation and preferences for conventional combat missions.[30]

Time and time again, faced with similar stabilization and reconstruction challenges, U.S. military forces have had to adapt, often with ad hoc responses, to accomplish tasks such as the restoration of basic order and area security, rebuilding basic infrastructure, the reconstitution of indigenous security forces, and the shaping of new political and administrative structures.[31] Despite the recurring nature of these challenges—indeed, the U.S. military has faced such requirements repeatedly at least since the mid-1800s—the military made few lasting organizational changes to prepare systematically for the challenges posed by stability operations. Eventually, prompted partly by the crises in Somalia and later in Bosnia, the defense policy community began to pay more attention to the many "nonstandard missions" that the armed forces found themselves undertaking. In the 1990s the various missions were discussed under such rubrics as peace operations, humanitarian assistance, small-scale contingencies, military operations other than war, peacekeeping, and stability and support operations.

A dominant feature of this discourse was that such operations, and preparation for them, were considered "lesser included missions": tasks that well-trained and disciplined conventional forces could execute effectively. Those terms did not distinguish operations in the midst of wars and other violent conflicts from responses to those in more benign security environments, such as a natural disaster or a static cease-fire situation. Despite the new attention, some expressed concern that the military's combat capabilities would be degraded by being asked to conduct noncombat tasks.[32] These concerns were a reflection of the continued influence of the Huntingtonian view of the military profession.

Efforts in the 1990s to update and develop new doctrine related to operations other than war and peace operations did not sufficiently improve the military's conduct of stability operations. Inadequate doctrinal and organizational preparation for stability operations contributed to the difficulties of U.S. forces in both Afghanistan and Iraq. Uncertainty and indecision hampered responses to challenges such as the reconstitution of indigenous defense forces, the establishment of area security, and the reestablishment of political order in key towns and cities. It soon became apparent that the wars in Iraq and Afghanistan would be intensely political struggles, with progress in each country dependent upon helping local populations work out political arrangements, while simultaneously managing ongoing violence. Both wars revealed the skill with which our adversaries could use both kinetic and nonkinetic advantages asymmetrically to outmaneuver U.S. forces.

Before the U.S. invasions of Afghanistan and Iraq, there had been little momentum in military or civilian circles to press for real organizational changes to ensure more sustained attention to stability operations. The doctrinal changes in the 1990s had not gone far enough to establish the idea that stability operations are central to war. The wars in Afghanistan and Iraq, however, sharpened the policy community's focus on the fundamental differences in national security challenges in the post–Cold War period and challenged the preferred military emphasis on conventional combat operations. These wars revealed that the threat from nonstate actors such as Al Qaeda derives partly from their ability to operate among and draw support from disaffected populations. Thus, in failed states there is an increased need for the military to operate effectively in the realms of stability operations. U.S. armed forces will not be the only U.S. government agencies involved, but where contingencies involve the imminent threat of violence, as most do, the U.S. military will remain the key instrument for a significant period of time.

Operations in Iraq and Afghanistan helped many begin to see that stability operations would be integral to all military operations and a necessary complement to combat operations at every stage of conflict, thus requiring specific planning and preparation. A variety of policy documents, including those from semiofficial entities, such as the Defense Science Board, and especially within Army and Marine circles, acknowledged that stability operations were a core part of the military's mission.

For example, the summer 2004 Defense Science Board Report on *Transition to and from Hostilities* urged the services to exert "management discipline" over stability operations. The same effort and planning that goes into preparing and planning for combat operations must, it urged, be extended to stability operations. The report described key areas, such as contingency planning and strategic communications, that the military and the U.S. government as a whole—particularly the State Department—should develop.[33] A year later, the same group completed a second review examining institutional requirements for the effective conduct of stability operations, such as the explicit acceptance and resourcing of high-level organizational leadership and the development of metrics for measuring and reporting readiness. That report argued that the United States could not afford to "maintain two separate forces, one dedicated to major combat, the other to stability operations."[34] In response to these studies, and after extensive staffing, the Defense Department issued DoD Directive 3000.05 in November 2005. In a dramatic conceptual break from the past, the directive declares: "Stability operations are a core U.S. military mission that the Department of Defense shall be prepared to conduct and support. They shall be given priority comparable to combat operations and be explicitly addressed and integrated across all DoD activities including doctrine, organizations, training, education, exercises, matériel, leadership, personnel, facilities, and planning."[35]

Recent revisions to Joint, Army, and Marine Corps doctrine also reflected a much greater integration of stability operations concepts. The September 2006 version of a key doctrinal manual, Joint Publication 3-0, *Joint Operations*, reflects revision of the joint planning construct to incorporate stability operations through all phases of military operations.[36] The most important change in new doctrinal statements is a shift from "separation" to "integration": formerly, stability operations were considered separate endeavors, discrete from combat and generally to be undertaken only in narrow circumstances, as a follow-on effort to combat operations, and now they are regarded as a set of tasks integral to combat that must be considered and resourced in all phases of operations, in peace, crisis, or war.[37]

There have also been some changes to training for the Army and Marine Corps. Considerable efforts to improve and focus training on counterinsurgency (COIN) and stability operations for units scheduled for rotation to Iraq and Afghanistan have included an extensive reorientation of the Army's premier combat training center, the National Training Center, with improved training in urban warfare and guerrilla-type capabilities, and learning to fight against an enemy that uses smaller and less predictable operations.[38] Improvements have also taken place at the Army's Joint Readiness Training Center at Fort Polk, Louisiana, and at the Marine Corps Air Ground Combat Center at Twentynine Palms, California, where there has been less emphasis on conventional force-on-force combat training and much more use of role-playing and ambiguous training scenarios involving combatants and noncombatants.

Although these are positive developments in the overdue effort to improve stability operations and counterinsurgency skills, these changes may not be strategically significant. They reflect tactical-level refinements. Broader changes are still needed, such as keeping units in place for a longer period of time. Frequent rotations result in a recurring loss of gains made by individual soldiers who have developed contacts and established trust in towns where they patrol.[39] Tactical improvements and competencies cannot compensate for broader strategic flaws.

The U.S. military's experience in Iraq illustrates the disconnect between planning for conventional combat against similarly structured and controlled national armed forces and planning for dealing with unconventional or irregular opponents (including nonstate and transnational groups). It reveals the need to develop a more comprehensive approach that combines combat and stability operations rather than treating them as separate and distinct activities. In Iraq, the two sets of activities have been inseparable and have required simultaneous and well-integrated execution. The military's failure to incorporate historical lessons from past stability operations contributed to the challenges: the absence of area security in key areas; confusing command arrangements in the theater, involving military headquarters such as CENTCOM and civilian organizations such as the Office for Reconstruction and Humanitarian Assistance and the Coalition Provisional Authority; the decision to demobilize Iraq's army; and problems with training and equipping a new Iraqi army. Failure to undertake stability operations during and immediately after major combat operations left openings that opponents deftly exploited. Excessive focus on the defeat or destruction of the armed forces of the state neglected the sectarian tensions that would prove even more challenging in Iraq. Local disaffection provided fertile terrain for insurgent activities and the creation of militant strongholds. Failure to build upon early successes in places such as Mosul and Ar Rutbah and an excessive reliance on "kinetic" operations did much to hamper subsequent efforts and put American strategic goals at risk.[40]

The Bush administration's adoption in early 2007 of a new strategy for Iraq suggested an affirmation of the requirement to link security, stabilization, governance, and reconstruction in the war effort. The president announced "major changes" in U.S. strategy in Iraq, with a primary emphasis on helping Iraqi leaders to "secure their population" so that Iraqis could enjoy a basic measure of security.[41] Until this was accomplished, the White House acknowledged, it would be difficult to achieve political and economic progress. A key rationale behind the surge of additional troops to Iraq was to implement a new strategy focused on "providing security and opportunity to the Iraqi people," and security and stability would then expand outward, "hence the image of an expanding oil spot."[42] Whether or not the surge ultimately succeeds, its adoption by U.S. civilian and military leaders signaled recognition of the link between stability, security, and ultimate victory in war.

Remaining Challenges and Opportunities

The imperatives of Afghanistan and Iraq, recent significant changes in doctrine, and some changes in training and education notwithstanding, several other barriers—many of them intellectual—hinder full acceptance of stability operations as an integral part of the military profession. Significant improvement in the military's ability to conduct stability operations will require changes in three main areas: overcoming remaining conceptual barriers to stability operations in American military culture, improving training and professional education, and making organizational changes. The recommendations in all three areas are interlocking and reinforcing.

Overcoming Conceptual Barriers

The American armed forces, and in particular their officer leaders, must take ownership of stability operations. This is a prerequisite to effective incorporation of stability operations into the core of the profession.[43] Although recent high-level policy and doctrinal statements reflect steps toward this goal, there remains great resistance in many quarters of the military to accepting the central features of stability operations as integral aspects of military operations in general, and of war in particular. The Army's emerging new doctrine in Field Manual (FM) 3-0, *Operations*, goes far in its discussion of full-spectrum operations. "Commanders employ offensive, defensive, and stability or civil support operations simultaneously as part of an interdependent joint force to seize, retain, and exploit the initiative, accepting prudent risk to create opportunities to achieve decisive results."[44] Nevertheless, there is still a tendency to consider stability operations as outside of the military's primary "war fighting functions."[45] Stability operations will not be accepted as a core part of the military profession until they are considered as integral and recurring, like intelligence or command and control.

The political element of war embodied by stability operations is not unique to counterinsurgency, but there is a tendency to relegate the political aspects of war to the COIN realm. There has been significant attention over the past two years, particularly in the Army and Marines, to updating doctrine for counterinsurgency operations.[46] The counterinsurgency manual, FM 3-24, lays out the comprehensive nature of counterinsurgency warfare and the specific challenges for which the military needs to be prepared, but many of these tasks—from security to basic control of local populations—are actually characteristic of stability operations as well. It is difficult to imagine a future in which the Army could be called upon to conduct large-scale conventional combat that did *not* involve political problems. These are inherent to all wars, not just counterinsurgency and irregular warfare.

The tendency to consider stability operations as outside the realm of full-scale combat operations encourages views that preparations for stability operations are a distraction or waste of resources; in fact, they should be seen as a force multiplier. The military's ambivalence about stability operations contributes to a lack of consensus regarding the training and organizational changes that would be required to entrench stability operations as a core expertise of the military.

Training and Education

Stability operations are not a science. Timelines and transitions will be tough to predict, especially at the outset of a conflict. However, key areas of expertise can be identified to shape the development of the organization's competencies. Expertise can be gathered from soldiers and training presented to them to improve their ability to respond to the full range of challenges they will face. In accounts of experiences in Iraq, a recurring complaint has been the lack of preparation for the security challenges of the war and the shaping of the political environment.[47] As one Army major described it,

> The average citizen [in Iraq] didn't care about the coalition's strategic advances in developing the country; the amount of oil flowing through the pipeline in Baji didn't interest the average Iraqi citizen. Whether or not there was propane available for cooking dinner or electricity for powering fans were the true concerns. We soon recognized that we had to address their concerns if we were going to persuade the locals that we were in Iraq to help. They needed to see action, not hear rhetoric.[48]

The main categories of challenges that constitute stability operations include establishing and maintaining security and public order, providing essential public infrastructure, providing governance, and rebuilding basic economic capabilities.[49] The commissioned officer corps must develop a deeper understanding of these areas of expertise, just as it works to ensure its expertise in elements of combat power.

Debate will certainly occur as to how "expert" a particular individual must become in these areas. Every soldier learns to shoot a rifle but not all are expected to become expert snipers. The services acknowledge that an individual cannot "achieve and sustain proficiency on every possible training task," and they leave the commander to "identify those tasks that are essential to accomplishing the organization's wartime operational mission."[50] It will therefore be a challenge to reach military-wide agreement on the areas of expertise essential to stability operations.

The good news is that many of the skills and specialties developed within military organizations are readily applicable to the demands of stability operations. For example, there is a close relationship between the requirements for stability operations and those for counterinsurgency. Stability operations may require a difference in balance or emphasis. In many historical examples of military effectiveness in stability operations, military leaders and their organizations have made necessary adjustments and adaptations. For example, the successful military occupations after World War II in Germany and Japan were accomplished under military leadership and with the extensive adaptation of headquarters to direct stability operations and with the adaptation of military units to conduct constabulary duties.[51] In the Vietnam War, the Civil Operations and Revolutionary Development Support (CORDS) program was a very effective adaptation of military leadership and organizations to focus on stability operations.[52] The development of Provincial Reconstruction Teams in Afghanistan and Iraq demonstrate similar adaptations. The current challenge is to institutionalize such adaptations to address contemporary national security requirements.

The first and most basic task in stability operations is security. The use of organized armed force to deter violence, or to achieve dominance if violence occurs and maintain dominance if violence escalates, is the most important feature of attaining stability. The security function is already at the center of the military profession. Expanding upon this expertise to include area security for local populations, not just traditional force protection, uses well-established and demonstrably strong American military skills. The ability to control large swaths of territory and significant populations in destabilized areas is very demanding, even more so when armed groups are vying with military forces for control. The military skills to achieve such control are resident in the force; the main need is for appropriate scope and definition for application in a particular environment.

The military will face the challenge of using all available networks—political, economic, social, and military—to defeat enemy armed forces and to convince political leaders and populations to act in accord with American strategic aims. While the military may not be able to master all of the types of expertise required to prevail in such a complex environment, it must develop a basic skill set in some of the critical recurring stability operations tasks. For example, the reconstitution of security requires the capacity to rebuild indigenous defense and police forces, adapt to differing rules of engagement, take new approaches to intelligence collection and integration, use strategic communications and information operations, and reestablish basic political functions. These steps are necessary to the initial phases of establishing a secure environment within which other U.S. government agencies such as the State Department, aid agencies, and nongovernmental organizations could assist reconstruction.

The most important focal point for training and education is the leaders of the American armed forces, that is, the officer corps. Officers must be educated and trained to operate effectively at the nexus of civilian and military professional expertise. This is a quintessential civil-military relations challenge for officers and will require continued attention to the education of officers from all of the services throughout their careers, from precommissioning to strategic leadership.

Guided by national policy, the officer-leaders—the military professionals— must exercise judgment in applying the capabilities of their organizations to national policy aims. The instrument of violence officers wield on behalf of the state serves broad purposes, but violence is not the end sought. Hence, officers must be able to judge the manner in which violence or potential violence might serve or might compromise national aims. Competence in executing stability operations similarly represents a complementary capacity the armed forces must bring to bear on achieving national objectives. Given the broad responsibilities that officers assume on behalf of the nation, a narrow focus on the means of combat alone is insufficient. The link between the use of military operations and the attainment of national policy aims requires leaders who have mastered the intellectual complexity of integrating combat and stability operations through military education and training.

A second important aspect of training should focus on the integration of stability operations into the mission-essential task lists and into the associated training activities of all joint headquarters. These headquarters are responsible for the integration of combat and stability operations into military operations that support the achievement of American policy aims. The emphasis on battle alone has ill served the United States. Nowhere has this been more evident than in the command and control mechanisms that have governed American military operations abroad. An acute and emblematic illustration of this came in the immediate wake of major combat in Operation Iraqi Freedom, when there were extremely poor connections and working relationships between General Franks's CENTCOM headquarters (and its subordinate military headquarters) and the Office for Reconstruction and Humanitarian Assistance led by Jay Garner. CENTCOM's problems persisted in the relationship with the successor organization, Coalition Provisional Authority, led by Ambassador Paul Bremer.

Many of the tasks involved in stability operations, particularly those related to governance and economics, are not ones for which the military has unique expertise. The most appropriate source of expertise for getting key systems up and running (sewers, electricity, courts, and so on) is more likely to be found among civilians. However, two practical aspects make it important for the military to develop some expertise in these areas.[53] The first is the practical aspect that, as armed forces come in contact with foreign populations in the midst of operations, there is an immediate need for recognition of civilian requirements. Second is the simple fact that the capacity of civilian expertise, although it may be preferred, is severely limited. The deployable civilian capacity to influence populations throughout all the areas in which the armed forces operate does not come anywhere near meeting the magnitude and influence of armed forces. In recent years, much has been written about the need to develop more U.S. governmental civilian capacity that can be deployed overseas in violent or unstable settings.[54] The Civilian Stabilization Initiative, announced by the State Department in early 2008, envisages the creation of three types of deployable civilian units: a small Active Response Corps of around 250 people drawn from civilian government employees; a Standby Response Corps drawn from a larger pool of employees; and a Civilian Reserve Corps, which would draw from experts outside of government.[55]

It remains unclear, however, how such civilian teams would operate in insecure environments without a significant military presence.[56] In most stability operations, particularly in unstable environments, armed forces would be supporting civilians who would be providing expertise and guidance in domains such as governance, economics, and other aspects of societal functioning. Military support to civilians includes security forces and activities to permit the civilians to operate in unstable, war-torn settings but also includes more general enabling capabilities such as transportation, communications, and even just well-disciplined and organized labor. More likely, however, armed forces must be prepared to substitute for such civilian expertise, at least as an expedient, until more appropriate long-term arrangements can be established.[57]

Furthermore, stability operations inform other aspects of war fighting. For example, war planners must consider the impact of core combat functions such as intelligence on broader political aims. Just as in counterinsurgency operations, in stability operations all soldiers become "eyes" and "ears." Moreover, "the population's potential to provide valuable information means that perceptions—the public's image of security forces and their activities—have operational consequences."[58] Understanding the local population—its allegiances and needs, its opinions of the security forces, and the like—as part of a broader intelligence picture for a town, city, or region is critical to the mission's success.

Organizational Changes

Meeting the demands of effective stability operations training is ameliorated somewhat by the fact that they involve many tasks for which the American armed forces already possess basic capabilities and competence. For example, to perform combat missions in the most disruptive and austere environments, the armed forces already have capacity to provide for their own practical needs such as food, water treatment, and communications; this capability may be applied to benefit the local populations in the areas where the forces operate. Also particularly valuable is the ability of organized and disciplined combat forces to provide physical security from violence in a particular area. The capabilities of military police, engineer, civil affairs, medical service, and logistics units are readily applicable to support of local populations. The capabilities inherent in the effective command, control, and support of a large, disciplined body of manpower constitute a valuable resource that can be applied to the needs of local populations.[59] The ability to lead complex military organizations also provides the foundation for many of the skills required as the armed forces interact with local populations and civic organizations, such as neighborhood associations, tribal councils, local governments, business associations, educational administrations, and various interest groups. Although the specific tasks and formal structures may differ markedly, thoughtful leadership can be put to good use in many ways in stability operations.

There have been new efforts to train military personnel for advisory duties in support of Iraqi and Afghan forces, but it is unclear whether such developments reflect permanent changes or are merely ad hoc responses to immediate requirements. The current approach in both the Army and Marine Corps has been to train existing units to perform stability operations in addition to their other well-established, predominantly combat-oriented tasks, rather than creating units specialized or optimized for such operations. Although this approach offers some evidence of a growing acceptance of the importance of stability operations, these training fixes are insufficient to address more demanding aspects of stability operations. There is a need to develop forces optimized for stability operations as a recurring and complex demand of war.

American special operations forces recognize the demand for both exceptionally skilled combat formations and adept, culturally aware teams focused on foreign military training, civil affairs, and support to local populations. This recognition should extend to the American armed forces more broadly with the creation or reorientation of a significant pool of units specialized for stability operations. Restructuring of headquarters and staffs should include more stability operations expertise in shaping overall operations. We advocate more expertise for all formations, but it is not enough. Fully integrated teams should be created to focus on stability operations and include at least one expeditionary headquarters at each of the regional combatant commands, focused on the specific conditions and needs of the particular region, and the affiliation of multiple brigade-sized joint operational teams for each regional command, comprising security forces, advisory teams, foreign-area specialists, engineering, military police, basic governance capacity, public communications and outreach, and other civil affairs specialties.[60] The organizations could be task-organized to include traditional combat forces (such as infantry, armor, artillery, and aviation elements) if required to deal with the threats in the particular area of operations. The expeditionary headquarters and the brigade-sized elements should be structured as joint units prepared and configured to integrate readily with interagency and multinational partners.[61] This configuration should include the integration of U.S. and allied government interagency partners within the headquarters; the establishment of civil-military operations centers[62] or other mechanisms to facilitate coordination with civilian agencies and representatives of multinational organizations, other governmental agencies, nongovernmental organizations, and representatives of local populations in the areas where operations take place; and the availability of well-trained and organized units that can provide security to appropriate civilian activities. A promising approach to the integration of military and civilian activities is the development of provincial reconstruction teams (PRTs) in Iraq and Afghanistan.[63] Although not as extensive or comprehensive as the Vietnam War CORDS program, PRTs are a valuable mechanism for using military means and civilian expertise to support key stability operations tasks.

The successful development and refinement of capabilities needed for stability operations will require rewarding personnel for achieving this expertise. The military can do this only with changes to the organization's beliefs about what tasks it values. Tasks are seen to have value if they are represented on par with other tasks in organizational structures. Consistently strong expertise will be created and sustained only if an organizational structure shapes, promotes, and rewards individuals in stability operations comparably to those in other combat specialties now appreciated in the military.[64] All of the major innovations undertaken by the U.S. military, particularly in the Army, since World War I have required changes in organization, personnel, training, and education. Organizational changes should be instituted to reward the military cohort now being shaped by experiences in Iraq and Afghanistan for building their skills and their expertise in stability operations. Otherwise, these hard-won skills will be lost.

Requirement for Integration

These recommendations are interlocking. Greater conceptual clarity about the integral role of stability operations to American national security requirements and success in war is necessary to broaden the profession's foundations. Training and education are the primary means of infusing the armed forces with this understanding, particularly the officer corps that guards the profession's essence. Organizational changes will be necessary to raise the performance of the force, to develop awareness of and familiarity with stability operations imperatives, and to increase the readiness and capacity of the armed forces to address the most demanding aspects of stability operations. Organizational improvements should provide pathways for individual development, promotion, and other rewards to perpetuate long-term organizational innovation and adaptation to the national security demands of stability operations.

Conclusion

The military today may have its best chance yet to incorporate stability operations successfully into the profession. Supportive conditions exist if military leaders are willing to exploit them. Literature on how organizations adapt and innovate suggests that internal drivers as well as external civilian-led change are central to innovation.[65] General David Fastabend pointed out that "cultural change begins with behavior and the leaders who support it."[66] The problems in Iraq and in Afghanistan and the generation of military leaders they are shaping may provide an unprecedented opportunity. Thousands of military personnel have experienced firsthand the critical role of stability operations in Iraq. The relative successes of the military governments in Japan and Germany after World War II did not create a constituency for change, but the requirements of recent wars and the widespread involvement of military personnel across a range of specialties in stability operations suggest that today there may be a much stronger opportunity for real innovation.

There is, further, a growing recognition outside the military of the need for change. Civilian leaders must make decisions (including funding decisions) about a civilian corps of government personnel, contractors, or nongovernmental organization personnel. The military can and should help influence this effort by actively shaping the parameters of the military's expected role in stability operations. Many military leaders still express the notion that the military "does not do nation building." Instead of standing back from such missions, however, or worrying that, if it becomes too adept at them, it will be asked to perform them all of the time, the military should recognize that a subset of the tasks usually subsumed under the label "nation building" is actually intrinsic to the conduct of war: it should embrace them, therefore, as an integral element of military professional practice.

The military has an opportunity today to shape the scope of nation-building operations by differentiating broad humanitarian assistance and nation-building missions in nonwar situations from the stability operations that are a part of virtually all kinds of conflict and war. The latter will always involve an element of instability and insecurity, especially in cases in which stability must be restored before political and economic reconstruction can begin to take hold. By shaping the determinants and requirements for the latter, the military will be in a stronger position to argue against being committed to the former, that is, to situations that do not present unequivocal national security challenges.[67] Such humanitarian and nation-building operations can and should be handled by a civilian corps, as the Department of State is now considering. Many in the military continue to hope that other elements of the U.S. government will step up to resolve the problem. This is not just unrealistic, but professionally inappropriate and irresponsible: the military must continue to play a central role in stability operations that serve long-standing and enduring national security interests. Stability operations are a critical component to winning wars. The military should not seek to rely solely on others to implement tasks so central to success in war.

Continued adherence to Huntington's excessively narrow formulation of the military profession and his related prescriptions of half a century ago would impede efforts to fully transform the U.S. military to address current challenges. Useful as *The Soldier and the State* was in providing a theory of civil-military relations, it was steeped in a Cold War context; now it is inadequate to the challenges facing the U.S. armed forces, particularly those of stability operations. War—whether conventional or irregular—is an intensely political endeavor. The military's conduct of stability operations is integral to the nature of war, and the military must always be prepared to serve as a complete instrument for realizing war's comprehensive political aims.

CHAPTER SEVEN

Professionalism and Professional Military Education in the Twenty-first Century

Williamson Murray

T wo of the major issues required for contemplating and intellectually preparing for war in the twentieth century are the historical continuities and discontinuities within the relationship between war and peace since the Treaty of Westphalia, and the implications of potential changes in that framework for the professional military education (PME) of American officers in the twenty-first century. On the basis of the paradigm set out by Samuel Huntington in *The Soldier and the State* for understanding the profession of arms,[1] here I review the historical framework within which the concept of peace and war have existed, consider the development of the military profession and the framework within which its practitioners have exercised their talents, and examine the implications for officership in the twenty-first century.

The crucial issues raised by Huntington have as much to do with the military profession as a *profession* as they have to do with the contentious issues involved in civil-military relations. In terms of America's security over coming decades, the former may prove more important than squabbles over whether generals should speak their minds in public or should resign when they find themselves to have fundamental disagreements over policy or strategic matters. The issue on which senior military officers should be in the position to advise their civilian leaders—namely, the utility or the unsuitability of their instrument—has profound implications for civil-military relations. Officers who know only the tactical and operational framework of conventional military forces might offer faulty advice and then prove incapable of adapting to the real conditions of the conflict they have been asked to fight.

The concept of the profession of arms—especially in the Anglo-American strategic culture—has developed within a political and strategic framework that began in the seventeenth century and has evolved, with considerable vicissitudes, to the present time. Moreover, in the Anglo-American world, it has found itself strongly influenced by societal expectations and an understanding of that, since the mid-nineteenth century, has been increasingly shaped by the drawing of a stark dichotomy between the ideas of peace on one side and of war on the other.[2] American and Allied soldiers and marines have meanwhile run up against cultures and societal attitudes in the Middle East and Afghanistan that represent a fundamental rejection of Western concepts concerning peace and war. Thus, a major portion of my task in this chapter is to examine the implication of that rejection for how we in the United States, and more largely in the developed world, need to rethink the basic requirements for officership and the profession of arms.

Given how much has happened since its publication, *The Soldier and the State* remains an impressive examination of the military as a profession as well as a starting point for an examination of civil-military issues in the United States.[3] Developments and new discoveries in military history over the past five decades might have altered Huntington's picture of military professionalism, particularly if he had known what we now know about the German military.[4] But that has to do with historical details, not substance. The larger picture that Huntington painted—that military professionalism is inherently connected to serious education and thinking—remains valid today, as the current debacle in Iraq illustrates.[5]

As Sir Michael Howard has suggested, the military profession is not only the most demanding of all the professions physically but the most demanding intellectually.[6] Senior officers must not only understand war in terms of its harsh unforgiving environment but also see and understand the relationships between politics and war and between means and ends, the nature of the conflict, and the larger framework within which they must conduct military operations. It is this larger framework that is crucial to military effectiveness at the strategic level. In the last book of *On War*, Clausewitz suggests that "no one starts a war—or rather, *no one in his senses ought to do so*—without being clear in his mind what he intends to achieve by that war and how he intends to conduct it."[7] Clausewitz's qualification is precisely the point: few statesmen and military commanders in history have paid much attention to what wars should achieve, much less how to end them in a fashion that ensured the peace for the long term.[8] For most of history they have simply not cared. That is the depressing history of Western wars over the past three and a half centuries. History suggests that there were even darker times before that, when peace, at least as we think of it, simply did not exist. Unfortunately, events over the past decade suggest that we may be returning to that darker past.

For those in the West, including much of the military profession, understanding of peace and war has to a considerable extent been formed by the peculiarities of the nineteenth century and by the intellectual traditions of Britain and the United States.[9] It has also rested on the fact that the British and American island empires have only on their fringes felt the lash of foreign military invasion or military operations. The result has represented a fundamental break from the impact of war on the human condition and the Hobbesian picture of human life, "where every man is enemy to every man . . . [with] continual fear, and danger of violent death; and the life of man, solitary, poor, nasty, brutish, and short."[10] Moreover, it has also led to a neglect of the reality that one of the primary drivers of the human condition has always been war and its devastation.

Michael Howard has lucidly laid out the requirements that underlie "peace" as we now understand it:

> Peace, as we have seen, is not an order natural to mankind: it is artificial, intricate and highly volatile. All kinds of preconditions are necessary, not least a degree of cultural homogeneity (best expressed through a common language), to make possible the political cohesion that must underlie a freely accepted framework of law, and at least a minimal level of education through which that culture can be transmitted. Further, as states develop they require a highly qualified elite, capable not only of operating their complex legal, commercial and administrative systems, but of exercising considerable moral authority over the rest of society. Where these conditions do not exist, or where they have decayed, there may well be no community of interest in creating, or capacity for sustaining, a peaceful international, or indeed domestic, order.[11]

Even the developed world of the twentieth century found it extraordinarily difficult to replicate such conditions. Two world wars and the ensuing Cold War came close to causing a general collapse of civilized behavior, as we understand it, because of the inability to conclude a lasting peace in the wake of the destruction the military profession had wrought. The difficulty for military professionals in the twenty-first century will lie in the fact that they must develop a historical and cultural awareness of the world they must defend—a world that believes that peace, international as well as domestic, is the norm—while they must operate in and deal with, over periods of decades, a Hobbesian world that reflects how most of mankind has lived in the past and will live for the foreseeable future. To bridge the gap between these two views of the world will require an extraordinary professionalism that emphasizes not only intellectual acuity but also war-fighting capabilities and expertise. This in turn demands farsighted programs of professional military education and uniformed leaders at multiple levels seeking to use them to fullest advantage.

History and the Framework of War

For those who live in the twenty-first century, even aware of the horrors of our own time, it is difficult to grasp the ferocity with which humans waged war before the Peace of Westphalia. A mixture of religion, ambition, and the warrior societies of Europe turned war in the West into unimaginable horror. The internecine war of Protestant versus Catholic in the Thirty Years' War destroyed much of Central Europe, and the wars of Islamic civilization against the infidel threat, which began in the seventh century, have continued almost unabated since.[12]

This was a world in which the fanaticism of religion triumphed over the necessities of politics or economics. During the cleansing of heretics in southern France in the thirteenth-century Albigensian Crusade, the inquisitor bishop ordered his crusader knights to slaughter everyone, declaring that in the end God would sort out the true believers from the heretics. Similarly, during the Thirty Years' War the Catholic Hapsburg army slaughtered 20,000 citizens of Magdeburg largely for the "sin" of being Protestants.[13] The political results of that murderous action were to frighten the surviving Protestants in Germany into allying themselves with King Gustavus Adolphus of Sweden, thus insuring that the Hapsburgs would not realize their dream of placing all Germany under their sway and restoring the Catholic Church to its former dominance in north and central Germany. It was a world in which the most brutish of human behavior triumphed over the simplest of religious prohibitions.[14] The war continued for another two murderous decades after Magdeburg, as armies roamed over the prostrate body of Germany. By the end of the Thirty Years' War, approximately 20 percent of Germany's population had been slaughtered by marauding armies of mercenaries, by disease, and by famine.

Out of this catastrophe, the Peace of Westphalia achieved two substantial aims: it removed religion from the framework of European war[15] and limited the nature of conflict to a contest between states. In other words, the Peace of Westphalia defined war as the conflict between states, and that definition, loosely constructed, has provided an international framework for the conduct of most conflicts through to the end of the twentieth century.[16] As for its creation of a larger framework of limits within which the European state system could function, historians of the conference note:

> [Although] France decided that conquests were more important than legitimacy, and the Spanish treaty was left unresolved . . . the concept of an international peace conference lived on. Henceforth, international conflicts were usually resolved by international negotiations: Nijmegen, Rijswijck, and Utrecht, were all consequences (of a sort) of the Congress of Westphalia. As late as the 1760s, it seemed to the incurable Romantic, Jean-Jacques Rousseau, that the entire state system of his day rested on a: "[solid] foundation, namely the German Empire, which from its position in the heart of Europe keeps all powers in check and thereby maintains the security of others even more, perhaps, than its own. . . . Despite its imperfections, this Imperial constitution will, while it lasts, maintain the balance in Europe; no prince need fear lest another dethrone him."[17]

After 1648, wars between and among the Europeans represented a return to the military organization of the Romans but with limited aims and results: armies consisted of trained soldiers under civil as well as military discipline.[18] As Clausewitz wrote, "In the eighteenth century . . . war was still an affair of governments alone, and the people's role was simply that of an instrument."[19] Yet there was, as Huntington notes, no real profession of arms. Rather, at best, armies were led by nobles, whose culture and frame of reference were still shaped by the medieval world as much as by the Enlightenment, even as they led the forerunners of modern military organizations. Military effectiveness in officers represented a combination of luck, experience, and the inexplicable result of genes, the prime example being Napoleon.

That situation of limited war changed dramatically in reaction to revolutionary events in France in 1789, as the people became participants in war. Wrote Clausewitz: "Instead of governments and armies as heretofore, the full nation was thrown into the balance. The resources and efforts available for use surpassed all conventional limits; nothing now impeded the vigor with which war could be waged, and consequently the opponents of France faced the utmost peril."[20]

However, it took the lessons of the French Revolution and Napoleon, expressed for the Prussians in their defeat at the double battle of Jena-Auerstadt in October 1806, to prompt creation of the basis of a real profession of arms: Huntington quite rightly identified the creation of Prussia's Kriegsakademie by Scharnhorst and Gneisenau as the seminal event in the creation of a true military profession.[21] In effect, the Prussian military reformers institutionalized military effectiveness. They understood that their generals could not possibly match Napoleon's genius, but they did grasp that organization and education, along with the mobilization of the Prussian people and those of other nations, offered the potential to defeat the French marshals and France, if not a military genius like the emperor.[22]

Ironically, despite the changes in how the French and then their opponents fought, the Peace of Westphalia still exercised its influence, if not for the French revolutionaries and Napoleon, then for the victors at the Congress of Vienna.[23] That congress, subsequently so reviled by liberal historians, attempted with some success to put the genie of nationalism back into its dark bottle and to reestablish limits on the waging of war. The twenty-five years of war that had preceded the meetings in Vienna persuaded most Europeans that the establishment of order was in their interest. For the next fifty-five years that order persisted; even when broken, it did not shatter entirely.

In 1870, with the outbreak of the Franco-Prussian War, nationalism again became the dominant feature of war. Otto von Bismarck, Prussia's "Iron Chancellor," deliberately unleashed the dogs of German nationalism for domestic political purposes.[24] He had not incited nationalism in the two earlier wars that Prussia had waged against Denmark and Austria, but against France it was a different matter. Nevertheless, during the Franco-Prussian War, Prussia remained within the larger framework of conservative European politics. For example, Bismarck refused to allow the Prussian army to approach Belgian territory or the Channel Coast for fear of upsetting the British. But, having whipped up Prusso-German nationalism, Bismarck found that it made it impossible for him to grant the Third Republic the kind of peace that might have assuaged the French desire to take revenge and to regain the "lost" provinces of Alsace and Lorraine.

The collapse of the limits on the conduct of war, set by the Treaty of Westphalia and reaffirmed by the Congress of Vienna, began with World War I. Here the two great military and social revolutions of the previous century, the Industrial Revolution and the French Revolution, exacerbated by failures in statesmanship and generalship, came together to create a catastrophe.[25] The hideous offspring of World War I were the ideologies of the Right and of the Left: fascism, communism, and Nazism; they were, in effect, religion in modern garb.[26] The reintroduction of modern religion into warfare was epitomized by the ferocity of the fighting on the eastern front from 1941 through to the end of the war in 1945.

The Cold War followed hard on the heels of the second, even greater, world war, but the awesome power of nuclear weapons dampened down the competition of its modern religions. The mere existence of those weapons at least persuaded its major contestants that nuclear war was not a viable way to seek their goals. Nevertheless, much of the history of the twentieth century represented a massive effort to control the explosive aggression of ideologically motivated powers, which aimed at the complete realignment of civil and political society. Only with the collapse of the Soviet Union did the ideological contest end. However, now appearing in the Middle East and other Islamic areas is a reemergence of religion and the fanaticism with which it drives conflict. As such, it could represent a return to the ferocious and merciless conflicts that marked international relations in the period before the Peace of Westphalia. It may even herald a return to an era of ceaseless conflict, broken by occasional truces, with neither end nor closure.

The Rise and Fall of American Military Professionalism

Real military professionalism began to emerge in Europe as the devastating victories of the Prussian military in the Wars of German Unification in 1870–71 worked their way into European consciousness. The advantages to the Prussian army from having a well-trained staff were obvious on the battlefield. Unlike the Austrians and the French, the Prusso-German armies of 1870 were able to utilize modern technologies fully, both in the movement of military force to the battlefield and in action on it.[27] While the Europeans attempted to copy the Prussians, for the most part they missed the essential concept underlying the system of Gneisenau and Scharnhorst: the careful selection of officers for the general staff on the basis of the applicants' professional knowledge, and the ruthless intellectual evaluation of all who actually attended the Kriegsakademie.[28]

Much of Germany's success in combined-arms warfare in the last two years of the First World War rested on the ability of its general staff to analyze and then adapt solutions to the actual conditions of the front.[29] Immediately after the First World War, the Germans were the only army then willing to examine the lessons of the preceding war minutely to see how military organizations could fight the next war. On the basis of that effort—with more than fifty-seven different committees studying those lessons—the commander in chief of the army, General Hans von Seeckt, issued a basic doctrinal manual in 1923; "Leadership and Battle with Combined Arms" would be the basis for German combined-arms, mechanized warfare throughout the Second World War.[30]

Nevertheless, although the Germans learned the tactical lessons of the preceding conflict, in World War II Germany did appallingly badly in many crucial areas of military professionalism, including strategy, logistics, intelligence, and the wider application of military power beyond the tactical application of ground power. Here the performance of the American military during the interwar period looks far more impressive. Perhaps one of the most useful portions of Huntington's discussion of American military professionalism lies in his examination of its roots, where he gives Upton, Sherman, Luce, Mahan, Bliss, and Sims the credit they richly deserve.[31] These visionaries saw as essential the intellectual preparation of officers in their profession, to avoid the amateurish blunders that had marked so much of the conduct of the U.S. Civil War.

The creation of staff colleges, war colleges, and then the Army Industrial College in the late nineteenth and early twentieth centuries underline an American approach to professionalism that emphasized the study not just of the tactical battlefield and military campaigns but of strategy, logistics, and intelligence as well.[32] What historians are beginning to understand, and what was not available in any form in the 1950s when Huntington wrote *The Soldier and the State*, is how innovative and adaptive the American military services were throughout the 1920s and 1930s. While one might conclude, looking at the curriculum of the Command and General Staff Course at Leavenworth during the interwar period, that the American Army's approach to war was pedantic and narrow, such a conclusion would miss the larger picture: in fact, serious professional learning led to the development of major concepts such as carrier warfare, amphibious operations, and precision strategic bombing.[33]

The army's creation of an Industrial College in the early 1920s to study the problems involved in the mobilization of the American economy may well have been one of the major factors that would contribute to the successful mobilization of America's immense potential so quickly in the early 1940s.[34] In January 1930 Captain Walter Warlimont of the German army, later to be a senior general in the German Armed Forces High Command (Oberkommando der Wehrmacht), told the students of the U.S. Army Industrial College, "To you . . . the only officers of the world fortunate enough to be able to devote yourselves to a regular study of procurement questions, it is hardly necessary to emphasize that the German economic history of the late war *can not and does not want to be regarded as a model.*"[35] Warlimont could not have realized how ironic his words would sound after the Second World War, which once again underlined the failure of the Germans to plan their war economy in any coherent fashion, especially compared to the American efforts.[36]

Historians have rightly seen George C. Marshall's tenure as the vice commandant at the army's Infantry School at Fort Benning as a period of intellectual ferment among both students and faculty, one that allowed Marshall to identify many of the Army's future leaders in World War II. The Army War College's six faculty members in 1940–41, at the outset of the massive buildup for war, included both Major J. Lawton Collins, who would become one of the most competent corps commanders in World War II and then chief of staff of the army, and Colonel W. H. Simpson, future lieutenant general and commander of Ninth Army.[37] This fact suggests how important Marshall felt professional military education to be. Moreover, after World War II, he would comment that his biggest mistake during the war had been to close the Army War College at Leavenworth for the duration.

A number of other indicators suggest the degree to which the American military connected serious intellectual preparation with professionalism, which a substantial number of officers defined as the business of preparing for war.[38] Historians and political scientists have emphasized the U.S. Navy's successful innovations with carriers throughout the interwar period.[39] Beginning with war games at Newport, initially pushed by Admiral William Sims, president of the Naval War College, U.S. naval officers developed the crucial concepts involved in carrier war before the Navy possessed a single aircraft carrier.[40] The work at Newport in the interwar period extended far beyond carrier development: it identified virtually all the major aspects of a war in the Pacific against the Japanese. After the war, Fleet Admiral Nimitz would claim, with considerable justification, that the work at Newport had foreseen virtually all of the major factors in the coming conflict, with the possible exception of the kamikaze.[41] Similarly, in the face of the presumed military wisdom revealed at Gallipoli that amphibious warfare was impossible in the modern age, the U.S. Marine Corps developed the conceptual basis for such warfare.[42]

What makes these contributions ironic was the fact that in the period from World War II through the 1980s, with only a few exceptions, professional military education simply collapsed as a vehicle for professional enhancement. Before the war, professional military education had formed a crucial element in an officer's career; by the 1980s, extracurricular sports and time spent with family had become more important than serious study of the profession of arms at America's professional military education institutions.[43]

A partial explanation lies in the fact that the Soviet and nuclear threat changed so little over the course of the Cold War. But the real explanation more probably lies in the fact that so many junior officers, who had not yet attended a professional school in the 1930s, returned from the Second World War as colonels or even brigadier generals, with the attitude that *they* had not needed professional military education to do well in their military careers.[44] Thus, while the leaders of World War II returned from the conflict praising the role that education in the profession of arms had played in their successful campaigns, their juniors soon turned the entire professional military education system into a backwater, where the faculty, no longer competitive for flag or general officer rank, could spend their time searching for civilian jobs, and the students could play golf and tennis while taking a break in the midst of their busy careers.[45]

General William Westmoreland was all too typical of such officers. Upon being informed in the immediate postwar period that he was scheduled to attend the Army War College, he replied that he had no intention of attending as a student, but he might consider an assignment to that institution as an instructor.[46] A comment in the general's memoirs suggests the narrowness of his conception of professionalism, at least on the intellectual side: "Beside my bed [in Vietnam] I kept . . . several books: a Bible; a French grammar; Mao Tse-tung's little red book on theories of guerrilla warfare; a novel, *The Centurions*, about the French fight with the Viet Minh; and several works by Dr. Bernard Fall, who wrote authoritatively on the French experience in Indochina and provided insight into the enemy's thinking and methods. *I was usually too tired in late evening to give the books more than occasional attention.*"[47]

A report in 1988 by Congressman Ike Skelton's subcommittee on professional military education underlined the dismal state to which professional military education had fallen by the 1970s and 1980s.[48] There were a few exceptions: Admiral Stansfield Turner's majestic reform of the Naval War College in 1972 introduced a graduate-level curriculum, especially in the study of strategy, and hired some of the world's leading scholars in a number of areas.[49] Unfortunately, Turner's reform had little long-term influence on the Navy, which over the past three decades has refused to send many of its best officers to war college. The Naval War College reforms sparked little interest from the other war colleges, which even today remain less than impressive academic institutions.[50] The Army did create a School of Advanced Military Studies.[51] The latter prompted the foundation of equivalent schools at Marine Corps Base Quantico (the School of Advanced Warfighting) and at Maxwell Air Force Base (the School for Advanced Airpower Studies).

But those improvements, if substantial, were for the most part on the margins.[52] Moreover, since the late 1990s, professional military education has steadily decreased in service interest and focus.[53] It still largely remains an arena that the services merely tolerate; for the most part, it neither challenges the students nor employs first-class intellectuals from within or outside of the military. In the largest sense, professional military education at staff and war colleges offers an incomplete system for the preparation of senior officers for the challenges of the twenty-first century. It can form only a portion of a larger framework that must include the efforts of officers themselves, graduate schooling in civilian institutions of higher education in disciplines that relate to war and international relations, and fellowships and tours of duty working with the military organizations of other nations.

The End of the Peace of Westphalia?

At present, the world confronts a number of "wicked" problems, none of which are susceptible to simple or clear answers.[54] Across the Middle East, reaching all the way to Indonesia and the Philippines, the developed world confronts an Islamic insurgency, brought about by the startling challenges of modernity to a culture still emerging from its medieval past. The second set of wicked problems results from the proliferation of nuclear weapons, in an arc of nuclear instability from the Middle East through South Asia to North Korea, where those gaining nuclear weapons appear to possess few of the inhibitions that restrained the nuclear powers during the Cold War. Third, the emergence of China, India, the European Union, and perhaps even Brazil as major economic, political, and eventually military powers adds significantly different challenges to the mix of threats that might confront the United States and its military in the twenty-first century.

What appears to be emerging is a world divided between functioning states and failed or failing states.[55] In the case of the functioning states, possibly including China and others as emerging peer competitors, the verities of the Westphalian framework will remain largely in place. War in the developing world would result only from the grossest incompetence and miscalculations on both sides. Instead, the competitions of the future within the developed world are most likely to be economic and political, as has been the case since the ending of the Cold War with the collapse of the Soviet Union. However, the problems of failed and failing states, in a world so closely interconnected, will present the greatest difficulties at every level of exchange, particularly in the political and military realms. Above the use of military power will always hang the questions of how, for what purpose, and at what cost.

Here the problems in the Islamic world are crucial, complex, and virtually insoluble, at least in political terms.[56] In the twenty-first century, groups within the Islamic world remain in agreement with the analysis, at the onset of the nineteenth century, of the Bey of Algiers, pointing out that if the United States wished to end the depredations of the Barbary pirates it had just three choices: like the European powers, the United States could pay protection money; it could convert to Islam and then the pirates would cease their attacks; or, because there was an eternal conflict between the Muslim community of believers and the unbelievers, it could wage eternal war.[57] Today, paying protection money is not even an option.

The extent of the difficulties that the developed world will confront in dealing with the jihadist portions of Islam is suggested in a recent report on Marine Corps professional education:

> The problems in the Islamic World stem from the past nine centuries of history, which witnessed "the rise of the West" and solidification of Western values in governance and human relations. In effect, the Islamic World confronts the need to adapt to a world of global interdependence created by the West. Often led by despotic leaders, denied political participation, shackled to commodity-based economies that offer little prospect of supporting the development of a broad middle class, and bombarded by Western media, many Islamic states have fallen further and further behind not only the West, but South Asian and East Asian countries as well. Their rage feeds on the lies of corrupt leaders, the rhetoric of their radical imams, the falsifications of their own media, and the images of the prosperous developed world. If the tensions between the Islamic World's past and present were not enough, the Middle East, the heartland of Islam, is riven with tribal, religious, and political divisions, creating an explosive mixture that makes continued instability and conflict all but inevitable.[58]

Unfortunately, because this region also holds much of the world's reserves of petroleum, the Middle East will remain a primary focus for America's military efforts for much, if not all, of the coming century.

Over the past two decades, America's interventions in that region, from the horn of Africa to the Caspian Sea, have been less than successful. In Somalia in 1993, U.S. military intervention helped considerably in ending mass starvation, but when American forces intervened in the politics of Somalia, the result was the disaster of "Blackhawk Down." The death of nineteen U.S. soldiers resulted in the rapid U.S. retreat from Somalia.[59] The vacuum then provided an attractive shelter for Al Qaeda, prompting the United States to intervene again in early 2007, this time with proxies and air power. The American misadventure in 1993 resulted from gross ignorance of the cultural and religious situation that made efforts to establish a political settlement irrelevant and then disastrous.

The pattern of events in Iraq has been similar but, in the long run, probably even more serious. At first, coalition conventional operations in 2003 overthrew Saddam Hussein's pernicious regime in less than three weeks in a masterful campaign.[60] It was evidence that the American military is the master of conventional major-unit warfare.[61] No other military in the world is in a position to compete with U.S. forces. That capability has emerged from three decades of operational and tactical as well as technological preparation and efforts in training.[62] What came afterward, however, proved a catastrophe that threatens to unravel not only America's place in the Middle East but the stability of the region as well.[63]

The American effort to stabilize the postconflict phase was from the start oblivious of the cultural, political, and religious sensibilities of Iraq and its people.[64] The crack-up was not the fault of the U.S. military alone: meddling in the effort from both the White House and the Department of Defense was almost entirely flawed.[65] Virtually all of the errors resulted from ignorance, by too many U.S. military and political leaders, of the Middle East's history, politics, and culture, reflecting the general American lack of knowledge about the area.[66]

Events in Iraq made it seem that the U.S. military had learned nothing from its time in Vietnam or from Operation Just Cause in Panama.[67] This sad state of affairs resulted from the fact that the study of the Vietnam War received only the most cursory attention over the three decades since the end of the conflict, even from schools of professional military education. The U.S. experiences in Panama, too, appear to have made little if any impact on American thinking.

The record of U.S. forces in terms of wars of insurgency over the past half century has been dismal.[68] The nature of counterinsurgency suggests that there are systemic problems when military organizations intervene in societies separated from them by deep cultural chasms. Such interventions ask for political disaster, military defeat, and, in the long run, failure to protect U.S. national interests.

Here the warning from Iraq is clear. At the beginning of postconflict operations in May 2003, there was substantial goodwill among many Iraqis for the American achievement in overthrowing Saddam Hussein.[69] But the badly handled postconflict occupation provided the ammunition from which the insurgents were able to kindle an impressive resistance movement. In spite of heroic efforts of those in the field, the situation spiraled out of control. American leaders in Iraq have had to rediscover the most basic lessons of counterinsurgency—lessons that had cost so much blood in Vietnam.

The Emerging Strategic World and Professional Military Education

In a world where one of America's major enemies—Islamic jihad—has already globally dispersed itself, and where the United States will soon no longer be the world's sole superpower but just one among a number of major powers, the use of military power will demand cultural, historical, linguistic, and political knowledge as well as tactical and operational competence. The fundamental nature of war will not change, but the challenges to America's military will broaden, ranging from deterrence and great-power competition to irregular war and the systematic pursuit of terrorism. Huntington's belief that serious education and intellectual preparation must lie at the heart of the profession of arms is thus even more timely than when he wrote in the 1950s.

> While all the nations of Europe by 1875 had acquired the basic elements of military professionalism, in Prussia alone were these elements developed into a rounded and complete system. Requirements of general and specific education for entry; examinations; institutions of higher military education; advancement by merit and achievement; an elaborate and efficient staff system; a sense of corporate unity and responsibility; a recognition of the limits of professional competence: these Prussia possessed to an extraordinary degree.[70]

Now, too, in a world where religion and violence will dominate the global landscape, how U.S. forces address problems that may have little connection to their traditional role of destroying conventional forces will critically affect America's ability to mold a more peaceful century or at least to mitigate the ravages of war: conventional, civil, and insurgent.

The quality and depth of professional military education then becomes of critical importance in preparing officers for these challenges:

There are two elements to a successful program in Professional Military Education. The first is imparting an ability to think critically and creatively, both in operations and in acquisition or resource allocation. The second is the ability to draw from a breadth and depth of education in a range of relevant disciplines to include history, anthropology, economics, geopolitics, cultural studies, the "hard sciences," law, and strategic communications. A significant difficulty that the staff and war colleges have confronted over the past half century lies in their attempt to teach everything—the "Pecos River approach," a mile wide and an inch deep. Even that approach has missed major studies such as Islamic studies and culture.[71]

Such an ambitious educational effort requires a fundamental rethinking of the systems of professional military education, as well as their place in promotion, and of the entire personnel systems of the services. The American military will find itself, for much of the coming century, involved in a battle of ideas with a ferocious and tenacious religious enemy; thus, it *must* address the mental aspects of the most demanding profession of all. If it does not do so now, it must learn on the battlefields of the future by filling body bags.[72]

The Bottom Line

In the irregular war in Iraq that emerged after the destruction of Saddam's regime, the United States and its military—particularly the Army and the Marine Corps—have paid a terrible price for the failure of all too many senior leaders, political as well as military, to adapt to the actual conditions.[73] It is as if Operation Just Cause in Panama, the Vietnam War, or the British experiences in Iraq in 1920–21 had never occurred. All too many senior leaders, at brigade command level and above, simply lacked a knowledge of history or even the capability to examine the past.[74] The troops on the ground in Iraq in summer 2003 saw what was happening, but their experiences were only rarely converted into knowledge among staffs and higher commanders. Without an understanding of the past, senior leaders had no intellectual framework to comprehend the reality that was happening before their faces.[75] The failure of understanding can be blamed on the failure of professional military education.

The world of the twenty-first century—a world that will look more like the pre-Westphalian world—will demand a senior leadership for America's military that is far better educated.[76] Senior American military leaders must possess the ability to understand and deal with the "other," in whatever the cultural and historical form the "other" appears. There is an enormous intellectual and conceptual gap between the views of most of the American elite on issues of war and peace and the views of much of the rest of the world. Only senior officers who are deeply educated in the issues surrounding the use of military force can bridge this gap.

Military leaders must acquire a knowledge of history through intensive study. In the inevitably tense dialogues with their military advisors, civilian policymakers might be both historically and militarily illiterate, given the current lack of military experience among America's political leaders and the collapse of the study of history in America's elite institutions. Because policymakers may have even less understanding of the "other" that is the adversary, it is essential that they receive nuanced, perceptive advice from their military advisors. Whether they take it or not is another matter, but an intelligent dialogue between political leaders and their military advisors based on deep historical knowledge is essential for successful civil-military relations in coming decades.

In the largest sense, this will require a fundamental reform of the service personnel systems. Only when professional military education becomes as important in an officer's promotion prospects as service as a general's aide or battalion executive officer will there be some prospect that the culture and ability to adapt at the highest levels will improve over the hit-and-miss system that currently governs promotions. And while service as a battalion executive officer is important in the tactical education of officers, only serious professional military education can prepare general and flag officers for the intellectual challenges of understanding the enemies of the United States in the Hobbesian world before us.

CHAPTER EIGHT

Responsible Obedience by Military Professionals

The Discretion to Do What Is Wrong

James Burk

Property cannot be taken from its rightful owners. People are free to worship and speak according to their beliefs. Citizens have a right to vote for their political leaders. Military professionals must obey lawful commands from civilian political leaders. All these are bedrock principles observed by liberal democratic states and embraced as characteristic features of their regimes. Nonetheless, they are principles not always absolutely observed. Property may be taken by the government if the owners are compensated. Freedom of worship and speech may be limited when their exercise might cause grave public harm. Citizens may forfeit their right to vote (at least for a time) if they are convicted felons.

But can there also be exceptions to the duty of military professionals to obey lawful orders from the civilian political elite? I do not mean historical exceptions, when the principle has been breached as a matter of fact, as it was in the iconic case of General Douglas MacArthur's insubordination toward President Harry Truman over how to wage the Korean War. I mean principled exceptions, allowing us to say—speaking loosely—that under some conditions military professionals may have discretion to do what we usually and ordinarily would say was wrong, or to do what they were not plainly authorized to do. Although it may seem contrary to accepted tenets of civil-military relations theory, I argue that there are such exceptions: that having discretion to commit some kinds of wrong underlies the military profession's moral responsibility for its acts.

To explain this position, I examine Huntington's argument about justifications for obedience or disobedience to orders that the military receives from the state. I show that Huntington's claim that obedience is the supreme military virtue cannot support a reasonable conception of military professionalism or account for the military members' obedience to the state. I further examine the claim that obedience is an unmixed virtue by considering the problem of "blind obedience" and arguing that Huntington's model of how military professionals should relate to the state allows for a more contentious (and morally based) relation than he acknowledged. This contention raises the question of what the limits to obedience should be. Here, Huntington's narrow conception of expert knowledge, according to which there are clearly separated domains of action for the military and others,[1] allowed him to ignore the moral responsibility of military professionals. I propose that their moral responsibility depends on the exercise of moral discretion, which may entail the possibility of permitting some (but not all) kinds of military wrongdoing, and briefly consider what practical implications follow if we take seriously the idea that military professionals are moral actors exercising moral discretion.

My argument rests on two claims. First, although he acknowledged the need for it, Huntington fails to provide an adequate account of how or when military obedience may and may not be limited. Second, because he believed that military professional competence rests solely on the possession of expert technical knowledge, Huntington neglects the role played by choice—particularly moral choice—in deciding how and how well that expert knowledge is applied. To redress these deficiencies requires telling why a morally responsible military depends on an exercise of discretion that may sometimes lie in a conceptual space between obvious obedience and obvious disobedience to civilian control.

Obedience and Military Virtue

Huntington believes that obedience to the state is the supreme virtue in the professional military ethic. To say why that is so requires that we address two questions: why is obedience so important—why is it the *highest* virtue—for the military profession, and why should military professionals be obedient to the state?

Huntington and others answer the first question on consequentialist grounds:

obedience is a supreme virtue because it is required for the military profession to succeed at its task, managing the means of violence to protect the military security of the state. For Huntington, the military is essentially a hierarchy of obedience: "For the profession to perform its function, each level within it must be able to command the instantaneous and loyal obedience of subordinate levels."[2] Alfred Thayer Mahan, for one, had earlier expressed a similar view. He thought obedience made the military a unified force; obedience was necessary to ensure that soldiers cooperated effectively, making many wills act as one, to avoid defeat in battle.[3] Max Weber also noted the importance of military discipline—his word for obedience—as the decisive factor for creating a powerful military force.[4] Obedience was not the only military virtue, of course, but it was the highest, the one on which all the others depended.

I argue that this position is overstated. This strict standard of obedience suggests that professional soldiers should suspend all thought and give no time to deliberation about whatever they are commanded to do. As Huntington puts it, "When the military man receives a legal order from an authorized superior, he does not hesitate, he does not substitute his own views; he obeys instantly."[5] That sounds right: certainly, a military engagement is no place for a debating society. Still, we should not take this claim too literally. To the extent that the military is a profession, military competence and success depend on the mastery and application of expert knowledge about how to manage the use of force to achieve particular policy objectives. Yet if the application of professional knowledge is an ingredient in military competence, there must be room, however small, even in the midst of a military engagement, for the exercise of thought: thought about matters of uncertainty that require a choice about how to proceed. If that is so, then we as observers, or as professional soldiers, must consider at a minimum whether the choice made accords with the best professional knowledge and whether it conforms with or is obedient to the given command. The act of obedience does not entail a simple yes or no.

On January 16, 1864, during the American Civil War, General Ulysses S. Grant sent an order to Major General George H. Thomas directing Thomas to "send Foster all the provisions you can. The question of provisions alone," Grant continued, "may decide the fate of East Tenn[essee]." The order was simple, yet Grant anticipated that Thomas might wonder why it was necessary. He did not expect unthinking obedience but gave a reason for the order. Even without the reason, Thomas could not simply have followed the order instantly or without thought: both expert knowledge and moral judgment were required before Thomas could decide what provisions in what amounts could be gathered from his supplies or from the stores of civilian noncombatants and shipped for Foster's use. Formally, the order was clear but, like a blueprint to an electrician, it provided only a bare sketch of what needed to be done.[6] As a result, whether Thomas's choice about how to proceed was adequately obedient might not have been known immediately or easily. The example shows that the discretionary application of professional knowledge cannot depend on unthinking obedience. This does not deny an important role for military obedience. It simply says that something other than blind or uncritical obedience is wanted. Though Huntington knows this, he is not always careful to incorporate it into his argument.

Granting that the military requires obedience, why should military professionals be obedient to the state? Huntington answers this question on functionalist grounds. His general theory is that the professions are instrumental occupations; they perform a service, on the basis of expert knowledge, to gain some important social good such as health, justice, religious guidance, education—or, in the case of the professional soldier, military security. Ideally, the professional's responsibility to produce a social good takes precedence over other considerations, such as financial rewards or any other self-interested goal, and this disinterested responsibility for the welfare of the client is part of what distinguishes the professions from commercial occupations.[7] Professions thus perform a moral or fiduciary function, in which they are concerned first of all with securing some particular aspect of the well-being of their clients. Because the client of the military is the state, the military is morally responsible to apply its professional expertise in the service of the state; it must provide the state with the degree of military security it wants to the fullest extent possible. But why is the state the military's client? Why should the military not use its power to dominate the state, creating a military regime or a garrison state?[8]

Huntington would think military rule of the state was a kind of perversion. The military profession's relationship of subordination to the state is based on what Huntington calls a "natural division of labor."[9] He fails to define this phrase, but I take him to mean that there are certain domains of activity and competence that are inherent to each function and that no actors do well to stray outside their respective domains.[10] The state's natural domain is politics, where it deals with setting the goals of state policy. Politicians possess legitimate authority to decide what the goals of state policy should be; to the degree they are competent, they consider the broad range of interests and people that affect or are affected by decisions they make. The military's natural domain has two elements. One is constant, dealing with strategy. It is defined by unchanging and unchangeable principles of war, which are derived from permanent features of human nature—for Huntington, a Hobbesian nature—and from constraints imposed by a particular physical environment. The other element is variable, dealing with tactics and logistics, and defined by invention and flexibility in the use of military resources as means to implement state policy consistent with the requirements of strategy. Ideally, this sharp division of labor, assigning different functions to the statesman and the military professional, means that the statesman gives political guidance to the military professional about the goals of state policy but does not presume to say how—with what strategies and tactics—the military professional should achieve those goals.[11] It also means that the military professional is politically neutral, viewing decisions about state policy as beyond her or his competence. The result of this natural division of labor is that the statesman and the military professional each retain loyalty to, and act within, their respective spheres of competence, with the military professional responsible for implementing the security policies of the state. It is to respect this division of competence that the military is properly subordinate to the state.

As there was with the earlier argument that entailed a too-strict standard of obedience, there is a problem with this argument: whether we can reasonably accept Huntington's claim that a sharp division of competence exists between the military and political domains. Notice that Huntington's claim is historically contingent and not a universal claim that this division of labor always exists. It did not exist, he says, until after the professionalization of military science in the nineteenth century. Before then, one might qualify as both a statesman and a warrior, but not since. Perhaps that is true historically. There is no doubt that the division of labor has increased greatly over the past two centuries, straining the assertions of many to possess competence in more than one realm. Yet I am not sure that those strains apply so neatly in this case; neither, for that matter, is Huntington.

Huntington notes, in the very section of *The Soldier and the State* from which we have been quoting, that the top military leaders "inevitably operate" in an "intermingled world of strategy and policy" and they must be alert to "the political implications of their military attitudes." This does not mean that the military elite is no longer subordinate to the state. This elite must still "be willing to accept the final decisions of the statesman."[12] But it calls into question the degree to which we should think about the military and politics as separated (or fully separable) domains, as if in policymaking the ends—military security—were one thing and the means—military action—were another. In a later section of *The Soldier and the State*, Huntington acknowledges that "military policy and political policy were much more closely interrelated in the postwar world than they had been previously."[13] In my view, Huntington is much more persuasive with this empirical observation than he is with his theory of the natural division of labor. Which ends it is possible to think about depend to a large extent on the means by which they are to be pursued, as is painfully evident in an era beset by weapons of mass destruction. It is no less evident, however, when contemplating the use of force to achieve limited political objectives, whether force is used (as it was by NATO in Kosovo) or not used (as by the UN in Rwanda). As a practical matter, this means that Huntington's reliance on the distinction between a political domain, where ends are decided on, and a military domain, where means are deployed in pursuit of ends, is at least highly misleading.[14] It is misleading, especially because it makes military professionals seem less responsible than they really should be for decisions about when and how to use force.

Yet without the sharp division between policy ends and military means, it is no longer clear why and how the military professional is obedient to the state. The problem is not that the theory leaves too little room for the exercise of discretion, as with the argument for a strict standard of obedience. It is just the opposite. Once we reject the theory of a clear division between the military and political domains, we seem to give the military too much room for the exercise of discretion. Without a clearer understanding of what counts as obedience to the state, there is no good standard to tell us when the military professional has gone astray. Obviously, it is no solution to change our minds and accept a doubtful theory simply to avoid facing the consequences of rejecting it. What is needed is a different way of thinking about the exercise of discretion, with all its risks that military professionals might act beyond the bounds of their responsibility. Before embarking on that course, however, we consider a little further why a too-strict conception of military obedience is untenable. We should do this if only to reassure ourselves that we really do want a military that exercises professional autonomy.

Blind versus Responsible Obedience

The phrase "blind" obedience is pejorative: it suggests a kind of obedience that should be avoided. Earlier, I associated it with "thoughtless obedience." My assumption is that this is a kind of obedience we think has gone too far. It is not just that obsequiousness is unbecoming, even somewhat degrading, although it is. The problem is political as much as personal. At its most acute, blind obedience occurs when public servants suspend their critical judgment about the good, which makes them available to serve unjust ends.[15]

To illustrate the point, we may think about Adolf Eichmann as described by Hannah Arendt. If anyone was an obedient servant, Eichmann was: his conscience as a Nazi SS officer was pricked "only if he had not done what he had been ordered to do." He was ordered to engineer part of the machinery of genocide, to ship millions of men, women, and children to their death, and that was no problem for him.[16] Here is not the place to examine the details of the case, but two specific matters now require attention. One is that Eichmann believed acts like his were justified because they were approved, not only by Hitler and his party but also by the "elite of the good old Civil Service [who] were vying and fighting with each other for the honor of taking the lead in these 'bloody' matters."[17] There are social forces that encourage us to put on blind obedience and that punish those who fail to do so.[18] Moreover, Eichmann acted as he did not simply because he succumbed to social pressure: rather, he was unable to think, "namely to think from the standpoint of someone else."[19] The only ideas he had in his head were the ideas—the clichés—of others. This is a serious moral deformity. Arendt concluded that it was Eichmann's "sheer thoughtlessness—something by no means identical with stupidity—that predisposed him to become one of the greatest criminals of that period."[20]

Defenders of the military's obligation to obey the state are not promoting blind obedience of this kind, nor are they arguing for a suspension of critical thought. Nonetheless, when it comes to making decisions that lead (or might lead) to war or any other policy objective, we can agree that the judgment that counts is that of democratically elected political leaders, making their decision according to the rules of law. Once their decision is made, the military professional is obligated to carry it out. Martin Cook states the rule forcefully: "There is no question that military members are obligated to follow legal orders of their superiors and to serve American society as society's civilian leaders see fit." The military is not free to determine its own mission. Rather, the military professional is committed, if needed, to sacrifice his or her life to complete all "legally assigned missions." This commitment of selfless service for the society is the essence of military professionalism, "the root of the nobility of the profession, and the source of American society's trust in and respect for the profession of arms."[21] If this is not counsel for blind obedience—and it is not—what is it?

Notice that Cook is careful, when defining the obligation to obey, to insist on the lawfulness of the order. If it is an order to wage war, customary law has long assigned responsibility for that order to the political leaders who make the decision. The military is not responsible for that decision when it follows the order. The responsibility of the military is limited—especially the responsibility of those in the military's rank and file—to the way war is conducted, adhering to standards of *jus in bello*. This is the point of the often-quoted lines exchanged by soldiers in Shakespeare's *Henry V*, that even if the king's "cause be wrong, our obedience to the King wipes the crime of it out of us."[22] Something like but not equal to blind obedience to the state's declarations of war is approved and expected. Political leaders do not want soldiers to ponder whether a war is just, or even whether it is legal, before they follow orders to fight. Soldiers might do it nonetheless and might refuse to obey orders they think are wrong, but such refusals are unwelcome. When First Lieutenant Ehren Watada publicly refused to obey orders to deploy to Iraq because he thought the war was illegal, he was court-martialed for missing his deployment and for conduct unbecoming an officer. His commanding officer repeated the traditional view that soldiers "don't get to pick and choose which war we go to."[23] That is a matter for political leaders to decide. Any other course, said the sixteenth-century legal theorist Francisco Vitoria, would leave the state in "grave peril."[24]

Where does the peril lie? If there is a conflict in judgment between political leaders and military professionals over the wisdom of a policy to use armed force, it is not necessarily the case that the political leader is right and the military professional wrong. Often, the matter will be surrounded by enough uncertainty that no one could be sure which judgment should be preferred. Yet, in the end, someone must decide, and typically there are established rules to tell who that is. In the United States, these rules are embedded ultimately in the Constitution; it gives Congress authority to raise the military, to set the rules for military conduct, and to decide whether to authorize war, and it places the president at the top of the military hierarchy as commander in chief. In this context, if military professionals arrogated to themselves the right to decide whether to fight this war or to deploy on that humanitarian mission, these constitutional provisions would be undercut. It would pose a constitutional crisis. The country could no longer be sure that the fundamental agreements on which it was based still held.

Constitutionalism depends on our accepting the idea that some principles are not on the democratic agenda.[25] These principles are not available for debate; observing them is a precondition for establishing and maintaining a liberal democratic society. They include respecting people's basic liberties of speech and belief and their rights to property and to privacy, allowing all who wish and can to participate in deliberation about the laws by which they live, refusing to treat people merely as means but treating them instead as worthy of respect, and relying on reason and persuasion rather than coercion and violence to decide who should lead and what public policies should be pursued. The Constitution establishes particular institutional arrangements to help secure these commitments. Civilian control over the military is just such an institutional arrangement. It helps to secure, for instance, the preference for reason over coercion in public policymaking as it subordinates the will of military professionals, who are specialists in violence, to that of elected officials, who are specialists in persuasion.

So, in the end, for sound second-order reasons, obedience to civilian authority is required to preserve democratic values, even if the civilian authority is mistaken in what it orders the military to do. The obedience is not a result of "thoughtlessness"; it is not blind obedience, as if there were no limits to obedience. It is responsible obedience to a constitutional principle.[26] Obedience to principle, moreover, does not preclude debate and reflection about what the military security policy should be but rather establishes a framework for it. At the highest ranks, the military professional contributes to this debate. Huntington alludes to this when he writes about the military professional's three responsibilities to the state: to represent the condition of the country's military security, to advise what the likely outcome of adopting various policies might be, and then to implement the policy chosen by the state.[27] These are analytic and static distinctions: they make matters sound neater than they are. Political processes are often ambiguous in reality, and they unfold over time. Who has a mandate to do what, exactly, whether in uniform or not, is often negotiated in the midst of conflict and is subject to revision. All this is implicit in Huntington's discussion and is worth making explicit.

What Huntington imagines is a world of three phases: before the decision is made to use the military, the time of decision, and after the decision has been made when policy must be implemented. The constitutional principle that the military must obey decisions by political elites is in essence a claim that the military has no right to make this decision but should remain silent in this second phase. Yet, as Martin Cook argues, to fix attention on the point where obedience to civilian authority is required "fails to articulate what is important about the military as a profession . . . [and] actually eliminates the very space in which the exercise of professionalism can and does occur."[28] In the first and third phases of Huntington's model, before the decision is made and then during its implementation, military professionals have the opportunity or space to review their expert knowledge, consider how that knowledge may apply to the given policy issue, and negotiate with others what the military's jurisdiction or domain of action should be.[29] The military's participation in these processes is often contentious and often strains trust between military and civilian leaders; neither side simply takes at face value the arguments or actions of the other.[30] Yet that is just the point. Obedience to the principle that civilian leaders rule does not necessarily create a world of blind obedience, not so long as the military profession retains its autonomy to cultivate its expert knowledge and to introduce it into policy deliberations.

That said, however, responsible constitutional obedience can be and historically has been displaced at critical moments by something like blind obedience. In 1965, for example, the Joint Chiefs of Staff, out of obedience to the president, "deliberately misrepresented their own estimates of the situation in Vietnam" to members of Congress. In discussion with members of the House Armed Services Committee, the service chiefs dramatically understated their professional assessment of how many troops would be needed for how long to win the war.[31] On July 27, 1965, at a meeting of the National Security Council, President Johnson outlined what action he thought was appropriate to meet the situation in Vietnam. Although presented as if it were designed to promote a diplomatic settlement of the conflict, the president's plan was actually designed primarily to prevent a mobilization for war from upending his Great Society program. The president asked if anyone in the room opposed that course of action. None of them spoke up, including General Earle Wheeler, who was chairman of the Joint Chiefs of Staff and who knew that the Joint Chiefs did not think this was a wise course of action. Ten minutes later, in a meeting with House and Senate leaders, President Johnson and Secretary of Defense Robert McNamara misrepresented the scale of General Westmoreland's request for money (by billions) and troops (by half) for use in Vietnam by the end of the year. Once again, President Johnson depended heavily on the silence of General Wheeler to give the appearance of truthfulness to those misrepresentations and of support for a policy limiting new troop deployments for Vietnam.[32]

The historian of this event did not mince words about what had happened. "The president's plan of deception depended on tacit approval or silence from the JCS. The Chiefs did not disappoint the president."[33] Because they did not, the president was able to distort the views of the Joint Chiefs publicly, misrepresent the mission of American forces in Vietnam, and lie to Congress about the costs of the military action in Vietnam. Without doubt, responsible obedience would require the Joint Chiefs to obey orders to fight in Vietnam with whatever resources the president and Congress decided to send. But there is no constitutional obligation to cooperate in deception before a decision—in this case on how to escalate a war—is made. On the contrary: "Because the Constitution locates civilian control of the military in Congress as well as in the executive branch, the Chiefs could not have been justified in deceiving the people's representatives about Vietnam."[34]

If this is not an example of blind obedience, it is a case of taking far too many steps away from responsible obedience toward blind obedience. At a minimum, such obedience distorts the exercise of military professional judgment based on and legitimated by expert knowledge. At worst it is a social force that encourages a collapse of thought in response to orders, allowing the military to do under pressure what would otherwise be morally unthinkable.[35]

Huntington on the Limits to Obedience

If blind obedience is problematic, on what basis can military professionals limit their obedience without at the same time violating their commitment to responsible obedience? Where can they draw the lines to keep from doing either too little or too much? In an effort that is difficult to reconcile with his earlier assertions about the supreme virtue of instant and unthinking obedience, Huntington tries to define the limits to obedience.[36] To do this, he returns to the problematic theory of separate realms, once more distinguishing political or other kinds of ends from military means. Huntington first examines conflicts between the claims of obedience and the claims of professional competence in military means. Then he turns to conflicts between the claims of obedience and the claims of nonmilitary or political values.[37] What matters is whether we are dealing with conflicts about the proper technical use of military means or with conflicts about the priority of nonmilitary ends, goods, or values that, by Huntington's account, the military profession is not competent to judge.

Huntington believes that conflicts of the first kind, between military obedience and professional competence, arise within the military chain of command when a military subordinate believes it is necessary to challenge the command of someone higher in rank. The basis of the challenge may be either operational or doctrinal. Operational problems arise when the subordinate believes that following orders will result in military disaster. The officer has no time to make this known to the superior or has made it known without changing the superior's mind. Normally the officer in this situation should obey the order, because disobeying would wrongly disrupt the authority of the chain of command, with a cost that would outweigh any benefits of the disobedience. It is assumed that those superior in rank have greater competence and knowledge to decide what to do. But obedience is a means, not an end in itself, and its end "is to further the objective of the superior."[38] Disobedience—doing what is ordinarily wrong—may be justified in the rare case that the subordinate is thoroughly familiar with the superior's objectives and has knowledge that the objectives can be achieved only if the orders are disobeyed. It is a kind of tactical disobedience that remains obedient to the higher strategic end. Doctrinal problems arise when a subordinate believes that "rigid and inflexible obedience may stifle new ideas and become slave to an unprogressive routine."[39] This can happen when those senior in the chain of command have not kept up with new knowledge about tactics and technology, and thus the subordinate's professional competence is greater, at least in some respects, than that of the superior. Here, Huntington claims, "the hierarchy of command . . . [has been] prostituted to nonprofessional purposes," that is, to purposes other than cultivation of professional expertise. In this situation, the subordinate officer may appropriately disobey and introduce the new technique but only if the gain in military efficiency outweighs the costs of disrupting the chain of command. In both cases, real professional competence may trump the claims of obedience, but the decision to trump is not easily made. In neither case can one calculate the costs and gains of disobedience until after the disobedience occurs.

Conflicts of the second kind, pitting claims of obedience against the claims of nonmilitary ends, are more challenging.[40] The central issue is whether there are limits on the obedience of military professionals to the authority of civilian political leaders. What if the ends sought by the policy were political folly, or military folly? What if the orders issued appear to be illegal? What if the orders call on military professionals to do what transgresses commonly accepted standards of morality? These are hard cases. In general, Huntington approaches them by asking whether the end sought falls strictly in the domain of military action, with no political implications (which would be quite unusual). If so, then judgment whether to obey should be based solely on the grounds of military professional competence, without deference to the statesman. Orders of this kind interfere with the application of professional expertise and may be disobeyed. By analogy, a decision whether to undergo surgery must ultimately be made by the patient, but the patient cannot tell the doctor how the surgery should be done. If the end sought falls outside the sphere of technical military competence, the presumption is that the military professional should obey. The military professional must defer to the political wisdom of the statesman and obey orders, even when he or she believes that following them will result in political folly. Likewise, military professionals must defer to the judiciary (or, in the worst case, their own understanding of the law) to determine the legal adequacy of an order. In any case, the presumption must be that the statesman's opinion is valid and that the order is legal.

What about the case of conflict with commonly accepted standards of morality? Huntington poses a troubling example: "What does the military officer do if he is ordered by the statesman to commit genocide, to exterminate the people of an occupied territory?"[41] I do not know what empirical case brought this particular conflict to Huntington's mind. The example is horrifying to contemplate. Yet Huntington reminds us of what we all know, that statesmen often feel justified to reject the claims of conscience and instead to act for so-called reasons of state. They may well regret the fact but feel compelled to do it anyway, because all the choices they have are bad—"destructive of values"—to use Arnold Wolfers's phrase, and they are forced not to do good but to do the least harm.[42] They have "dirty hands." Must the military professional go along? The choice is stark. "As a soldier," Huntington writes, "he owes obedience; as a man, he owes disobedience." What then should be done?

The answer Huntington gives is far from clear: "Except in the most extreme instances it is reasonable to expect that he will adhere to the professional ethic and obey. Only rarely will the military man be justified in following the dictates of private conscience against the dual demand of military obedience and state welfare."[43]

It is no help to say that "except in extreme circumstances" the military professional should obey. The example under discussion is an order to commit genocide. If genocide is not an "extreme circumstance," one wonders what would be. A decision to begin a genocide is impossible to justify under any moral paradigm, and so it cannot constitute a lawful order. Even if the order were (mistakenly) thought to be formally lawful, to commit genocide violates the criteria for waging just war. It would be an order that the professional soldier would rightly choose to disobey.[44]

In brief, while Huntington accepts there are some limits to the obedience of a military professional, in his view there are not many. Disobedience is justified only when the orders affect the domain of military action, have no political implications, and clearly violate technical standards of professional military competence. Even then, the reasons of professional competence must be weighty enough—measured by objectives reached, gains in mission efficiency, or the avoidance of military folly—to outweigh the costs of upsetting the chain of command. Otherwise, the virtue of obedience is maintained.

At least two flaws in Huntington's arguments make them unreliable guides on this matter. One flaw is to discuss the limits to obedience only in crude binary terms. The choice we face, Huntington supposes, is between obedience and disobedience, one or the other. But that view of the problem is too narrowly drawn and too restrictive; it is a one-dimensional view. We have seen already there are at least two kinds of obedience to distinguish, a responsible or constitutional obedience from a blind and unthinking obedience. I argue that other more subtle distinctions allow us to identify departures from obedience that are not simply disobedient. Yet nothing like these nuances enter into Huntington's account. The second flaw is that Huntington too quickly dismisses moral reasoning and finds no place for moral responsibility within the military professional's role. However, his unstated assumption—that moral considerations lie outside the military professional's domain—is unwarranted. Even the simplest order may have moral implications. Consider Grant's simple order to send provisions to Foster. If one assumes conditions of scarcity—which the order implies—it was not a matter of moral indifference how to distribute the provisions among all who needed them and who would bear the cost. The moral stakes are higher when we recall the role of the Joint Chiefs in the escalation of the war in Vietnam, and higher still in the hypothetical command to commit genocide. Yet Huntington's discussion provides no way—and no reason—for us to think about the moral responsibility of military professionals. The autonomy of military professionals is restricted to the application of their knowledge of the technology of war as means to achieve unquestionable ends of the state's military policy. Huntington has not thought enough about these issues. He has grasped too firmly onto the theory of separated military and political realms and cannot bring himself to let it go.

The Military Professional's Moral Discretion

Military professionals require autonomy, including moral autonomy, to be competent actors who can be held responsible for what they do. By autonomy, I mean the ability to govern or control one's own actions with some degree of freedom.[45] Autonomous action is a precondition for responsible obedience and implies the opposite of blind obedience. To the extent that military professionals are autonomous, they exercise discretion, choosing how to respond to the situation in which they find themselves and how to obey what are usually lawful orders. As we have seen, orders and regulations determine just so much; decisions remain about what they mean or how they apply in any particular case. Decisions may be purely technical, about how to manage the use of violence for a purpose. But they are often also moral, concerned, for instance, with the protection of troops and noncombatants, just procedures for interrogating detainees, or how much force is needed to disperse an angry crowd. This moral element is the issue now before us. Here my aim is to map a conceptual space within which military professionals exercise moral discretion. The map includes a definition of responsible obedience and disobedience. It also encompasses two types of action that do not fit classic definitions of these alternatives. Each exhibits a defect: discretion is used either to do what is morally wrong or to do what was not explicitly authorized. Nevertheless, they are not simply forms of disobedience. They are "protected" actions—protected, because the discretion to commit them preserves the autonomy on which the moral responsibility of the military profession depends.

To map this space, we can make two simple distinctions. The first distinguishes what military professionals are explicitly authorized to do from what they are not explicitly authorized to do.[46] For instance, under the terms of the Posse Comitatus Act, the U.S. military is not authorized (with certain exceptions) to engage in law enforcement within the United States.[47] Yet it might be authorized to do so outside the United States if it were sent, say, on a peacekeeping mission to Haiti. More generally, authorization refers to explicit instructions about what to do, received through the chain of command. The second distinction has to do with whether a particular act, judged in relation to an objective standard, is morally right or wrong. We need to say, in other words, whether the act (a moral fact) lives up to or is an instance of behavior expected by the standard (a moral principle). Making this judgment is easier said than done, even if we assume there is no controversy over what standards of morality to follow or how they should be applied. But the difficulties are not insurmountable. The moral principle that prohibits using people merely as means to our ends, for example, allows us to say that torture is wrong. Disagreement about whether some particular acts are instances of torture does not mean we are confused about whether torture is wrong or what acts typically count as torture.[48]

These two distinctions can be treated as orthogonal to one another. William Edmundson tells us that "there is a difference between *having a right to do something* [what is explicitly authorized] and that something's *being the right thing to do* [what is moral]."[49] Taken together, the two distinctions allow us to describe four conceptually independent types of action, shown in table 8.1. Ideally, military professionals will be responsibly obedient. They will do what they are explicitly authorized to do in a way that they, and we, judge to be morally right, that is, con-

Table 8.1.   Four Types of Moral Action

Types of action	Explicitly authorized	Not explicitly authorized
Morally right	Responsible obedience	Conscientious intervention
Morally wrong	Authorized misconduct	Disobedience

forming to a moral principle. But if they choose to do what is not explicitly authorized and what they and we judge to be morally wrong, violating a moral principle, then they are simply disobedient. These are the conventionally expected types of action, and they merit little attention here. A theory of moral discretion must address the two protected but defective actions: conscientious intervention and authorized misconduct.

Conscientious intervention—doing what is right even though the action was not explicitly authorized—should be distinguished from other kinds of conscientious actions. It is not a conscientious refusal like that of First Lieutenant Watada, who refuses to fight in the Iraq war because he believes to fight there is morally wrong. It is true that Watada's refusal is not authorized and that he thinks the refusal is morally right. The problem is that his judgment runs against constitutional commitments to secure certain moral principles by means of civilian control over the military. It ignores what we earlier called "sound second-order reasons" for obedience to civilian authority. On these grounds, Watada's act must be called disobedient. Nor is conscientious intervention meant to be like conscientious objection, involving an appeal to the majority to reform their judgment of what should count as just or morally correct action. Rather, conscientious interveners assume that they are acting in conformity with a moral principle already embraced by the Constitution or in law. They use moral discretion to act, albeit without explicit authorization—without a direct command—to ensure that their action protects or is an instance of the principle at stake.[50]

Consider the case of Chief Warrant Officer Hugh Thompson, who piloted a small reconnaissance helicopter flying over My Lai in Vietnam on March 16, 1968.[51] From the air, Thompson saw evidence of the massacre then occurring as American soldiers shot wounded civilians and hunted down children and the elderly. Thomas had no explicit right to interfere because the soldiers engaged in moral wrongdoing were not under his command. He landed and met briefly with a platoon leader, Second Lieutenant William L. Calley, to object to these actions. Calley, who outranked Thompson, told Thompson to mind his own business. Thompson began to leave, but then decided to intervene. The decision was his alone. He was not directly commanded to intervene. He landed his helicopter be-tween the American troops and the Vietnamese those troops were pursuing. He confronted the soldiers, demanded that they stop their chase, and ordered his crew to fire on the soldiers if they continued their pursuit. He arranged for the safe evacuation of surviving Vietnamese. Thompson did what was right, protect-ing the lives of innocent noncombatants. Although he was not explicitly author-ized to do what he did, it was an appropriate exercise of moral discretion when he chose not to ignore the platoon's criminal acts; he had no explicit authority to act but defended the larger values, embedded in military regulations and the laws of war, opposed to massacres.[52]

Calley was later court-martialed and convicted of murder. Calley's command-ing officer, Captain Ernest Medina, was found not guilty for lack of evidence. It was thirty years before Thompson and his crewmembers were officially com-mended and awarded the Soldier's Medal for their actions. The thirty-year wait before the commendation reminds us that institutional leaders may look on con-scientious interventions with a wary eye, perhaps because they distrust action without authorization more than they embrace a defense of what is right. This suggests one important reason why conscientious intervention should be re-garded as a protected act: to encourage military professionals to exercise moral discretion to do what is right despite institutional doubt.

More difficult to defend is the second type of defective action, authorized mis-conduct, or doing what is morally wrong even though one has been explicitly au-thorized to do it. What is defective here is the choice to do what is wrong. For leaders, a tempting response to the problem of wrong choice is to deprive mili-tary professionals of any choice, insisting that they should do only what, and ex-actly what, they are ordered to do, as if they were robots or automatons. We have already seen that it is not entirely possible to eliminate the exercise of moral dis-cretion by military professionals. Even if it were possible, it should not be desired. The result would replace responsibility with thoughtless obedience, opening the door to greater horrors.

Consider the case of Major Hal Knight, who provided ground control direct-ing B-52s to their targets during the Vietnam War.[53] On March 17, 1969, he re-ceived orders that his commander told him to follow carefully. The orders in-structed him to give bombers coordinates for a raid into Cambodia, territory that U.S. forces were not authorized to raid by their current rules of engagement. These were to replace the coordinates for that night's bombing runs that had been sent from Washington as usual. When the mission was complete, Knight was to shred all evidence of what he had done. He was also ordered to cover his tracks by recovering the coordinates he had originally received and entering them into the Strategic Air Command computer system as if they had identified the mission's targets. Knight followed the orders to the letter and continued to do so for a dozen additional raids. In doing so, Knight did what orders gave him a right to do. Following Huntington's analysis, Knight could and should assume the lawfulness of the orders coming through the chain of command. Operating on that assumption, however, Knight chose to do what we would judge as wrong, helping to wage, by fraudulent means, what came to be known as a "secret war" in Cambodia.

The problem did not arise because Knight lacked expert knowledge. It arose (and not only with Knight) when the choice was made, higher up, to act against rules and to cover up that action with fraud, violating the principle of civilian control by trying to deceive Congress. Colonel Ray Sitton, the planner in the Pentagon who sent Knight's orders, was initially pressured to do so by Colonel Alexander Haig, as instructed by his boss, National Security Advisor Henry Kissinger. At first, Sitton refused to act outside of the usual system of accountability, and rightly so. Kissinger and Haig pressed further, allowing Sitton to believe that the request came from President Nixon. Sitton then wrongly chose to comply.

Why should these acts—acts of misconduct—be protected? They could not be protected on the basis that the outcome was, by some account, militarily effective. Knight believed that restrictions against bombing Cambodia were wrong and harmful to U.S. forces, and thus it was easier for him to think it was right— would limit harm—to falsify the coordinates. It was easier, but it was still wrong. In 1973 Knight testified before Congress that—apart from the illegal bombing— the cover-up was wrong because it placed "an oath to support the military" over "an oath to support and defend the Constitution." That, he rightly thought, was the wrong priority. His belief was not based on scholarly arguments in constitutional law. It seemed based rather on an intuition that his actions betrayed a moral trust in the capacity of the people to rule themselves, a capacity that constitutional arrangements were meant to protect, even in war.

In a second example of authorized misconduct, in 2003, Lieutenant Colonel Allen West, an artillery commander in the Iraq War, was penalized for using harsh tactics to interrogate a detainee; he was fined $5,000 and retired from the Army. The interrogation had sought information about a planned ambush on West's convoy, with West himself designated as a primary target. West's position in the chain of command explicitly authorized him to conduct such an interrogation. When interrogation by others produced no results, West intervened, threatened to kill the detainee if he refused to talk and fired his pistol beside the head of the blindfolded detainee. Reports vary on whether these harsh tactics led the detainee to give information enabling West to prevent the ambush.[54] But the putative utility of his choice of means is not the point. The military effectiveness of a morally wrong action, whether bombing targets in Cambodia as in the first example or mistreating detainees in Iraq in this example, does not justify misconduct nor warrant protection. Misconduct is partially protected when the actions are or seem to be authorized. It was not unreasonable for West to believe he had authority to interview a detainee who might have information affecting the safety of his troops. He chose the wrong means to gain the information. His culpability for the interrogation would have been greater had he done the same thing without explicit authority, but he was culpable nonetheless.[55] Yet here is the main point: West could be held responsible for his action because he had discretion—the autonomy to choose—how the interrogation would be conducted.

Odd as it may sound, it is essential to provide institutional protection for the exercise of discretion, even though that exercise sometimes leads to acts of authorized misconduct that are rightfully subject to punishment. To be sure, the exercise of discretion is often difficult. Military professionals must choose among alternatives that run the gamut from clearly appropriate to clearly not, and the appropriateness of many of these alternatives may not be evident. The actors must balance competing moral values, often facing urgent pressure to choose under conditions of uncertainty that leave little time for reflection. They may make the wrong choice and may be subject to criticism or punishment as a result. That is the risk. The benefit is that, by protecting this capacity for discretion, we preserve the moral accountability of the military profession. Military professionals act under orders, and yet they remain responsible for their actions.

Taken one step farther, the argument is not that *any and all* wrongdoing is protected. It is an all too troublesome problem that the military might sometimes abuse its power, serving its own interests rather than the ends chosen by democratically accountable political elites. Theory cannot prevent this, but it can make clear how the problem will be defined. In terms of the framework introduced here, there is no justification of any kind when military professionals do what they are not authorized to do and what they do is morally wrong. The military in such a case is acting without competence; it is engaged in disobedience or a kind of professional abuse. The obvious example is the coup d'état. The abuse of power occurs when the coup succeeds, as it did in 1973 when General Augusto Pinochet deposed Salvador Allende, Chile's democratically elected president. But it also occurs even when the coup fails, as happened in 1961 when four generals moved to overthrow the government of France because they disagreed with its policy to negotiate Algerian independence.

Harder cases deal with more subtle processes through which the military might influence the formation of public policy. In 2006, for example, senior military officers reportedly opposed, some quite strongly, developing U.S. plans for a bombing campaign against Iran that reportedly included the possible use of a nuclear device. One reporter called this opposition "a major victory" for the military over the White House.[56] This is unfortunate rhetoric, as if it were a sporting event in which the issue was who won or lost. The real questions are, Were the officers doing what they were explicitly authorized to do or not, and were they doing what was morally right or not? Evaluation of their action depends on the answers to these questions.

Practical Implications

As I read them, Huntington's arguments about the supreme virtue of military obedience and the limits to obedience should be rejected. Whether reflecting on obedience or on limits to obedience, he leaves no room for military professionals to accept moral responsibility for their actions. That is so whether we think narrowly in terms of how the war is waged or more broadly about the influence of senior military leaders on decisions to go to war. Huntington seems untroubled by this omission. Moral responsibility, he apparently thinks, is a problem for the statesman, if anyone, and he sharply separates in theory (although he cannot separate in fact) the military from the political domain. The military's role is not moral, as he sees it, but purely instrumental, to serve the ends of the state—whatever they are—so long as they do not interfere with the military domain. What the military profession is responsible for is maintaining its expert knowledge of the means of war and of techniques for employing them.[57] That asks far too little from the profession, whose acts never fail to invite moral judgment.

My argument, in contrast, is that the application of expert knowledge unavoidably requires military professionals to exercise discretion in what they do and how they do it. To the extent that they exercise discretion, choosing the course of action they will follow, they are moral agents who are responsible for what they do, and that means they can and ought to be held to account for their actions. To say that they are free to exercise discretion does not mean that they are completely free to choose whatever action they will, no more than a judge's powers of judicial review allow her to say that a law means whatever she wishes.[58] The exercise of discretion is real, but its exercise must be justifiable in light of the moral values and customs associated with the constitutional design of liberal democracy and with the customary laws of war that are a part of that design. These values and customs define the moral standards we expect military professionals to meet. Thompson was ultimately commended for his actions in My Lai because he used discretion to defend standards prohibiting the slaughter of noncombatants. West also used discretion, but he was punished, because his interrogation techniques failed to defend standards requiring the humane treatment of prisoners.

What practical implications follow from this emphasis on the moral responsibility of the military professional? First, the kinds of warfare we are likely to face in the foreseeable future will pose difficult and novel moral problems whose resolution will affect the course of the conflict. Dealing with these will tax the military professionals' powers of moral reasoning, especially when they involve balancing moral conflicts that arise from clashes with different cultures. There will rarely be textbook answers. Nonetheless, military professionals will be expected to act with discretion and will be held morally accountable for their actions. To help them meet that expectation, they should take part in an extensive program of moral education.[59] For officers, this program should begin at the undergraduate level, before commissioning, and continue periodically throughout their professional careers as an essential part of their military education. Some may be skeptical whether a large bureaucracy can establish programs attempting to improve moral reasoning, but there is evidence that moral reasoning can be taught within the military's academies.[60] Broader programs encompassing reserve officer training at the junior level or formally incorporated into higher military education for senior officers have yet to be established. How much could be accomplished is difficult to say. A sustained effort at the moral education of officers stretching across the military educational system would be subject to bureaucratic pressures to routinize the program, to turn away from the opened-ended uncertainties of serious moral education toward the less useful (but more easily measured and controlled) practice of indoctrination. These pressures can be resisted, but they will be resisted only insofar as military leaders are persuaded that the quality of their troops' moral reasoning is essential for professional and institutional success, despite the risk of wrongdoing.

Second, moral education must be augmented by an institutional climate within which moral reasoning is taken seriously. That climate will be fostered if the military provides routine oversight to judge whether moral standards that guide the exercise of discretion are neglected or met. Doing so is a challenge for many institutions, as recent scandals in business and religious organizations suggest. It is difficult within the military in part because it exists in a political arena where few rewards are given for uncovering "scandals." A temptation for those in uniform and for civilian leaders in the Department of Defense is to avoid publicizing actions that could show the military in a bad light. The temptation should be resisted.[61] Oversight that reveals events truthfully and deals as quickly as possible to correct moral failures will cultivate belief and confidence in the military as a moral institution. When oversight is lax, it breeds cynicism and distrust. Examples from the Iraq war are too many, including delayed and distorted reports about Pat Tillman's death by friendly fire, failure by senior leaders to notice and correct abusive conditions at Abu Ghraib even after credible reports of wrongdoing, attempts by Marines to cover up the massacre at Haditha, and inadequate treatment and respect for veterans suffering from post-traumatic stress disorder.[62] Such failures have broad consequences. Programs of moral education will not be taken seriously if members of the military doubt that the institution holds itself to high standards of moral responsibility.

Two objections might be raised against drawing such implications from my argument favoring broader limits to obedience than Huntington proposed and permitting some discretion to do what is wrong. One objection is that there is nothing new in the argument. After all, military professionals have long been taught that they are morally accountable for their acts. Here is one example: at least as far back as 1956, one year before *The Soldier and the State* was first published, it has been part of U.S. Army doctrine that obeying orders from superior authorities is no defense to excuse violations of the law of war or committing war crimes.[63] In this view, the discussion here may have relevance for academic debates about how to read and evaluate classic texts, but it has none for the military profession. The other objection (which Huntington might make) is that my argument is irrelevant because it is too ideal, too perfectionist in its expectations: it fails to treat human beings as they are and institutions as they might be, and so it cannot be and will not be acted on. As Huntington argues, the truth is that we live in a world of conflict, a Hobbesian world, a world inevitably at war because states are driven by the pursuit of self-interest "to unlimited acquisition of wealth, overstepping the bounds of what is necessary."[64] In such a world, moral considerations are thought to be of little worth.

Both objections cannot be true. One holds that the idea that military professionals are moral agents and morally accountable for their actions is already established. The other holds that that idea is not and cannot be established in the real world of Hobbesian conflicts where what matters most is brute military strength.

But both could be wrong. I have argued that Huntington was mistaken to embrace a Hobbesian view, treating the military professional as a morally neutral instrument of violence obedient to the state. Against the other objection, let me note simply that establishing a rule or standard of conduct does not complete, but at most begins, a process of moral reasoning. The process is open-ended, not determined by rule. The ongoing task is to use reason to choose a course of action that is militarily effective and that is justifiable by the values and customs held by liberal democratic societies. This is not something done once and for all. It must be renewed, even at the risk of doing what is wrong, in each new encounter with violence.

CHAPTER NINE

The Military Mind

A Reassessment of the Ideological Roots
of American Military Professionalism

Darrell W. Driver

The military mind has long been shorthand for the kind of hyperconservative, illiberal, and decidedly un-American ideology feared in an insulated professional military caste. Ironically, it is for this reason that Samuel Huntington found this ideology so important for the preservation of American democracy. Unlike the dominant American liberal tradition, which had grown out of the desire to guard against tyranny, the military professional's classic form of conservatism offered, said Huntington, the requisite ideological resources both to prevent the military from usurping democratic governance and to defend American democracy against the grave new Soviet threat. While traditional American liberalism could accomplish the former, it was poorly suited for the task of the latter. Liberal ideology could not support the functional demands of a military organization that relies on strict obedience to orders, perseverance through extreme hardships, and absolute commitment to the group. According to Huntington, America required military leaders with an ideological inventory that was better suited to the task, that is, a less liberal ideology. Huntington thus saw military effectiveness, military professionalism, and ultimately healthy civil-military relations as intimately connected to and dependent on a set of classically conservative beliefs about public life.

In assessing whether military professionalism is—as Huntington argued—inevitably linked to a coherent, distinct, and functionally reinforcing ideological framework, I argue that this model construct does not fit with what we have come to understand about the nature of deeply held views toward public life. Emerging understandings of such beliefs reveal that there is no singular or linear connection among individual views on public life and professional functions. Instead, through the use of narrative, human beings are surprisingly capable of connecting a diverse range of behavioral choices, such as vocation and even voting, to eclectic beliefs.[1] This pliability in the connection between function and ideology has been confirmed by experimental data, presented in this chapter, that reveal not agreement centered on classically conservative beliefs but a surprising ideological heterogeneity.

This decoupling of a distinct conservative ideology from military professionalism weakens Huntington's contention that what keeps professional officers out of mainstream liberal politics is an alien, uniquely military ideology capable of ensuring civilian control. For a military struggling to keep up with recruiting demands in an increasingly diverse American society, this is fortunate: a singular ideology appears to be neither a prerequisite for nor a natural result of military service. Instead, the experimental sample of officers presented here shows only two basic ideological characteristics that were shared almost universally: first, a broad commitment to public service and, second, the ability to reconcile a diverse range of public beliefs with the requirements of military forms of public service.

The Connection between the Military Mind and Military Professionalism

The chief dilemma Samuel Huntington tackles in *The Soldier and the State* is a long-standing one in democratic governance. How does a state develop the requisite military power to fend off external threats without creating a military so strong that it threatens internal political control?[2] Huntington's response was to contend that both military effectiveness and continued political control could be ensured by maximizing military professionalism. According to Huntington's definition, professionalism entailed mastery of a designated field of expert knowledge, a corporate sense of identity with and loyalty to other members of the profession, and social responsibility to serve the needs of the client state. Into the latter criterion Huntington smuggles his definition of professionalism as a basic bargain between military and political leaders within the state. If military leaders want the autonomy to practice expert knowledge and cultivate their own corporate identity, then they must accept the requirement of unquestioning obedience to the state. With this definition, Huntington effectively rests civilian control of the military on the agreement that the military will remain loyal to the state in exchange for autonomy within a separate and distinct sphere of military professional jurisdiction. The single answer, then, to the dual requirements of maintaining a strong military and maintaining civilian control was to cultivate an intense professionalism in the military.

Huntington's theory has been criticized for placing all of the responsibility for ensuring civilian control on this strict definition of military professionalism. First, it is argued, loyalty to the state may not necessarily be taken by military professionals to mean loyalty to the existing government. Samuel Finer points out that, far from being a guarantee against military intervention in political affairs, militaries have historically often used social responsibility and state loyalty as a justification for intervening against the existing political arrangements.[3] Additionally, the attempt to answer the problem of civilian control with professional internal self-policing alone falls short of the kind of guarantee that might satisfy a suspicious polity. On the definition of professionalism, Huntington rests all of the weight of civilian control: that is, if civilian control and military professionalism are synonymous, it is impossible for a "professional" army to challenge such control. By definition, a professional military that challenges civilian political control becomes unprofessional; thus to ensure civilian control one need only maximize professionalism and its concomitant respect for civilian control. Because it is true by definition, it is impossible to disconfirm Huntington's theory. Consequently, in order to avoid begging the question, what Huntington's model requires is for something other than internal professional self-policing to bear some of the weight of assuring military separation from and subordination to political authorities.[4] This is the role for ideology in Huntington's model.

The existence of a distinct military ideology derived from the unique functional demands of military service would aid Huntington by reinforcing the separation between military professionals and civilian political leaders. This natural ideational distinction would make it less likely that military professionals could successfully contend for influence in the very different world of civilian political life.

Thus, as described in chapter 4 of *The Soldier and the State*, ideology is an important intervening variable in Huntington's model. To begin with, he argues, there are two basic types of ideology: pro-military ideologies are supportive of the military's functional tasks, and antimilitary ideologies are not. Fascism is excluded from pro-military ideologies because its belief in the ability to rationalize and control human events conflicts with the uncertain and often highly irrational domain of war. Marxism, with its overly positive view of human nature, cannot be reconciled with the military professional's war-informed belief in the baseness of humankind. Thus, no military could be effective on the field of battle if it were imbued with either of these decidedly unmilitary ideologies. Liberalism, too, is antimilitary, according to Huntington, because its focus on the individual undermines military-unit cohesion and the necessary allegiance to the group. Thus, the U.S. military must always guard its battlefield effectiveness against the effects of an antihierarchical, radically individualistic, and power-distrusting American liberalism. Classical liberalism was the soul of America, in Huntington's view, but it could never be so for America's military.[5]

The only ideology, in Huntington's view, that served the demands of military service was the ideology of classical conservatism. Huntington's description is precise: "In its theories of man, society, and history, its recognition of the role of power in human relations, its acceptance of existing institutions, its limited goals, and its distrust of grand designs, conservatism is at one with the military ethic."[6] In the public philosophy of a long-eclipsed European aristocracy, Huntington found a belief system that appeared to fit well with the dictates of military service and function.[7] Conservatism provided the ideological resources to support the demands of war that the American liberal consensus could not. To deviate from this conservative philosophy was to put military effectiveness at risk.

The ideological pieces to the puzzle were thus identified. Military leaders needed conservatism to foster an effective military. If they wanted the public legitimacy that would put them in a position to threaten civilian political control, they would have to wave the banner of American liberalism. This clear distinction between the necessary public philosophies of these two worlds—the political and the military—meant that neither military officers nor political leaders could be effective actors in the domain of the other. For either to be effective in the other's world, they would need to leave behind the ideas and convictions that had made them successful. For the military, this would mean an officer corps that abandoned the principles of leadership, hierarchy, and discipline to espouse those of self-actualization and maximum individual liberty. To gain political success, military officers would be forced to trade away military professionalism, casting aside subordination to the state and betraying the expertise associated with effective military leadership. In this way, Huntington argued, the necessary conservatism of the military mind, nested in a dominant liberal political culture, assisted in establishing a division between civilian and military roles.[8]

The remainder of this chapter examines these connections. Does ideology correlate so firmly with military experience and function? Can military professionalism depend on the presence of a distinct ideology to help ensure its separation from the de-professionalizing effects of liberal-state politics? Is this distinction empirically demonstrable, or are there many officers who do not share in some sort of a conservative ideology? If so, do such officers undermine military professionalism? Do they put healthy civil-military relations at risk? These are but a few of the questions invited by Huntington's reliance on ideology to bolster his theory of civilian control through civil-military separation.

Function and Ideology: Connecting Public Beliefs to Individual Action

Within a decade after *The Soldier and the State* appeared, other sectors of American political science were beginning to come to a better understanding of the nature of beliefs and ideology. On the basis of large-scale surveys, a number of researchers concluded initially that the glaring inconsistencies noted in respondents' opinions were a clear indication that the average American citizen held no coherent ideology.[9] Philip Converse, for instance, looked for a belief system, that is, "a configuration of ideas and attitudes in which the elements are bound together by some form of constraint or functional interdependence."[10] When survey data showed, instead, that the average citizen's beliefs were not consistently linked in such a system, Converse concluded that the possession of a coherent ideology was the exception rather than the norm. Without an "internal constraint or functional interdependence" between ideas, people had random and chaotic collections of attitudes about the world, rather than a coherent ideology. In response to these findings, other researchers began to look harder for the kind of functional interdependence between ideas, attitudes, and actions that would reveal that ideology or belief systems were, in fact, more widespread than the initial polling data had suggested. The results of their research changed views of the role and nature of public beliefs; it has important implications for how we understand the connection between ideology and military professionalism.

Robert Lane was among the first to suggest that the consistencies sought by survey researchers were merely products of existing social biases and expectations about how beliefs "ought to" hang together.[11] When the discrete responses to survey questions did not relate in the way that conventional wisdom predicted, researchers presumed that the respondent was simply inconsistent. As Lane demonstrated, however, careful attention to how an individual reconciled his or her ideas revealed far more consistency in the relationships among ideas and between an individual's ideas and his or her actions. It was not that individuals simply held discrete, unconnected, or inconsistent beliefs; instead, the way that they connect those beliefs to one another and to their everyday experiences and actions is far more idiosyncratic than the dominant survey instruments had been capable of capturing. More in-depth qualitative approaches to understanding ideology made it increasingly clear that people were capable of reconciling all sorts of superficially inconsistent beliefs into a personally coherent view of the world.[12] The important matter was not the degree to which individuals' beliefs corresponded easily to publicly accepted ideologies but the idiosyncratic ways in which beliefs were connected to one another and were made to satisfy an individual's psychological needs. In this task, personal narratives proved to be an important means of reconciling beliefs into a functionally interdependent whole. As this qualitative research on the empirical study of ideology has matured, it has become increasingly accepted that an individual's own "stories" or "morality tales" provide a flexible means of organizing beliefs and of connecting those beliefs to actions.[13] These connections often fail to fit with external expectations.

These conclusions are important because they tend to vitiate the ideology-from-function argument inherent in the military-mind claims of Huntington and others. The malleable nature of beliefs and of the narrative-based way in which individuals hold beliefs and relate them to observed reality means that any attempt to deduce an ideology from the functional requirements of military service alone would give very uncertain results. One cannot presume, for instance, that because military service requires hierarchical discipline, therefore, individuals in military service must embrace hierarchical political beliefs. Instead, this more pliable view of ideology suggests that individuals in military service have to reconcile their beliefs with the military's need to maintain hierarchical discipline; they do not simply transpose, unaltered, military requirements into all of their ideological commitments. Moreover, by means of narratives, this reconciliation might take any number of paths as it conforms to individual psychological needs. Recognition that the connection between an individual's ideology and lived experience are idiosyncratic and imprecise decouples the connection Huntington tried to make between conservative ideology and military service. If individuals can, in fact, reconcile an expansive range of individual public beliefs with the demands of military service, an ideological division between civilian society and military professionals is not inevitable. This undercuts the argument that clearly distinct ideologies will keep military professionals and civilian leaders in their respective military and civilian spheres.

Against this criticism, however, one might still argue that the nature of military service is altogether different, that it is perhaps unique in being able to transform broad aspects of an individual's beliefs about public life in ways that other professional experiences do not. Even if a maturing understanding of human beliefs and ideology cautions us against drawing clear lines, perhaps the military experience could nonetheless have the effect that Huntington and military-mind proponents predict.

This assertion can, however, be tested, and in this testing we can consider two contending claims. The first, as Huntington asserted, is that military professionalism is firmly linked to conservative ideology, and this conservative ideology helps to keep military professionals out of a thoroughly liberal American politics. The counterclaim is that the connection between military professionalism and ideology is not so firm: military professionals might hold a number of different beliefs and ideologies, and if so, then ideology cannot provide a reliable bulwark against military interference in politics. The question then is whether there exists a demonstrable connection between military professionals and a distinct, coherent ideology, and if there is such a connection, whether this ideology conforms to the description of conservatism Huntington contends is fundamentally incompatible with American political life.

Function and Ideology: Testing for a Military Mind

To test the relationship between military service and political beliefs, the typical solution has been to turn to public opinion polls and survey instruments. For several reasons, however, this approach does not help with the task of exploring the presumed connection between a military-mind conservative ideology and military professionalism. First, public opinion polls are mostly looking at contemporary forms of politics: left and right or Democratic Party and Republican Party. To use these questions, however, would mischaracterize what Huntington and earlier observers of ideology and military service meant by the terms liberal and conservative.[14] Huntington's argument is not that the American military is on one side of the American party-political spectrum, but that military professionals share a coherent conservative ideology that is off the American political spectrum altogether. Military ideology, unlike mainstream American beliefs about public life, is not based on broad, classically liberal tenets; it returns to Edmund Burke rather than John Locke for its philosophical underpinnings.[15] This kind of distinctiveness and isolation is what is required if the military mind is to put up a barrier between the military and political spheres of action. An effective test would be one that can determine whether military professionals do hold such a distinct ideology.

A second reason that traditional surveys and polls do not help is that the military-mind argument is not simply that the individual beliefs held by military professionals are unique when compared to the individual responses of typical Americans; it is that they hang together in a comprehensive view of the world—or, in Max Weber's term, *Weltanschauung* or world view—that is holistically unique. This holistic quality of a belief system or ideology is what Philip Converse suggests when he talks about the functional interdependence of ideas in a belief system. Ideology is not just a collection of discrete ideas and beliefs aggregated as data points; it also involves the manner in which those beliefs relate to, build on, and support each other. Because the claim in question involves an ideology, the test must be able to account for this holistic functional interdependence of ideas.[16]

Thus, given that the priorities among and the relationships between ideas are just as important as the beliefs themselves, an effective test must allow subjects to identify these relationships themselves, building and explaining their worldview as they see fit, rather than forcing them to select from a limited menu of options chosen by the researcher. This is particularly important given the topic of concern here. Do military professionals choose the conservative label because of perceived expectations that they will do so? Or does that characteristic exist organically? Respondents must be allowed to construct their own ideologies—independently and with few constraints—and the researcher must be able to compare those constructions systematically with the claims of the military-mind thesis.

This was the goal of a study on military and civilian beliefs about public life I conducted between 2004 and 2006. This public beliefs study made use of two instruments: a public beliefs sorting exercise was followed by semistructured interviews. The sorting exercise included a collection of fifty statements taken from earlier studies on political attitudes and civil-military relations and from the broader literature on political ideology. (These statements appear in the appendix at the end of this chapter.) The statements were chosen for the degree to which they fit with or contradicted existing descriptions of the military mind as inimical to classical liberalism: traditional, anti-individualistic, authoritarian, nationalistic, and prone to embrace physical power as the path to security.[17] The sorting exercise itself, in what is known as Q-method, required the respondent to arrange a collection of statements (according to a normal distribution) from those with which they agreed the most to those with which they agreed the least.[18] Patterns in the correlations between responses allowed me to identify ideological categories and to group individual respondents into categories according to their responses.

This sorting exercise was followed by interviews to clarify the stated priorities and to understand the relationships among those priorities. If something like a military-mind ideological archetype really exists, it should be demonstrable with an approach of this kind. In a reasonably large sampling of military professionals and civilian leaders, if Huntington's theory is correct, one should see discernible and relatively coherent agreement on value priorities and justifications among military professionals. This agreement would adhere to the classical description of the conservative military mind offered in the literature, and it would place the military outside of the liberal mainstream of American political life.

One sample was taken from among senior Army officers at the U.S. Army War College in Carlisle Barracks, Pennsylvania, and the National War College in Washington, D.C., and from midgrade Army officers on temporary assignment to the U.S. Military Academy at West Point, New York: forty-five officers in total.[19] The civilian comparison group—forty-five senior to midlevel civilian leaders—was selected from several American cities, including metropolitan New York, Chicago, and Richmond, Virginia. To weight the test toward manifestation of the distinction between, in Huntington's terms, business-oriented liberalism and a military-supporting conservatism, the civilian sample was predominantly drawn from business leaders from both corporate and small businesses.[20] The ethnic, racial, and gender composition of both the military and civilian samples approximated that of their respective populations overall.[21] Within these constraints, respondents were randomly selected for the exercise. The goal was not to develop a sample large enough to be generalized across the American population or across the U.S. military services but to provide a reasonable empirical test for the presence of something like a distinct, coherent, and classically conservative military ideology that differed from the civilian ideology thus revealed. If military professionalism requires very different ideological resources, this approach should have identified the nature of this distinction. Perhaps broadly liberal or even markedly heterogeneous beliefs would abound in the civilian control group, but if ideology is as connected to function as military-mind claims suggest, the forty-five senior and midlevel U.S. Army officers should have displayed a strong tendency toward consensus in their responses. In fact, however, they did not.

Whether divided into two broad ideological categories or four narrower ones, the sample revealed no distinct conservative-like world view dominated by the military respondents. Emerging instead from the ninety-person sample were various public perspectives that generally fit with earlier theoretical and empirical attempts to map the contemporary American ideological terrain.[22] These perspectives ranged from the more social-centric to the libertarian, and from more hierarchical views on the social and political ordering of society to the thoroughly decentralized. The U.S. Army officers in the sample were not markedly different from the civilians in this attitudinal pluralism. Military service proved to be a poor predictor of where an individual ended up on the ideological spectrum. No ideological archetype—conservative or otherwise—captured the heterogeneity of the public beliefs and the values of these Army officers.

On the basis of the respondents' performance on this exercise, it was possible to divide the ninety-person sample into two broad ideological categories: one with generally stereotypical left-leaning priorities, the other with right-leaning priorities. The first category emphasized values such as international cooperation in foreign policy, shared service to common societal goals, collective discussion and debate in public problem-solving, religious neutrality in the public sphere, belief in the basic goodness of most people, and the importance of values such as justice and equity. The second category emphasized traditional values, hard work, and moral character as the key to public problems; a punitive approach to crime; the benefits of a vibrant consumer society; the preemptive use of force in foreign policy; and the benefits of international cooperation so long as the United States was militarily and economically dominant.[23] It is here that one should have begun to see a military-ideological separation predicted by the military-mind thesis. There was none. The first or "left" ideological category comprised eighteen Army officers and twenty-two civilians, and the second category, on the "right," had twenty-one Army officers and twenty civilians.[24] While this hinted of a slight military lean to the right, it fell far short of warranting claims of an organic, isolating military conservatism.

Even if the ideological categories were further divided with finer distinctions (see table 9.1), it was still impossible to separate the political attitudes of the mil-

Table 9.1. Distribution of 90 Respondents into Four Ideological Categories

	Libertarian	Communitarian	Traditional conservative	Active, pro-government conservative	Not significant on any of the four categories
Army, midgrade	3	6	6	7	6
Army, senior leader	2	5	5	1	4
Army total	5	11	11	8	10
Corporate-business leader	1	8	3	5	8
Small-business leader	1	10	1	6	2
Civilian total	2	18	4	11	10
Total	7	29	15	19	20

Source: Steven R. Brown, Political Subjectivity (New Haven, CT: Yale University Press, 1980), p. 223.

Note: Labels derived from interpretation of the shared positions of the participants in these categories, together with explanations obtained in follow-on interviews. Significance is obtained according to the following: the Standard Error is obtained with the expression $1/\sqrt{N}$, where N equals the number of statements. Consequently, the $SE = 1/\sqrt{50} = .14$. Factor loadings exceeding .36 are significant at the .001 level. This is obtained with the following expression: $2.58(SE) = .36$, where the $SE = .14$.

itary respondents from the civilian portion of the sample. The responses of the ninety participants could be divided into four ideological categories, with perspectives that tended toward communitarianism, libertarianism, traditional conservatism, or a more active and progovernmental conservatism. Here again, one could find points of both similarity and dissimilarity with the military-mind thesis. However, there appeared little support for the most basic claim that there exists a distinct, coherent military ideology.

In short, when comparable samplings of Army officers and of civilian leaders were asked to reconstruct their ideologies from the ground up, military service turns out not to be a significant predictor of where each respondent would end up in the resulting ideological architecture. This finding is consistent with the literature from the empirical study of ideology discussed previously, which demonstrates that beliefs are not bound to each other, to experience, or to action according to one universally acceptable or even recognizable blueprint. Individuals find innumerable ways of connecting their professed ideas and beliefs to a variety of different public and private behaviors. This idiosyncratic relating of commitments and actions to ideas and vice versa is especially prevalent in the realm of politics, where the basic concepts themselves, as Robert Grafstein warns, do "not have a separable fund of factual content, an objective link to an independent world."[25] Concepts such as freedom, justice, and liberty are, in Walter Gallie's term, "essentially contestable."[26] They may be broadly agreed upon in word, but the meanings of those concepts are matters for interminable debate.[27]

Consider, for example, a brief examination of the two terms at the center of this debate: liberalism and conservatism. Observers of American political thought, Samuel Huntington included, have long contended that the U.S. political tradition is firmly rooted in a strong liberal consensus.[28] Nevertheless, defenders of the idea of an American liberal consensus have had to explain a host of contradictions. If there is such a liberal consensus in America, why do Americans argue so much about deeply divisive matters of public policy? If America is so liberal, why was there slavery, and why at times have U.S. citizenship laws been so race-based?[29] The answer suggested by J. David Greenstone was that liberalism is America's linguistic tradition, meaning that it provides the grammar for political life in America, effectively setting strictures on what is and is not acceptable according to how well a desired public action or policy can be described in terms of liberalism's core commitments.[30] Attempts to describe one's ideas and commitments with widely approved liberal language are, according to Greenstone, the essence of the American liberal consensus, a linguistic or nominal agreement within which deep and important debates over meaning remain. If we understand liberalism as an agreement on public language, the question becomes whether military professionals share in a liberal nominal consensus with other Americans. The answer is unequivocally yes.

Greenstone's conclusion is not disconfirmed by the priorities and explanations of the respondents to the public beliefs study just described. There was a wide degree of diversity in the sorting exercise, but when asked to explain the reasons for their ordering choices, all of the respondents—military and civilian alike—drew on the same classically liberal vocabulary. Consider a few examples from the subsequent interviews. One Army captain used the grammar of American liberalism precisely in stating his belief that "each individual knows best how they want to run their business; each individual knows best what makes them happy; each knows best how they want to live their lives." Similar language and concepts such as liberty, individual rights, and equal treatment under the law were central to the language used by all of the interviewed respondents. Even concepts such as the common good were negotiated through language infused with deference to the individual. In describing how self-interest results in the common interest, the same Army respondent claimed that "the way I understand this dynamic is that . . . the common good is maximized when individuals work for their own self-interest." Another Army captain, whose response grouped him solidly in the more conservative ideological categories, did not agree that there could ever be any benefits to self-interest but was nevertheless careful to stress the centrality of individual choice in all matters: being concerned "with the common good, of what's going to improve society, not just what's good for me. . . . That's a good thing . . . [but] I see more of the individualist mentality. Yeah, that's the way I look at it; individuals themselves should be committed to the common good. I don't believe it should be imposed." Consequently, in terms of both their attitudinal pluralism and the shared liberal grammar employed to describe and justify their beliefs, the Army officers in this sample do not display any holistic attitudinal distinctions that support military-mind claims.

The term conservative is similarly problematic. Called by Clinton Rossiter "one of the most confusing words in the glossary of political thought and oratory," it too is a term that approaches the realm of the essentially contestable.[31] Huntington employs the term to describe the philosophy of British parliamentarian Edmund Burke, an Old World aristocratic plea for traditional order from a time when liberal ideas provided justification for capitalist expansion. In contemporary America, however, both "conservative" and "liberal" have taken on quite different meanings: conservatism often refers to a set of beliefs that endorse regu-latory regimes on social or moral issues, while embracing a laissez-faire state on economic matters, in contrast to liberalism's preference for economic regulation over social regulation. These multiple meanings for the term "conservative" lead to confusion. Much of the recent literature in the area of military ideology has fo-cused on whether military professionals have drifted to one side of the American political-party spectrum. This would be an interesting and possibly troubling phe-nomenon, but it still would not account for the more ambitious claim that military officers are professionally insulated because they agree on a deeper philosophical conservatism that is outside the boundaries of American political debate alto-gether. Given the prominence of the politically conservative American Right in recent decades, it seems unlikely that identification with this contemporary con-servative coalition alone could fulfill the isolating role expected by military-mind claims. But this too largely misses the point.

This public beliefs study reveals that there is a deeper heterogeneity of beliefs and attitudes among Army professionals; thus, even the most expansive contem-porary reading of the term conservative cannot serve as a useful shorthand for military beliefs. It is true that in recent and well-publicized polls, military officers identified overwhelmingly with Republican Party politics and the conservative label, and in the limited sampling of Army officers in my public beliefs study, twenty-three (62 percent) of the thirty-seven military respondents who provided a political self-description chose some variant of "conservative" or "Republican," similar to the percentages found in polling data.[32] Nevertheless, of these twenty-three self-identified conservatives or Republicans, seven of these embraced ideo-logical priorities that grouped them on the more left-leaning ideological category in the two-category solution. When the responses were divided into four cate-gories, these twenty-three respondents were distributed across the ideological terrain: two libertarian; six communitarian; six traditional conservative; and five with more active, pro-governmental conservative leanings. Thus, the military re-spondents employed the term conservative to describe a broad array of public be-liefs. Conversely, in the civilian portion of the sample, the label conservative was used with a much more precise meaning; only one of seventeen self-identifying conservatives or Republicans fell outside of the right-leaning category in the study. In sum, although as a label of self-identification conservatism enjoys broad mili-tary support, it is employed with highly divergent meanings and thus often ob-scures more than it clarifies.

While the preceding discussion reveals that there is a fair degree of ambiguity to negotiate in order to explain the use of terms like liberalism and conservatism in military-mind claims, doing so reaffirms the basic arguments forwarded here. First, experience and actions are not as simplistically connected to ideology as the military-mind logic contends. The way in which individuals interpret meaning, draw connections, and then hold beliefs (and, one might add, describe divergent beliefs with a similar liberal grammar) is often much more complex and idiosyncratic than suggested by the military-mind model. Second, this is confirmed by the Q-method part of the public beliefs study: military service turns out not to be a good predictor of an individual's position on the ideological spectrum. Third, all of the respondents in this exercise shared a broad classically liberal vernacular. There were no variant grammars of description that might identify military professionals as somehow unique or antithetical to a liberal setting. Finally, while military respondents' tendency to adopt a conservative political self-identification does suggest a level of consensus about labeling among military professionals, it is, nevertheless, a thin consensus under which there is considerable attitudinal variety. This brings us back to the role that ideology plays in Huntington's thesis and, more importantly, to the practical issue of how contemporary military officers ought to think about their profession and its relationship to their deepest public beliefs.

Ideology and the Military Profession

The classic conservatism supposedly shaped by military service would, Huntington argued, confirm the incompatibility of military professionals with the politics of a thoroughly liberal state such as the United States. Like oil in water—or, as Huntington said, like "Sparta in Babylon"—a healthy separation between the military and political spheres of action would be established by differences in ideology. Beliefs and commitments necessary for success in one sphere simply could not apply to the other. In a liberal democracy, therefore, healthy civil-military relations would require us to embrace and even cultivate this difference.[33]

On the basis of the research described here, however, ideology would be a poor insurance policy for civilian military control: it cannot fulfill the role Huntington assigns to it. There is no separate specific ideology coherent and distinct enough to keep military professionals from encroaching on political terrain. The connections between belief and military function are too uncertain, while the collection of military attitudes and value priorities are not appreciably different from those of other citizens in their degree of dissimilarity, disunity, and discord. Thus, the military profession appears much more capable of accommodating a diversity of ideologies and public beliefs than claimed by military-mind arguments.

This brings one to the inevitable question: if the military reflects no functionally driven ideological archetype, where does that leave us? Can beliefs about public life play any role in fostering a more effective civil-military relationship? The answers to these questions invite a rethinking of the connection between military professionalism and the realm of normative beliefs in a pluralistic American democracy.

The desire to design a professional military ethic or shared values base for the contemporary force pushes us to look more carefully for those normative beliefs that might be truly fundamental to effective military service. What beliefs support task cohesion across the full spectrum of military missions? What beliefs can provide a shared normative foundation for a diverse professional force? This challenge is similarly faced by contemporary democratic theory itself, to find in the modern, deeply diverse, and pluralistic liberal state a basis for consensus or a point of agreement upon which to base collective action. The extreme pluralism of the modern state has caused many liberal political theorists to dismiss any hope that there could ever be such a broad consensus on substantive matters.[34] But, as Robert Dahl contends, what the modern liberal state requires is not that citizens share in common normative beliefs about public life but that citizens, especially those charged with public decision-making capacity, share an acceptance of democratic norms and processes.[35] In evaluating democratic civil-military relations, Marybeth Peterson Ulrich arrives at similar conclusions: "An officer's allegiance . . . is not just to the state, but to the democratic character of the state." She argues that professional military development ought to include a plan for "the incorporation of democratic values in an officer's overall set of internal values," instilling a "professional obligation that links the special requirements of service to a democratic state to an officer's overall professionalism."[36] This turns the inquiry into public beliefs and values from a focus on identifying a comprehensive and potentially exclusionary ideology, such as the military mind, to one focused more broadly on inculcating a commitment to the democratic process, and to valuing that process enough to engage in professional military service on its behalf.

This approach already enjoys broad support among the military professionals queried here. Although there were no "consensus statements," that is, statements that were statistically similar (either acceptance or rejection) across the full ninety-person sample, when the sample was narrowed to only military respondents, one consensus statement did emerge: *societies run best when individuals are committed to the common good and service to common societal goals.*[37] This statement was the only shared normative position that the military leaders examined here held in common. Though their explanations of what is involved in this "common good" and "service to common societal goals" took different forms, the fact that this commitment was shared by the military respondents does offer hope for a professional military normative consensus founded on a commitment to democratic public service.

Such an ideational foundation would also provide better support for both the military's functional imperative to maintain military effectiveness and its societal imperative to be broadly representative of society's core characteristics. Even if it were possible to draw clear lines from the military function to an interdependent ideology, the expanding spectrum of military missions over the past half century makes it uncertain what such an ideology or ideologies would look like.[38] Between 1991 and 1999 alone, fifty-four military operations were carried out by Western countries.[39] The United States undertook operations for such purposes as drug interdiction, restoring domestic order, peacekeeping, infrastructure development, disaster relief, and rescuing foreign nationals, along with traditional combat operations. The increasingly combined (multinational) and joint (multiservice) nature of these operations leads to a much more complicated picture of the military profession's function and context than in the past. A professional normative military ethic drawn from traditional high-intensity ground combat alone might or might not produce the military-mind attitudinal construct Huntington describes, but it is unlikely to meet the needs of an adaptable, capabilities-based, full-spectrum force. For those who look for connections between experience, ideology, and action, ideological uniformity may be neither demonstrable nor desirable in the present full-spectrum operating environment. A professional military ethic for the contemporary force would instead need to spring from values common to and supportive of all forms of contemporary military service.

The societal imperative is supported by similar arguments for a more appropriate ideational foundation. Given the increasingly diverse nature of the people on whom the military profession will draw for future members, successful military professionalism is likely to be measured less by commitment to a narrow, distancing ideology than by the ability to reconcile diverse belief systems with the demands of democratic military service. In the past, efforts to accommodate the societal imperative have been denigrated as coming at the expense of functional military effectiveness.[40] However, as recruiting demands become more difficult to meet and as the competition for professional talent grows more intense, societal imperative concerns such as inclusivity have direct functional implications. A high-quality officer corps that draws on the best and brightest of all of America is a functional imperative. Recognition that ideational commitments central to effective military service are not only reconcilable but indeed central to Americans' deepest and most widely shared normative beliefs will assist in this effort.

Conclusion

In the end, the American professional military ethic is best served not by searching for a comprehensive ideology in which all military professionals might share but by recognition that military service is compatible with a broad range of political commitments. Military professionals must reconcile their various beliefs and commitments with the demands of military service, but fortunately this is already happening. With an eclectic mix of value priorities and normative positions, the military professionals examined here drew on disparate public philosophies to support their shared commitment to the military profession. The common belief within this ideational diversity was a shared dedication to democratic public service, in a theme the respondents sounded often. "I think the beauty of our nation is that people —some people—will be willing to subjugate their own self-interests for the greater common good." That statement came from an Army captain identifying with the more left-leaning ideological categories, while another, from the right, said: "I think military officers must be about selfless service, complete service . . . because if they had a fair degree of self-interest they would not be a military officer." Future attempts to understand, describe, and teach about the American military ethic should start with this basic foundation.

The continued promulgation of the notion that military professionals share some distinct and professionally necessary ideology that isolates—and by some accounts elevates—military professionals is not empirically demonstrable, nor is it conducive to meeting the military-functional and democratic-societal demands of a twenty-first-century force. Instead of clarifying the military professional's duties and roles, attempts to locate a unique and separate military ideology have confused them. Today's professional military education system must instead emphasize ideational principles that correct these missteps.

An important first step, then, is to begin the work of recrafting the image of the "military mind" from its perception as the antithesis of basic American liberalism to a more realistic appreciation of ideational diversity within a military that is held together by public service themes. Such themes have deep roots in the American experience: the individualism, commercialism, and social atomism in America's liberal tradition that Samuel Huntington pointed to, following Louis Hartz and others, coexists with the America of town hall meetings, barn raisings, and citizen-soldiers. For many historiographers, the latter list of traditions indicates that liberalism alone cannot fully account for the American political experience.[41] More recent histories of American political culture have highlighted the central importance of such community-focused civic-republican political traditions. These traditions have been described in many ways and through a number of lenses, but at their core are a set of values that emphasize common good, community service, and civic commitment.[42] The findings of the ideological study described here suggest that, while not the citizen-soldier highlighted in this republican lore, today's military professional is no less committed to community service and no less entitled to draw on the rhetorical resources of America's civic-republican tradition. Shifting the debate regarding military professionalism and ideology in this direction may not provide the parsimony of a monolithic military-conservatism thesis, but it promises both an easier fit with reality and a more useful ideational foundation for twenty-first-century military professionalism.

Appendix: Statements Used in the Public Values Sorting Exercise

[This appendix lists the fifty statements that were sorted in the exercise by forty-five military officers and forty-five civilian business leaders.][43]

1. Most people can be trusted and are inclined to help others.

2. You can't be too careful in your dealings with others, as most people are inclined to look out for themselves.

3. Societies run best when individuals all try to maximize their own self-interest.

4. Societies run best when individuals are committed to the common good and service to common societal goals.

5. Citizenship cannot be given; it must be earned by service to one's community; duty begets rights.

6. Citizenship is an inherent right of being human, and you should not have to do something in order to get citizenship rights.

7. Voting is a democratic obligation, regardless of the chances your party has to win.

8. If a person doesn't care how an election comes out, he should not vote in it.

9. The decline of traditional values has created significant problems for American society.

10. It is necessary for each generation to define their own values and ways of life.

11. Morality is rooted in social norms and beliefs and is, consequently, ever changing.

12. Morality is constant and does not depend on what people think is or is not moral.

13. Social and political change must come slowly and carefully, less we risk destroying the successes and accomplishments of past generations.

14. Social and political change must be focused on the fulfillment of important core values like justice and equity, even if that means a significant departure from the status quo.

15. Pervasive selfishness and consumerism represent alarming threats to the future of American society.

16. A vibrant consumer society should be encouraged because it sustains American economic prosperity.

17. No weakness or difficulty can hold us back if we have enough will power.

18. Many individuals face a host of social and economic impediments to success in life that are not their fault.

19. A few strong leaders could make this country better than all the laws and talk.

20. Collective discussion and debate is the only way the country can move forward.

21. The business professional and the manufacturer are much more important to society than the artist and the professor.

22. Science has its place, but there are many important things that can never be understood by the human mind.

23. The United States is justified to use force against a country suspected of developing weapons of mass destruction, even if these countries do not currently pose a threat to the United States.

24. The United States should avoid using military force against other countries if they do not pose an imminent threat to the U.S.

25. American foreign policy should focus first on fostering international cooperation through the United Nations.

26. American foreign policy should focus primarily on the expansion of capitalism and free markets.

27. American foreign policy should focus primarily on bringing a democratic form of government to other nations.

28. American foreign policy should focus first on maintaining American economic and military superiority.

29. The best hope for peace in the world is a strong America to keep the peace.

30. The best hope for peace in the world is strong cooperation between nation-states.

31. In times of threat, democracies often have to forgo consultation and deliberation and turn over decision making authority to one strong leader.

32. In times of threat, deliberation and democratic decision making are most important.

33. Most of the time the majority of Americans are unable to determine what is in their own best interest, much less the interest of the country.

34. Average Americans are generally stable and rational guides for decisions regarding governance and public action.

35. We should repeal regulations on sex for consenting adults.

36. Some regulations on sex—even between consenting adults—is necessary in a good society.

37. Tariffs are necessary to protect important sectors of the national economy and American jobs.

38. People are better off with free trade than with tariffs.

39. Minimum wage laws cause unemployment; repeal them.

40. Minimum wage laws prevent the exploitation of the least advantaged workers.

41. Affirmative action is little more than reverse racism, because it disadvantages some individuals simply on the basis of skin color.

42. Affirmative action is a necessary device to ensure healthy diversity, which inevitably benefits all Americans.

43. Our treatment of criminals is too harsh; we should try to rehabilitate them, not punish them.

44. Crimes of violence should be punished severely; this is the only way to stop most criminals.

45. In the future the US would do well to avoid identification with any particular religion.

46. In the future the US should be careful to remain a Christian nation.

47. Government action is the key to solving the major problems facing America today.

48. The improvement of moral character and individual hard work are the keys to solving the major problems facing America today.

49. Democracy is about citizen participation in government; it should not be made to mean other things like social justice and relative resource equality.

50. Democracy must be judged by its product, such as the degree to which it equitably distributes justice and resources.

[Respondents were asked to order the above statements by placing them into thirteen separate piles from those with which they agree the most (assigned a value of +6) to those with which they agree the least (assigned a value of −6). Respondents were limited as to the number of statements that could be assigned to each pile according to the following constraints: +6 = 2 statements; +5 = 2 statements; +4 = 3 statements; +3 = 4 statements; +2 = 5 statements; +1 = 6 statements; 0 = 6 statements; −1 = 6 statements; −2 = 5 statements; −3 = 4 statements; −4 = 3 statements; −5 = 2 statements; −6 = 2 statements. The result was a normal distribution of statement values from each participant that could be statistically compared using factor analysis. Participants could then be grouped according to the degree of similarity or dissimilarity between their priorities and those of other respondents. It was this technique that is exploited by the exercise to determine the existence and disposition of a military-mind consensus.]

CHAPTER TEN

Changing Conceptions of the Military as a Profession

David R. Segal and Karin De Angelis

The publication of Samuel P. Huntington's *The Soldier and the State* in 1957 and Morris Janowitz's *The Professional Soldier* in 1960 altered the way American social science views the military profession, the armed forces more generally, and the nature of civil-military relations.[1] Although the theories, methods, and concepts of mid-twentieth century social science have largely been displaced, these books made marks on the social science agenda that have lasted to this day. Here we place these books in the context of social science research on the military and the sociology of professions at the time they were written, and then describe how these fields and the military profession have changed over time, in part as a result of these scholars' work.

In light of today's All-Volunteer Force and the twenty-first century operational demands placed on its personnel, it is time to update the foundation that Huntington and Janowitz provided for the study of military professionalism. More specifically, we should rethink the boundaries of the military profession and consider expanding them beyond active-duty commissioned officers to include reserve commissioned officers as well as active-duty and reserve senior noncommissioned officers.

Military Social Science in the Early Twentieth Century

Social science research on the American military during the first four decades of the twentieth century was minimal, both because the social sciences were not particularly well developed and because the military was not a major institutional presence in the United States during a period when the country was not at war. The size of the military surged through mobilization of the militia and conscription when the United States was engaged in combat; it declined with demobilization during interwar periods.[2] For these reasons, the study of the military developed more slowly than other institutional areas in the social sciences. Bernard Boene, for example, notes that only 5 percent of the publications in the field of American military analysis that he cataloged as of 2000 were published before 1942.[3] He attributes this to ideological liberalism in the field, a widespread meliorist orientation to social problems, and war weariness after World War I.

This is not to say that war and the military were completely disregarded by the social sciences. Many of the early contributions to the military subfield were made by psychologists and political scientists, and this work produced an interdisciplinary orientation in social science analysis of the military that continues today.[4]

Much of the research that was done during this period focused on enlisted personnel—primarily conscripts—who composed 85 percent of the force. Psychologists, particularly during World War I, focused on individual abilities and behavior and sought to make practical contributions through aptitude testing for the military and improving understanding of performance effectiveness.[5] A focus on individual soldiers has continued to dominate social science research on the military.

Political scientists, for their part, sought to understand war as part of the process of international relations. This is reflected, for example, in Charles Merriam's project on the causes of war, a project that led to Quincy Wright's seminal study of war.[6] However, before World War II, little attention was paid to the military as a social institution—an organization, an occupation, or a profession—or to the structural linkages between the military and its host society.

The World War II period was a turning point for the social-scientific study of the military, for the social sciences generally, and for the institutional presence of the military in the United States. The social sciences experienced a behavioral revolution, in which the focus of analysis was shifted from historical events and organizations to systems of social behavior. America, more than other nations involved in the war, mobilized large numbers of economists, psychologists, political scientists, and sociologists in a variety of research and analysis roles in support of the war effort. Thus, the emerging field of military social science was initially dominated by Americans. Because the problems studied, like most important social issues, were not contained within the boundaries of a single discipline, these researchers established a pattern of interdisciplinary collaboration. Because the Army was the largest service, military social science emerged primarily (but not exclusively) as the study of ground combat forces. And because the research was aimed explicitly at helping to manage the army and the war, it emerged primarily as an applied field: one oriented toward organizational and small-group processes rather than toward national or transnational concerns. As a policy science, it was concerned with the military's policies regarding soldiers and small units rather than national policies regarding civil-military relations and the use of force. Because of the nature and the size of the mobilization, it looked primarily at the enlisted ranks rather than the officer corps.

Government research efforts were dominated by psychologists, whose work expanded beyond selection and classification testing into training research, human engineering, social psychology, and physiological psychology. During World War II, the War Department drew on the knowledge of manpower economists to help manage the personnel assets of the nation in support of the war, again focusing primarily on enlisted personnel.[7] The major substantive sociological knowledge base in the field during the World War II period came from reports of the results of experiments and surveys conducted by the Information and Education Division of the War Department. The four-volume *Studies in Social Psychology in World War II*, including the two-volume *American Soldier* studies authored by Samuel A. Stouffer and his colleagues, covered a range of topics at the individual and small-group level such as cohesion, leadership, and morale.[8] The surveys, observations, and field experiments conducted by Stouffer and his team constituted major methodological advances in the social sciences, and were important factors in the behavioral revolution in the social sciences.[9]

After World War II, in contrast to past patterns of surge and decline in the force structure, America did not demobilize to the same extent. The armed forces became a continuing institutional presence in American society. In the mid-twentieth century, there were occasional attempts by scholars to describe the emerging structural relationships between military forces and their host societies in the modern world. C. Wright Mills's book *The Power Elite* and Harold D. Lasswell's developmental model of "the garrison state" were among the most important of these.[10] Mills saw the military elite simply as one actor in a national power structure. For Lasswell, the changing role of the military was driven by changes in the technology of war that increased the importance of security concerns on national agendas, but his focus was also on the elite. It was not until the late 1950s, on the cusp of the behavioral revolution in the social sciences, that political scientists and sociologists concerned with the military changed their focus from individual soldiers to the corporate organization of the military and its relationship to the broader society. This focus thus became a viable area of academic inquiry, while maintaining its applicability in the policy arena.

The Sociology of Professions in the Twentieth Century

The post–World War II period was also a period of growth for the sociological study of professions. Modern professions had developed in the early era of European capitalism. Professions differed from other occupations in that they were seen as vocations involving performance of tasks of great social value based on knowledge and skills that set the members of professions apart from other workers.[11] In contrast to the theme of capitalist occupations, *caveat emptor* (let the buyer beware), the service ethic of the professions could be characterized instead as *credat emptor* (let the taker believe in us).[12] Those occupations designated as professions had license to act in ways forbidden to other members of society because their activities served society. They enjoyed special status, autonomy, and privilege, constrained by a mandate not to use that privilege to further their own interests. The medical profession, for example, had special authority to touch and to cut human bodies. The legal and clerical professions had authority to enforce social order and to judge the righteousness of behavior. The military profession had the right to kill in defense of the state. What was crucially important in these early conceptualizations of professions was that professional status was a dichotomous variable: an occupation either was or was not a profession.

The sociological study of professions was at its zenith in America during the period when the analyses by Huntington and Janowitz of the military profession came to the fore. Theorists during this period agreed, more or less, on a set of characteristics to describe this set of occupations. Goode offered the most comprehensive list:[13]

- "The profession determines its own standards of education and *training*" (1).
- "The student professional goes through a more far-reaching adult *socialization* experience than the learner in other occupations" (2).

- "Professional practice is often legally recognized by some form of *licensure*" (3).
- Members of the profession *run their own licensing* and admission boards (4).
- The profession *shapes most legislation* concerned with that profession (5).
- "The occupation gains in *income, power, and prestige,*" and draws high-caliber students (6).
- The practitioner is relatively *autonomous* from outside control (7).[14]
- Members demonstrate very strong *identification* and affiliation with their professions, more so than others with their occupations (8).
- "The profession is more likely to be a life-long career or *terminal occupation*" (9). "Members do not care to leave it, and most assert that if they had it to do over again, they would again choose that type of work."

Interestingly, the characteristic of serving an important social need does not appear in Goode's inventory, perhaps because it was assumed. The characteristic of *political neutrality* (10)[15] and a tendency toward *specialization* within a profession (11)[16] have also appeared in the literature on professions, and both have particular applicability to the military profession. All of these characteristics of professions can be viewed as tendencies, rather than as hard-and-fast criteria for the recognition of an occupation as a profession.

Abrahamsson notes two approaches—typological and gradualistic—to the study of professions.[17] The typological approach attempts to identify the characteristics that distinguish professions from nonprofessions.[18] In this approach, the professional status of an occupation (or its absence) is seen as a dichotomy. The gradualistic approach, by contrast, sees occupations as being more or less professionalized along a continuum.[19] A third approach balances the first two by subdividing into several categories those occupations seeking to be recognized as professions: old established professions, new professions, semiprofessions, would-be professions, and marginal professions.[20]

To understand the status of the military as a profession and where it is situated along the continuum of professional occupations, we first consider how Goode's and others' criteria apply to the American military, and particularly to the American officer corps:

- The armed services set their own standards of education and *training* (1) for both officers and enlisted personnel.
- The American military has an extensive system of *continuing education* for

officers (2), requiring completion of specific courses and schools for advancement in rank.

- The right to command is based on receipt of an officer's commission (*licensure*, 3).
- Military boards determine whether to accept someone into officer programs, and whether to grant a commission (control of the profession's own *admissions and licensing*, 4). The military maintains considerable control over who enters its ranks, who is excluded, and who advances in rank.[21]
- The military plays a major role in shaping *legislation* (5) to be included in Title 10 of the U.S. Code, which deals with military personnel issues, although many other parties are also called to testify in congressional debates on such legislation.
- The military has been acknowledged as a major player in the American *power* structure (6), and the military has regularly been noted as one of the most respected American social institutions, even though a military career is not a path to great wealth in the United States.[22]
- A characteristic that distinguishes the military from other professions is autonomy, or *self-regulation* (7). The degree of independent practice characteristic of other professions has never characterized the military profession: structurally an agent of the state, the military is, at one level, under outside civilian control; indeed, the issue of how society controls its military has remained a central concern in the study of the military profession. On the other hand, the military, at least in the United States, has been exempted from control by the criminal and civil-law processes that bind other occupations (including the professions) and has been allowed to control itself, largely autonomously, through its own system of regulations, laws, and courts-martial. The broader judicial system has deferred to it on the basis of the functions that justify the existence of the profession: national security concerns.[23]
- Military officers tend to regard themselves as members of a brotherhood of arms that extends across services and even national boundaries (8, *identification* with the profession).
- The other main way in which the military differs from other professions is that it is not so likely to be a lifelong career or *terminal occupation* (9). While the established professions experience relatively low mobility out of the occupation, the American military shares with new professions, semi-

professions, would-be professions, and marginal professions a high rate of movement to other occupations.[24] The armed forces require only five years of service from graduates of their military academies, and the average length of service of all American military personnel is only about ten years.[25] One could argue, however, that this is because the military is a newer profession than medicine, law, or the clergy, and because the professional requirements of military service place a premium on youth over experience.

- *Political neutrality* (10), that is, impartiality and neutral service of the professions, is seen by some as an additional criterion of professions. Involvement in politics has become increasingly accepted in cases such as medicine and law. However, the control of the military over the legitimate use of organized violence as an agent of the state imposes an imperative to avoid partisanship.
- In the case of the military profession, internal *specialization* (11) can be seen in the organizational, cultural, and doctrinal differences between (and sometimes within) services.

Thus, the profession of arms, particularly as manifested by the American officer corps, reflects many of Goode's characteristics defining a profession. Changes in the enlisted ranks, in the use of reserve forces, and in the civilianization of previously military functions,[26] as well as changes in other professions, suggest that it is appropriate to examine whether the boundaries of "the military profession" should be expanded beyond officers to include, perhaps, senior noncommissioned officers and reserve officers.

Cold War Reconceptualization of the Military Profession

During the Cold War, Huntington's *The Soldier and the State* and Janowitz's *The Professional Soldier* reflected the empirical side of the sociology of professions early in the second half of the twentieth century, which involved case studies of specific occupations.[27] These two books shifted the focus of social science analysis of the military from the enlisted force to the officer corps.[28]

Interestingly, like Stouffer with *The American Soldier* and Moskos with *The American Enlisted Man,* both Huntington and Janowitz used singular nouns to identify their object of analysis.[29] This reflected their participation in the behavioral revolution in the social sciences. After World War II, both had been graduate students at the University of Chicago, Huntington in political science and Janowitz in sociology. Chicago had been one of the centers of the behavioral revolution.[30] Janowitz had written his doctoral dissertation after World War II, on the dynamics of prejudice, under the direction of psychoanalyst Bruno Bettelheim and was disposed to take the individual as his unit of analysis. Huntington's master's thesis was "The Politics of the Nonpartisan League," and he published a political-behavior paper based on it.[31] He was about to undertake a study of American voting behavior when Harvard, where he served on the faculty, hired V. O. Key, a prewar Chicago Ph.D. and arguably America's premier political behaviorist. As a result, Huntington had to identify a different intellectual domain for himself. He had written his doctoral dissertation on "clientalism," describing how federal agencies get co-opted by the industries they are supposed to regulate. In an era of increasing concern over the relationship between the military and industry, examination of how the state maintains control over its military force was not that far afield from Huntington's earlier interest.

Despite the titles of their books and their inclinations as behaviorists to see individuals as their units of analysis, neither Huntington nor Janowitz was primarily concerned with the individual American officer as a professional. Rather, they were both concerned with the occupation of officership as a profession. This somewhat subtle distinction was consequential. At the individual level, the adjective *professional* has multiple meanings. It may connote someone who performs an activity for money rather than another motivation—a professional athlete as compared to an amateur, for example. From this perspective, the mercenary would be the true military professional. It may connote a level of expertise or success at one's occupation, regardless of the legitimacy or social esteem of that occupation. Thus, one could be a professional thief.

This is not the sense in which the professional military has been analyzed. Rather, the object of analysis has been the profession of arms as an occupation that is designated by society to be a profession and is privileged by virtue of that designation. Society has historically identified particular occupations as professions because of the value and characteristics of those professions. Because the designation as a profession is socially valued, it has been sought by an ever-widening number of occupations.[32] Because it is bestowed on the military profession by the society that the military defends, it is an important thread in the fabric of civil-military relations. Thus, the focus of sociological studies of the military profession is not on how the military produces a professional officer but rather how society produces a professional military.

Huntington did not explicitly apply most of the characteristics of a profession specified by Goode and others, although most clearly did apply. He defined the military profession in terms of three specialized characteristics: responsibility, which was the basis of early formulations but overlooked by Goode; expertise, which subsumes Goode's first two characteristics (training and socialization), and corporateness, representing Goode's ninth characteristic (identification and affiliation). Expertise is the knowledge and skill specific to an occupation, requiring robust, historically grounded education and training. Liberal arts education, Huntington argued, forms the foundation of military expertise, followed by ongoing technical training staged to coincide with specific ranks and skill sets. The military professional's specialized area of expertise is, in Harold Lasswell's terminology, "the management of violence."[33] Military professionals must know how to execute and control the application of violence within a variety of unpredictable scenarios; thus, expertise is a never-ending professional pursuit. Indeed, military forces in Western democracies have for far longer had more extensive systems of continuing professional education than other traditional professions, which only recently established norms of continuing education, certification, and licensure.

Equipped with expertise, the professional military officer does not operate in an intellectual vacuum but must use knowledge within the framework of service to society. As an agent of the state, it is the officer's professional responsibility to serve when called upon. Service is provided not for monetary gain but as the fulfillment of a service ethic shaped by professional values and ideals. With violence and threat of violence as their primary tools, military professionals operate with oversight from the organization to which they are responsible: the state or, more specifically, its civilian leaders. A critical feature is that the military professional may utilize expert knowledge only at the state's discretion and never for personal benefit.

The standards of expertise and responsibility are enforced through the third specialized characteristic specified by Huntington: corporateness. Corporateness, or group unity, develops through shared training and educational experiences, common work obligations, and the profession's unique social responsibility. It provides cohesion within the ranks and is enforced through external bureaucratic management. Like the physician who is constrained by the hospital administrator, but more consequentially and for different reasons, the military profession is constrained by a process of civilian control manifested in management by elected and appointed government officials. And, like the medical profession, it must constantly wrestle with the issues of identifying which decisions should be based upon professional military expertise and which must be determined by a professional commitment to civilian control.

In *The Professional Soldier*, Janowitz accepts Huntington's basic premise that expertise, responsibility, and corporateness form the foundations of military professionalism. He agrees that professionalism requires the acquisition and refinement of skills through ongoing education and training. Ethics that guide military decision making and action are similarly reinforced through internal bureaucratic administration and institutional allegiance.

Despite these intellectual affinities, the ideas of Huntington and Janowitz differ on the proper application of military professionalism within the state, creating important distinctions within their overall definitions of military professionalism. On the issue of autonomy, Huntington's vision is that military professionalism must operate under "objective civilian control"—the formal lines of authority that make it an agent of the state—to achieve superior mission effectiveness. If subjective aims, such as political bias or individual political aspirations, were to dictate mission definition, this would compromise military autonomy and, thus, military effectiveness. By maximizing military professionalism, the soldier is trusted to fight wars without the compromises that would come from muddled civilian management of "purely military" decisions.

Rather than demarcate civilian and military spheres as incompatible, Janowitz, by contrast, argues that in a democracy soldiers should reflect the society they serve; thus, the military must represent society as well as the state and not be separated from it. With the global stage complicated by the increase in weapons of mass destruction, Janowitz sees the military developing into a constabulary force. In response to global changes, the military must be ready to act toward the goal of stable international relations rather than military victory. New technology, particularly the development of precision high-lethality weapons systems, commits the military to the use of minimum force in conflict resolution. Accompanying this change is both a narrowing of the skill gap between military and civilians and open recruitment so that the military reflects the diversity of the state. The military officer must merge the heroic-warrior identity with management responsibilities, developing a political ethos alongside its military expertise. In Janowitz's view, the military remains an independent force but does not hold as much autonomy or distance from politics as reflected in Huntington's objective civilian control. Indeed, political sensitivity becomes an important tool of the military professional.[34]

The End of the Mass Armed Force and the Redefinition of the Military Profession

Mobilization for the Vietnam War, achieved primarily through an increase in military conscription, focused the attention of social scientists again on the enlisted ranks.[35] However, opposition to the war crystallized into opposition to conscription and led to the end of the military draft in America. The volunteer force that replaced it, seen by many as an increasingly professional force, raised questions about whether the military profession was limited to the officer corps, as Huntington and Janowitz suggested, or whether there were conditions under which the enlisted ranks should be included in the profession of arms.[36] The reserve components of the American military had not been mobilized for the Vietnam War, in contrast to previous conflicts, and after the war they were defined as a strategic reserve for the newly conceived Total Force.[37] Thus, the role of the reserves did not figure into the post-Vietnam debate on the nature of the military profession.

Early in the All-Volunteer Force era, Charles Moskos, whose analyses had focused on the enlisted force, suggested three alternative models for understanding the direction in which the American military was moving. These were a *calling*, legitimated in terms of institutional values; a *profession*, legitimated in terms of specialized expertise; and an *occupation*, legitimated by the marketplace.[38] In using the label of profession, Moskos reflected the thinking of Huntington, Janowitz, and other analysts; he noted that the label is most commonly applied to the officer corps, that it is characterized not only by expertise but also by a level of autonomy and corporateness (manifested, said Moskos, in professional military associations), and that it usually connotes a commitment to a career—a characteristic that, as we have noted, is associated with the old professions, but does not characterize most American military personnel, or even most officers. Moskos noted as limitations of the applicability of the concept to the military the fact that relatively few officers remain in the military for a full career; that the label implies that soldiers who are not officers are not professional; and that the factors that he saw eroding the sense of military service as a calling, rooted in the end of military conscription, also eroded the professional nature of the military.

When Moskos, shortly thereafter, published what became the most frequently cited statement of his institutional and occupational models of the military, the professional model had disappeared from the typology, although he argued that "the military variant of professionalism historically has been consistent with the institutional model," citing Huntington and Janowitz.[39] As in subsequent statements of his institutional and occupational models, he appears to have conflated the individual level of analysis, the soldier as a professional or as an employee, with the organizational level—the military as an institution, a profession, or an occupation. He thus opened up the issue of whether "other ranks" (nonofficers) should be recognized as members of the military profession.[40] In response, Janowitz suggested that Moskos was hypothesizing a deprofessionalization of the military, "moving [it] from a profession . . . to an occupation." He argued that there was no basis for such a formulation: "To shift from a profession to an occupation the officer corps would have to undergo a number of changes which are most unlikely."[41] Janowitz was continuing to focus on officers as constituting the profession, but Moskos was at least raising the question of whether the professional boundaries should be expanded. This question remains central to the nature of the military profession today.

The discussion regarding the boundaries of the military profession encompasses the officer-enlisted dichotomy and also extends into the role of specialization, as reflected in the different missions of each service branch, or combat environment, such as submarine, surface warfare, or aviation in the Navy. George Kourvetaris and Betty Dobratz broaden this concept with a "pluralist" model that divides professions into subsegments based on occupational specialty.[42] In the medical profession, this would highlight differences between physicians and surgeons and, more specifically, between cardiologists and cardiothoracic surgeons.

This model, applied to the military, leads to examination of divisions based on military specializations and not the current distinction between commissioned officers and others. Including specialization in the definition of the profession of arms places boundaries around military specialties directly connected to combat arms, such as infantry, and would tend to exclude from the definition of profession those specialties such as support branches that usually operate further back from the conventional line of battle and that can often be outsourced to a civilian work force.[43] It raises the issue of how to classify military service members who are simultaneously members of other professions, such as attorneys, physicians, and clergy. Thus, the validity and usefulness of a single uniform paradigm of the military profession may no longer be useful.

Through his models, Moskos approaches the role of specialization within the broader context of civil-military relations.[44] His "convergent" model assumes a Janowitzian framework; the "divergent" model builds on Huntington's objective civilian control. His third formulation, the "segmented" military, is based on occupational specializations.[45] In this model, the military is viewed in subsegments that differ from one another in their convergence or divergence from civilian society. Divergent forces (Moskos uses the Marine Corps as his example) are those that cultivate the traditions and beliefs that separate the military from the state it serves. Convergent forces, exemplified for Moskos by the Air Force, share education and occupational functions with civilian institutions. Technology and growth in the spectrum of military missions will continue to foster such occupational specialization. The question becomes whether this will lead to two or more different militaries and, as a result, two or more different conceptions of the military profession.

The Military Profession Today

Current security demands place the All-Volunteer Force in a historically unique position that has significant implications for the military profession. In the period following World War II, the growing institutional presence of the armed forces gave rise to the officer-centered discussion of the military profession opened by Huntington and Janowitz. The post–Vietnam War era, coupled with the implementation of the All-Volunteer Force, shaped Moskos's institutional-occupational model and opened the discussion of expansion of professional boundaries. Current counterterrorism operations and utilization of the Total Force, including reserves and civilians, require an updated discussion of the military profession beyond the officer-centric and occupational focus of past research. Specifically, the definition of who is considered to be part of the profession of arms may need to be broadened beyond active-duty commissioned officers, potentially to include reserve commissioned officers as well as active-duty and reserve senior noncommissioned officers.

The boundaries of the profession are consequential because society privileges people who are regarded as members, and expansions would affect such privilege. Huntington's work serves as the starting point for our discussions of expansion and of the present and future direction of the military profession.

Senior Noncommissioned Officers

We examine in this section whether it is appropriate to extend Huntington's conceptualization of the profession, which, although fundamental to this discussion, is dated in its narrow focus on the commissioned officer. In *The Soldier and the State*, Huntington wrote this now-controversial statement: "The enlisted men subordinate to the officer corps are a part of the organizational bureaucracy but not of the professional bureaucracy. The enlisted personnel have neither the intellectual skills nor the professional responsibility of the officer."[46] With a conscription-era force as his model, Huntington viewed enlisted draftees as short-term specialists with limited responsibilities; in contrast, officers are trained as experts responsible for directing violence. He envisioned enlisted personnel and officers as belonging to separate entities with distinct organizational vocations and hierarchies. Officers embodied military professionalism through the occupational characteristics of expertise, responsibility, and corporateness. These characteristics, as defining features of the nature of the profession, continue in today's officer, but they also, we argue, extend to today's senior noncommissioned officer corps: those at or above the ranks of sergeant first class in the Army, gunnery sergeant in the Marine Corps, master sergeant in the Air Force, and chief petty officer in the Navy.

Past literature on the military profession may not have recognized the professional standing of these noncommissioned officers, but this is not to say that the military institution holds the same viewpoint. Even as the sociology of professions waned, the military's reconceptualization and development of the profession of arms began to acknowledge the prestige and knowledge of noncommissioned officers. The demands of staffing a technologically complex All-Volunteer Force linked retention of enlisted personnel to readiness, demonstrating the military's reliance on the expertise of noncommissioned officers. The education of noncommissioned officers reflects this transformation: schoolhouse curricula now include specific readings and discussions about military professionalism as applicable to the noncommissioned officer corps. The skills taught in noncommissioned officer academies extend beyond technical specialization to include conceptual knowledge such as leadership and international affairs. The noncommissioned officer creed makes explicit the importance of expertise: "I will remain tactically and technically proficient."[47]

In addition to the transformation of noncommissioned officer education within military-run academies, expectations have also increased regarding off-duty educational attainment. More than 50 percent of the most senior enlisted personnel now hold associate's degrees.[48] As most enlisted personnel join the armed forces with only a high school degree, it is clear that the increase in educational attainment occurs during uniformed service. Higher education is not a direct requirement for promotion within the service branches, but it does play a role in promotion rates; higher-educated personnel have an edge over their similarly qualified counterparts lacking higher education.[49]

Levels of higher education within the enlisted corps are not equal to the educational levels of officers; this educational disparity is one of the differences be-tween officer and enlisted accessions. Commissioned officers, although having less postcollegiate professional education before entering their profession than do physicians or attorneys, are a highly educated force: approximately 92 percent come into the service with bachelor's degrees and 15 percent with advanced de-grees.[50] Twenty-three percent of active-duty commissioned officers obtain ad-vanced degrees while in the service. The higher educational attainment of offi-cers supports Huntington's focus on expertise, particularly in his call for a liberal arts foundation. Huntington also acknowledges the importance of ongoing tech-nical training for development of occupationally specific knowledge and skills. Though educational attainment levels differ, it is nevertheless now reasonable to say that both commissioned and senior noncommissioned officers fulfill the ex-pertise requirement of military professionalism.

To justify extending Huntington's definition of military professionalism to senior noncommissioned officers, the nonquantifiable characteristics of respon-sibility and corporateness must also be addressed. Society privileges certain oc-cupations as professions based on the perceived values and characteristics of that profession. In March 2005, for example, 87 percent of Americans polled had fa-vorable opinions of the military; this proportion remained virtually unchanged in 2007 (84 percent).[51] Military professionalism reflects this distinction through its privileged capacity to manage and use violence in service to the state. Huntington describes officers as the executors of violence and enlisted personnel as auxiliary specialists. He states that the "management of violence" distinction applies to all officers regardless of their air, land, or sea affiliation, although he acknowledges that different forms of application lead to "subprofessional specialization."[52]

Huntington distinguishes between levels of responsibility: large, complex execu-tions of violence mark an officer with high professional competence, whereas an officer in charge of an infantry squad has lower professional responsibility. To Hunt-ington, however, differences in scope do not alter the overall professional criterion of managing personnel and equipment to accomplish a purpose using a violent means. Thus, we argue, his inclusion of small-group leaders within the definition of a profession opens the door to similar inclusion of noncommissioned officers re-sponsible for leading squad- and platoon-level organizations. This activity has be-come more important in twenty-first-century military operations, which are usu-ally small-unit operations in which a noncommissioned officer is the senior U.S. authority on the ground, making rapid decisions regarding the utilization of force.

Corporateness, which is defined as group unity, develops through common experiences, obligations, and the profession's unique responsibility to manage violence. Huntington defined corporateness as cohesion; Moskos pushed this interpretation to include the physical manifestation of professional military associations.[53] Regardless of which definition is used, senior noncommissioned officers are often cited as the "backbone" of the military, critical to mission success.[54] This suggests that senior noncommissioned officers display sufficient "corporateness" to fit within the definition.

The Reserve Components

The role of the reserve components, too, has evolved to include the characteristics of military professionalism. The reserves have played a significant role in all major American conflicts of the twentieth century, with the exception of the Vietnam War. The establishment of a standing military after World War II led to the subsequent development of the reserve components as an expansion base for global conflicts. After World War II and Korea,[55] the reserves constituted a "strategic force," and they were rarely called upon to serve alongside their active-duty counterparts.[56] They were not mobilized in large numbers for overseas combat duty during the Vietnam War. Treated as "weekend warriors," reserve units were not funded or equipped at levels comparable to active-duty units because they were not used regularly in operational missions.[57]

Things began to change in the 1990s. Reserve units were activated for Operation Desert Storm, although no combat brigades actually participated in the conflict because of its short duration.[58] In the mid-1990s, the military deployed reserve personnel overseas as part of the American contingent to the Multinational Force and Observers in the Sinai Desert in support of the Camp David accords.[59] Reserve success in that operation led to increased use of reserve personnel for contingency operations such as Bosnia.[60] These involved small proportions of overall personnel deployed and were generally limited to six months.[61]

Operations Iraqi Freedom and Enduring Freedom established the reserve component as an operational force critical to continuous operations. In mid-2008 reserve forces constitute 40 to 50 percent of American military personnel serving in the area of responsibility for counterterrorism operations.[62] The military now stresses continued reliance on the reserve component and the importance of incorporating it as a full operational partner.[63] The Army, for example, states that full integration of reserve units with their active-duty counterparts is critical for mission success. The Army has institutionalized this paradigm shift by recasting the reserve component as an equal-partner operational force through its Army Force Generation Model (ARFORGEN), which guides preparation and deployment of both active and reserve brigade combat teams for global missions.[64] To accomplish this, Army and civilian leadership must structure, equip, train, staff, and resource reserve units at full and equal levels.[65] This involves reciprocal relationships of active-duty and reserve personnel where skill sets are developed and exchanged equally. For example, drill sergeants within the Army are predominantly reservists.[66] On the basis of current doctrine and strategy, the reserve component will continue in its role as operational partner; the reserve is no longer just a strategic force.

As full partners within operational missions, the reserve components merit recognition as members of the profession of arms. Regardless of active-duty or reserve status, officers, both commissioned and noncommissioned, must undergo rigorous professional development through general military education and specific occupations. Compared to their active-duty counterparts, reserve leaders carry equal responsibility in managing violence and are equally accountable for the safety of their personnel. Reserve personnel experience less geographic mobility than active-duty members, and so they develop greater corporate identities based both on military professionalism and their geographic affiliations.

Profession or Semiprofession?

The discussion of whether senior noncommissioned officers and reserve commissioned and senior noncommissioned officers should be included within the profession of arms does not require a dichotomous approach. As Reiss showed, it can be useful to view the profession of arms as a continuum of characteristics and designations. Commissioned officers represent the old, established profession of arms in the tradition examined by Huntington and Janowitz. However, it could be argued that company-grade officers, who are at the beginning of their service, should be regarded as the equivalent of medical interns or residents, not yet having the expertise or commitment to a career that is required to be counted as full members of the military profession. However, current operational demands and the amount of responsibility carried by company-grade officers as they make tactical decisions at the small-unit level suggest that they should be included within the boundaries of the military profession. Similarly, some might argue that only senior commanding officers working within the combat arms truly carry the responsibility for managing strategic violence and thus embody the characteristic of responsibility. Once again, however, current operations challenge this interpretation of military professionalism, as specialties outside the combat arms, such as intelligence and logistics, shape the battlefield through their actions; indeed, many personnel outside the combat arms of the services, such as convoy truck drivers in Iraq, are frequently called upon to engage in infantry operations.

The same questions also arise about senior noncommissioned officers. If they are to be included within the profession of arms, should they be considered part of the old, established profession, or do they constitute something new? Senior noncommissioned officers are the experts in their occupational specialty; however, they also have responsibilities regarding personnel and equipment that extend beyond the limits of most occupations. Thus, they may well be said to fit within a category of "semiprofession," as Reiss defines it: occupations that "replace theoretical study of a field of learning by the acquisition of precise technical skill."[67]

Conclusion

In the middle of the twentieth century, as American sociology was increasingly focusing on those occupations that are privileged by society because they are identified as professions, Huntington played a key role in reorienting analyses of the American military from a concern with conscripts to include research on the profession of arms, then identified as the officer corps, and a concern with civil-military relations. Although he did not focus on the full range of characteristics used to identify the professions by the sociological literature, his analyses, and the military institution itself, were compatible with case studies of other professions of the time. As a result, the research agenda of military studies was dramatically altered.

The analysis of what constitutes a profession altered during that period and in subsequent years. In the context of these changes, it is reasonable to ask whether the boundaries of military professionalism extend beyond Huntington's focus on active-duty commissioned officers and what the consequences might be of such an expansion.

From the outset, the American military differed from other traditional professions: it was always being practiced in a bureaucratic setting, was composed of people who did not all have a lifelong commitment to their occupation, had its autonomy constrained by responsibility to extraprofessional (state) authority, and was explicitly politically neutral. Since Huntington wrote, other professions have become increasingly bureaucratized, their autonomy has been challenged by extraprofessional criteria and judgments, and other occupations have begun to intrude upon their traditional areas of professional jurisdiction. Thus, there has been some convergence among professions.

Moskos introduced into the debate the issue of what role enlisted personnel play in the military profession. Clearly many senior noncommissioned officers have made career commitments to the military and have participated in a process of continuing professional education, while many junior officers have not made a career commitment and have only minimal postcollegiate professional education.[68] Judgments must be made about the point at which officers are full members of the profession of arms, and whether noncommissioned officers constitute members of the same profession, a different profession, or a semiprofession within a community of common professional practice.

The recent transformation of the reserve component from a strategic force to an operational force raises the question of whether personnel in these forces are full members of the profession, even though their primary employment is in another sector of the economy. Like their active-duty counterparts, reserve commissioned officers and senior noncommissioned officers carry equal responsibility in managing violence. We argue that they merit equal recognition within the profession of arms.

Even more interesting is the increasing presence of civilians, both civil servants and contractor personnel, in combat theaters. The conflict in Iraq has as many civilian contract personnel as uniformed military personnel in the combat theater.[69] If specific "professional" expertise is shared between military personnel and civilians, are the civilians in the same profession (or professional community) as the military personnel?[70] This has consequences in terms of the self-regulation of the profession. For example, does the Uniform Code of Military Justice or the international law of armed conflict extend to civilians, whether Department of Defense employees or contract personnel?[71] It also has consequences in terms of the nature of a military career. For example, a Defense Science Board task force recently recommended that the boundary between active service, reserve service, and service as a civilian employee of the military departments be made more permeable, so that personnel could, over time, move among these components, in a career of service to national security but in a variety of roles.[72] This would open up the possibility of more people serving a full career in this arena and changes in the norms that govern civil-military relations.

We believe that the broader the definition of who constitutes the profession, in the views both of society and of military personnel themselves, the greater the likelihood that the behavior of the force will meet the professional standards to which it is held, and the more effective the military will be.

CHAPTER ELEVEN

Militaries and Political Activity in Democracies

Risa A. Brooks

When individuals join the armed forces, they commit to act in service of the country as a whole and to forgo political activity. Military personnel are charged with protecting the security of the country and with performing their functional responsibilities with efficiency, commitment, and skill. Officers are socialized to believe that the world of politics is exclusively a civilian arena. Most officers in democratic states might find it uncomfortable, or at least unusual, to discuss their military establishment's "political" activities.

Yet historically in many democracies, including the United States, we find many instances in which military officers and their organizations have engaged in activities that are indisputably political. Whether self-consciously or not, but always with the intent to influence policy outcomes, officers have adopted particular positions on issues and have employed a variety of tactics to increase public exposure of their views. Some observers might assert that these activities are natural, or perhaps inevitable, for any large organization or profession like the military, especially when significant resources, informational complexities, and stakes are involved.

Other than a few early studies that sought to conceptualize the military's political power on a continuum, remarkably little time has been spent reflecting systematically on these political activities or their implications.[1] This may be due, in part, to the significant normative influence of Huntington's *The Soldier and the State,* especially within the United States.[2] Huntington argued that political activity by militaries was harmful for a country's military security. Such activity was associated with a form of relations between military and political leaders—what he called subjective control—that entailed a trade-off between controlling the military establishment and ensuring its effectiveness in war. Huntington advocated an alternative model—objective control—with a division of authority whereby military leaders would concentrate on the art and science of "managing violence" and would abstain from participation in civilian politics. Today, the culture of the officer corps of the United States military is infused with these ideas; they are mirrored in the Uniform Code of Military Justice and Defense Department regulations, which prohibit partisan activity and proscribe openly political behavior.[3] These normative and legal constraints may explain why political activity by military leaders and organizations in democracies, which Huntington argues are inconsistent with appropriate norms of professional behavior, get little attention in the practical and scholarly literature on civil-military relations.[4]

Nevertheless, despite the dearth of analysis, the phenomenon of officers who engage in political behavior is increasingly salient in the United States. Recent years have seen many high-profile incidents capturing headlines. Among these are the controversies associated with Admiral William Fallon's March 2008 resignation as head of Central Command after he expressed publicly skepticism at Bush administration policy toward Iran;[5] the outspoken criticism of the management style and errors in judgment of Secretary of Defense Donald Rumsfeld by six prominent retired military leaders in April 2006;[6] and the congressional testimony of Chief of Staff of the Army General Eric Shinseki in spring 2003 that contradicted standing Bush administration views on the second Iraq war.[7]

These controversies capture attention because they speak to debates about appropriate norms of behavior by active and retired officers in expressing their private views in public forums. Yet underlying the debate are also profound concerns about how we can best safeguard the security of the United States, and what role military leaders should play in ensuring that the country adopts sound political-military strategies. In short, these events and the associated controversies raise an important question: does political activity by officers harm or help U.S. national security?

Perhaps the first place we might turn for an answer to this question is *The Sol-*

dier and the State. Indeed, Huntington's book implies a clear answer to the question: political activity, because it harms professionalism, is detrimental to military security. It involves military officers in debates about policy issues, undermines meritocratic norms, and thereby compromises military members' technical-tactical skill and effectiveness in the "management of violence."

Huntington raises an important point about the impact of political activity on professionalism and military skill. However, his book is less than satisfying in evaluating the full implications of how the military's political activity influences national security; he misses several critical considerations essential to any contemporary debate about the issues. For example, while he was fundamentally correct in pointing out some potentially damaging effects of political activity, he neglected possible positive effects. Especially on issues related to military strategy and policy, political activity is not intrinsically harmful, and in certain forms it can, in fact, benefit the United States. Given the significant information asymmetries between citizens and their political leaders, military leaders are important sources of expertise whose contributions can further debate about security issues. Through their political activities, they can signal efforts by civilian defense authorities to promote bureaucratic and other policy change, spurring investment in search and analysis in those proposals. By helping set the agenda and creating an audience or a forum for individuals who have new ideas, such political activity can also facilitate innovation in intraorganizational processes and in force development. The lesson here is clear: political activity by military leaders can at times benefit U.S. national security by generating better-informed and considered military strategy, plans, and defense policy.

Yet the debate and discussion about the issues should not end there. Several underappreciated complications may also arise when military officers and leaders engage in political activity. One is that any consensus about the appropriate use of political tactics is complicated by disagreement over the ends to which those tactics may be put: what may appear normatively acceptable in one context may not be perceived that way in another. Hence, the "principle" of what is appropriate behavior by military leaders is frequently redefined, depending on the political setting in which it occurs. Moreover, the potential benefits of a military member's political activities hinge on its leaders' capacity to inject needed information into the public sphere, but this role can be problematic in the United States or other places where military leaders have substantial latent political influence in the polity, because of the substantial social esteem their organizations enjoy.

With these complications also come costs and risks. When military leaders engage in political activity, it can harm the organizational interests of the military as a whole because citizens may increasingly view the entity as cynically as they see other public institutions. Political activity also threatens strategic assessment at the civil-military nexus by undermining trust between political and military leaders. Even more important, it complicates the capacity of elected political leaders to execute their constitutionally mandated roles as the final decision makers about military and security issues, potentially prompting them to conciliate military opinion, whether or not that opinion deserves consideration and benefits the country, rather than face generals and admirals mobilizing against their policies.

How are we to assess these pluses and minuses of political activity by military officers? Ultimately, I conclude that the negatives outweigh the positives. Evaluated against the potential benefits for strategy during a particular international event should be the cumulative, long-term complications, costs, and risks, as well as the corrosive effects on principles of civil-military relations and democratic practice that political activities invite. For these reasons, I argue that political activity by both serving and retired officers should be discouraged across the board. This conclusion may resonate well with existing norms of civil-military relations in the United States (in theory, if not always in practice). Indeed, it may strike some as a reiteration of conventional wisdom. Yet the goal of this essay is not just to offer a recommendation but, by making explicit the costs and benefits of political activity, to yield a better informed debate. Moreover, for any recommendation against officers engaging in political activity to wield influence, we must more openly and explicitly acknowledge—*and we must ultimately accept*—the risks and costs that come with it: if military officers and their leaders forgo political activity, it may mean that the United States sometimes pursues more risky and less well-conceived military actions abroad than had those officers engaged in more forceful and explicit efforts to shape public debate about the issues. This is a price we must pay, I argue, to maintain healthy civil-military relations in the long run.

I begin this chapter with a brief overview of Huntington's notion of objective and subjective control and the linkages he posits with military security. I then introduce a typology of different political tactics that militaries employ in the United States and other democratic states. I analyze the implications of those tactics, highlighting some of their benefits for policy and strategy. I also point out some particular complications, costs, and risks to consider as we analyze the implications of political activity by military officers. I close the chapter with my conclusions in which I advocate that military officers refrain from engaging in political activity.

Subjective and Objective Control

The view that political activity by militaries is to be avoided is widely held in democratic states, especially in the United States. This view, at least in the modern era, is due at least in part to Huntington. Among his central contributions, he proposed two alternative conceptions about how the military might be "controlled" by its civilian overseers—that is, how civilians could solve the dilemma of maintaining a powerful armed force to protect the state from external adversaries, while keeping the republic itself safe from forcible meddling by those holding the guns. In what Huntington called objective control, the military operates within its own defined sphere, with significant autonomy in the tasks essential to preparing for and conducting military operations, whereas its role in politics is sharply circumscribed. Politicians have the power to debate and authorize the use of force and then can hand off the execution of those decisions to military authorities. The division of labor implied by objective control is sustained by the military's professionalism: military leaders refrain from intervening in politics and focus on issues within the realm of their professional expertise. This focus allows them to hone the technical and tactical skills essential to war fighting. Objective control is advantageous, from this perspective, because it both protects the republic from a military coup and ensures its military security.

The other approach, subjective control, entails "civilianizing" the military, such that the military is identified closely with the values of the civilian group holding power in the state. It presumes that the military is intimately involved in politics and that affiliation and identification with civilian authorities keep its officers politically quiescent and disinclined to engage in military takeovers. Absent, in this approach, is the clear division of labor between politics and specialization in the military arts. A central problem intrinsic to subjective control for Huntington— and the reason he considered it inferior—was that it required a compromise between the goals of insulating the state from internal military interventions and the goals of protecting its military security externally. Within the model of subjective control, he argued that "intensified security threats result in increased military imperatives against which it becomes more difficult to assert civilian power. The steps necessary to achieve military security are thus viewed as undermining civilian control. On the other hand, the effort to enhance civilian control in the subjective sense frequently undermined military security."[8]

Subjective control—or the military's enmeshment in political life—undermines military security. Although Huntington did not explicitly define the meaning of military security, his usage of the term suggests that he meant the capacity of the state to protect itself from external challenges. He referred frequently to the importance of safeguarding military efficiency or skill, implicitly because this helps promote military security, noting that "a military specialist is an officer who is peculiarly expert at directing the application of violence under certain prescribed conditions." By implication, the absence of that professionalism, and of the conditions of objective control that support it, are bad for security of the state.

Political Strategies of the Military in a Democracy

Before investigating the potential implications of political activity for military activity, it is essential first to lay out what this might entail. The idea of militaries engaging in politics might bring to mind military coups or interventions in domestic politics. This is one extreme form of activity, but focusing on an extreme obscures the diversity of political activities in which militaries do engage without ever overtly challenging the rights of civilians to govern. In fact, the military's political power and its activities operate on continuum.[9] Even where civilian control is assured, militaries can be political, employing a variety of tactics (see table 11.1).

Among these tactics are what I term *public appeals*—military leaders' use of statements or opinion-laden commentary to convey information to the public about a government's strategic or policy choices and its judgments about them. This may involve interviews with the print and news media, speeches, or leaks to the media. Two things distinguish a public appeal, in the sense that I use the term, from the regular dissemination of information about military affairs: the scope and nature of the commentary, and the public nature of the appeal. For example, a military news briefing might involve a statement of expected costs, risks, and benefits of military options and alternatives; a public appeal, however, also attaches a value judgment about how to weigh those risks, costs, and benefits and hence, implicitly or explicitly, conveys support for or opposition to a policy alternative.

Among the most colorful, historical cases of a military leader resorting to public appeals to influence civilian policy choices occurred in the post–World War I era, when Army Brigadier General William (Billy) Mitchell launched major publicity campaigns in favor of establishing a large, independent air force. Mitchell often gave interviews and authored articles and editorials on air power.[10] In these articles, Mitchell regularly criticized the Navy and War Departments, going so far as to publicly accuse the Navy Department of fraud in the test air bombing of the naval ship, the *Ostfriesland*.[11]

Table 11.1.   Political Activities of the Military

Tactic	Nature of activity	Audience	Examples
Public appeal	Public, value-laden commentary	Mass public	Colin Powell's 1992 statements on intervention in Bosnia
Grandstanding	Threat or actual resignation in protest of policy	Mass public; Congress; executive branch	Hypothetical: if Eric Shinseki had resigned in 2003
Politicking	Retired officer endorsements; organizing vote drives	Mass public	Crowe's endorsement of Clinton in 1992; Franks's endorsement of Bush in 2004
Alliance building	Military leaders form ties with civilian interest groups	Congress	Air Force and Lockheed-Martin alliance over procurement of F-22 Raptor
Shoulder tapping	Military leaders setting an agenda by bringing issues to attention of politicians and engaging in lobbying-like activities on behalf of those issues	Congress	Military mobilization of key members of Congress over gays in the military in early 1990s

General David Petraeus has recounted a number of instances in the mid-1980s in which military leaders used speeches, as well as interviews, to specify requirements for using force in Central America. He also cites a widely publicized graduation address at the Naval Academy, in which a chief of naval operations outlined his views on the conditions under which it would be appropriate to use military force to retaliate against terrorism.[12] In June 2001, when Bush administration officials announced they would end bombing exercises on the Puerto Rican island of Vieques in 2003, senior Navy and Marine officials used such terms as "outrage," "sold out," and "betrayal" to describe the decision in interviews, thus going public with news of their opposition to the Bush administration's political decision.[13]

Activities of Chairman of the Joint Chiefs of Staff Colin Powell in the early 1990s provide a more recent example of public appeals. He granted an interview to the *New York Times* and authored an article in *Foreign Affairs* in which he publicly stated his reluctance to intervene in Bosnia.[14] Powell, an extremely popular military leader, made his comments during the 1992 presidential election season, while one of the candidates, Bill Clinton, was advocating greater involvement in Bosnia. Many analysts, even those who agreed with Powell's strategic view, were alarmed by the public advocacy of his views.[15]

Within the notion of a public appeal I do not include one important activity— some might say obligation—of military leaders: to speak out forthrightly within the corridors of the Pentagon and executive offices about their views on military issues. This private dialogue does not invite the public as an audience. Moreover, some activities fall in a gray area: an example is congressional testimony by senior military leaders. Although this testimony is necessarily public and therefore might be considered in the category of public appeals, we must also look at the qualitative nature of the statements offered. All testimony is going to be at least somewhat value laden; this is inherent in any reporting process. Yet some testimony can look less like responses to questions from Congress and more like a public appeal if it involves such characteristics as the selective presentation of facts, self-censoring of one's statements to support or to undermine an administration's position or congressional opinion, or failure to distinguish opinions and conjectures based on uncertain premises from those based on established facts. Responses to explicit questions that are forthcoming and not shaped to support a preexisting policy are less likely to constitute public appeals. Eric Shinseki's February 2003 congressional testimony about the Iraq war is thus not what I would term a public appeal.

A second tactic, which I label *grandstanding*, involves a senior military leader's threat to resign when a major policy initiative is in dispute. A threat is grandstanding when the dispute is well publicized, and the senior officer involved is well regarded and is directly affected by the policy decision. Resignation, in this context, is the military equivalent of a vote of no confidence in the political leadership. It is meant to send a signal to the opposition and the public that the political leadership is pursuing what the military leader perceives to be inappropriate or ineffective military policies. Resignation is a political act in the following sense: faced with the threat of resignation of an esteemed military officer, a political leader may be forced to retreat from a policy not because of a change in his or her convictions about the merits of the policy but because the resignation by a senior officer compromises domestic support, mobilizes the opposition, and makes it politically difficult to maintain the policy, regardless of its merits.

Not all military leaders perceive resignation as grandstanding and, when done quietly, without public commentary about the controversy or media attention, resignation may have few political ramifications.[16] Many have interpreted H. R.

McMaster's book *Dereliction of Duty* (popular among military officers) to claim that military leaders have a moral responsibility to resign if politicians pursue policies they believe will put the country at risk.[17] Such an interpretation has, however, been greeted by civilian analysts with significant apprehension.[18] Feaver and Kohn caution that "resignation accompanied by protest . . . give[s] a whip to the military ('do it our way or else')."[19] In other words, although military leaders may perceive resignation as a personal act of conscience or of frustration, it can also be a political act.[20]

A third set of political behaviors we might place under the category of *politicking*. Conventional wisdom associates a military's overt participation in leadership politics with the autocratic states of the Third World. Consolidated democracy, by contrast, demands an apolitical officer corps in order to secure civilian supremacy over the military. In democracies, there are substantial checks against the military's overt participation in politics. In the United States, for example, officers and enlisted personnel are explicitly prohibited from participating in campaigns and engaging in partisan activity.[21] The Uniform Code of Military Justice also prohibits speaking contemptuous words against the commander in chief, members of Congress, and the secretary of defense. The strict enforcement of these policies perpetuates norms of nonpartisanship and civilian supremacy.[22]

Military leaders may nonetheless at times play an influential role in leadership politics in democratic states, with influence achieved not through the threat of force but through the collective power of military personnel at the ballot box. Military influence in electoral politics has two principal dimensions. First, it involves the indirect or "structural" power of the military in elections, which is largely the result of the size of the military, its reach into the community, the number of veterans in the electorate, and veterans' membership in veterans' organizations.[23]

Second, politicking may involve open support for candidates and efforts to influence election outcomes through retired officers' endorsements and public statements of support, especially by prominent and senior former military officers. Such endorsements have become increasingly common in the past several elections in the United States, beginning, by one observer's estimation, with the 1988 Bush-Dukakis presidential race.[24] For example in 1992, two years after her retirement, Brigadier General Gail Reals (who had been the first woman selected for promotion to that position in the Marine Corps) publicly endorsed Bill Clinton for president, along with twenty other retired senior military officers.[25] Among the other Clinton endorsements in 1992 was that of William J. Crowe, a former chairman of the Joint Chiefs. In the 2000 election season, the George W.

Bush campaign was able to claim numerous endorsements by senior officers, including those who had served in influential positions during the Clinton-Gore administration, a fact the Bush administration publicized.[26] More than a dozen prominent generals and admirals signed a statement endorsing George W. Bush in the 2000 election season.[27] Recently retired commandant of the Marine Corps Charles C. Krulak, who had served during the Clinton administration, organized "Veterans for Bush-Cheney." In the 2004 elections, both John Kerry and George Bush courted retired officers for support.[28] Twelve retired generals and admirals endorsed Kerry at the Democratic national convention. Among the endorsements Bush received at the Republican national convention was that of recently retired General Tommy Franks.[29] So pervasive was the practice that one newspaper warned that the election race "could become a war of the generals."[30]

Some observers might contend that endorsing a political candidate is the prerogative of every citizen, to which retired military officers are entitled as much as their civilian counterparts. This raises an important issue about how the political activities of retired military leaders bear on the military organization as a whole. Certainly a leader who retires is released from the legal and regulatory constraints that limit serving officers' participation in partisan politics: the individual enjoys the rights of every citizen, including the prerogative to campaign on behalf of a favored candidate. Krulak, for example, defended his actions in the Bush-Cheney campaign on the grounds that, as a retired officer, he had the right to express his political preferences just like every other citizen.[31]

Such a view neglects two critical considerations. First, some military endorsements matter precisely because they are made by prominent, recently serving officers; hence, to argue that the retired officer is just exercising his or her rights in campaigning for a candidate neglects the fact that those efforts particularly matter—are publicized and have extra influence—because the person served in the military. It is hard to imagine that "citizen Krulak" would have captured the same publicity had his military career been unknown to the media and public. Second, these individuals may be perceived as speaking on behalf of some broader constituency in the military: by endorsing a candidate, they create the impression not just that the individual officer favors this candidate but that the military, or some significant subsection thereof, does as well.[32] These endorsements send powerful signals to active-duty military personnel suggesting how to cast their votes. Former assistant commandant of the Marines General Richard Neal put it this way: generals and admirals "are mentors, they're former role models, they represent the institution from which they came. [And] they still have significant impact on the uniformed military."[33] In fact, one could argue that this is precisely why these endorsements are so prized by the candidates who receive them.

In short, to say that these partisan activities by retired officers are legally appropriate is accurate; however, it would be inaccurate, at best, to deny at least their potential import as political activities that bear on the military organization as a whole, and they should be carefully weighed in that light.

Alliance building, a fourth tactic, refers to efforts by the military services and leaders to court civilian groups and constituencies, as a way of indirectly leveraging their influence in policy processes. These activities vary in the degree to which they target specific audiences or focus attention on specific issues. It seems reasonable to expect some general public relations activities by military establishments; to what degree these acts are "political" is debatable. For example, all the U.S. services engage in activities designed to familiarize military families and citizens at large with military life and facilities; the Navy allows citizens to tour its vessels when they are in port during "Fleet Week."

More significant are cases in which the military services target civilian "influentials" in politics, public life, or private industry as part of efforts to influence civilian opinion and attitudes through visits to ships and bases. These activities verge on the inappropriate if, as Vice Admiral John Shanahan suggests, they are targeted "specifically to some elite group of organizations as say a payback or an award for services rendered, or to gain support for the budget, the bottom line of the budget, or for a specific weapons system."[34] In 2000, for example, the U.S. Navy's Pacific Fleet allowed upwards of 8,000 civilians on trips aboard its vessels.[35] Many of these were people with actual or potential political or social influence, not just ordinary citizens.[36]

Among the more powerful civilian partners available to the military are defense industry officials. The growth of the U.S. arms industry in the latter part of the twentieth century has created a natural civilian ally for the military. The Pentagon and civilian defense industries regularly team up to promote weapons programs.[37] The target audience is usually Congress; anxious to protect jobs and local economies, its members are susceptible to the military's lobbying tactics. These alliances—what some have called an "iron triangle" of influence in defense policymaking—can be formidable.[38]

A fifth tactic I label *shoulder tapping.* Shoulder tapping refers to activities by military leaders taking the initiative to seek support for a policy from members of the country's legislative branch. Some military-legislative interactions are not shoulder tapping: military personnel may be called upon to consult with members of the legislature and, in the United States, this is constitutionally mandated. Accordingly, all the U.S. service branches, as well as the Joint Chiefs, maintain legislative affairs offices charged with overseeing consultation with members of Congress.[39] These offices provide information and expertise about issues of concern to the services and their civilian overseers. Most of this activity is not what I would call shoulder tapping.

At some point, however, liaison activities cross the line into advocating on behalf of a particular policy. It is more likely to look like advocacy when military leaders "volunteer" information through informal contacts with legislators than when they are explicitly asked for data or when they fulfill their constitutional duty of speaking forthrightly in congressional testimony.

There is evidence of shoulder tapping when the military takes the initiative in framing an issue for Congress, in a pattern some might call agenda setting. Take, for example, the military's efforts to promote congressional mobilization against ending the ban on homosexuals openly serving in the armed forces that began soon after Clinton's announcement in July 1992 (before the November presidential election) of his intention to change the policy. Opposition from Congress was muted at first, and little was heard in the campaign season, but the controversy exploded in late January 1993. Senator Sam Nunn, then chairman of the Senate Armed Services Committee, began to organize opposition to ending the ban in close collaboration with Pentagon officials. By mid-January 1993 military personnel had taken highly visible stands in opposition to changing the ban. Right after the presidential election, Pentagon officials began to report to the press the "nearly wholesale resistance among the military brass," to changing the policy. In the days after Clinton's inauguration, the service chiefs were so aggressive in stating their opposition to the policy that some Pentagon aides suggested that it bordered on insubordination. During this time, a fifteen-minute video titled *The Gay Agenda* was circulated among members of Congress by active-duty military personnel. The Marine spokesman confirmed in January 1993 that the commandant of the Marine Corps, General Carl Mundy Jr., had also distributed copies to other members of the Joint Chiefs of Staff. The Marines, as one former Pentagon official put it, "are passing [the video] out like popcorn."[40]

Positive Implications for Military Policy and Strategy

All five of these political tactics clearly contradict the tenets of objective control. In each, military leaders and their organizations are expressing clear preferences about policy and other issues, and they take initiatives and employ tactics to ensure that the public and special constituencies are aware of their views on these issues. In such cases, militaries are behaving like political actors, contrary to Huntington's normative prescriptions for military professionalism. For that reason, we might be inclined to conclude they are wholly inappropriate and look no further, but this leaves unanswered the question of whether, or when, there might be certain advantages to the public or the polity of having militaries engage in political behavior. Here I outline three effects of the military's political activities and how they affect policy and strategy.

The Expertise Effect

Military officers can help offset the significant information asymmetry between citizens and politicians in evaluating military activity. They may do so by means of tactics that are associated with public appeals, as I define the term previously, such as public commentary and back-channel leaks to the press that contain judgments about military strategy and policy options. They can also foster better analysis of military strategy and other dimensions of military activity and their integration with political goals.[41] Military leaders can supply essential expertise in wartime about the merits of alternative strategies and war plans. In peacetime, they can offer insight into issues associated with organizational reform, force structure, and other aspects of military development. This expertise can help citizens make more informed decisions about whether to support particular candidates and their ideas about how to manage a military conflict or reform military forces. These dynamics, in turn, condition political leaders' incentives to invest in research and analysis and to avoid pursuing flawed policies, war plans, or strategies in the first place.

Citizens often lack the information and expertise necessary to evaluate military activity. This seems to undermine a key premise of American civil-military relations: that civilian political leaders, and not military leaders, should retain the prerogative to make decisions about the use of force because citizens can hold them directly accountable for their actions. Political leaders are elected by citizens, who delegate to them the responsibility to make decisions about the use of force on their behalf. If citizens do not like the policy civilians pursue, they can vote them out of office.

But what happens if that accountability function goes awry? Today, few citizens are educated in the complexities of military strategy, operations, and activity, and they may not understand the basic organizational structure of the military. As a result, it is much harder to hold politicians accountable for decisions they make in the military realm. On what grounds can regular citizens judge the justifications that political leaders offer for their military strategies and war plans? How can citizens hold their politicians accountable for decisions they are ill prepared to evaluate for themselves?

One solution is that military leaders might provide information and evaluation to the public at pivotal moments, especially when it is critical to the strategies and policies adopted by their civilian leaders.[42] Military leaders have expertise and access to information that should improve the value of their opinions. When they engage in public appeals, they make those informed opinions available to the citizenry at large. Citizens are better equipped to identify the weaknesses when political leaders propose military operations based on poorly conceived plans or flimsy assumptions. The political activities outlined in the previous section may facilitate political-strategic-operational integration by providing information to citizens, who can then check their political leaders if they are pursuing flawed strategies and policies.

This seems to be the motivation for those who applauded (or, perhaps more accurately, were not alarmed by) the April 2006 "revolt of the generals." Several recently retired generals, many of whom had occupied key command positions in Iraq, made public statements and comments criticizing Secretary of Defense Donald Rumsfeld, his management of the Iraq war, and especially the war-planning processes.[43] Among the charges were that Rumsfeld stifled advice and that he intimidated potential dissenters, thereby contributing to the adoption of flawed strategy in the war.

In response, many argued that the generals' public commentary violated norms of appropriate behavior by military officers and that, whatever the merit of the claims offered, it should be condemned. Others, however, were not alarmed but instead emphasized the usefulness of the information and expertise inherent in the commentary.

The justification for the generals' public appeal was spelled out by Lieutenant General Gregory Newbold, one of the outspoken generals, in an essay in *Time* magazine in which he criticized Secretary Rumsfeld. Suggesting that in offering his comments, he served as a mouthpiece for those still on active duty who were alarmed by Rumsfeld's inadequacies and strategic misdirections, he described his actions by claiming that, "with the encouragement of some still in positions of military leadership, I offer a challenge to those still in uniform: a leader's responsibility is to give voice to those who can't—or don't have the opportunity to—

speak."[44] He continued, "I am driven to action now by the missteps and misjudgments of the White House and the Pentagon," and by the desire to hold them accountable for what he called "an unnecessary war" in Iraq. In short, Newbold justified his actions on grounds that they were essential to check misguided civilian war strategy.

Retired Lieutenant Colonel Ralph Peters presented a similar argument in his public defense of military dissent, asking "if former officers cannot speak out on complex military issues, to whom can we turn for expert advice? To politicians who never deigned to serve in uniform themselves? To pundits equally lacking in military expertise? To defense industry publicists? Surely, lifelong expertise should hold some value in our specialized society."[45]

Some popular reaction to the commentary expressed the same theme. In a public debate on a popular Internet site soon after the revolt, for example, a participant said that "the military, and most especially general officers, should express their opinions, whether it belongs in the realm of strategy or tactics—which are parts of a continuum, and not well defined by bright lines. Those officers come with a wealth of experience and a broad spectrum of knowledge. We should endeavor to make the best use of that knowledge and experience; 'shut up and soldier' is not an answer." Internet columnist Kevin Drum wrote that "feedback from retired generals is really the only feasible way to keep the civilian leadership accountable." More colorfully, another participant declared that "there are unnecessary wars and there are unwise wars, but Iraq is a criminal, bogus, evil war [and] honest Army and Marine generals have an obligation to speak out."[46]

In short, military officers can play a critical role in providing expertise and facilitating the accountability of public officials. Public appeals can in this way promote more extensively considered and potentially superior policies and strategy than would have resulted absent the intensified public awareness and debate.

The Fire Alarm Effect

A second mechanism through which the military's political activity could affect military policy and activity is by what I call here the fire alarm effect.[47] Military officers may alert outside experts or Congress when political leaders are contemplating significant changes in doctrine, organization, force structure, or other critical areas of military development or activity. This, in turn, can prompt investment by Congress and civilian analysts in research and analysis of these critical issues. This fire alarm function is closely related to the informational role the military can play for citizens, but here the focus is less on providing essential and otherwise missing expertise, and more on signaling when proposed changes or factors could affect the military's organizational competence or capabilities.

Shoulder tapping and alliance building with civilian constituencies can be powerful ways to attract attention to an issue. Congress has a constitutional mandate to oversee and regulate the military yet, for a variety of reasons, it may not be well positioned to identify and pursue issues that bear on the military's organizational competence or capabilities. Military leaders could, actively and on their own initiative, alert representatives and senators to change that is contemplated by the civilian secretary of defense and his or her staff. Congress may be more inclined as a result to investigate the issue, through hearings, debate, or legislation. Through alliances with interest groups, military organizations can alert a group with a vested interest in monitoring military affairs, although, of course, those interest groups will convey information consistent with their own preferences. Similarly, when military leaders shoulder-tap—for example, when they solicit congressional support for their policy views—they can be expected to communicate information in ways consistent with their own preferences about a given issue. This is not inherently negative; it might be so only if politicians did not seek alternative sources of information. Nevertheless, in principle, shoulder tapping and alliance building could play an important role in signaling potential areas of change that should be explored and debated. They can help ensure that changes and reforms are more likely to enhance efficiency, have the desired effects, and prepare the country better to address threats and challenges. In short, political tactics can produce more informed and potentially superior military strategy and activity.

The Innovation Effect

A third potentially beneficial effect of a military's political activity is facilitating peacetime innovation. Analysts have conceived of the process of innovation in a variety of ways. Stephen Rosen argues that innovation can occur through the development of an alternative theory of war and the advancement, within the military hierarchy, of individuals advocating that theory. Barry Posen argues that innovation is often spurred by mavericks from outside the military mainstream who challenge authorities and who push novel, unconventional, or even unpopular approaches to warfare.[48]

Military political activity could be helpful in three ways in facilitating this innovation process. First, it can help with agenda setting. If bureaucracies have a status quo orientation, then making the case for change within a bureaucracy is an inherently uphill battle. By alerting Congress directly through shoulder tapping and by offering public appeals, those who can articulate a coherent case for change can raise awareness and build momentum for examining new issues. This activity can at least raise the stakes, by forcing those holding to the status quo to articulate better defenses of their positions.

Second, political activity can make it easier for civilians to identify and support innovators. Rosen and Posen suggest, in different ways, that those capable of being effective innovators within the military must be empowered and supported by civilians outside it. Whether by creating opportunities for innovators to attain leadership positions within the military, as Rosen recommends, or by singling out and empowering a military maverick on the fringes of conventional thought to shake up the bureaucracy, civilians play a critical role in promoting change. Political activity by senior officers who advocate new concepts and approaches to warfare can help mobilize support from civilians in this process. As a result, civilians might be more inclined to support new specializations or make other regulatory changes that facilitate the rise of these individuals and promote their influence within the bureaucracy. They might appoint to key positions individuals who advocate these alternative visions of warfare.

Third, innovators might mobilize and build constituencies in favor of innovation through alliance building. If defense industry interests, for example, identify a benefit for themselves in proposed changes, they may organize to raise awareness in Congress or through contacts with members of the Department of Defense. Through close relationships with these corporations and industry officials, military leaders with novel ideas might be able to gain essential support for those ideas. As a result, the country might become better prepared to seize technological or other opportunities to enhance its capabilities and the effectiveness of its military forces.

Negative Implications of Political Activity

Thus, we can identify some advantages if military leaders and their organizations engage in political activity. However, the implications are inevitably more complicated, and also entail some costs and risks.

Objective Expert Knowledge, or Subjective Values?

The first complication is that the tactics described here may be used in support of good causes or bad. In each, military leaders and their organizations arrive at and express some policy preferences, and do so publicly and forthrightly. Yet any judgment about a policy or strategic option is inherently that: a judgment. Consequently, civilian analysts and politicians are unlikely to agree consistently about what constitutes the injection of military expertise into debate or is instead the introduction of bias and misinformation; what constitutes a fire alarm of change or is instead an inappropriate effort to mobilize opposition to policy redirection; whether a proposed change in military activity is a promising innovation or is instead an ill-conceived distraction from essential priorities. While the tactics are neutral, the ends to which they are put are not. Military leaders and organizations can use political tactics for parochial self-interest as well as for the public interest; this is common, for example, in the realm of military procurement. In short, how one judges the value of military leaders employing political tactics may depend on one how one views the policy outcome they advance.

An important recent example can be seen in the 2006 "the revolt of the generals." Some argue that these six retired generals were justified in speaking out against Rumsfeld and his strategies in Iraq, but even those individuals might not view as appropriate General Douglas MacArthur's efforts to challenge President Truman's strategy in Korea in the 1950s.[49] Similarly, those who might support the six dissenting generals might be less approving of Colin Powell's efforts to mobilize opposition to U.S. intervention in the Bosnian civil war in the early 1990s, or of Powell's and the military's subsequent efforts to mobilize opposition to ending the ban on gay individuals serving openly in the military.[50] Powell and other supporters of the ban apparently believed that they were protecting the health of the organization and that their political mobilization was essential to achieving that end. As many saw it, however, Powell's reaction reflected a particular value system and beliefs, not "expertise."[51]

The subjectivity inherent in judging policy outcomes thus complicates debate about where to draw the line defining the political means military leaders may appropriately employ on their behalf. One can see this ambiguity in debate about the statements in the lead-up to the 2003 Iraq war of Chief of Staff of the Army Eric Shinseki. As Matthew Moten discusses in chapter 3 in this volume, Shinseki was one of the few public figures to speak publicly about the inadequacy of troop deployments for the postwar occupation. In congressional testimony in February 2003, he did so while fulfilling a constitutionally mandated obligation. Some suggest, however, that he might have taken more forthright steps to express those views. He might, perhaps, have issued a broader public appeal, or resigned in protest of the administration's strategic choices. Whether those tactics would be appropriate, however, depends on subjective interpretations of the issues at stake:

the fact that Shinseki was right, in the eyes of many, helps make the case that he could and should have spoken out more.

There are three potential approaches to this problem of subjectivity. First, one could conclude that a strict principle against engaging in any of the tactics outlined in this chapter is ideal, whatever the potential costs to the public in being unable to draw directly on the military for help with expertise, search and investment, and innovation. Second, we might discriminate among the tactics and choose just some as tolerable. Some types of political activities might be seen as more costly than beneficial. The costs of public appeals and politicking might always be seen as overriding their positive contributions to policy outcomes, while alliance building and shoulder tapping are less worrisome. Others might contend that one can judge the appropriateness of political activity only by the context and circumstances in which it is used, examining the issue, the specific actions taken, the stakes, the nature of domestic reaction, and so on.[52] Yet this option fails to give explicit guidance to help a military leader know when to speak out. Although looking at context may introduce more nuanced standards of appropriateness, it does not escape the problem of subjectivity. In different ways, all three options are unsatisfying, which underscores the difficulty of separating an abstract decision about appropriate means from values about ends.

The Latent Political Influence of the Military

A second complication originates in the unique position of the military, especially in the United States. The military enjoys substantial latent political influence in society, which magnifies the impact on policy outcomes of the tactics discussed.

This political influence stems from a number of sources. First, the U.S. military enjoys substantial structural power as a result of its size, measured in active-duty members, guard and reserve forces, veterans, families, and the communities and civilian employees of the defense establishment. Substantial base facilities house and train military personnel, heavily influencing local economies both economically and culturally.[53] The United States is home to large numbers of veterans and organizations representing their interests. A substantial constituency has an interest in protecting the military organization and sees security issues through the lens of that interest.

Second, the United States has a sizable domestic arms industry, comprising a civilian constituency with interests in supplying the military services with weapons systems. Substantial sectors of the economy depend on the activities of these industries and the jobs they generate. This creates another interest, as well as a natural ally for military organizations in lobbying politicians over procurement decisions.[54]

Third, institutional and partisan divisions render the political system especially permeable to civilian interests that might ally with military organizations. It also engenders substantial opportunities for lobbying and influence within Congress by military services. Systems like that of the United States, in which the president and legislature are elected separately and are not dependent on each other for their positions in office, and where political parties tend to be relatively weak, create natural points of access for military organizations and for the civilian constituencies with which they may cooperate.

Fourth, the U.S. military enjoys substantial social prestige. In the contemporary United States, the military is among the most respected of public institutions. It is regularly rated higher than Congress in public opinion polls. In European democracies, the military's profile is much lower.[55]

This social esteem has a significant effect on how the U.S. military's political activities might be received by the public. When military leaders speak out or protest through resignation, their views are likely to gain substantial attention from a population that tends to respect military opinion. Citizens may be inclined to believe military leaders if they assert that political leaders are not effectively supporting the military establishment, or are risking the security of the country. Social prestige also enhances the influence of retired military officers and the significance of their political endorsements during campaigns. Social prestige facilitates alliance building and lobbying efforts by industry and the services; public opinion is likely to be more responsive to claims about weapons systems and other military "necessities" made by a military that is perceived as an institution of high credibility and integrity.

Fifth, the U.S. military is currently closely identified with a political party. In general, we might expect a military's political power to be enhanced when a particular political party is identified closely with a pro-military platform, both by the party leadership itself and by military personnel. This relationship might incline military leaders to appeal to members of that party if they feel that their interests are at risk. In turn, a political party whose ideological and political platform is tied to military interests might be prone to push harder for policies advocated by military personnel. These dynamics increase the risks to other politicians who might question military policy, by reducing debates about matters such as strategy and force structure to partisan issues.

Studies by the Triangle Institute for Strategic Studies (TISS) on the growing partisanship of the American officer corps help us understand this set of issues. For much of the twentieth century, the American military was decidedly nonpartisan and became more professionalized over time. By the 1970s, officers were more likely to identify as independents, rather than profess support for any single political party.[56] In recent decades, however, these norms and conventions of nonpartisanship appear to have relaxed considerably. TISS and others have found that, since the Vietnam War, officers are increasingly likely to identify with a political party.[57] Moreover, there is a decided bias in their affiliations, relative to the population at large: 62 percent of the U.S. senior officer corps identified itself in the mid-1990s as Republican, 10 percent as Democrat, 18 percent as independent, only 9 percent gave no preference.[58] More widespread party identification, and especially with one particular party or another, may foreshadow a greater willingness to express political views and opinions if officers no longer see themselves outside the realm of politics but as participants within it. Although TISS did not directly examine the relationship between partisan affiliation and partisan activity, it did find anecdotal evidence that suggests a greater willingness by officers to express their political views.[59] It notes, for example, a number of cases in which active-duty senior officers identified their party affiliations in discussions with junior officers or in letters to the editor of civilian newspapers criticizing a political party.

In sum, the nature of the political system, along with the military's social prestige and current identification with the Republican Party, affords military leaders and their organizations substantial if mostly latent political influence in the United States. All of this matters because it affects how the information military leaders may supply through public appeals, grandstanding, shoulder tapping, alliance building, and politicking is received by the public at large and by political officials. The playing field is not level: military leaders are not just another voice, but a particularly loud and clear voice. As a result, military opinion might be given substantial, even undue, weight. Consequently, beyond just providing information, signaling change, or pushing for innovation, their political stature may mean that military leaders and their organizations can wield substantial influence over policy outcomes.

Costs and Risks to a Military's Political Activities

Finally, beyond these complications, we can identify some major costs and risks if the military engages in political activity. The first risk is that the military's political activism may have a negative effect on civilian society's perceptions of the military organization. One of the reasons that the military enjoys the esteem of the U.S. population is that it is viewed as impartial and as operating above or apart from politics. If it is seen as a participant in political processes, the organization becomes vulnerable to the same cynicism and questioning of motives that affects other public institutions in United States. This could be damaging: for example, it could make it difficult for the military to defend funding choices if the armed forces are perceived as just another special-interest group vying for resources. In briefings or essential communications to the public, its leaders might be dismissed as the mouthpieces of a self-interested bureaucracy. These dynamics, moreover, could be exacerbated if the officer corps is increasingly identified with one political party. Bacevich notes that "the more the military becomes identified with one party, the more likely government officials and the voters are to perceive its recommendations as part of a political agenda—rather than the considered judgment of disinterested professionals."[60]

A second major risk is that such political activity might affect civilian incentives in making appointments to leadership positions within the military and in how military leaders are engaged in consultative processes more broadly. In order to preempt opposition and safeguard his or her reputation with the electorate, the secretary of defense may be more apt to choose individuals whose preferences align with those of the administration. If military leaders are appointed because they are perceived (whether rightly or wrongly) as loyal to a particular administration, it could complicate those leaders' credibility in intragovernmental debate. They might no longer be perceived as independent contributors of objective expertise. Political leaders might become more reluctant to air controversial ideas or to be forthcoming in discussion with military leaders, even those they have carefully selected, out of fear that the latter might publicly criticize them or their proposed policies. These dynamics would harm the strategic assessment process at the civil-military nexus. They would reduce both the degree to which alternative or dissenting views could be heard in the evaluative process and the productivity of consultation and debate. Consider the April 2006 revolt of the generals: after several retired officers criticized the secretary of defense for being dismissive of his military leaders' advice, civilian leaders may have been motivated to engage their military counterparts in the future better than Rumsfeld apparently did. Also possible, however, is that future civilian leaders, especially those pursuing controversial reform programs or military actions abroad, might become more risk averse, reluctant to share information with their generals, choosing to speak only to those they can be sure will not speak out against them or their policies. This would clearly be harmful to strategic assessment at the civil-military nexus.

A third potential negative effect of political activity is on military professionalism. If professionalism both reflects and promotes, as Huntington argues, the military's technical efficiency and specialization in the instruments of violence, engaging in political activity could distract from and undermine those proficiencies. In other words, as Huntington projects, the military might be less expert on the battlefield if its senior officers are distracted by political involvement.

Moreover, political behavior may be damaging to meritocracy. Senior officer promotions might reflect considerations of the political and perhaps even partisan positions of candidates if the military were more involved in political debate. We know, moreover, from numerous historical cases that when political criteria become paramount in appointments and promotions, it can undermine the quality of the officer corps. When military leaders engage in political activity, it can send mixed signals to those under their command: if, for example, their superior officers have questioned a policy decision by the civilian leaders, should enlisted personnel or junior officers have questions about executing it? Consequently, if political activity by military leaders, occurring now only in isolated instances, were to become more common, those officers who engage in them—or who express sympathy for the positions of others who do—might thus undermine morale.[61] These are just some of the potentially negative effects on military professionalism of political activity by military leaders.

Finally, and arguably especially important, allowing political activity by military leaders could undermine their deference to elected civilian leaders on issues of policy and strategy. As Huntington pointed out, the autonomy the military enjoys under objective control shapes the culture of the officer corps, making deference to civilians in these decisions paramount. If, however, military leaders engage in the political tactics discussed previously, officers may increasingly feel justified, even compelled, to speak out about issues where they feel the stakes to the country or their services demand it. The more political tactics became customary, the more it might seem natural and appropriate that military leaders should play a central role in deciding matters of national security. Yet, if they are not ultimately answerable to their civilian masters, they are answerable to no one: unlike their civilian masters, they are not answerable to the polity. This dynamic could undermine the capacity of elected civilian leaders to make major policy decisions and to remain accountable to citizens.

This problem is compounded in a country like the United States where the substantial social prestige of the military means that citizens may be overly persuaded by military opinion. In enough volume and at the right moment in domestic politics, public appeals, endorsements, mobilization of allied interest groups, and shoulder tapping by military leaders could have enormous consequences for civilians' policy decisions. Political leaders might refrain from pursuing policies that might be criticized by service chiefs. A central problem is that the military's political tactics might do more than increase information and inspire further analysis about important issues; they might also excessively influence the decisions leaders make, by putting pressure on them to conform to military opinion or risk losing popular support. Political leaders might then accommodate military opinion even if they did not agree with it and even if it was not necessarily in the best interest of the country.

It was this dynamic that some found so alarming when Colin Powell spoke out publicly against intervention in the Bosnian civil war during the 1992 election season, and when, after Clinton's election, military officials mobilized in opposition to the proposed end to the ban on gays in the military. Clinton's compromise decisions on both issues suggest he may have been swayed unduly by military pressure.

The Balance Sheet

How should we weigh the costs and benefits of a military's political activities in the democratic United States? One metric looks at the implications for policy and strategy. In this light, there are potential benefits when military officers and leaders engage in these activities. They can facilitate better public debate and analysis as political leaders survey alternative means to achieve their international goals. They may provoke useful debate about the merits of organizational reform or other changes within the services or the Defense Department. They may allow the country to seize upon innovations in doctrine or weaponry, or to check ill-conceived transformations. In each of these cases, the primary mechanism through which political activity improves policy and strategy is by generating more information and investment in research and analysis about the alternatives. Given the significant informational disadvantages and lack of expertise among citizens, civilian analysts, and many politicians, the military's political activity can, in principle, be beneficial to the polity, by providing information and by signaling key issues through public appeals, threats of resignation, shoulder tapping, and third-party monitoring induced by alliance building and even by endorsements of candidates in elections.

These benefits, however, must be weighed against a second metric: the effect of political activity on the long-term principles that guide civil-military relations and democratic practice in the United States, combined with the significant costs and risks they could generate.

Among these, perhaps most important, the military's political activity threatens conventions of democratic accountability and decision making in the United States. They do so not by increasing the threat of direct military takeover of government, the problem with which Huntington was primarily concerned. Instead, at some point, military leaders may go beyond just contributing to debate through public appeals, grandstanding, and the like to fundamentally influencing policy debate, in the process privileging outcomes they favor. Here, we must return to the fact that it is political leaders who must, by constitutional mandate, make final decisions about military and security policy and strategy, because they, not the military, are answerable to the electorate.

In *The Soldier and the State*, Huntington correctly recognized that there are severe downsides to allowing militaries to engage in political activity in that it compromises their professionalism and therefore technical competency, but his analysis missed crucial dimensions of the issue. By failing to recognize the potential positive effects of political activity, he obscured the central dilemmas involved in prohibiting these activities. There is a serious trade-off involved in calling on officers to abstain from political behavior, but it is one that must be made. The threat to long-term principles of civilian control and the importance of civilians' deciding major national security issues, without acceding to pressure from a politically powerful officer corps and outspoken military leaders, demands that we require officers to refrain from political activity and that we do so across the board.

Some might see this conclusion as overly inflexible, neglecting the fact that the temptations to engage in political behavior are great and sometimes may appear to officers and the public as overwhelmingly compelling. Yet the other options are worse. Approving the use of some political tactics while ruling out others, or leaving it to officers to judge when the context for action is appropriate is problematic. Both alternatives require subjective judgments about what is appropriate in a given circumstance—judgments that will inevitably be colored by the opinions of the individuals and outside observers on the issue at stake, as we often already see.

To be clear, the costs and risks of this across-the-board rule are potentially substantial. Moreover, they must be acknowledged and accepted for the officer corps to embrace the rule. If military leaders refrain from political activity, the state may as a result sometimes pursue misguided or less informed military strategies and operational plans; it may miss opportunities in defense policy, procurement, or organizational restructuring. These are costs we must bear—and hope that other actors and institutions can help alleviate them—to maintain the long-term framework of civil-military relations upon which the republic is based.

CHAPTER TWELVE

Enhancing National Security and Civilian Control of the Military

A Madisonian Approach

Christopher P. Gibson

The U.S. involvement in Iraq has prompted widespread and contentious debate over what went wrong, who should be held accountable, and what course corrections should prevail.[1] Various writers have already offered explanations and narratives.[2] Some of the reasons why the United States has experienced such difficulty in Iraq, I argue, are issues at the core of civil-military relations.[3]

Functional civil-military relations do not guarantee successful policy outcomes, but dysfunction in this critical area is sure to produce incomplete options and ineffective outcomes. In my estimation, dysfunction is an accurate term for the U.S. situation circa 2002–6, as Defense Secretary Donald Rumsfeld dominated Joint Chiefs Chairman General Richard Myers.[4] The United States had not learned the lessons of history: this was not the first time that political appointees at the Pentagon practiced dominating methods of civilian control. Forty years earlier, Defense Secretary Robert McNamara employed similar strategies, to the detriment of policy and effectiveness.[5]

Why did the United States not learn from history? I argue that part of the blame lies with the lack of an effective normative construct to guide the organization of U.S. civil-military relations. Such guidance must come from the nation's elected leaders, not from the secretary of defense. The latter, like the nation's top general officers, is a servant or "agent" for the nation's elected leadership, the president and Congress; they, by constitutional design, share the duty to lead and control the military. Thus, it is also inappropriate for top generals to shape the relationship.[6] It is not the subordinates who should arrange and characterize interactions.

Elected leaders have a dearth of options to choose from when it comes to organizing their relationships with the national security establishment. They need more help. Scholars could play an important role by helping elected leaders articulate a coherent set of structures and norms to guide key civil-military relationships.

The topic of civil-military relations has taken on greater saliency in the public discourse since the end of the Cold War. As national leaders, including presidential candidates, develop their philosophies toward "civilian control of the military," and what exactly that means in practice, they should be able to turn for advice to the scholars who have devoted much of their professional lives to studying these questions. I believe that this scholarly community can bring well-considered arguments to the debate. In this chapter, I offer a "Madisonian approach" to help stimulate the discussion.

In the prevailing literature, there are really only two well-articulated options for arranging civil-military relationships: subjective control, of the type employed by McNamara and Rumsfeld, and objective control, first outlined by Samuel Huntington with great promise, but flawed by faulty assumptions about the nature of the civil-military nexus where options are generated, analyzed, and conveyed, along with advice, to elected leaders.[7]

Upon closer examination, objective control is revealed as a false choice, because it fails to provide insights useful to the preponderance of civil-military interactions. It does not help at the nexus where civil and military leaders share responsibilities for helping elected leaders to understand the strategic environment and to sort through issues and options before making decisions. Thus, subjective control is the only fully developed model. However, most presidents have not followed the subjective control approach, because micromanagement of the profession by political appointees, who generally have lesser practical experience, could result in reduced levels of effectiveness (as during the McNamara and Rumsfeld eras).

More often than not, presidents and Congresses have operated without a clearly articulated model or established norm to guide civil-military relations, which often leads to confusion and ambiguity.[8] At times, critics have charged that one or both sides of the relationship have not performed their duties fully and effectively, or that one side has overreached into the sphere of the other.[9] But without clearly established expectations and standards and an agreed-upon framework, how can we agree what constitutes dereliction or inappropriate behavior?[10] Today, with subjective control freshly discredited, elected leaders are in need of a clearly articulated method to organize civil-military relations.

Samuel Huntington and the Objective Control Model

In *The Soldier and the State*, Huntington sought to provide new normative theory to help elected leaders arrange their civil-military relationships effectively to solve national security problems.[11] Unfortunately, his policy recommendations were flawed.

In the early 1950s, Huntington recognized the U.S. dilemma as it struggled with the Soviet threat. Never before had the United States faced an existential threat. It lacked a coherent theoretical approach to organize the national security establishment adequately. The United States had, up to that point, generally eschewed large peacetime standing armies and expansive defense budgets as threats to civil liberties and other domestic priorities. Large armies and expenditures were the necessities of wartime, but after wars, both were downsized, or "extirpated," as Huntington put it. Yet the communist threat meant that now disarmament was not an option. This created philosophical confusion. If remaining armed to the teeth was required to prevent communist takeover, some feared that the country would be unable to retain its "Americanness."[12]

Huntington recognized the need for a normative theory or guide that would provide a way to combat Soviet aggression without substantially altering the U.S. way of life. Huntington offered the "objective control model," called this because it relied on the military itself to refrain from politics, retaining professional objectivity by abjuring political partisan struggle. Civilian forces, Huntington maintained, were not in a position to manage the day-to-day military adherence to civilian control effectively, as their voices were fractured among the executive and legislative branches of government. Guidance and supervision would be inherently conflictual and contradictory, whether they came from within the same political party, from opposite parties, or from the congressional and executive branches of government. These branches were, by constitutional design, expected to counterbalance one another and could be expected to disagree widely on many topics, including how best to limit the military's role in politics. The minority political party would always face the temptation to draw the military into the political sphere to alter the power balance in its favor, at least temporarily on a particular issue.[13]

To escape this dilemma, Huntington maintained that military professionalism, which he defined as inherently apolitical, could be advanced by allocating to the military a "narrow sphere" of autonomy on tactical and operational matters. The military would make the decisions on a number of issues deemed to be purely military. This bounded freedom, he argued, would inspire the military to focus mainly on maintaining combat readiness while staying out of politics. The military, Huntington theorized, would see the virtue in this, because aligning with a particular political cause, position, or party, useful one moment, might prove useless the next as political fortunes changed. Particularly because the military would be held accountable for its assigned and clearly defined domain of military matters, it would recognize and avoid the trap of politics. Moreover, because of the corporate nature of military professionalism and the inherent accountability associated with it, Huntington posited that those who got out of line would be policed from within the ranks.[14]

Huntington thus offered a model designed to secure the country, but to do so in a way that would preserve civilian control of the military and U.S. values. Huntington's objective control model became broadly popular and was largely internalized within the military for many years, taught at the U.S. Military Academy and in Reserve Officer Training Corps (ROTC) instruction.[15] Aspects of the theory were somewhat idiosyncratic, such as his description of officers as "managers of violence," but on balance his ideas found a welcome among members of the military, especially his emphasis on professionalism, the fostering of expert knowledge, and the study of the history of warfare. Huntington argued that expertise came through training and reflection, fostered by a lifelong commitment to acquiring professional knowledge.[16] Huntington's objective control model appealed to the warrior: it described the kind of soldier that most soldiers wanted to be. Having accepted his arguments about professional knowledge, it was not much of a move to embrace his view of politics, too; it all seemed logically consistent. As the much-expanded Cold War military embraced objective control, civil-military relations appeared to have a normative guide; however, it was not so.

Objective control was fundamentally flawed from the outset because it presumed that the military and political spheres could be distinguished in a comprehensive and meaningful way. This ignored all that Clausewitz had contributed to national security and strategy over a century earlier.[17] It is true that there are some clear distinctions. The U.S. Constitution and statutes provide that elected leaders make such decisions as the military's size, composition, and funding levels and when to commit the military to battle. Members of the armed services take on the hazards of battle, but much of how they are prepared for battle, even the rules of engagement that guide their behavior when committed, are shaped and crafted by civilian leaders: members of Congress and the president. Thus, a central problem with Huntington's objective control model is that few actions fall neatly into one sphere or the other. Nearly all civil-military interactions occur at the nexus where roles and responsibilities are shared between general officers and politically appointed advisors who provide analysis, generate options, and convey recommendations to elected leaders on all matters related to the common defense.[18]

A normative theory that addresses only a very small fraction of the interactions of the participants provides little real help on crucial day-to-day matters that shape decisive moments. At the upper tiers of the national security decision-making process, there is too much overlap between the roles of top-level civilian and military leaders for a normative model of civil-military relations that is based on splitting duties and staying out of each other's sphere.[19]

It is understandable how Huntington could get this wrong. In the early days of the Cold War, the Eisenhower administration was advancing strategies of massive retaliation and reorganizing the Army into Pentomic Divisions to survive on the nuclear battlefield. The pervasive belief was that conflicts in the future were less likely to be limited. The bipolar world and the advent of nuclear weapons and their devastating effects on armies and populations meant, it was believed, that future war would escalate quickly and might include an atomic exchange. Under these assumptions, it was not radical to think that analysis and recommendations in support of decisions pertaining to war and peace could be kept largely in the civilian realm, because tactical and operational military advice appeared irrelevant in the expected scenarios. It was the civilian national security experts with extensive background in nuclear physics and weapons who would provide the essential support for decisions by elected leaders.[20]

Experiences since the 1950s, however, have demonstrated the flaw with these assumptions. Every generation seems to need to relearn that the nature of conflict has remained unchanged, even if the way it is waged evolves over time. Controlling land and populations still requires large formations of ground troops. The advent of nuclear weapons did not obviate the need to prepare for conventional and unconventional war. Presidents need insight, analysis, and advice from their military commanders. The commanders must adequately represent the military profession in the civil-military nexus during the decision-making process. This requires expert knowledge not only about war, campaign planning, and force development but also in the political-cultural domain. Applying such expertise goes beyond the norms of the objective control model.[21] (There are other problems with the objective control model, but for the sake of brevity I treat only the most problematic one in this chapter.)[22]

Morris Janowitz and Subjective Control

Huntington helped shape views of the main alternative to the objective control model; he described and categorized as "subjective control" the method employed by U.S. leaders during times of war. When the armed forces dramatically expanded, civilian leaders practiced subjective control. They essentially civilianized and politicized the armed forces through a widespread draft, direct commissioning of officers throughout the ranks (even of general officers) without the benefit of reserve officer training (ROTC) or academy preparation, careful screening of senior military leaders to match the civilian leaders' political leanings, large-scale use of the National Guard (and, before that, militias), and invasive management by presidential appointees working within the War and Navy Departments. All of this served to force the military to embrace civilian values and to reflect administration positions and direction.[23] Huntington did not recommend employing this as a long-term strategy because he hypothesized that, under such a regime, military professionalism and effectiveness would decline. Janowitz, however, disagreed.[24]

Like Huntington, Janowitz focused on military professionalism, although he was primarily interested in elite analysis, the officer socialization process, and elite and military cultures and their interaction.[25] Janowitz fundamentally disagreed with Huntington's assumption regarding the possibility of delineating separate roles for top-level civilian and military leaders. Indeed, a major point of his 1971 book *Professional Soldier* was his detailed description of the blurring of civilian and military responsibilities in what he described as our nation's "constabulary" force (rather than "military" force), one that is "continuously prepared to act, committed to the limited use of force, and seeks viable international relations, rather than victory."[26] Janowitz envisioned that such a constabulary force would be employed in limited ways during the Cold War, such as irregular war and conventional battle to achieve carefully defined limited objectives in the Third World as the superpowers vied for power among developing nations.

Under Janowitz's scheme, civilian leaders would be expected to get into the details of military organization, doctrine, leader development and selection, and even ongoing military operations, in part because the pursuit of limited objectives would require constant oversight and restraint: military leaders could no longer be turned loose to pursue "victory." Military leaders, similarly, could be expected to contribute in the political sphere, both in the national debate before the commitment of U.S. forces and thereafter in critiquing the effectiveness of ongoing operations.[27]

Because his assumptions led him to reject the possibility of objective control as a means of civilian control, Janowitz went the other way, arguing for civilian penetration of military culture to tame it so that it would comply with civilian direction. This approach was in essence what Huntington had described as subjective control of the military, but Janowitz proposed it for perpetual use, not just in times of war. As Janowitz described it, his constabulary would inherently have competition and friction among the three major types of leaders in the military's officer corps: the traditional "heroic leader," the "military manager," and the "technical specialist." Janowitz's advice was that civilian leaders should exploit these divisions to maintain civilian control and get the most out of their military leaders.[28]

Janowitz described the ongoing ideological struggle in the military as it emerged from the Vietnam experience as an instance of the "absolutist" versus "pragmatist" debate. Historically, the former was represented by MacArthur, a heroic leader, and the latter by Marshall, a military manager. The heroic leader was typified by MacArthur's desire to expand the war in Asia and to fight a total war until receiving the Chinese unconditional surrender—the absolutist position. Marshall, the military manager, recognized the potentially disastrous effects of nuclear war among the superpowers and the resulting need to limit conflict and develop realistic foreign policy and war goals—the pragmatist position.[29]

In the years just after Vietnam, Janowitz argued, it was in the nation's interests for the pragmatists to win this struggle within the military. He argued that subjective control of the military would ensure this outcome, as civilian leaders assured that only those with the right world view and philosophy would climb the ranks. Moreover, he said, political leaders needed to undertake indoctrination about the virtues of civilian control, both of the leadership of the armed forces and as far down the ranks as possible, and to establish civilian counterparts for military leaders with domination over them in functional areas where responsibilities overlapped. Janowitz pointed to the British army as his example. The Soviet Union, too, had employed a similar strategy to maintain civilian control over the Red Army: the deputy commander of regimental units and higher was a political commissar who had the functional responsibility for political training and tactical oversight.[30]

Huntington and others argued that, however, such subjective control would weaken military professionalism and effectiveness over the long haul.[31] Fostering a politically correct force would result in fewer warriors steeped in expert knowledge about how to combat the opponents of the U.S. way of life. Such concerns are reflected today, for example, in the existence of a Washington, D.C., think-tank dedicated to stopping efforts to use the military as a tool of social progress and experimentation or to "civilianize" the military.[32]

Because the primary responsibility of militaries is to win their nation's wars, such positions should not be rejected out of hand. However, the history of the military, as it relates to protecting our way of life while simultaneously supporting cultural initiatives designed to foster positive changes to it, is long established and fairly positive. Modern examples include the integration of African Americans within the armed forces after World War II. Similarly, throughout the 1980s and 1990s, there was marked controversy over the role of women in the armed forces, with some activists expressing grave concern over the effectiveness of the military if the numbers and roles of women were expanded.[33] Yet during the Global War on Terror, women have performed very well, even in situations where, despite organizational impediments meant to preclude such incidents, close combat with the enemy occurred unexpectedly.[34] From this we can conclude that politically directed social change in the military (a dimension of subjective control) does not always result in significant drops in effectiveness. However, policymakers should be careful how they approach such initiatives; any proposals should be thoroughly examined and weighed against the potential impact on the military's first-order responsibilities and its effectiveness. Huntington described this tension between the functional imperative (the requirement to win wars) and the societal imperative (attempts to make the military look like or be more representative of society). There is, he said, no final answer on this score.[35] What is clear from the standpoint of civil-military relations is that any decisions on these matters must come from the country's elected leadership. The Constitution specifically assigns jurisdiction over the military to the Congress. Military leaders have a responsibility to advise the Congress and the president about the anticipated effects, positive and negative, of proposed social change affecting the military, but once decisions are taken by civilians, full compliance by the military is expected.

At either end of the spectrum, there will be some distinctions between the roles of the civilian and those of the military. Elected leaders must give direction and make decisions, and soldiers must have knowledge of and competence in defeating the country's enemies in combat and all the associated command and staff functions that facilitate that capability. Toward that end, Huntington was right in recognizing that the military benefits by focusing on fostering its expert knowledge. However, Janowitz was also right in recognizing that, at the nexus, military and civilian advisors share many responsibilities.

To accommodate both of these points, I propose a Madisonian approach. It accepts political penetration of the force by civilian leaders, including political appointees at the Pentagon. Even with this close supervision and involvement, military effectiveness and battlefield success are expected from the profession of arms.[36] I disagree with Janowitz, however, in his recommendation for not just civilian penetration but domination of the military by politically appointed counterparts. My research supports, instead, the position that a more balanced approach at the civil-military nexus within the Department of Defense (DoD) would better serve our elected leaders and the country.[37]

A Madisonian Approach for Civil-Military Relations

To develop an effective model for civil-military relations, it is helpful to look at how the Founders grappled with similar questions. They had the difficult challenge of designing a government that could control the governed but also control itself.[38] They were mindful that the history of mankind is devoid of example where absolute power did not corrupt or disappoint. For the Founders, even the most virtuous man (in those days widely believed to be George Washington) would be corrupted with unlimited power. James Madison concluded that the only solution to this problem was to put the virtue into the system. Man's ambitious inclinations should be arranged in such a way that they negated or attenuated man's tyrannical tendencies: use of countervailing forces was the way to prevent tyranny. Institutions with overlapping responsibilities that shared power and inspired the best efforts for those they serve is the very animating concept of the U.S. Constitution. It could provide the logic we are seeking to improve the design of U.S. civil-military relations. Such an approach at the Pentagon could prevent the accumulation and abuse of power by either set of "agents": top-level civilians or their military advisors.

The function of civil-military relations is to enhance national security and civilian control of the military. Civilian control is defined as the exercise of the will of the country's elected leadership over the armed forces. It seems desirable, therefore, to maximize the relationships between and among the top-level political appointees and the highest-ranking generals and admirals at the Pentagon, those who support national leaders at the critical civil-military nexus. This way of conceptualizing and thinking about civil-military relations, though significantly different from the current paradigm, is actually not new in the American experience. Two historical examples of U.S. civil-military relationships illustrate the relative advantages of a partnership-like approach, rather than structured domination by top-level political appointees at the Pentagon: I am referring specifically to the functional and effective relationships between General George Washington and the Continental Congress, and between General George Marshall and Secretary of War Henry Stimson.[39]

In this Madisonian approach to civil-military relations, first-order principles reinforce constitutional provisions. The first principle is that elected leaders always have the final say and nothing is beyond their purview. Second, members of the military must always remain nonpartisan in their public life. Third, like many other facets of the U.S. constitutional arrangement, civilian control of the military is shared between the president, who serves as the commander in chief of the armed forces, and the Congress, whose vast authority over the military is outlined in Article I, Section 8 of the Constitution. Together, these elected leaders control the military establishment, providing it with guidance, funding, and supervision.

This model would specifically guide interactions within the Department of Defense. There, the Madisonian approach would provide a new guide for the key relationships in top-tier positions, those between the president's political appointees and the nation's top military officers. Top civilian and military leaders would work together to provide the nation's elected leaders with the best possible military advice and information to guide executive decisions. Although the top military officer would still report to the secretary of defense, this approach would discard the dominating model practiced during the McNamara and Rumsfeld years for the more collaborative approach employed during World War II, in recognition of the inadequacies of both the objective and subjective control approaches to civil-military relations.[40]

Here the model is the relationship between General Marshall and Secretary Stimson. Any relationship can appear healthy in the good times, but what marks excellence in this regard is how the parties deal with adversity and disagreement. Marshall and Stimson handled these moments as well as anyone and each ex-

tolled the virtues of the other. A deep mutual respect provided the basis for a relationship that could survive significant disagreement. Stimson, although the
civilian, even deferred to Marshall's judgment on occasion, as with how best to
expand the officers corps and the U.S. Army during World War II. Personal tem-
perament was critical to this relationship, but structure and norms also played
prominent roles. By Executive Order of July 5, 1939, General Marshall had been
authorized to go around Secretary Stimson and deal directly with President Roosevelt, but he almost never invoked this option. Instead, Marshall wisely chose to
work through his civilian secretary, a member of the opposition party, which enhanced his stature among both Democrats and Republicans on Capitol Hill and
certainly endeared him to Secretary Stimson. But the existence of that executive
order helped shape the relationship, particularly early on as norms were being
formed. Together, Stimson and Marshall made an excellent team, helping President Roosevelt and the Congress evaluate the strategic landscape and sort through
options before making difficult decisions.

In this model, guidance and direction would come from elected leaders, most
immediately from the president as the commander in chief, but shared over the
long run with the Congress, within their respective jurisdictions. Under the Madisonian approach, the national security experts within the Department of Defense—civilian and military—would develop competing plans to accomplish such
directives. These national security experts would critique each other's ideas and
concepts and would offer their analyses, replete with accounting of advantages
and disadvantages, to the president and Congress for review, comment, and decision. There is no requirement for consensus at the civil-military nexus; separate
and even competing proposals for executive deliberation would be encouraged.
The relationship between Secretary Stimson and General Marshall provides the
historical guide.[41]

Sometimes issues within the civil-military nexus might clearly have a lead pro-
ponent. During conflict termination activities at the end of the first Persian Gulf
War, for example, political appointees within the Departments of State and Defense should have been more involved and should have taken the lead. In the
event, General Norman Schwarzkopf was the principal player, despite his concerns expressed later that he needed more civilian help.[42] For matters of policy in
general, political appointees should be out front but, before matters are elevated
to national decision makers, military advice should be incorporated and adequately considered. Especially when dealing with foreign leaders, the civilian secretary of defense should be the lead within the Pentagon. Most of this work is at

the civil-military nexus, where responsibilities are shared. However, the Madisonian approach recognizes that professional preparation in these instances generally favors political appointees, while professional military advice provides the support, by thoroughly reviewing proposed courses of action for plausibility of assumptions, feasibility of proposed implementation, and analysis of second-order and third-order effects.[43]

There are also instances when military officers should be in the lead, as with operational planning. These activities, too, reside at the civil-military nexus; political appointees and their civilian national security experts also play a prominent role, critiquing military plans, their assumptions, and implementation feasibility and analyzing second- and third-order effects. The Madisonian approach improves on existing processes, in that elected leaders would be presented with more fully developed options, often multiple ones, supported by analysis. The civil-military nexus, thus restructured, would not require compromise and consolidation of options before reaching the president or Congress.

This normative framework builds upon the work of others. It begins with Peter Feaver's agency theory.[44] The president and Congress are the principals: as such, they provide guidance, render decisions, and then choose how best, including how much, to supervise the implementation of policy to achieve desired goals and objectives. Feaver's agency theory specifies an array of supervisory methods that principals can choose from; I carry them over to the Madisonian approach.[45] In their relationship with the military, Feaver argued, civilians must make trade-offs between tighter control or oversight and the advantages of trust or morale-based teamwork, mindful of second-order impacts on loyalty and effectiveness.

Where the Madisonian approach differs from Feaver's agency theory is in its conception of the "agents." The secretary of defense is not treated as a principal along with the president and Congress but is instead considered an "agent" along with the military. Both are responsible to the will of the nation's elected leaders.[46]

This arrangement opens up opportunities for employment of more noninvasive monitoring techniques, such as inter-DoD rivalry, or what Feaver characterized as internal "fire alarms," moments when players inside the organization bring problematic behavior to the attention of the principal. The nature of the relationship at the Pentagon would be such that the competition of views of civilian and military agents would keep elected leaders better informed and armed with more fully developed divergent options from which to choose. A Madisonian approach to civil-military relations at the Pentagon might provide a way to balance the intrusiveness of oversight techniques, the level of compliance, and effectiveness, aspects of the dynamic that, as Feaver points out, are highly inter-related. Where principals are faced with difficult trade-offs between compliance and morale-related effectiveness, the Madisonian approach might offer better possibilities. By setting up countervailing forces within the Pentagon itself, we may at once get more accountability (or, in Feaver's parlance, less shirking) and more effective policy outcomes, because there would be both more freedom dur-ing initial stages of policy development and better vetting of options during war gaming and other planning involving both civilian and military officials.[47]

The Madisonian approach also pulls in ideas from other scholars. From Hunt-ington and Kohn, it incorporates the military's primary focus on the development of expert knowledge, warrior skills, and the cultivation of the profession at arms.[48] Congress would provide general guidance on the kind of military force the nation should develop and maintain. National security experts within the DoD, both civilian and military, would collaborate with the Congress to flesh out the details of force development and the specifications for required professional knowledge. Indeed, all hands would collaborate in helping define the future of the profes-sion.[49] In the Madisonian approach, I expand the definition of professionalism to include joint-services competencies, integration with multinational forces, gov-ernance skills, and appreciation for the U.S. national security decision-making process.[50] Huntington would see these duties as part of the civilian domain. The experiences over the past four decades, however, and the examples of General Washington and General Marshall, show that in the main these are duties exer-cised at the civil-military nexus. Having senior military officers with expert knowledge of the political-cultural arena benefits the nation, even and especially its elected leaders.[51] Another element from Huntington incorporated into the Madisonian approach is the requirement that officers must remain publicly non-partisan. The instant this is violated, even the most virtuous acts would be viewed with suspicion.[52]

From Janowitz, the Madisonian approach acknowledges the futility of an at-tempt at strict separation of the roles and responsibilities of civilian and military leaders at the Pentagon.[53] The military officer must have broad competencies: he or she must be able to fight and win wars, big and small, and be employed in any way that the nation's elected leaders decide. As Janowitz argued, the military must have a constabulary capacity: a full spectrum of capabilities from police forces for application of limited force up to overwhelming military forces.

Statutory Revisions

To implement the Madisonian approach, there would need to be changes in law, as well as the changes in norms. Changes in structure would be needed to facilitate pluralistic views and strengthen the ability for military voices to be heard at appropriate times. Changes in norms alone would not be sufficient to ensure that the president and Congress get the kind of military advice they need. Revisions to the Goldwater-Nichols Defense Reorganization Act of 1986 are needed to prevent the reemergence of domination and dysfunction in the relationship.[54]

The top military leaders of the services—the Joint Chiefs of Staff—must be included in a more meaningful and systemic way in the deliberations and drafting of war plans and in all facets of military preparedness, such as force development, programming, and budgeting, so that when their advice is sought by the elected leadership, they speak from a personally informed and invested perspective.[55] Thus, the combatant commands should be realigned to fall under the command of the top military officer. This officer would be called the commanding general (CG) of the U.S. Armed Forces, a position that would replace the post of chairman of the Joint Chiefs of Staff.[56] The position of CG would be reinstituted, this time as a joint billet in charge of all U.S. forces. The CG would be placed above the Joint Chiefs and the Joint Staff as well.

The Army had the position of commanding general about a century ago, but it was eliminated in 1903 in favor of an Army chief of staff, a move that, perhaps counterintuitively, was made in order to strengthen the nation's top Army officer. The catalyst for the realignment was to address the disastrously weak support of the Field Army by the War Department during the Spanish-American War. The solution was to make the commanding general the chief of staff, giving the nation's top Army officer power over the War Department, something the CG had previously lacked. This reform was implemented to bring about more responsiveness from the logistical and support side of the service. In the Madisonian proposal, converting the position of chairman to commanding general is meant, similarly, to enhance the responsiveness of the DoD to the fielded forces.[57]

Reestablishing the position of commanding general, and requiring all combatant commanders to report to one military officer who has the benefit of the Joint Chiefs and the Joint Staff to develop and vet courses of action, would ensure that the individual who has the statutory responsibility to advise the president and Congress is materially and substantively involved in the development and assessment of war plans.[58] Converting the role of chairman of the Joint Chiefs to the role and title of commanding general would underline the obligation of the secretary of defense to consider the CG's advice and would help make sure that the advice gets to the nation's elected leaders unfiltered.[59] The secretary, of course, would be free to disagree with the CG's advice and to offer his or her own independent analysis, supported by the under secretary of defense for policy or perhaps other military voices. But the civilian leadership at the DoD should recognize and accept that, even when there are major disagreements at the civil-military nexus, the views of top military officers, including the CG and the Joint Chiefs, will always be among the positions conveyed to the president and, when it has jurisdiction, to Congress.[60]

To enhance the commanding general's effectiveness across the services and to promote "jointness" in development of campaign plans and support for peacetime force development, the service chiefs should report directly to the commanding general, who in turn reports to the secretary of defense. The commanding general would retain the role of principal military advisor to the president, National Security Council, Congress, and secretary of defense. The Joint Chiefs, too, would retain its advisory role to the president, National Security Council, Congress, and the secretary. Annual and periodic meetings with the president and the National Security Council would continue, as would testimony by service chiefs and service secretaries before the Congress. The commanding general would exercise command authority over the combatant commanders and the services, but the advice of each service chief would also be conveyed to the president and Congress, along with the views of the secretary of defense. Elected leaders, then, would receive multiple sets of advice and analysis from which to decide policy, and they would have one commander to hold accountable if expectations were not met.

This reform would enhance operational and contingency planning and execution, force development, and programming and budgeting, as combatant commanders and the service chiefs could channel their advice to the commanding general, for whom the Joint Staff could vet and review recommendations. When the CG presented recommendations to the secretary of defense and the rest of the National Security Council, including the president, those recommendations would reflect the joint perspective that has been absent from many such discussions in the past.

The service secretaries, under this model, are teamed with their respective service chiefs as a countervailing force to the commanding general and secretary of defense. The model for this relationship is that of the Army Chief of Staff General Marshall with Secretary of War Stimson.[61] In recent times, too, chiefs of staff have recognized how crucial civil-military teamwork within the services is. In remarks at his retirement ceremony, speaking of recently departed Army secretary Thomas White, General Eric Shinseki said:

> Leadership is essential in any profession, but effective leadership is paramount in the profession of arms—for those who wear the uniform and those who do not. We, in The Army, have been blessed with tremendous civilian leadership—most notably the service of Secretary Tom White, whom we farewelled last month. We understand that leadership is not an exclusive function of uniformed service. So when some suggest that we, in The Army, don't understand the importance of civilian control of the military—well, that's just not helpful—and it isn't true. The Army has always understood the primacy of civilian control—we reinforce that principle to those with whom we train all around the world.[62]

In some respects, the Madisonian proposal would provide more centralization and unity in such steps as bringing the combatant commanders and service chiefs under the commanding general. In other respects, at the highest levels of the DoD, it would diffuse and balance power, providing for competing advice from the CG and the secretary of defense and competing advice from the services and the DoD leadership. This would result in giving the president and elected leaders in Congress pluralistic advice, from both civilian and uniformed advisors.

This is not an argument for weak cabinet secretaries, nor should we abandon the possibility of perfecting the best aspects of so-called cabinet government to enhance efficiency and responsiveness: we need the strongest possible leaders in charge of our government departments. However, we should have structure and norms so that cabinet leaders get the most out of the professions that work under their charge, and a decision-making process that ensures that our elected leaders have access to the best professional knowledge and experience. Toward that end, it would be helpful for scholars to examine and analyze how a reconstructed cabinet government approach could better incorporate professional analysis and judgment. What is needed is a balanced approach across the departments of government that provides for political direction from the elected leaders of our country, without being antiprofessional in practice.

Rough Parity in Professional Preparation Is Essential

A pluralistic, Madisonian approach to civil-military relations requires that officers have adequate professional preparation, in terms of education of the right kind, and grooming in assignment history, to perform effectively at the civil-military nexus of the national security decision-making process.[63] It also depends on a rough parity in professional preparation between the civilian and the military leaders who are the nation's national security professionals. Asymmetries could lead to domination and dysfunction, which historically has dampened creative options and advice. Active management and constant review of professional preparation of both civilian and military participants is needed. Out of concern with whether the military is as experienced and educated as its civilian counterparts, and vice versa, Congress, in its oversight role, should track the professional preparation of nominees for top-level positions in the DoD.[64]

A Madisonian approach to civil-military relations thus requires an investment in the development of leaders among both civilian and military officials. Imbalance in professional preparation has a deleterious impact on the relationship's dynamic. Janowitz has pointed out that detailed attention to the selection and grooming of senior leaders is an important dimension of subjective control of the military. The Madisonian approach differs from that of Janowitz in that its intention is balance, not domination, and the salient characteristic for selection is competence, not political fealty.

The services are already investing in developing leadership skills. The civilian side, too, needs a comprehensive development program for national security specialists; it could build upon successful initiatives such as the Joint Civilian Orientation Conference.[65] More expansive programs are needed, such as regular professional military education assignments for political appointees and Senior Executive Service personnel, and other fellowships and exchange experiences throughout the national security establishment.[66] Political appointees should have a professional development program dedicated exclusively to them; it should require at least four to six weeks of residency at the National Defense University for exposure to a curriculum of civil-military relations, grand strategy, the strategic planning process, the joint operational and crisis action planning process, and the program and budgeting process.

Senior Leadership Development offices of the respective services should be expanded to include the civilians in the Senior Executive Service of each branch of the military as well. War College attendance, Joint Professional Military Education, and joint assignments should be mandatory for promotions, as is already required of senior military officers. Such initiatives might be linked with the sorts of academic and scholarly efforts already underway at nonpartisan think-tanks such as the Council on Foreign Relations, the U.S. Institute of Peace, and elsewhere. Security studies programs among the nation's top-tier graduate schools might be improved by more comprehensive and standardized curriculum. National security conferences and fellowship opportunities could be enhanced. Outstanding developmental institutions for future civilian national security professionals, such as the Center for International Security and Cooperation at Stanford, the Olin Institute at Harvard, and the School of Advanced International Studies at Johns Hopkins could be linked to the Office of the Secretary of Defense, similar to the ways in which the Arroyo Center at RAND helps the Army or RAND's Project Air Force assists the U.S. Air Force.[67] We need to invest more in developing the human capital of our civilian national security professionals and then develop and exploit their expertise with assignments of increasing responsibility in the Department of Defense and the Department of State.

New Norms for Officers under the Madisonian Approach

In addition to changes in law and the reforms in human development and personnel management, new norms are also needed. Top-level military officers must approach their responsibilities in a way that enables their voices to be heard and their views to be considered by elected leadership.[68]

Norms must be seen in the context of the unique role of the military professions and their strategic leaders, who are responsible for virtuous and effective performance at the civil-military nexus. A leading scholar in the effort to renew the military professions is retired Army colonel Don M. Snider, now at West Point. He identifies four broad fields of expert knowledge that officers must possess in order to apply their expertise properly and effectively, in accordance with their oath of office: military-technical, moral-ethical, political-cultural, and human development. These areas of expert knowledge correspond with the self-identity of the officer corps: that of the warrior (military-technical), leader of character (moral-ethical), servant of the nation (political-cultural), and member of a profession (human development). Learning and applying this knowledge will make an officer's service more effective, virtuous, and honorable—values at the core of the trust relationship between the military professions and their civilian clients. Thus, norms for the proper conduct of officers at the civil-military nexus reside within the political-cultural domain of expert knowledge; officers use this knowledge and expertise as servants of the nation.[69]

The following list of proposed norms can serve as a departure point for an extended investigation and a professional dialogue about how military officers should conduct themselves in accordance with a new model of civil-military relations. The list is meant to be illustrative and not exhaustive.

Develop Expert Knowledge

To ensure that one can adequately represent the profession during joint, multinational, and interagency deliberations, officers must develop expert knowledge and practical expertise across the spectrum of conflict,[70] accompanied by an appreciation for the different roles and responsibilities of all parties at the civil-military nexus.[71]

Offer One's Best Advice

An officer has an obligation to put forward his or her best advice when participating in deliberations that are shaping U.S. policies and plans. This advice should be informed by past experiences and professional study and should be unconstrained by politics, although an officer should be cognizant of political sensitivities and limitations. An officer's expert knowledge includes a political-cultural understanding of the policy process.

Offer Candid, Well-Supported Assessments

An officer should be expected to put forward candid assessments in deliberations designed to review ongoing operations for effectiveness and for progress toward declared strategic aims, goals, and objectives. Closed-door meetings should move beyond initial "talking points" to extended interactions supported by quantitative and qualitative analysis pertaining to progress, or lack of progress, of ongoing operations. An officer should create recommendations or insights on possible solutions, should never speak beyond his or her expertise, and should not let any elevated moral status a soldier might enjoy in time of war serve as license for inflating the value of the military perspective over the other perspectives that civilian decision makers will seek.

Be a Team Player with Civilian and Military Alike

An officer should be a team player in interagency meetings; should listen carefully to and help civilian participants develop effective policies, plans, and programs; and should facilitate civilian national-security professional expertise. The central idea of the Madisonian approach is to facilitate a range of options and provide exhaustive and candid review of their respective advantages and disadvantages, so that elected leaders can make the best choices possible for the American people. There is little value in simply winning bureaucratic competitions or advocating careerist agendas; rather, the goal is the adoption of the courses of action that are best for the nation.

Be Responsive to Congress as Well as to the Executive

The officer's first duty is to uphold the Constitution and serve the American people. Toward that end, although officers work for the administration, they must also be responsive to and serve the Congress. Balancing these dual civilian masters has proved difficult over the years, but for the officer seeking truth and the common good, and committed to fulfilling his or her duty, conscience and professional judgment will provide the guide.

Understand and Accept the Subtleties of Our Democratic Processes

Officers should develop an appreciation of the complexities and nuances that come with a representative democracy. The Founders devised a complex system of checks and balances so that liberty could prevail in a system of government that responds to the will of the people while respecting minority rights. Matters of the highest import, such as matters of war and peace, were meant to be debated and deliberated before public votes were taken, on record, by duly elected representatives of the people. The officer is duty-bound to ensure that this debate is fully informed and accurate. The nation's top military officer is directly responsible and accountable for this requirement. National security may, at times, require secrecy, but the need for operational security does not justify political machinations to obscure or truncate the debate about matters of war and the use of force. A soldier's duty in this regard is first to the administration but includes the Congress as well.

The press in a free society plays a critical role in ensuring that a full and informed debate occurs on matters of high import. Should there ever be a case when the American people are not adequately aware of information so critically important that it would substantially alter the public debate about the worthiness of whether to go to war or to use force, then the officer is duty-bound to make it known through the executive and legislative branches, regardless of any personal concerns over the potential career impact. This does not change the basic nature of how officers render military judgment and advice: these activities are to be primarily in private. The advice of military leaders to the president, the National Security Council, and Congress should stay within those circles whenever possible. Hearings before the Congress, however, are often open to the public and media. Should there be a case when sensitive topics are to be discussed, military leaders may request a private meeting with the leaders of both parties before the hearing, to convey sensitive information more discreetly. How members of Congress handle the information after military officers convey it is not an officer's responsibility, beyond clearly stating whether such information is classified and offering an assessment as to the potential harm that could occur should such information become public. In no case is it permissible to tell less than the full truth to the Congress or press, or to anyone else for that matter, assuming security classifications are appropriately followed.

Above All, Serve the American People

The American people are the ultimate clients of America's military professions. Thus, the military's principle of unity of command still applies in a Madisonian approach to civil-military relations. The interests of the people and their Republic are paramount, even if they speak through the multiple voices of the executive and the Congress. It may feature more friction and debate at the civil-military nexus during the process leading up to decisions, but once decisions are made, providing they are legal and ethical, all officers should fully support them and do their best to secure successful implementation. Officers who have met their service obligations and who feel they cannot fully support a chosen course are duty-bound to retire, or to resign if they are not eligible to retire. Otherwise, their best effort is required.[72]

Stand Aside from Partisan Struggles

Military officers must not take a side in partisan struggles. A counterexample is General Powell's op-ed in the *New York Times*.[73] While it was arguably not a legal violation, because it was cleared first by his chain of command,[74] it was not appropriate under this norm, both because of its content (it gave the perception of endorsing the views of President George H. W. Bush, a candidate in the presidential campaign just finished) and because of its timing (publication just before the start of the new Clinton administration). The perception of nonpartisanship is just as important as the reality. All those serving on active duty should understand and comply with the regulations pertaining to permissible and prohibited political behavior, which are spelled out in DoD Directive 1344.10 issued in 2004.[75]

Military officers are also bound by Article 88 of the Uniform Code of Military Justice (UCMJ), which prohibits contemptuous words about or personal attacks on designated top-level federal officials. In public settings, officers should always display respect for the leaders of the Republic and especially for the people's elected representatives within both the executive and legislative branches.

None of this, however, should be construed to mean that officers must refrain from candid assessments of ongoing operations when participating in meetings designed toward that end or when providing feedback on plans and proposals being debated before decision and implementation. The stipulation in the UCMJ exists to limit comments of a personal nature, but disagreement about matters of professional knowledge or expertise is not personal, nor is it disrespectful. Before Congress, officers must be forthright with their assessments and opinions. In the past, there has often been a norm that officers should conceal their views from the Congress if those views were not in line with administration positions. However, Congress shares in the constitutional role of controlling the military, and it is the duty of officers to put forth their judgments candidly and to back them up with analyses drawn from their expert knowledge and experience. Officers adhering to a Madisonian approach may struggle mightily with their civilian counterparts at the DoD while working at the civil-military nexus but, once policies are decided upon, they are still duty-bound to work indefatigably to make those policies successful regardless of whether military advice was followed. Officers in academic settings should be afforded the freedom to critique all aspects of national security decision making and execution, so long as it is for the purpose of perfecting such matters in future endeavors.

Use the News Media Only for the National Interest

Military officers must not use the news media for advancing policy positions that are not in the best interests of the American people. In other words, using the news media to advance the interests of one's service, when not also in the interests of the American people as a whole, is entirely inappropriate, as are off-the-record comments to journalists made to similar ends. The limits will inevitably be fuzzy, particularly when conveying budget or programmatic positions. Thus, before a media engagement, whether on or off the record, it is a good idea to have a "devil's advocate" offer feedback, to confirm adherence to the pertinent norms. The benefit of the doubt should always go to the side of the public good, rather than the interests of one service over another.

Military officers should not give the appearance of directing policy or of taking advantage of a new administration as it transitions to power. The way that the "gays in the military" controversy was handled in 1993, leading to public confrontation between civilian and military leaders, was not helpful to anyone, although it is possible that such a confrontation might have been unavoidable, given that the media, not the military, raised the issue shortly after the election. Still, object lessons can be drawn: military officers should be actively looking for ways to support a transition to a new administration.

Military officers must avoid inadvertently undermining ongoing U.S. efforts at policy formulation or diplomacy in their public statements and published works. In the Madisonian approach to civil-military relations, military officers have a role in educating elected leaders and the populace about the advantages and disadvantages of potential military options. However, a special effort must be made to ensure that these educational efforts do not undercut administration policies or efforts. Clarity on this point can be elusive and controversy may not be avoidable, even when an officer is acting appropriately and in accordance with duty. Still, it is elected leaders who decide the course of U.S. foreign policy, and military leaders who must follow their direction and implement policy. If the process of educating elected leaders and the U.S. populace gives adversaries the impression, for example, that the military is balking at the use of force, this could undermine administration efforts at coercive diplomacy based on threatening to use force while hoping not to have to.

Final Thoughts

The Rumsfeld-Myers period at the Pentagon was a low point for civil-military relations. The U.S. preparation for conflict with Iraq suffered as a direct consequence. The U.S. national security establishment abandoned firmly established procedures for campaign planning. Instead, a Rumsfeld-dominated process resulted in a plan presented to the president and the U.S. public as the plan of CENTCOM commander General Tommy Franks, but it was so twisted and contorted from its initial conception that it no longer represented best military judgment.[76] Military officers, including General Franks and General Myers, acquiesced to this. Why?

It seems to me that at least a partial explanation was that the civil-military foundation was flawed. To correct this will require both changes to structure, such as the Goldwater-Nichols revisions, to strengthen the position of the top military officer, and new norms to clarify and enhance the military's ability to represent the profession at the civil-military nexus. During periods when McNamara and Wheeler or Rumsfeld and Myers presided at the Pentagon, top officers accepted the notions that disagreement equaled disloyalty and that the role of the soldier at the civil-military nexus should be restrained and reactive.[77] These norms contributed to a dynamic whereby elected leaders were inundated with civilian-dominated military options and analysis from the Pentagon. This approach has not delivered for the American people. In contrast, under the norms practiced by General Washington and General Marshall, military leaders played appropriate and effective roles at the civil-military nexus and ultimately helped contribute to victory. Washington and Marshall both recognized the critical contribution that top-level military officers make at the civil-military nexus, particularly to the advisory component of the national security decision-making process and in helping elected leaders sort out options and make effective decisions. Washington and Marshall helped shape norms conducive to effective policy.

In the Rumsfeld-led Pentagon, by contrast, what was considered appropriate behavior by top military officers at the civil-military nexus was very limited. This dysfunctional normative framework and inappropriate conception of civilian control was, to some degree, presented to the officer corps by scholars with a view on the subject that was different from that of the military heroes whom even those scholars cited as examples of what the conduct for officers ought to be.[78] Scholars did not do this alone; this brand of subjective civilian control has also been advanced at various times in our recent history by politically appointed leaders at the Pentagon. However, this time in particular military officers were complicit in the abrogation of their responsibilities to provide elected leaders with decision-making support analysis and advice.[79]

The highest ranking generals certainly should continue to act with decorum and deference when dealing with civilian leaders, but they also should ensure that, as war plans are being developed, their views, analysis, and best military judgment reach the nation's decision makers, including the president, regardless of whether their views square with those of the defense secretary or any other political appointee in the administration. The first proposal briefed to the president by a military officer should be a concept devised by military professionals, and not significantly altered to meet the wishes of a political appointee. There will always be a time and place for the defense secretary to make his or her proposal. However, the president should not be told that he or she is receiving a concept briefing from a military officer that represents best military judgment when it is actually a concept that has been substantially shaped and altered by the political appointee. If needed or desired, proposals significantly shaped by the thinking of political appointees should be presented, instead, by the defense secretary or by his or her designated representative. This would enable the president to weigh multiple options and analyses properly and carefully before deciding.

Another area that needs improvement is articulation of the military's proper role with the Congress.[80] The Founders devised a system that allocated shared responsibilities for national security and the military among the executive and legislative branches in a political structure that employed countervailing forces to guard against the consolidation and abuse of power. To ensure unity of effort, the president was made the commander in chief, but Congress, too, was expected to be central, devising policies for the armed forces, providing for their funding, and deciding when they would be committed in the defense of the country. Beyond that, Congress was granted the authority to help decide the essence of the military: its policy-making powers give it jurisdiction over the development of the military's expert knowledge. Congressional powers are often referred to today as defining the military's "roles and missions," but in fact they go well beyond that to include working with the armed forces to make explicit choices about what kind of military the United States should possess. Military leaders should recognize the instrumental role that Congress plays and work with members accordingly to build a stronger national security establishment.

As the United States struggles in Iraq and Afghanistan or takes other actions to protect the U.S. homeland and way of life, new defense secretaries will take over, and there may well be periods of improved civil-military relationships characterized by mutual respect and trust.[81] We should not, however, allow any period of momentary comity to lull us into neglecting the need for long-term structural and cultural change within our national security institutions. Personalities will always play a key role at the civil-military nexus of the national security decision-making process, but without anchoring those relationships with structural and cultural reforms, we will be doomed to repeat the wild oscillations in civil-military relations of the past forty years.[82] It will only be a matter of time before a dominating personality takes the reins of power in the Office of the Secretary of Defense and once again embraces a dysfunctional form of subjective control. If history is any guide, this will be done in the name of civilian control of the military and of bureaucratic efficiency, and it might again be accompanied by a long, painful, and costly military misadventure.

We need to take the necessary steps now to put our civil-military relations on a foundation that can withstand the powerful winds of domineering personalities. By reforming the civil-military nexus of the national security decision-making process through revisions to the Goldwater-Nichols legislation and embracing new norms and a more balanced approach to civil-military relations within the Pentagon, we can better secure the state. We should not delay.

CHAPTER THIRTEEN

Building Trust

Civil-Military Behaviors for Effective National Security

Richard H. Kohn

When Samuel P. Huntington published *The Soldier and the State* in the mid-1950s, he revolutionized the study of civil-military relations, turning it away from concerns over military coups d'état and toward an examination of the role and functioning of the military in society, particularly in the United States.[1] Huntington identified the central dilemma of the relationship: how to assure sufficient military influence to protect a nation while at the same time maintaining the supremacy of civilian political authority. "The role of the military in society has been frequently discussed in terms of 'civilian control' yet this concept has never been satisfactorily defined," Huntington wrote. "Presumably, civilian control has something to do with the relative power of civilians and military groups. . . . The basic problem in defining civilian control is: How can military power be minimized?"[2] In perhaps his greatest contribution, he characterized the relationship between military and civilian as one of inherent conflict. To him it arose from differences in values and ideology: a "functional imperative," in which a military that thought and behaved in whatever ways resulted in military effectiveness, as opposed to what he labeled a "societal imperative," which reflected the norms, values, and behaviors of a liberal society. His solution to the conflict was "objective control": delegating to the military as much autonomy as possible for successfully waging war, in exchange for the military's abstention from politics. Implied was a perpetual struggle between civilians, trying to define how much autonomy to delegate, and soldiers, striving to maximize that autonomy in order to fulfill their function.

Although Huntington identified the larger truth that conflict was inherent in American civil-military relations, his explanation that the struggle lay rooted in a clash between the ideologies of a conservative military and the values of a liberal American society was never wholly persuasive. Instead, I argue, the conflict between the most senior military and political leaders at the top of government arises from their differing needs, perspectives, and objectives in peacetime and in waging war. What follows is an analysis of that conflict that examines the deficiencies of Huntington's argument and the sources of conflict, beginning with a look at two secretaries of defense whose tenures produced the most friction— even hatred—between civilian and military. I conclude with a guide for the behavior of both sides that would minimize distrust and aid in constructing an effective partnership. The solution, as this chapter argues, to maximizing military influence on policy and decision making (as a way of maximizing security), and also maximizing civilian control, lies not in theory or the structure of society but in the more mundane and situational personal relationships that develop between military and civilians at the highest levels of the American government.

The Soldier and the State

From the very beginning of its extraordinary scholarly life, *The Soldier and the State* contained numerous contradictions and errors that undermined its argument. Huntington's "objective control" assumed clear boundaries between policy and strategy, on the one hand, and tactics, operations, training, and military administration, on the other, that were diminishing in the dawning era of nuclear weapons and limited war. A second problem with his analysis was that military autonomy in fact limited and lessened civilian control of the military. A third problem was Huntington's interpretation of the U.S. Constitution; he conceded that it made "objective" control impossible because it explicitly drew the military into political life by dividing control over the military between the branches of government and by giving the military leadership access to the highest civilian authorities. Fourth, Huntington's analysis, brilliant as it was and based on wide and eclectic reading, derived its picture of military thinking, values, and perspectives from an abstract analysis of the function of military institutions, rather than from comprehensive research into the military profession in the United States, which was, in reality, far from homogeneous.[3] In many ways, even then, the American military deviated from the conservative model Huntington posited. Contrary to his contentions, moreover, senior officers espoused ideas that were consonant with basic American values and thinking (and do so today—a point made by Darrell W. Driver in chapter 9 in this volume). Thus, "the professional soldier," in the words of one scholar, has shared, "rather than [opposed,] the Liberal democratic tradition that dominated American life from (at the very least) the collapse of the Federalist party to the coming of the New Deal."[4] Fifth, Huntington's characterization of American history was, even when he wrote, contested among historians and since has been largely repudiated by the discipline. In the 1950s when Huntington wrote, the "consensus" school of American historiography was at its zenith, notably at Harvard where Huntington studied and wrote, and in its Government Department where political scientist Louis Hartz, the author of a leading text in the movement, taught. Their interpretations emphasized agreement on basic values and systems of thought: what Huntington called liberalism. Their picture of an American society without deep conflict began to be replaced less than a decade after Huntington wrote by renewed emphasis on the political, economic, intellectual, and social disagreements and struggles among groups, regions, classes, ethnicities, races, ideas, and schools of thought.[5]

Subsequent historical investigation since Huntington wrote contradicted some of his most important characterizations of the American military. For much of the nineteenth century, the army was not isolated from society in spite of deployment largely in small units on the western frontier.[6] Professionalization occurred not after the Civil War but before, when West Point graduates began to dominate the service, seeing themselves as servants of society in uniform for entire careers and divorced from partisan politics, even though some of their top leaders (who were not graduates of the Military Academy) sought high political office.[7] The Navy possessed a professional officer corps, devoted to service to the nation and abstaining from partisan politics as an institution, as early as the War of 1812.[8] Contrary to Huntington (and to C. Vann Woodward, in an influential article published three years after Huntington's volume), security "from the second decade of the nineteenth century to the fourth decade of the twentieth century" was not "a given fact of nature and circumstance, an inheritance rather than a creation," at least in the minds of Americans of those generations.[9] The United States did face the possibility of foreign war and maintained a national military establishment that included a coast artillery system, arsenals, an army and navy, and provisions to mobilize the military-age male population. The nation's expenditures and vulnerability were modest only by comparison with European great powers.

Huntington's analysis of the Constitution, particularly the thinking of its framers, was almost exactly wrong. The men in Philadelphia in the summer of 1787 feared standing armies but lacked confidence in the military efficacy of the militia, and as a result provided for a national military establishment explicitly under civilian control, both to keep the military subordinate and to prevent any individual or one branch of government from overturning the Constitution and establishing tyranny. Indeed, the framers did envision a separate military profession, a concept already known to the eighteenth-century Atlantic world, even if based on an aristocratic officer corps appointed and promoted by purchase and personal influence. Their concern for civilian control pervaded the Constitution so completely as to amount to an obsession.[10]

Some of Huntington's other generalizations have not withstood the passage of time. Huntington claimed, for example, that "the public . . . hardly conceives of the officer" in the same way as other professionals, "and it certainly does not accord to the officer the deference which it gives to civilian professionals."[11] The respect accorded military officers (and soldiers in general) and the military as an institution since the late 1980s indicates quite the contrary.[12]

If, then, much of Huntington's historical analysis has proved deficient, and American society was indeed so diverse and its military so in tune with many basic social ideas, then the argument that civil-military conflict originates in the differences between a conservative military and a liberal society collapses and, with it, the necessity for "objective control" in order to reconcile military professionalism and civilian control. What then explains the inherent conflict, and what can be done to alleviate it?

The Sources of Civil-Military Conflict

Secretary of Defense Donald Rumsfeld resigned in November 2006, just as the history office of his department published the first of two volumes on Robert S. McNamara's tenure as secretary of defense in the 1960s.[13] No two secretaries of defense have been more often paired in the public mind and national security community. While most of the similarities are more apparent than real, in civil-military relations the congruence seemed striking: both officials alienated, disparaged, and to some extent ignored Congress and the uniformed military. Both were secretaries of enormous drive, energy, and ambition: competitive (both relentless squash players), domineering, arrogant, dismissive, manipulative, hardworking, bullying, contemptuous, intimidating, ruthless, humiliating, and aggressive.[14] Both at times accused of lying, neither was ever caught unambiguously in an obvious untruth, but both would mislead by omission, prevarication, redefinition, or other rhetorical prestidigitation. Both were hands-on secretaries who acknowledged no boundaries to their power or authority within the Department of Defense. Neither granted the armed services the kind of autonomy Huntington thought necessary for "objective" civilian control in any area they believed important to policy or war fighting. Both secretaries were willing to meddle in minor details—the selection and assignment of flag officers down to the two-star level, strategy and operations, and virtually anything of significance by their own definition. Both were centralizers in the extreme; both disempowered their service secretaries and the Joint Chiefs. Both ruled by fear. Both gathered tightly around them a group of civilians who operated with a kind of closed, cohesive loyalty to their boss and to each other, and with suspicion and distrust of the uniformed military. Both asserted civilian control of the military with relentless determination, often peremptorily, believing with considerable justification that it had eroded significantly under their predecessors.[15]

The problem that these two larger-than-life figures present for civil-military relations is whether the assertion of such extreme civilian control is functional: that is, whether it can lead to effective policies and wise decisions. Much of their management of the Pentagon remains in dispute, but in strategy and war making, the consensus—and the essence of Huntington's thesis about civil-military relations—suggests that such peremptory exercise of civilian control is not functional. Indeed, relations under Rumsfeld were so poor that the Iraq Study Group, a bipartisan commission convened to reassess the Iraq campaign, called upon his successor to "make every effort to build healthy civil-military relations, by creating an environment in which the senior military feel free to offer independent advice . . . to the civilian leadership."[16]

Yet given the unwavering support for civilian control—an understanding shared by critics and by supporters of both, that civilian control must prevail in all circumstances—two essential questions arise: how should military people respond to leadership of this sort, and how should senior civilians treat the military in order to achieve the most positive outcomes in policy and decision making?

These questions are extraordinarily important, for effective civil-military relations are indispensable to national defense, and dysfunctional relationships between the topmost civilians and the most senior military officers—particularly lack of candor, consultation, coordination, and collaboration—can be disastrous for policy and decision making, in peacetime and in war. Poor civil-military relations have in the past undermined military professionalism and led to dangerous military policy and astonishing wastes of money. Poor communication can cause the United States to undertake unnecessary wars, prosecute them unwisely, and pile up hundreds or thousands of dead and wounded Americans, not to speak of many times that number of enemies and innocent civilians. Dysfunctional civil-military relations can undermine the position of the United States in the world and even endanger the nation's very existence. The history of American national defense since World War II abounds with costly mistakes attributable in whole or in part to broken civil-military relations, most glaringly in the Vietnam War and the campaigns in Afghanistan and Iraq. And yet everyone believes in, and supports, the idea of civilian control. How can the country reconcile civilian control with civilian leaders who behave as McNamara and Rumsfeld did, and still produce successful policies and decisions in national defense? The answer is "with great difficulty."

There are many reasons why it is difficult to establish trusting partnerships between the military and civilians in American government. Positive collaborations have occurred in American history, even if that history is littered with instances of conflict. But much of the problem lies in certain constants about civil-military relations in the United States.

To begin with, civilian control can be absolute and thus conducive to abuse. Eliot Cohen has called the interaction "an unequal dialogue."[17] Civilians in the executive branch and in Congress possess nearly all of the power should they choose to exercise it. As one staff officer put it at the height of concern within the Army about McNamara's centralization, "Should he [the secretary of defense] be thought of primarily as a business manager of a $50 billion-plus operation? Or should he be considered as a statesman primarily concerned with military affairs, directing enormous resources, and acting as a Deputy for the Commander-in-Chief?" McNamara, concluded this officer, "strove to fulfill both roles."[18] So, too, did Donald Rumsfeld. Civilians determine the extent of military responsibility and authority and what will be delegated, and even whether to listen or consult. They are subject only to the limitations they impose, for various reasons, upon themselves; to the legal checks of the other branches of government when they disagree; and to the military and political conditions at any given moment that might cause civilians to fear, defer, or listen to military perspectives and recommendations. Thus, civilian control means that the elected leadership, and those whom they appoint, have both the right and the authority to be wrong, and it is neither the role nor the function of the military to prevent their mistakes other than by advice. Indeed, it is utterly improper for the military to attempt to hold the civilians accountable. At the same time, an unspoken truth rarely even recognized by scholars, government officials, and the military itself is that no single individual, institution, or organization "controls" anything in American government. In other words, military leaders have little recourse against not only decisions they oppose but also the process by which those decisions are made. As the opposition inside the Pentagon to bombing policy in Vietnam was peaking, for example, John P. McConnell, the Air Force chief of staff, explained the president's thinking to his new brigadier generals, pointing out that "many non-military factors . . . must be considered by the President along with the JCS [Joint Chiefs of Staff] recommendations." McConnell was adamant about the system: "I want to make sure you understand that the opinions and recommendations of the JCS are being fully considered. . . . National policy is *not* being made in ignorance of JCS recommendations. . . . Once the President has made his decision, it our duty to carry it out to the best of our ability. Either support it or turn in your suit."[19]

The truth is that McNamara and Rumsfeld were not *sui generis*. Civilian leaders who believe they should always defer to the military in its areas of professional expertise, like Harry Woodring, the Kansas banker who served as Franklin Roosevelt's secretary of war in the 1930s, have long since left the scene.[20] More typical was the second secretary of defense, Louis Johnson (1949–50), who was motivated mostly by personal and political ambition. "He nearly always did what he thought would be politically expedient and what he believed would advance his own personal ambition." He was "a difficult and complicated man. His arrogance was legendary. He was cocky, self-righteous, and imperious. He rarely raised his voice, but he could silence a room or intimidate a visitor with his icy stare and tight-lipped intensity." Yet "he had a remarkable ability to befriend not only" presidents "but hundreds of powerful people in business and government, individuals on whom he lavished his attention because they would help him succeed."[21]

As secretary of defense, Johnson provoked the "Revolt of the Admirals" in 1949 by canceling construction of a new "super carrier," without consulting the Navy or its secretary, even though construction had already begun. In protest, the Navy secretary resigned, and the public outcry from the Navy became so intense—including challenges in Congress and the press to the Air Force's B-36 bomber program—that the chief of naval operations was fired amid widespread accusations against the Navy of insubordination.[22]

Presidents can also be difficult. Roosevelt had famously good relationships with his service chiefs. However, a conflict over the Army budget in 1934 led Chief of Staff Douglas MacArthur to such an angry outburst that he felt constrained to offer his resignation to the president on the spot; after the meeting, MacArthur was so upset he vomited on the steps of the White House.[23] Roosevelt did not fully trust the Navy, which he knew intimately from eight years as the number-two civilian official in the Navy Department during Woodrow Wilson's administration.[24] Similarly, Dwight Eisenhower so distrusted his chiefs that he replaced them all early in his administration, failed to renew his Army chief of staff, Matthew Ridgway, for a second two-year term, demanded that Ridgway's successor Maxwell Taylor toe the line (which he did not), considered in 1960 firing the Air Force chief of staff, and characterized the attitudes and statements of some senior officers as "damn near treason."[25] John F. Kennedy rapidly lost faith in the Joint Chiefs; he called out of retirement Maxwell Taylor—the chief who had failed to toe Eisenhower's line—to be special assistant and then chairman. Lyndon Johnson, in a 1965 private meeting, turned on his chiefs, "screamed obscenities, . . . cursed them personally, . . . ridiculed them, . . . called them filthy names—shitheads, dumb shits, pompous assholes—and used 'the F-word' as an adjective more freely than a Marine in boot camp would use it. . . . It was unnerving, degrading," remembered the Marine officer who happened to witness the meeting in the Oval Office. "After the tantrum," Johnson "resumed the calm, relaxed manner" of a few minutes earlier. "It was as though he had punished them, cowed them, and would now control them. Using soft-spoken profanities, he said something to the effect that they all knew now that he did not care about their military advice," but "that he did expect their help." He then demanded of each of them what they would do were they president. After they finished, he "suddenly erupted again, yelling and cursing, again using language that even a Marine seldom uses," telling them "he was disgusted with their naive approach, and that he was not going to let some military idiots talk him into World War III. He ended the conference by shouting, 'Get the hell out of my office!' "[26]

A second factor affecting trust in American civil-military relations has been the difference in perspectives inherent in the two worlds of political and military leaders, given their different purposes, responsibilities, careers, and methods. It would be a mistake to attribute conflict solely to the people involved, as important as that can be. Neither McNamara's or Rumsfeld's personalities, nor Bill

Clinton's fear of the military and his personal reputation (avoiding the draft, phi-landering, smoking marijuana as a youth), nor Eisenhower's immense experience in military affairs fully explain civil-military relations during their times in office. Officers want clear, definitive orders delivered quickly, and strong civilian lead-ership—particularly in providing a maximum of material and public support—yet at the same time as much freedom and autonomy to execute those orders as possible. Politicians want flexibility and choice. They want to know the costs so that they can calibrate ends to means. Often they want to delay decisions until the costs and implications are clearer, and the risks perhaps reduced. As one knowl-edgeable staff officer put it in 1966, "There are good reasons why decisions on crucial matters are not made until the last minute. No President wants to decide until he has to; he wants to leave as many alternative courses of action open to himself for as long as possible. The decision may leak to the press and tip the gov-ernment's hand before it can act" and might thus "invalidate the decision." And "if he makes a decision which is contingent on future developments, some indi-viduals who favor that course of action will try to compress the series of events so that he will have to take action sooner," while others who oppose it "may try to shape events so that the approved course of action will never be really executed." Either way leads to "frustration for the policy approved by the President."[27]

Civilians want, above all, to assure that the execution of a policy or decision—"not simply strategy but military operations themselves"—will be consonant with goals, costs, and risks, and with a wide variety of choices so that they can re-view and perhaps revise their goals in order to lessen costs and risks. The tension is thus natural and functional because statesmen in determining ends must be in-formed not only of what is possible but of the cost in blood and treasure. On their part, generals and admirals are duty-bound to shape their activity to the purpose and policy of the state, no matter what the cost or the character of the civilian leadership, even if that purpose or policy suddenly changes. That the relationship is therefore uneasy, and involves considerable distrust and mutual suspicion, is natural, and indeed this has characterized most of the history of American civil-military relations. Distrust can be beneficial if it leads each side to press the other for more precise, rigorous, unsentimental, and tough thinking.[28]

A third factor complicating civil-military relations is the enormously expanded importance of military affairs in the United States during the past seven decades. The presence of nuclear weapons, of worldwide interests, and of various threats has made national security issues far more important—on a continuing basis—than in the past, and thus deeply political in the generic, and increasingly in the partisan, sense. The size, composition, configuration, and use of the American military have to a large degree affected the allocation of national resources, the character of the American economy, the relationship of the United States to the rest of the world, and above all the fate of the American people. It thus has seemed almost natural that deep disagreements have arisen over these subjects, often forcing compromises and limitations that military and civilians alike have found disturbing, and that in turn have driven both sides, but particularly the military, into bureaucratic and political behaviors to fight for the resources and policies that uniformed leaders viewed as indispensable to fulfill their responsibilities.[29]

A fourth reason why is it difficult to establish trust is that the altered circumstances have increased the power of the professional military itself since the beginning of World War II. Struggles between the services over roles, missions, budgets, and weapons spun out of control almost immediately in the latter half of the 1940s. Then, divisions over limiting the war in Korea exploded in the firing of Douglas MacArthur. The military and political leadership fought among themselves and with each other over strategy and budgets in the 1950s; over Pentagon administration, weapons, budgets, and strategy in the 1960s; over Vietnam; and over various issues of foreign policy, arms control, weapons, and interventions in the 1970s and 1980s. In virtually all of this history, the military often acted in its own institutional interest; civilians bargained with the military leadership as much they led, directed, or controlled it. Inevitably the relationship was triangular, involving the Congress, which acted sometimes in its members' interests to dilute civilian control by the executive branch, to embarrass the administration over military affairs, or to force or prevent spending according to legislative desires. Beginning with the Vietnam War, these issues became increasingly partisan (although some had been so as early as the Truman administration), and the military itself, to a degree never before in American history, became politicized and identified with one political party.[30]

The Vietnam War did much to destroy trust between civilians and the military in the government. It led a whole generation of military people to distrust civilians and civilian control, and to vow never again to be sent into battle without adequate resources, a winning strategy, the support of the American people, and an exit strategy. Thereafter, the uniformed military rose tremendously in the trust and esteem of the American people. Since the Persian Gulf War, the armed services have enjoyed a level of prestige unprecedented in American history with the possible exception of the immediate post–World War II years.[31] Over the past forty years, officers inside the Pentagon have come to possess more education and experience in national security affairs than their civilian counterparts, giving military leaders both the ability and the inclination to work their own agendas.[32]

In short, the relative power between military and civilian has shifted over time, imperceptibly and sometimes inadvertently, while at the same time, the military's understanding of civilian control and its willingness always to accede to, and comply with, civilian policies and decisions lessened.[33] The issue is not a coup or any direct military intervention in American politics but a gradual change in the political life of the United States. The professional military, with its allies and communities, has developed into a potent political force in American government. Knowledgeable people, particularly those who, in each administration, are charged with the direction of national security affairs, recognize this, even if they cannot, for political reasons, admit it openly. Over a half century, bureaucratic maneuvering, end runs to Congress, sophisticated public relations campaigns, leaks, and alliances with contractors and with local communities and veterans groups have aroused the political leadership's suspicion and diminished its trust in the military, whatever its rhetoric of support for the military and national defense. Lieutenant General Charles Bonesteel, serving as Army Chief Harold K. Johnson's director of special studies, recognized this in 1966; in an anguished private memorandum, Bonesteel told Johnson that "the vicious, parochial 'internecine war' " between the services in the 1940s "began to undermine the nation's faith" in the traditional system of civil-military consultation. Bonesteel believed the "first steps" were begun "in large part by we in the military ourselves."[34] Secretaries of defense as different as Robert McNamara, Melvin Laird, Caspar Weinberger, Frank Carlucci, Dick Cheney, and Donald Rumsfeld all came into office suspicious of the military and determined to exercise control over the Department of Defense.[35]

Military Behaviors to Inspire Trust

Given that these background conditions will affect the relationship between soldiers and civilians, directly or indirectly, for the foreseeable future, what behaviors on both sides might lead to the kind of cooperative partnership that would produce both civilian control and wise, effective decision making? For the military, there are several steps to take.

First, the most senior military leadership must do everything possible to establish trust with civilian political leaders, not only above them in the Pentagon and White House but also on Capitol Hill: they can achieve this by avoiding all behaviors and activities other than advice that might give even the appearance of maneuvering to achieve policy outcomes or decisions according to the military's choice.[36] That would mean abstention from all activities such as leaking, denying information, failing to implement orders or policies or slowing them down, end runs to Congress or up the chain of command, or framing choices so as to limit or manipulate the options. The approach should be candor and openness in both appearance and reality. Military leaders have to assume that knowledgeable civilians come into office with considerable suspicion, aware that officers possess personal views, ideologies, ambitions, and institutional loyalties and perspectives and that they have historically pursued various military agendas. There has been so much politicization in the past few years that only civilians who were asleep might think otherwise. Senior officers should also recognize that while many politicians and their appointees fear the military, some also are jealous—about officers' accomplishments, achievements, bravery, rank, and prestige in American society—and this too inspires some distrust.

Building trust also requires obedience: communicating to the civilians that military leaders will carry out orders and instructions to the very best of their ability. There may be some space, as James Burk argues in chapter 8 in this volume, for principled opposition to civilian decisions, but the military must never fail to implement those decisions once the course of action has been set. Officers do need to resist civilian efforts to manage operations or interfere in tactical situations, but that cannot include blocking such involvement. One wise soldier who has studied this tendency admits that civilians have the authority, but he argues that the way to maximize the military's "operational autonomy" is to act openly, "*involve civilians in creative collaboration,*" and work in every way to build mutual confidence. Trust must be not only personal but institutional: the civilians have to be convinced that the military understands and accepts not only the decision but the thinking behind it and that therefore the orders will be carried out in a manner that will harmonize strategy, operations, and even tactics with the civilian intentions.[37]

Second, military leaders must speak up and insist on the right to give military advice *without varnish*, yet that advice must not be shaped so as to manipulate or dictate outcomes. Straight, thoughtful professional perspectives should be delivered in private up the chain of command and forthrightly to the Congress when officers are called upon to testify. In an address at West Point, Secretary of Defense Robert Gates told the cadets to "listen to me carefully—if as an officer you don't tell blunt truths or create an environment where candor is encouraged, then you've done yourself and the institution a disservice."[38] Flag officers should *speak up but not out,* that is, not speak out publicly but keep their advice confidential, prevent their staffs from leaking papers or advice, and not let either become public unless communicated in testimony when Congress asks for their personal views. Let the civilians make the military perspective public if they wish.[39] In front of Congress, however, military leaders are obliged to be fully forthcoming, frank, and responsive, even at the risk of retribution from their bosses in the Pentagon or White House. While avoiding undermining those bosses, senior officers nevertheless owe an equal advisory obligation to Congress. Although it is explicitly legal under Title 10 of the U.S. Code, it is unwise for members of the Joint Chiefs to volunteer their views to the Congress without the permission of the secretary of defense; however, once called before that body, senior military officers must not equivocate or, when asked their personal views, hide their disagreements with their chain of command.[40] When officers are not candid, or seem not to be, when they are not consistent in private and in public, they forfeit their effectiveness and diminish their credibility, not only with the political leadership but eventually with the public.[41]

Third, in order to remain the neutral servant of the state no matter which party or faction is in power, military leaders must do what is right from a professional perspective and must resist all efforts by civilians to have senior officers—or any military members—act otherwise. Officers have the duty to help civilians, and to help them avoid mistakes, but if, after frank exchanges, civilians insist, they have the authority to be wrong; it is neither the role, the function, nor the obligation of the military, once a decision has been discussed and made, to prevent those mistakes. Military judgment may not always be best in any given situation anyway, but to stop civilian officials from exercising their authority by any activity that undermines civilian control would threaten American government. The integrity of the system of government—promised by every officer in the oath they all take upon commissioning—supersedes any conceivable national security problem.

A fourth behavior that builds trust is to get ahead of the civilians in military policy in terms of change, reform, adjustment, innovations, and thinking through national security problems. Change, whether evolution or transformation, is ongoing. For over a century a chief function of military leaders has been to manage change, in response to shifting national priorities, new threats, altered international conditions, changing technology, and social change. Fashions come and go in national defense; change occurs at differing speeds, and arises from many sources, often suddenly and unpredictably. Officers who manage innovation, on the basis of what is best for the nation and its defense rather than from the perspective of a service, command, or the military as an institution, can often benefit the latter while increasing military influence. If something new seems deleterious, advising against it openly and forthrightly is the only proper course.

In forging these collaborative and sometimes intense relationships with civilian superiors, military officers face at least five pressures that must be resisted: careerism, institutionalism, politicization, manipulation, and resignation.

The first pressure to be resisted is *careerism*. The pressure to conform, to stay silent, to go along, or to do what advances one's career is the most prevalent and at the same time one of the most deadly behaviors for effective civil-military relations. Officers must not remain silent or suppress open discussion of significant issues in order to avoid angering civilian superiors. National defense requires that the armed forces communicate honestly inside their institutions, whether they are considering the proper courses of action, studying warfare and current and past operations, making projections about the need for weapons, devising doctrine and strategy and tactics, or addressing a large variety of other professional issues and concerns. Speaking up inside the institution on professional issues differs from speaking out to the public with the intent of affecting public opinion on matters of high policy or war making that have clear political or partisan implications. The possibility that the public may listen to unclassified versions of these professional discussions through the press or military professional journals should not be a deterrent. If such discourse angers civilian superiors, too bad. Officers cannot keep faith with the men and women under their care and command, or ably serve the nation, if they censor themselves in internal professional discussion. The military profession, above all others, respects and demands physical courage, but all professions require and respect moral courage.

A second pressure to be resisted might be called *institutionalism*: the urge to do what is best for one's service, command, unit, or organization whether it serves the larger national interest or not. Frequently such behavior grows out of limited or parochial experience or is reflexive, but often service interests have been pursued fiercely without regard for other needs. Few things arouse more suspicion or distrust from civilian leaders in Congress and the executive branch, or from the American people. Narrow bureaucratic agendas diminish the reputation of the military and the credibility of its advice and suggest that the military is just one more bureaucracy pursuing its own institutional needs. The public, and even a notable percentage of the military itself, seems to agree. When in 1998 the

Triangle Institute for Security Studies asked a representative sample of influential civilians and the general public if "civilian leaders order the military to do something that it opposes, [would] military leaders seek ways to avoid carrying out the order?" more than 45 percent of civilian leaders and over two-thirds of the public said they expected that the military would do so at least "some of the time"; some 11 percent of the civilian leaders (and 29 percent of the public) expected such disobedience of the military "most" or "all of the time." Within the military, more than a quarter of the up-and-coming military officers, active and reserve, who were surveyed in the resident courses at professional military educational institutions, answered at least "some of the time," as did nearly half of the cadets and midshipmen in the service academies and ROTC. Even at the highest ranks, more than a third of the active-duty brigadier and major generals in the sample expressed this expectation of passive disobedience.[42] Without question, behavior that blocks, undermines, or otherwise violates civilian authority, even though it may help an armed service, unit, or command, is simply unacceptable, and a clear violation of professionalism.

A third pressure that undermines the trust of the civilian leadership is *politicization*. In the past half century, in contrast to earlier norms of the profession in the United States, military officers have begun to vote in large numbers and to identify themselves with political parties; indeed, they do so at higher rates than the general public does.[43] Politicization has progressed to the point where Secretary of Defense Robert Gates, in his first graduation addresses at the Naval and Air Force academies, felt it necessary to warn the new graduates that, "as officers [they] will have a responsibility to communicate to those below [them] that the American military must be non-political."[44] Similarly, in his first message to the armed forces, the new chairman of the Joint Chiefs felt that he had to promise explicitly to "develop and deliver" his advice to the president and secretary of defense "independently, in private and in a completely apolitical manner."[45] Officers who are suspected by politicians and by the public of being influenced by their own ideology, or of possessing strong beliefs about the best policy, vitiate the credibility of their advice as being entirely professional. To function as the neutral servant of the state, the military must be seen not simply as nonpartisan but as "un-partisan": above, beyond, and oblivious to partisan politics. Discussion of partisan politics erodes professionalism because it politicizes. Voting, if pursued, should be an intensely private matter. In old Navy tradition, three subjects were out of bounds for discussion in the wardroom: sex, religion, and politics were all viewed as both personal and divisive; these topics are still likely to cause conflict in the officer corps and to undermine the neutrality and objectivity of the military as an institution with regard to what are still contentious issues in society. In the mid-1990s the White House personnel office approached a senior general being considered for a high civilian position requiring Senate confirmation, asking twice in the space of ten days for this officer's political affiliation. Both times the general instructed his aide to tell the White House that his party registration was "none of their business." His reply, while correct, did not go far enough, because it confirmed the assumption that the military is political. Better if he had responded: "As a flag officer in the American armed forces, I have no political affiliation."[46]

A fourth pressure officers must resist is *manipulation* by the political leadership, who often expect or even pressure senior officers to promote particular policies in public and to speak on issues beyond those which are professionally within the military sphere, such as defining who the enemy is, defending the necessity of war, championing a particular policy or decision, or reporting progress in ways that would provide political support for the prosecution of a conflict or intervention. Explaining a campaign or operation from anything other than a strictly military viewpoint inevitably politicizes the military, diminishing the nonpartisanship of the armed forces and identifying the commander with a particular administration. This gives rise to suspicions that this or that flag officer is a "Democrat" general or a "Republican" admiral. All of this undermines the confidence and trust of political leaders and the public.

Senior officers must resist inadvertently or unknowingly echoing their political bosses on partisan issues, as Chairman of the Joint Chiefs General Richard Myers did when calling terrorism the most dangerous threat the United States ever faced, hyperbole that was questionable as both history and nonpartisanship.[47] The more opposition or pressure, the more likely the politicians will want to use, or hide behind, the military, as did Lyndon Johnson when he had William Westmoreland report publicly on progress in the Vietnam War to shore up faltering public support in 1967.[48] Senior generals should stay out of the public media before elections, not publish prominent newspaper essays, as Colin Powell did while chairman of the Joint Chiefs in October 1992, about foreign interventions, or as David Petraeus did in 2004 about progress in training Iraqi security forces.[49]

Officers should avoid the sorts of political entanglement that Petraeus suffered during his confirmation hearings in early 2007, when he agreed that congressional debate might be encouraging the enemy. John Warner, the dean of Republican senators on national defense, responded with barely concealed anger:

"I hope that this colloquy has not entrapped you into some responses that you might later regret."[50] Senior officers should resolutely avoid political controversy unless their duties require exposure to it. The members of the Joint Chiefs had no call to defend either Secretary Rumsfeld or the troops, as they did in early 2006 by attacking *Washington Post* cartoonist Tom Toles for a savage caricature of Rumsfeld. Similarly, the Joint Chiefs of Staff chairman undermined the appearance of nonpartisanship when he provided the U.S. District Court with a character reference for Scooter Libby, the vice president's chief of staff subsequently found guilty of perjury in the case involving the exposure of undercover CIA officer Valerie Plame.[51]

The issue of progress in war inevitably ensnares a commander between bosses and war critics no matter how careful he might be, as happened in the summer of 2007 to Petraeus and some of his subordinates. Pushed forward by the Bush administration as spokesman for the "surge" strategy and forced by Congress to report on its progress, Petraeus was squeezed between his civilian superiors and their Democratic opponents in Congress. In his testimony he walked a tightrope, putting a positive spin on the situation in Iraq while at the same time scrupulously qualifying his interpretations so as to conform to the facts. Yet from the beginning of his command, by meeting frequently with the press and by permitting or encouraging his subordinate commanders to discuss the war publicly, Petraeus seemed to embrace the public role, provoking a predictable response from Democrats and from the press, both of whom questioned his political neutrality. One reporter called him "a political frontman" for the White House; a national columnist labeled him an "enabler" of the president. After his appearance before Congress, one scholar labeled it a "charade," while another called him "a political general of the worst kind." Senior officers recognized the problem: reportedly, "top military leaders at the Pentagon" were worried that "an incessant spotlight on one general" risked "politicizing the military and undermining the public's faith that military leaders will give honest assessments of the war's progress."[52]

As divisions sharpen, politicians cling more strongly to the military; difficult as it becomes, senior flag officers must resist. Matthew Ridgway defined the proper behavior in his valedictory letter to the secretary of defense in 1955, after not being renewed as Army chief over differences with Eisenhower's defense policies. Ridgway described his role as giving civilians "competent professional advice on the military aspects of the problems referred to him, based on his fearless, honest, objective estimate of the national interest, and regardless of administration policy at any particular time." He "should be neither expected nor required to give public endorsement to military courses of action against which he has previously recommended. His responsibility should be solely that of loyal vigorous execution of decision by proper authority."[53]

A fifth pressure, one that seems to be taking root in today's military, is the idea of *resignation*. Officers must resist, beyond giving forthright advice against them, what they see as wrong or mistaken policies, particularly decisions that will unnecessarily cost lives or violate an officer's personal moral or professional ethics; they can and perhaps should walk away from such policies, decisions, or orders by asking for retirement or reassignment. In 2006 several retired generals publicly excoriated Secretary Rumsfeld in the most personal terms, expressing regret that they had not done so earlier when on active duty or immediately upon leaving the service, and they called for him to be sacked.[54] At the Army War College, a retired general repeated three times that the military had "permitted" the civilians to take the country to war in 2003, implying that the military had both the power and the duty to have prevented it. When asked how, under our system of civilian control, that resistance could legitimately have been undertaken, however, the general had no answer.[55]

A respected retired lieutenant general advocated resignation in print, criticizing "the failure of the key military four-stars . . . to stand their ground over divided command in immediate post-conflict Iraq," and citing as examples the threats to resign made during World War II by General Dwight D. Eisenhower and General George C. Marshall, even though Marshall later called his own behavior in that situation "reprehensible." As additional authority, the writer cited Napoleon, not exactly a suitable model of high command for a democratic republic.[56] Equally worrisome, a National War College graduate who argued openly for the propriety of resignation in protest won the Alumni Association Writing Award for Ethics for 2006.[57] In recent articles, several respected scholars have stated outright or implied that under certain circumstances senior military officers can, and perhaps should, "resign" if ignored on crucial (by their own standard) issues.[58] Perhaps most disturbing, the chairman of the Joint Chiefs, in affirming strongly that the military must remain politically neutral and have "the moral courage to stand up for what's right" in providing candid, apolitical advice to civilian superiors, asserted the option of quitting if the decisions were unacceptable. "We give our best advice beforehand," he told the graduating midshipmen at Annapolis in May 2008. "If it's followed, great. If it's not, we have only two choices. Obey the orders, . . . carrying them out with the professionalism and loyalty they deserve or vote with our feet."[59]

This professional understanding differs altogether from that of the past. There is no tradition of resignation of any kind in the American military. Personal and professional honor do not require request for reassignment or retirement if civilians order one's service, command, or unit to act in some manner an officer finds distasteful, disastrous, or even immoral. The military's job is to advise and then execute lawful orders. One individual's definition of what is moral may differ from that of peers or of society. Even military officers at the very top of the chain of command (much less those below) cannot know all of the larger national and international considerations involved, a calculation that belongs properly to the political leadership, elected and appointed. Nor is there historical evidence that military judgment has been superior to that of the politicians. George C. Marshall reflected near the end of his life that "there are too many influences involved [in a political decision], and it is quite a question of how much of this would be familiar to the military participants."[60] Furthermore, if officers at different levels constantly measured policies, decisions, orders, and operations by their own personal moral standards, and acted on those assessments, the good order and discipline of the military would collapse.

Resignation—even the very hint of it, much less the threat or the act—is a direct assault on civilian authority. Civilian officials rightly interpret it as such. It inherently violates civilian control. Few things more explicitly injure civil-military trust. Officers who threaten resignation wield a power that is not consistent with the theory or historical practice of civilian control in the United States. In other walks of life, professionals can choose to resign their position, but in the military, an officer sworn to protect the country would, by resigning, abandon the American people, and the officer's own troops, for essentially personal reasons. There may be truly extraordinary or dire circumstances in which an officer cannot continue to serve, for example a decision that causes slaughter or indisputably jeopardizes the existence of the country for no explicable or conceivable reason. But even in such dire circumstances, the leaving must be accomplished silently lest it violate civilian control and thus an officer's oath to the Constitution. The fact that there is no tradition of resignation in the American military—and the realization that under our system of government the other branches of government and ultimately the American people hold the political leadership, not the military, accountable—should give pause to every officer who believes that resignation, either in silence or in protest, may sometimes be appropriate.[61]

Finally, certain professional obligations of top senior military officers extend into retirement. Most such obligations, while unwritten, are fully understood:

do not dishonor the uniform; do not undermine the national defense by word or deed. Similarly, some pertain to civilian control: the officer must not use the reputation of the American military (for disinterested patriotism, impartial service, and political neutrality) to commit political acts that would undermine civil-military relations and would contribute to the politicization of the military profession.

Officers do not take off their professionalism along with their uniforms, any more than do lawyers, doctors, or college professors. As a matter of law, officers carry many of the obligations of their commissions throughout their retirement.[62] To endorse presidential candidates, or to attack an administration in which an officer served at a senior level while it is still in office, is clearly improper, for it uses the legitimacy and the aura of impartiality to be partial and indeed partisan. It suggests to officers still on active duty that partisanship is acceptable. It suggests to the American people that the military is just one more interest group with its own agenda, rather than the neutral servant of the state. It suggests to politicians that they should choose generals and admirals on the basis of political and ideological compatibility, subservience, and compliance, rather than professional accomplishment, experience, candor, character, courage, and the capacity for highest responsibility. It suggests, moreover, that senior military officers cannot be trusted to keep confidences, not to abuse candid interchange, and not to undermine their bosses politically. Public attacks such as those on Secretary Rumsfeld in April 2006 by half a dozen generals who served during his tenure threaten to poison civil-military relations far into the future.[63] Even worse is a retired field commander who publicly attacks the administration he served while it is still in office and while the war continues, and who gives the opposition party's reply to the president's Saturday radio address, declaring that he speaks to the American public "today, not as a representative of the Democratic Party, but as a retired military officer who is a former commander of the Multi-National Force–Iraq."[64] Such behavior politicizes the military and degrades the profession.

The overwhelming majority of retired officers know this. In 1992, after retired Chairman of the Joint Chiefs Admiral William Crowe and other senior retired officers violated this norm by publicly endorsing candidate Bill Clinton for president, the head of the president's reelection campaign asked Crowe's predecessor, Army General John Vessey, to endorse President George H. W. Bush. Speaking personally to the president, Vessey said that "he would take a bullet for him, but he could not do that—make a public endorsement of a presidential candidate."[65] James L. Jones, the highly respected former commandant of the Marine Corps and NATO commander, has also followed this tradition in retirement. While making "no secret" of a desire to serve again in government, he has refused partisan affiliation. "I've been advised," he said, "that it's time to show your colors," and that "if you're going to survive in this town [Washington,] you have to decide what you are . . . Democratic or a Republican. But I don't agree with that."[66] Even General Norman Schwarzkopf, who had lent his name and presence to the Republicans after retirement, seems recently to have rediscovered the larger norm: when a newspaper columnist asked him how many troops were needed in Iraq, he responded: "Some of the best advice I was given is that when a general officer retired, he should never pass up an opportunity to remain silent."[67]

Civilian Behaviors to Inspire Trust

Civilians also possess obligations in civil-military relations, although it is unrealistic to expect consistent norms to be followed by an eclectic group of individuals appointed by different presidents at different times for a variety of reasons. Nevertheless, civilian officials have every incentive to want effective, collaborative relationships with the senior military leadership, and this depends on them following certain norms of behavior and attitude.

First, civilians need to understand the military—the people, the profession, the institutions, that is, the entire military world including its needs, assumptions, logic, and perspectives—in order to make proper and informed decisions on the myriad issues that constitute national security. Even with the benefit of long experience, this requires reading, travel, informal social interaction, and above all listening, as Rumsfeld's successor Robert Gates acknowledged when he immediately began meeting weekly with the Joint Chiefs on its turf, in The Tank.[68] While high-level Defense Department officials and members of Congress must delegate much authority and responsibility, they should not make the mistake of thinking that military issues, weapons, processes, behaviors, systems, strategies, operations, or even tactics are so esoteric or technical as to be beyond their understanding and thus requiring a surrender of authority. As much as they might wish on some occasions, the civilians cannot escape the responsibilities that accompany high office. They should ask questions continually until they hear answers that make sense. At the same time, the advisory relationship demands dialogue, characterized as much by open, frank conversations as by the formalities of recommendations, questions, and decisions in a relationship of authority and subordination.[69]

Second, civilians should recognize that the military is loyal and values loyalty, and will be loyal to its bosses of the moment, not to previous bosses. That is, there are no Democratic admirals, no Republican generals. Just because an officer faithfully served civilian masters of the opposite political party in a previous administration means nothing; that same officer can be expected to shift allegiance quickly to serve a new administration with equal loyalty. To assume otherwise would insult the officer and the military professional, and would provoke mistrust in return.

Third, civilians should treat military people and their institutions with genuine respect. If civilian officials cannot respect the military and what it does, they should serve elsewhere in government, or not at all. Like military officers, civilian officials must see to the needs of the troops as far as possible, for a priority in military service is that leaders take care of their people's physical and emotional needs, down to the lowest enlisted ranks and most recent recruits, before seeing to their own needs. Robert Gates exemplified this concern, adding personal comments to every letter of condolence sent to the families of soldiers killed in Iraq, and choking up while giving a speech about a Marine officer who died in combat.[70] In his confirmation testimony to the Senate Armed Services Committee, Gates said: "I think the other lesson that I learned over time was the respect for the professionals. . . . When you treat the professionals . . . who perform the mission of the organization with respect and you listen to them and you pay attention to them, I think that everybody is better served." Gates acknowledged that "they were there before you got there, they'll be there after you leave, and if you don't make them a part of the solution, they will become a part of the problem." This does not, however, mean automatically deferring to them, to their judgment, or to their advice. Few military officers, even at high rank, have the broad political picture or nonmilitary factors in mind, and they are often divided in judgment amongst themselves.[71]

Fourth, civilians should support and defend the military against unwarranted or unfair criticism and should represent the military's needs and viewpoints elsewhere in government, even when pursuing policies or making or executing decisions that the military dislikes, such as reductions in forces or resources. If politicians throw the armed services to the wolves, the military will reciprocate by failing to serve the political leadership loyally and candidly, even though professional obligation requires it. It is not the job of civilians in the executive branch to criticize the military or its members personally or institutionally. But high civilian officials have a responsibility both to insist that the military stay out of partisan politics and to avoid contaminating senior officers with partisan requests. The U.S. Supreme Court in 1976 explicitly noted a "constitutional tradition of a politically neutral military establishment under civilian control. It is a policy that has been reflected in numerous laws and military regulations throughout our history."[72] As Matthew Ridgway noted in a letter to the Secretary of Defense, the "political climate shifts and changes," and "differing assessments will be made of [a chief's] proper role, but whatever the situation, he must remain outside the field of partisan politics. It is incumbent upon civilian officials to see that he stays outside, and to protect him from becoming involved."[73]

A fifth obligation of civilians is that they must, at the same time, hold the military accountable for its actions, within the normal, legitimate processes of the services and the Department of Defense. Just three months into office, acting with speed and grace, Secretary Gates fired some generals and the secretary of the Army over the scandalous living conditions and bureaucratic frustrations suffered by wounded veterans at Walter Reed Medical Center.[74] Replacing people who did not perform their duties adequately—after due consideration, fairly, and in an appropriate manner—established the very same climate of accountability and strength of leadership that officers champion within their own professional ideals. However, officers who must be relieved need not be dishonored or disgraced for mistakes or malfeasance, after a lifetime of service that qualified them and earned them high rank, unless there is some pressing need to make an example. Firing is enough of a punishment unless law or regulations call for something more.

Sixth, civilians should also be accountable; they have no business hiding behind the military to cover for their own mistakes or those of other civilians. Given large or multiple missions with limited or insufficient resources, conscientious officers will make every effort to succeed, but in such cases even positive results will almost certainly stimulate controversy. Blaming the military for the outcome, in an attempt to avoid political heat or responsibility, imperils a civilian's legitimacy, inspiring disrespect and distrust. Leaving the military holding the bag for civilians' political decisions or unforeseen events risks warping civil-military relations to the point of dysfunction. If civilian control means that civilians have the ultimate authority, it also means that they have the final responsibility.

Last, civilian officials in the executive branch and Congress, including staff, must exercise their power gracefully, politely, and forcefully—not abusively, or peremptorily, or at the expense of others' personal or professional dignity. Gates set a good example when he communicated his displeasure without explicitly scolding the chairman of the Joint Chiefs for expressing in public the opinion that homosexual acts were immoral. Within his first six months in office, Gates replaced the military leadership in Iraq and on the Joint Chiefs, and in 2008 fired the secretary and chief of staff of the Air Force, all with quiet thoughtfulness and a plainspoken candor, with praise for the individuals, and without a hint of personal denigration.[75] Military people respect strong leadership. They want decisions, instructions, goals, and guidance in as explicit and comprehensive a form as possible and, above all, in a timely fashion so that money and lives are not squandered by indecision or uncertainty. If this is impossible, they deserve candid, honest explanations. Civilians should meet deadlines and keep to schedules, and act in such a fashion in every respect so that the military does not get the feeling that dealing with its political masters is itself a war.

Managing the Civil-Military Relationship

In the end, there are no cookbook recipes for civil-military relations, as diverse and unexpected as they can be. Both sides expect tension and suspicion because that is the historical experience, particularly in the past half century. If the system is working properly, both sides will work to alleviate the distrust. Even if the civilians refuse to make an effort from their side, however, the military leadership must not resist passively by constricting information or failing to communicate fully, by slowing implementation of policy or decisions or engaging in "shirking," as Peter Feaver has so insightfully called it.[76] Such behavior would inevitably produce bad policy and bad decisions.

Thus, while the responsibility for an effective partnership rests on both sides, ultimately it is the military that must make the relationship work. Senior military leaders have a professional duty to teach their civilian superiors and to shape the relationship, just as doctors do with their patients, lawyers with their clients, teachers with their students, and all professionals with those they serve. Officers are the long-term stewards of national security: they are the ones who, as a matter of professional responsibility, must think about and practice civil-military relations on a continuing basis, and recognize its study as necessary to fulfill their role in society effectively.

For soldiers, there can be no difference between Republicans and Democrats. Both political parties have proved that they can manipulate or even corrupt the military for partisan or policy ends. Neither party is the military's enduring ally or patron, or its enemy either. If one party believes the military to be a core constituency, and the other believes it to be hostile, neither will approach the relationship with any trust on either an individual or an institutional basis; as a result, relations are likely to be warped, perhaps to the point of dysfunction.

George C. Marshall faced many of these dilemmas in his seven years as assistant chief of staff and then chief of staff of the army. With Presidents Roosevelt and Truman and with Congress, Marshall was often brutally frank, sometimes even confrontational, but always cooperative and never dismissive. He was not above manipulating his bosses, sometimes even cutting a deal with a congressman or senator, but it was always done in private. "I thought it was far more important in the long run that I be well established as a member of the team and try to do my convincing within that team, rather than to take action publicly contrary to the desires of the president and certain members of Congress."[77] He opposed many presidential decisions—to send munitions to Britain and the Soviets during the desperate years of American rearmament, to occupy Greenland and Iceland in 1941, to invade North Africa in 1942—and as secretary of state he opposed the recognition of Israel in 1948, telling Harry Truman that if he, Marshall, were ever to "[break] his lifelong refusal to vote, 'I would vote against the president.'"[78] But Marshall was honest and straightforward; he never leaked a word or undermined his bosses' decisions. He insisted upon advocating the army's needs; indeed, he was relentless on the subject. Sometimes he opposed the president on personnel choices. But Marshall always acceded to the president's decisions. "I never haggled with the President," Marshall remembered. "I swallowed the little things so that I could go to bat on the big ones. I never handled a matter apologetically and I was never contentious."[79] He always maintained formality in his relationship with Franklin Roosevelt, to avoid being manipulated by the president's charm. As assistant chief of staff in 1938, Marshall openly disagreed with the president in a meeting, leading some to predict that Marshall's career was thereby finished. He maintained his distance from others, rejecting intimacy with his professional colleagues. By his bearing he discouraged President Roosevelt from calling him "George," often avoided going to the White House, and even refused to laugh at the president's jokes. When told by Roosevelt that he would be nominated chief of staff, Marshall "expressed thanks but added that there would be occasions when he would state disagreement with presidential views. Roosevelt said that was all right. 'You said "All right" pleasantly,' answered Marshall, 'but it may not be pleasant.'"[80] Roosevelt was difficult, his thinking often opaque to outsiders, "very much like chasing a vagrant beam of sunshine around an empty room," as Secretary of War Henry Stimson put it.[81] In a telling parallel to the silence of the military leadership in 2002–3 while President George W. Bush took the country to war, Marshall remained publicly silent in 1941 while Roosevelt misrepresented the aggressive U.S. posture toward Germany in the Atlantic and involved American forces actively in support of the British.[82] Marshall never permitted himself to be maneuvered into a partisan or inappropriate role.

Nearly thirty years after Marshall retired, a legal and legislative aide to the chairman of the Joint Chiefs of Staff advised his boss explicitly along the lines exemplified by Marshall. The chairman asked, "What do I do if in testifying before Congress I am asked a question that the President has ordered me not to answer or even discuss?" "Well, General," Colonel Zane Finklestein replied, "you roll your eyes, clutch your chest, and fall out of your chair. . . . And when you hear the door close on the Chairman's suite at Walter Reed, open your eyes, get out of bed, and go over and pick up the red phone. 'Mr. President,' you say, 'Sir, I will not perjure myself before the Congress of the United States. Please give me new orders.'"[83]

The Soldier, the State, and Huntington's Contribution

"*The Soldier and the State* put the issue of civil-military relations on the map," as foreign affairs writer Robert D. Kaplan observed in a 2001 retrospective of Huntington's work.[84] Certainly the scholarly community and the military profession owe Samuel Huntington an enormous debt for his writings on the subject. But today, a controversial secretary of defense and a deeply divisive war have made it all the more necessary to transcend Huntington's work, to build on his scholarship to delve deeper into the substance of civil-military relationships, and above all to impress upon soldiers and politicians the necessity of studying the subject and thinking through the norms and behaviors that will improve policy and decision making. When *The Soldier and the State* first came out, a particularly knowledgeable reviewer—Telford Taylor, who had been the chief prosecutor at the Nuremberg war crimes trials—praised Huntington precisely for his "impressive and provocative contribution" in "an area where iconoclasm is badly needed." What he said, unfortunately, remains true today: "Civilian Control has become a piece of cant that politicians mouth worshipfully but with little understanding."[85] Today, to paraphrase an aphorism long ascribed to Mark Twain, nobody talks about civil-military relations, but everybody does something about it. If this continues, particularly among soldiers and politicians, it puts the nation in peril.

CHAPTER FOURTEEN

Conclusions

Suzanne C. Nielsen and Don M. Snider

A fundamental premise of this project is that, as the military continues to play a central role in U.S. national security policy, democratically appropriate and strategically effective civil-military relations are vital; however, there is no consensus on many important aspects of these relationships. A second premise is that *The Soldier and the State*, published more than half a century ago, is still a useful starting point for thinking about current and enduring issues of civil-military relations, as amply shown in the work of the authors in this volume.

This final chapter draws from the analytical chapters a set of conclusions about the realities and challenges of American civil-military relations today. These conclusions are shaped in part by Huntington's conceptual framework, but they also reflect the insights of the volume's contributors. The nine conclusions of this work are summarized in table 14.1.

1. The Continuing Value of Huntington's Normative Model for U.S. Civil-Military Relations

- Five decades after its creation, the contributions of Huntington's objective control model continue to outweigh its shortcomings, although

Table 14.1.   Conclusions of the Project

1. The Continuing Value of Huntington's Normative Model for U.S. Civil-Military Relations

Five decades after its creation, the contributions of Huntington's objective control model continue to outweigh its shortcomings, although some of its core propositions deserve amendment. The most significant shortcoming of Huntington's construct was its failure to recognize that a separation between political and military affairs is not possible—particularly at the highest levels of policymaking.

2. Tensions between American Liberalism and the Military Perspective

Huntington's prediction that the moral absolutism inherent in American liberalism would create tensions between the societal and functional imperatives remains helpful in explaining current and likely future challenges in U.S. civil-military relations.

3. Military Professional Expertise

Huntington's description of the central expertise of the officer as the "management of violence" is too narrow. Instead, the military officer must be expert in "the threat or use of force to achieve the political purposes of the state." Nonkinetic skills, as well as traditional combat skills, are essential to success in modern war.

4. Professional Military Autonomy

Huntington was wrong to root the need for military autonomy in an unrealistic separation of political and military spheres but was right to suggest that for functional purposes some aspects of military culture would need to differ from dominant cultural norms in American society. His recognition of the need for moral autonomy in military professionals, however, was inadequate and deserves further exploration.

5. The Boundaries of the Military Professions

Huntington viewed active-duty officers as the only members of the military profession. It is time to consider whether membership should be expanded to include active-duty and reserve officers and senior noncommissioned officers as professionals. The legal and practical distinctions between America's military institutions and private security companies playing an increasingly critical role in U.S. military operations overseas are also urgently in need of analysis.

6. Political Participation and Behavior of Military Professionals

Under Huntington's objective control model, professional military officers would voluntarily refrain from participation in politics. However, since the end of the Cold War, there has been a marked decrease in partisan neutrality among the U.S. officer corps. Partisan behavior remains inappropriate, but military leaders do have an obligation to be effective contributors in a policymaking process that is inherently political.

7. The Interpersonal Dimension of Civil-Military Relationships

Although Huntington did not address interpersonal dynamics, mutual respect and a presumption of trustworthiness among military and civilian leaders are important to the crafting of sound national security policies. Democratically sound and strategically effective civil-military relationships are more likely when both sides are guided by a set of explicit and agreed norms and principles.

8. The Development of Senior Military and Civilian Leaders

Although largely unaddressed by Huntington, improved efforts to educate, train, and develop future senior civilian and military leaders for their respective roles at the civil-military nexus would make effective civil-military relations more likely.

9. Congress and the Executive as Coequals in Control of the Military

Although the U.S. Constitution gives Congress weighty responsibilities in military affairs, the manner in which Congress can best exercise those responsibilities is not broadly agreed upon. Military officers should respond to the shared responsibilities of the two branches by providing Congress with frank and expert military advice while, to the best of their ability, remaining loyal to the executive branch of which they are a part.

some of its core propositions deserve amendment. The most significant shortcoming of Huntington's construct was its failure to recognize that a separation between political and military affairs is not possible—particularly at the highest levels of policymaking.

The introductory chapter of this volume noted that one of Huntington's major contributions was to suggest a normative model of civil-military relations, which he called "objective control," that would "maximize military security at the least sacrifice of other social values."[1] However, Huntington's objective control model has proved to be far from perfect. Richard Betts (chapter 2), Chris Gibson (chapter 12), Richard Kohn (chapter 13), and others point out the most significant shortcoming of his construct: its failure to recognize that a clear distinction between political and military affairs is not possible. While Clausewitz notes that war is appropriately subordinate to politics, he also argues that at the highest level "strategy and policy coalesce."[2] Policy choices must be informed by military expertise, while military operations must be aimed toward and infused with political purpose, or they make no strategic sense. This reality, more complex than Huntington acknowledged, requires close and constant interaction between political and military leaders, who must be able, at the very least, to appreciate one another's roles, responsibilities, and respective areas of expertise.

Despite that significant shortcoming, we argue that U.S. civil-military relations should continue to be guided by the objective control model in at least two important ways. First, as Richard Betts emphasizes, Huntington's approach rightly rejects politicization of the military by civilian leaders as harmful to military effectiveness and professionalism. Adherence to the objective control model may well be what has prevented certain recent developments, such as the increase in partisan identification by military officers, from becoming a significant problem. If civilian officials began to practice forms of subjective control, such as selecting senior military leaders according to partisan criteria, serving officers would have incentives to make career bets in their choice of political party. The result would be detrimental to military professionalism in numerous ways: civilian leaders might begin to view military officers as competitors rather than partners; the broader American society might lose regard for the military institution; and advancement through partisan identification would diminish military cohesion as well as the priority currently accorded to professional competence in promotion and other selection processes.

Second, as Michael Desch points out in chapter 5, objective control allows for considerable autonomy in the practice of the military profession and highlights the importance of military expertise. While it is impossible to specify in advance precisely what degree of autonomy will be appropriate for any of an unlimited variety of potential contexts, Betts, Desch, and Kohn all caution civilian leaders to exercise prudence in recognizing that there is, in fact, a unique military expertise accruing to military leaders from long years of education and practice. As an example of the consequences of a lack of such prudence, Desch cites the relations with key military subordinates established by the civilian leadership team headed by Secretary of Defense Donald Rumsfeld. While noting that even exemplary civil-military relations would be no guarantee of military or strategic success, Desch argues, Rumsfeld's exclusion of key military members from the planning process and his general disregard for expert military opinion bear considerable responsibility for problems in Iraq after the 2003 invasion.

While many of the project's researchers see continued merit in the objective control model and consider it preferable to existing alternatives, at least two of the project's authors take a different view. Chris Gibson argues in chapter 12 that, because most civil-military interactions of importance occur in the realm of shared roles and responsibilities, objective control should be scrapped, not just amended. He offers instead what he labels the "Madisonian approach," which would require organizational changes to the role and responsibilities of the secretary of defense to facilitate the flow of military advice to the president and to the Congress. Richard Kohn, in chapter 13, suggests that the solution is not to provide a new theory or model of civilian control but instead to prescribe a series of norms to govern the actions of both partners to the civil-military relationship.

Given the merits of objective control as well as its shortcomings, we conclude, the best way forward is to preserve its underlying strengths while mitigating its weaknesses. Betts, for example, recommends that the U.S. civil-military relationship should be guided by a principle of "equal dialogue, unequal authority." Like the "unequal dialogue" that Eliot Cohen proposed in *Supreme Command*, this principle has the advantage of accommodating Clausewitz's insight that, in reality, no wall can separate political and military affairs.[3] Its reference to "unequal authority" reaffirms the primacy of democratic civilian political control over a subordinate military. Most valuably, however, the term *equal dialogue* is a reminder that civil-military interactions that are both vigorous and respectful—based on each side's trust in the other's competence and intentions—make it more likely that civil-military relations will produce strategically effective choices.

2. Tensions between American Liberalism and the Military Perspective

- Huntington's prediction that the moral absolutism inherent in American liberalism would create tensions between the societal and functional imperatives remains helpful in explaining current and likely future challenges in U.S. civil-military relations.

Our second conclusion rests on an analysis of the strategic environment and recent U.S. responses to it. As Richard Betts points out in chapter 2, the U.S. military did not demobilize after the Cold War as it had following other major wars; instead, American military activism actually accelerated. In the absence of great-power adversaries, the U.S. use of force abroad became increasingly diversified and discretionary, focused on spreading U.S. values and regulating world order rather than on realist goals relating directly to U.S. vital interests more narrowly defined. As a result, choices about the use of force became more contested among civilian groups and between civilian and military leaders. Political leaders who want to use strictly limited levels of force for discretionary and often humanitarian goals are likely to face resistance from military leaders who, if force is to be applied, are inclined to favor decisive and overwhelming means applied in conflicts that can be resolved quickly.

In addition to the discretionary aspect of the use of force, a second recurrent tension flows from the fact that American liberalism continues to exert a powerful influence on U.S. foreign policy. As argued by Michael Desch in chapter 5, the foreign policy views of both President Bill Clinton and President George W. Bush after 9/11 can be characterized as "neo-Wilsonian." Desch argues that this explains why the United States did not experience the decrease in civil-military tensions that some expected after the end of the Clinton administration in 2001. The neoconservative foreign policy of the Bush administration reflected, in form if not in name, classic tenets of American liberalism and its focus on exporting U.S. values and institutions abroad. Desch predicts that the idealism and moral absolutism of American political leaders will continue to come into conflict with the more conservative approach of the military.

The presumption that American liberalism necessarily clashes with the military perspective is consistent with Huntington's view of the beliefs likely to be embraced by a professional military. In *The Soldier and the State,* Huntington argued that an ideology of conservative realism characterized the "military mind."

By supporting the military's functional needs, this ideology contributed to military effectiveness and professionalism. It also contributed to civilian control because it counseled abstention by members of the military from participation in partisan politics. In chapter 9, however, Darrell Driver presents recent scholarship that undercuts the notion that ideology is derived from function: instead, it appears, a variety of professional activities can be reconciled, through individual narratives, with a diverse array of public beliefs. An experiment comparing views of military leaders and civilian leaders failed to find evidence of a consistent "military mind" among serving Army officers. These findings suggest that it would be a mistake to presume that conservative realism necessarily characterized the outlook of the U.S. military.

Instead of continuing to accept Huntington's construct of the military mind, therefore, it is more useful to examine the particular reasons for civil-military conflicts in specific contexts. As Richard Kohn points out in chapter 13, tension can be expected between civilian leaders and their military counterparts—even in the absence of ideological differences—simply because of differences in their personal backgrounds and in their official roles and responsibilities. Narrower propositions have been empirically established; for example, as he described in *Soldiers, Statesmen, and Cold War Crises,* Richard Betts found that, once force has been decided upon, the military generally tends to advocate fewer limits on means (an approach expressed both in the Weinberger Doctrine of the 1980s and in the Powell Doctrine of the early 1990s).[4]

For these reasons, tensions in U.S. civil-military relations are likely to continue, especially over use-of-force decisions, and especially when the decision is to undertake operations for purposes that can be seen as discretionary, with relatively tight limits on means.

3. Military Professional Expertise

- Huntington's description of the central expertise of the officer as the "management of violence" is too narrow. Instead, the military officer must be expert in "the threat or use of force to achieve the political purposes of the state." Nonkinetic skills, as well as traditional combat skills, are essential to success in modern war.

Huntington stated that officers shared an expertise that distinguished them from other professionals and from civilians. Borrowing Harold Lasswell's phrase, he said that the central skill of this professional expertise was "the management violence": "The direction, operation, and control of a human organization whose primary function is the application of violence is the particular skill of the officer . . . the management of violence, not the acts of violence itself."[5]

In the decades since Huntington wrote, several important debates regarding the military and its function have turned, in part, on this definition. Military officers disagreed over whether they should see themselves as "managers," as in Huntington's definition, or whether the identity of "leaders," often preferred, is more appropriate. Although in many respects this presents a false dichotomy— an effective leader must also be a good manager—this debate within the military has a rich history. It is significant because America's military professions use identity-based models to guide their leader-development programs. The identity they establish for the leader, such as that of "warrior," then becomes the central focus of both institutional and individual developmental efforts. It matters how officers see themselves because, absent an agreed-upon self-concept, it is much more difficult for officers to develop in their professional careers with the knowledge and the expertise needed to be effective in the prescribed role.

A second debate focuses on the word *violence*. Borrowing a phrase from Clausewitz, Huntington wrote that "the essence of war when considered as an independent science, as a thing in itself, is force. War is thus an act of force to compel our adversary to do our will."[6] A decade or so after World War II, and with the Korean War only recently past, Huntington's narrow focus on force and violence was understandable: although the Korean War ended in an armed standoff, it demonstrated that, even under the nuclear umbrella, conventional wars could occur.

From the perspective of the first decade of the twenty-first century, however, it is easier to see that Huntington's definition, though accurate, has always been incomplete. The U.S. experience since the end of the Cold War has been one of frequent engagement in complex contingency operations and irregular wars such as in Panama, Somalia, Haiti, the Balkans, Afghanistan, and Iraq. In these operations, capabilities for violent or "kinetic" forms of warfare, although necessary, are insufficient. As Clausewitz also pointed out, what matters in the use of force is the ultimate achievement of political goals: "the ultimate success of the whole."[7] For some purposes it can be useful to examine the management of violence as if it were an independent science, but such analyses would, as Clausewitz acknowledged, always be incomplete: "The political object is the goal, war is the means of reaching it, and means can never be considered in isolation from their purpose."[8]

Thus, Huntington's definition fails to encompass the actual expertise required of today's military professions. As Nadia Schadlow and Richard Lacquement emphasize in chapter 6, the U.S. armed forces increasingly require capabilities that are nonkinetic in nature. For example, if the central goals of a counterinsurgency campaign are to provide for the security of a population and to foster a sense that the supported government is legitimate, these may be ill served by a sole focus on the application of force to kill insurgents and terrorists. The U.S. military today must also be able to perform a variety of nonkinetic tasks, such as helping to secure basic services such as water, electricity, or medical care, or to provide for security against criminal elements, in environments in which the security situation is uncertain. Without skills such as engineering, policing, and the like, it will be almost impossible for the military to further the political goals of many U.S. military operations.

The implications of this challenge for U.S. civil-military relations are manifold. First, from the perspective of civilian policymakers, the nonkinetic measures that supplement combat efforts in complex contingency operations are often preferred. They create far less collateral damage, particularly in urban areas, and they thereby assist in achieving objectives abroad while lessening negative reactions at home to civilian casualties. Development of such nonkinetic capabilities, however, requires military organizations to invest resources and time that must be traded off against investments in the traditional combat capability needed to fight and win conventional conflicts.

Second, civilian leaders must be wary of trying to treat the military as an all-purpose instrument, or to rely on it for all needed capabilities that are not possessed by other governmental entities. Civil-military tensions have been heightened by military "mission creep" during the past decade, as State, Justice, Commerce, Treasury, and other U.S. executive departments lacked capacities needed to operate effectively overseas in support of tasks that the United States has undertaken, such as reestablishing governance by rebuilding failed infrastructure, local economies, and political institutions. Military leaders ask, quite rightly, how much their forces should be expected to do beyond the establishment of basic security, and for how long.

A third debate looks at the level of the individual officer or professional to ask what the domain of professional expertise should reasonably be. Is it possible to define a professional identity to help shape the development of professionals who are equally capable of practicing both kinetic and nonkinetic forms of warfare? Or does the way ahead for America's armed forces involve greater specialization of roles for officers and the units they lead? Such issues will continue to generate tension and require new policy and new research.

4. Professional Military Autonomy

- Huntington was wrong to root the need for military autonomy in an unrealistic separation of political and military spheres but was right to suggest that for functional purposes some aspects of military culture would need to differ from dominant cultural norms in American society. His recognition of the need for moral autonomy in military professionals, however, was inadequate and deserves further exploration.

One of Huntington's greatest contributions to the study of civil-military relations was his explicit consideration of the influence of the two imperatives—functional and societal—on the military institutions of any society: "Military institutions which reflect only social values may be incapable of performing effectively their military function. On the other hand, it may be impossible to contain within society military institutions shaped purely by functional imperatives. The interaction of these two forces is the nub of the problem of civil-military relations."[9]

In developing his theory of civilian control, Huntington relied on his own analysis of how the military became professionalized in the late nineteenth century, and on his own interpretation of Clausewitz's theory of war. Both analyses led him to conclude that to be effective the military needed, and should be granted, a significant degree of autonomy within the political structure of the state.

In the nineteenth century, he argued, military professionalism emerged because, among other influences, the creation of a constitutionally based state enabled "party strife and political conflict" to be moved "one step away from the military forces themselves." Political control of the military could then be channeled "through some accepted formal institution of government."[10] Explicating his analysis of Clausewitz, he wrote that Clausewitz's "concept of war as an autonomous and yet instrumental science implies a similar theory with respect to the role of the specialists in war. The fact that war has its own grammar requires that the military professionals be permitted to develop their expertise at the grammar without extraneous interference. . . . The ends to which the military body is employed, however, are outside its competence to judge. . . . War does not have its own logic or purpose. The soldier must always be subordinate to the statesman."[11]

Thus, his recommendation for the most effective form of civilian control—objective control—had at its core "the recognition of autonomous military professionalism." This professionalism, by minimizing the military's power within the state, had the effect of rendering the military "politically sterile and neutral."[12]

Over the decades, Huntington's recommendation of objective control has generated two major concerns. As discussed by Richard Betts, Michael Desch, and Richard Kohn, decision making at the civil-military nexus does not divide neatly between matters of state policy—ends—and military means. Williamson Murray adds to this discussion in chapter 7. Focusing on the military side of this relationship, Murray argues that officers operating at the most senior levels must have political and social knowledge as well as expert knowledge in military affairs. This is especially true in the current strategic environment, as the types of armed conflict are not just the conventional and nuclear confrontations central to Cold War planning, but encompass challenging new issues of terrorism and "holistic" or irregular war. Nothing on the horizon is likely to alleviate the complexity faced by military officers operating at senior levels or by their civilian counterparts. Identifying and developing those who will be best suited to respond effectively to today's national security issues remains one of the most vexing challenges as the nation elects, appoints, and, in the case of the military, promotes its future senior civilian and military leaders.

The second concern, foreshadowed by Huntington's argument for "autonomous professionalism," is the "gap" between America's armed forces under the All-Volunteer Force policy initiated in 1973 and the evolving values of the society from which those forces are drawn and in which they are rooted. Often articulated in the 1990s in topical terms such as gays in the military, women in combat, or the married military, these issues reflect how American cultural debates influence civil-military relations.[13] If military norms or values that differ from those of the society actually stem from or support functional requirements of the military, the senior leaders of the military professions must articulate and defend them.[14]

Among Huntington's provocative arguments for an autonomous profession with a degree of cultural isolation, there is an aspect of autonomy that he did not adequately address. As James Burk argues in chapter 8, serving military professionals "require autonomy, including moral autonomy, to be competent actors who can be held responsible for what they do." Burk's argument for the professional's autonomous "moral space" is a compelling one. Without clear recognition of its existence, it is difficult to make sound arguments about the exercise of this discretionary judgment. Burk's argument furthers the debate and is likely to lead to additional valuable research and analysis.

To have the most effective military in the future, the United States must have military professions, as they alone are capable of producing the expert knowledge, the military units, and the individual professionals able to apply that knowledge in the defense of the nation. Such knowledge and expert practice does not flow from ordinary governmental bureaucracies. But will the nation allow the professional, All-Volunteer Force to be sufficiently autonomous from the society it defends to be militarily effective? And can the military develop, within its own forms of social control—its professional ethic—moral norms for decision making and war fighting that the American people will find sufficiently trustworthy to grant them the needed autonomy? These abiding tensions between the social and functional imperatives, now more clearly focused, are not likely to go away.

5. The Boundaries of the Military Professions

- Huntington viewed active-duty officers as the only members of the military profession. It is time to consider whether membership should be expanded to include active-duty and reserve officers and senior noncommissioned officers as professionals. The legal and practical distinctions between America's military institutions and private security companies playing an increasingly critical role in U.S. military operations overseas are also urgently in need of analysis.

The question of boundaries focuses on just who is within the military sphere of American civil-military relations. Chapter 1 posited that today the United States has three military professions defined by domain of war fighting expertise—land, aerospace, and maritime—that are roughly equivalent to the three military departments in the Department of Defense—Army, Air Force, and Navy. Within these military institutions, Huntington's definition would limit membership to the commissioned officer corps of each service, as suggested by the title of the first chapter of his book, "Officership as a Profession."

Boundaries matter when dealing with professions and professionals: no one wants to undergo heart surgery by a retired surgeon who has not practiced for a half decade. Similarly, no parent wants to send a son or daughter to fight in an armed force whose company commanders have not been recently and rigorously certified to lead soldiers in mortal combat. The question of who is in a military profession is an important issue, morally, legally, and practically. In U.S. foreign policy today, however, it is not always clear who practices on behalf of the military professions.

David Segal and Karin De Angelis in chapter 10 explain why Huntington's delineation of the boundaries of the military profession may be too narrow for the All-Volunteer Force of today. They argue that many reserve officers and reserve and active-duty noncommissioned officers (NCOs) are doing "expert work" and that they have, to large degree, already been included in the "certification" processes that determine who is authorized to practice and who is not. In their view, reserve officers and all senior noncommissioned officers (NCOs in grades E7 through E9) should be considered professionals. In support, they point to the educational accomplishments typical of most of these individuals, as well as the professional education systems now in use for their progressive career development.

A second question of the boundaries of the profession is who speaks for the military in American political culture and civil-military relations. Is it just the active-duty commissioned officers who are the senior leaders of the professions, or does it also include retired, no-longer-practicing officers who offer commentary on the evening television newscasts?

In light of the vastly increased role of private security companies (PSCs) supporting U.S. operations overseas, a third and increasingly pressing question becomes how far the boundary of the profession should be moved. Who else should be included? While no researcher in this project addressed this subject directly, at the vetting conference there was broad and almost unanimous consensus that PSCs, although initially useful, now raise the specter of out-of-control mercenary militias acting in lieu of the profession of arms that has earned respect by defending the country's national security while protecting its values. The legal and practical effects of the expanding use of PSCs on U.S. foreign policy are huge, largely unexplored, and in urgent need of further research and policymaking.

This new issue turns upon understanding the societal imperative that Huntington introduced: just whom do the American people want to fight their wars, and what kind of armed forces do they trust for their security? As the research here suggests, the answer is evolving from citizen-soldier to a professional All-Volunteer Force, and expanding from commissioned officers to a professional corps that includes both officers and senior NCOs. But the status of PSCs remains urgently to be addressed by the Congress and the executive.

6. Political Participation and Behavior of Military Professionals

- Under Huntington's objective control model, professional military officers would voluntarily refrain from participation in politics. However, since the end of the Cold War, there has been a marked decrease in partisan neutrality among the U.S. officer corps. Partisan behavior remains inappropriate, but military leaders do have an obligation to be effective contributors in a policymaking process that is inherently political.

Huntington wrote that "the one prime essential for any system of civilian control is the minimizing of military power." As he explained it, "Objective civilian control achieves this reduction by professionalizing the military, by rendering them politically sterile and neutral. . . . A highly professional officer corps stands ready to carry out the wishes of any civilian group which secures legitimate authority within the state."[15]

If the military were purely a profession all of the time, its members might, consistent with Huntington's hypothesis, value their autonomy so highly that they would not want it weakened by the inevitable trade-offs involved in activities such as political deal making. However, since the end of the Cold War, the military—like many other institutions in the U.S. government and society—has become more sharply partisan and political. Absentee voting by deployed military personnel has been a politicized issue in recent elections. Retired flag officers increasingly undertake new partisan roles. Thus, our researchers sought to develop guidelines for what is and is not appropriate political behavior by military professionals.

Risa Brooks introduces and expands on the recent literature on the political activities of the military in chapter 11. She identifies potential benefits of increased political activities by uniformed military leaders. For example, such activities could enhance U.S. national security if they resulted in a more informed public dialogue on security matters, or if they served to alert political leaders to opportunities for innovation and adaptation of doctrine or military capabilities that might otherwise be missed.

However, she also points out problematic implications for democratic political control. Such activities might, for example, erode society's perception of the military as an impartial institution that operates above and apart from politics, and might increase the incentives of civilian leaders to appoint senior military leaders whose political positions agree with their own (converting objective control to subjective control, in Huntington's terms). In view of the potential risks and costs of such activity, Brooks and the other researchers in this project come down on the side of caution; several chapters recommend a stricter application by the military of its own existing norms, both explicit and implicit, that place limits on political activities by those in uniform.

Even if active-duty military officers adhere to very stringent norms against political involvement, challenges will be created by the partisan environment in which U.S. national security policy is made. Future military leaders must be capable of rendering professional advice within a process that is inherently political, yet as Williamson Murray points out in chapter 7, it is doubtful that current professional development processes within the services adequately prepare their leaders to do so.

Moreover, during the past decade, the proliferation of overt political activity by retired flag officers has muddied perceptions of who represents and speaks authoritatively for the military professions, potentially confusing the American public, junior military professionals, and even some in the policymaking communities. As retired flag officers appear in television newscasts or political ads, or actively endorse electoral candidates, it is often not clear that in doing so, they are speaking only for themselves as private citizens, not for the military profession as a whole.

These developments mean that the military profession has lost a large measure of control over its own certification processes, in that (unlike most professions) many who have relinquished their certification to practice because of voluntary retirement have not accepted that they can no longer speak for the military profession.

Thus, there is a need for clarity as to who speaks for the military profession to the American people, their collective client. Traditionally the representative function has been fulfilled by senior, active-duty leaders, specifically, the chairman of the Joint Chiefs, the service chiefs, and a very few of their senior active-duty commanders. These leaders must, we urge, reassert their exclusive role as representatives on behalf of their professions, in the process renewing control over their own certification processes. Such actions would provide a renewed basis for healthy civil-military relations by clarifying just who speaks for the military profession and who does not. Without such clarity in the senior ranks, it is doubtful that junior professionals will be willing, more broadly, to retain partisan-political neutrality, identified by Huntington as necessary for effective civil-military relations.

7. The Interpersonal Dimension of Civil-Military Relationships

- Although Huntington did not address interpersonal dynamics, mutual respect and a presumption of trustworthiness among military and civilian leaders are important to the crafting of sound national security policies. Democratically sound and strategically effective civil-military relationships are more likely when both sides are guided by a set of explicit and agreed norms and principles.

An example of an unsuccessful civil-military dialogue, described by Matthew Moten in chapter 3, was the relationship between Secretary of Defense Donald Rumsfeld and the Army Chief of Staff General Eric Shinseki. This failure stemmed not just from differences of opinion about military policy but also from interpersonal dynamics. Moten's study illuminates the manner in which dysfunctional relationships of just a few people can have far-reaching negative consequences for the country, particularly in time of war. The relationship between Rumsfeld and Shinseki was troubled from the start. Like several of his predecessors, Secretary Rumsfeld came into office with a perception that civil-military relations were out of balance and that an aggressive reassertion of civilian control was urgently needed. In an environment lacking mutual respect and trust, Army estimates of force requirements for post-invasion Iraq were dismissed as expressions of institutional interest and risk aversion, rather than credited as expert military advice.

Although the subordinate military participant may not always be able to remedy flaws in the interpersonal dimension of a civil-military relationship, several researchers in this project argued that it is their responsibility to attempt to do so. To prepare officers for this role, Moten advocates officer education to develop specific "political-cultural" expertise. This form of expertise would involve an officer's ability to represent the profession to people and institutions outside the service, including other agencies of government and other countries and their institutions of government.[16] Efforts to foster this expertise should be a deliberate component of the services' preparation of their officers for strategic leadership.

Richard Kohn also places interpersonal relations at the center of his analysis. He finds the sources of tension in the fact that the two participants, civilian and military, have quite different roles, responsibilities, and needs. Kohn argues that officers should seek to cultivate the reputation of neutral servant of the state, known for rendering their honest, well-reasoned advice in the best interests of U.S. national security, in order to build a relationship of trust with political lead-

ers and to assure a hearing for expert advice. As the best way to meet this enduring challenge, he suggests specific behaviors for each party, military and civilian,
to strengthen civilian control and to facilitate wise policymaking.

Institutional structures and organizational culture will continue to shape
American civil-military relations, but specific people and their particular dispo-
sitions will inevitably cause fluctuation in the relationships over time. Although
it is difficult to gain analytic leverage on concepts such as mutual respect and the
presumption of trust, it is undeniable that they will remain crucial to effective
civil-military relations.

8. The Development of Senior Military and Civilian Leaders

- Although largely unaddressed by Huntington, more intentional and
  robust efforts to educate, train, and develop future senior civilian and
  military leaders for their respective roles at the civil-military nexus
  would make effective civil-military relations more likely.

A number of the researchers in this volume, including Betts, Desch, Gibson,
and Kohn, identify specific qualities needed in the civilian and military leaders
who work at the civil-military nexus. These qualities include functional competence and trustworthiness, as well as respect for the same qualities in their counterparts in the processes of policymaking and policy execution. Richard Kohn's
discussion offers numerous specific examples, both positive and negative, from
the Vietnam era to the present. These qualities have been much talked about in
recent decades, even as they seemed to be often absent in key participants at the
civil-military nexus.

The policy issue here is whether and how much senior civilian and military
leaders should be trained and developed specifically for their roles in American
civil-military relations. As a group, civilian leaders are more diverse, whereas, as
Huntington often noted, military leaders develop within a more homogeneous
culture that is strongly influenced by the functional imperative of the military.
Thus, civilian leaders arrive at their policymaking roles from realms as diverse as
business, academia, the policy community, and the practicing professions, with
sets of concerns and perspectives that are quite different, and often much more
political in content, than those of military leaders. In the American tradition, this
is to be expected, and it is not normally a source of concern. The United States
has never adopted the strong civil-service system of some of its European allies

under their parliamentary systems of democratic governance, which create much more depth and continuity of expertise in civilian leadership positions.

At times, however, such as the start of a new administration, differences in preparation and experience place civilian leaders at a decided, if temporary, disadvantage.[17] In this book, we do not examine professional development and preparation of senior civilian leaders for their roles in crucial civil-military relationships, but we do consider whether professional military education needs an overhaul. As Williamson Murray writes in chapter 7, the United States has entered an extended period of persistent conflict with an adversary that holds fundamentally different conceptions of war and peace than do the United States and its Western allies. This demands significant change in the development of U.S. military leaders, he argues, with much greater emphasis on intellectual development and the political-cultural expertise of the military professional. Murray recommends redesigning professional military education and giving it a much more prominent role in an officer's advancement.

Also affecting the development of senior military and civilian leaders, as Nadia Schadlow and Richard Lacquement point out in chapter 6, are the new requirements of stability operations. These create the need at almost all levels for military professionals able to interact effectively with civilians, both governmental and nongovernmental. This degree of need for cultural and political acumen has not yet been addressed adequately by the personnel development systems of any of the U.S. military services.

9. Congress and the Executive as Coequals in Control of the Military

- Although the U.S. Constitution gives Congress weighty responsibilities in military affairs, the manner in which Congress can best exercise those responsibilities is not broadly agreed upon. Military officers should respond to the shared responsibilities of the two branches by providing Congress with frank and expert military advice while, to the best of their ability, remaining loyal to the executive branch of which they are a part.

Although the U.S. Constitution clearly gives Congress considerable responsibilities in military affairs, it is less clear on how Congress is intended to exercise those responsibilities. Congress has contributed to this ambiguity by not protecting diligently its constitutional prerogatives, such as its sole prerogative to declare war. In addition, while the military's obligation of obedience to civilian superiors within the executive branch is well understood as an extension of the military chain of command, and is reinforced in numerous ways in U.S. military culture and tradition, the obligations of military leaders to Congress, and the appropriate character of those relations, are not as settled. These ambiguities will continue to be a source of tension when, as has increasingly been the case since the end of the Cold War, military affairs are contentious between the two branches of American government.

Several chapters address this critical issue; they generally insist that military leaders must provide the Congress with frank and expert military advice while, to the best of their ability, remaining loyal to the executive branch of which they are a part. In chapter 3, Matthew Moten argues that there are proven ways for military leaders to work through the awkward aspects of such formal relationships, such as developing informal relations over time with individual members of Congress. Such efforts by military officers in appropriate positions to communicate with members of Congress demonstrate respect for the role of that institution in national security policy, enable military officers to improve their understanding of congressional perspectives, and facilitate communication on service needs and requirements.

In a similar vein, Richard Kohn points out that when officers are called to testify before Congress, they are duty-bound to give forthright military advice, irrespective of possible retribution from superiors within the executive branch who may have other opinions. It is up to the civilian authorities, including members of Congress, to decide whether to allow or to require the open airing of differences, if any, between civilian and military officials within the executive branch.

A closely related issue is how key committee leaders and individual members of Congress should exercise their responsibilities in the area of military affairs. For example, as Matthew Moten points out, members of Congress regularly reiterate their expectation of access to professional military advice in confirmation hearings for flag officers nominated to positions of significant responsibility. Yet, as Richard Betts suggests, this alone does not answer adequately the question of how far Congress should go in pushing senior military leaders to disagree in public hearings with their commander in chief or, more broadly, with administration policy.[18] There is no dispute, however, that in all circumstances officers should be frank, responsive, and consistent in their communications with civilians in the executive branch and in Congress.

The manner in which Congress executes its role in U.S. civil-military relations deserves more attention; it is clear that steps must be taken by civilian leaders to lessen partisan and other institutional tensions if the military is to be most effective in advising civilian officials in both branches of the U.S. government. Civilians must treat military professionals with respect and protect them from undue or partisan attacks. This is not to say, however, that they should give excessive deference to military views or fail to hold military leaders fully accountable for the advice that they give and for the effectiveness of the forces they prepare and employ.

Final Thoughts

Samuel Huntington's book, *The Soldier and the State*, clearly deserves its status as a seminal work in the field of civil-military relations. It spurred methodological as well as substantive progress, as chapter 4 by Peter Feaver and Erika Seeler explains, through its emphasis on rigor and its embrace of methodological ecumenism. Huntington—and a few years later Morris Janowitz with *The Professional Soldier* (1960)—played a leading role in the move after World War II by political scientists and sociologists to broaden their focus from individual soldiers and small groups to the corporate organization of the military and its relationship to the state and the society it serves.

Today, however, the United States operates in a strategic environment that Huntington could not envision in 1957. The Cold War that was Huntington's focus is over, but the United States remains broadly engaged in the world, exercising a singular and unprecedented level of power and leadership while continuing to rely heavily on the military instrument of national power. Until this context changes—which it is unlikely to do anytime soon—civil-military relations will remain significant. When managed well, they can safeguard the country's democratic values while enabling the development of effective military institutions and wise strategic policies. A civil-military relationship that can successfully accomplish these ends, however, cannot be taken for granted.

Notes

Foreword, by Jim Marshall

1. David G. McCullough, *John Adams* (New York: Simon and Schuster, 2001), p. 607.
2. Francis Fukuyama, *The End of History and the Last Man* (New York: Free Press, 1992).
3. See, for example, Qiao Liang and Wang Xianqsui, *Unrestricted Warfare: China's Master Plan to Destroy America* (Los Angeles: Pan American Publishing, 2002).

CHAPTER ONE: Introduction

1. Samuel P. Huntington, *The Soldier and the State* (Cambridge, MA: Belknap Press of Harvard University Press, 1957), p. vii.
2. James A. Baker III and Lee H. Hamilton, cochairs, *The Iraq Study Group Report,* December 2006, bakerinstitute.org/Pubs/iraqstudygroup_findings.pdf, p. 52.
3. Huntington, *The Soldier and the State*, p. viii.
4. The Army, Navy, Air Force, Marines, and Coast Guard are federal government agencies organized by Congress as hierarchical bureaucracies. Whether they are at the same time also vocational professions—organizations and individuals applying expert knowledge to the resolution of specific societal problems, such as national security—has varied over our nation's history. It is fair to say that today there are three military professions in America practicing with overlapping fields of expert knowledge but specialized in combat within specific domains—maritime, air-space, and land —and that a fourth profession is emerging, the joint military profession, with new expert knowledge and practices that integrate the capabilities of the other three into effective joint military campaigns. See Don. M. Snider and Lloyd J. Matthews, eds., *The Future of the Army Profession*, 2d ed., rev. and exp. (New York: McGraw-Hill Primis, 2005), chaps. 2 and 10.
5. Huntington, *The Soldier and the State,* p. 2.
6. Ibid.
7. Ibid., pp. 80–85.
8. Ibid., p. 11.
9. Ibid.
10. Ibid., p. 79.

11. Don M. Snider and Suzanne C. Nielsen, "The 44th Annual Senior Conference: American Civil-Military Relations Fifty Years after Huntington's *The Soldier and the State*," *Assembly*, September–October 2007, pp. 44–48.

CHAPTER TWO: Are Civil-Military Relations Still a Problem?

1. Richard H. Kohn, "Out of Control: The Crisis in Civil-Military Relations," *National Interest*, no. 35 (Spring 1994): 3–17.

2. Samuel P. Huntington, *The Common Defense: Strategic Programs in National Politics* (New York: Columbia University Press, 1961), p. 1.

3. Samuel P. Huntington, *The Soldier and the State: The Theory and Politics of Civil-Military Relations* (Cambridge, MA: Belknap Press of Harvard University Press, 1957), pp. 2–3.

4. The six principles of the Weinberger Doctrine were that commitment of U.S. forces to combat should be undertaken only on behalf of vital interests, "wholeheartedly, and with the clear intention of winning," with "clearly defined political and military objectives," if objectives and force requirements are "continually reassessed and adjusted," with "the support of the American people and their elected representatives in Congress," and as "a last resort." Secretary of Defense Caspar W. Weinberger, "The Uses of Military Power," speech to the National Press Club, November 28, 1984, pp. 7–8, www.pbs.org/wgbh/pages/frontline/shows/military/force/weinberger.html.

5. Regarding the decision on Laos in 1961, Roger Hilsman recalled: "Not all of the Joint Chiefs fully subscribed to the 'Never Again' view, but it seemed to the White House that they were at least determined to build a record that would protect their position and put the blame entirely on the President no matter what happened. The general thrust of their memoranda seemed to imply that they were demanding an advance commitment from the President that, if they agreed to use American force and there were any fighting at all, then there would be no holds barred whatsoever—including the use of nuclear weapons." Roger Hilsman, *To Move a Nation* (Garden City, NY: Doubleday, 1967), p. 129. Neoconservatives' impatience with military caution reflects their true colors: they are unreconstructed Wilsonian liberals on matters of international relations. After all, most neoconservatives began as Democrats in the Scoop Jackson mold and migrated to the Republican Party only when they came to feel isolated among Democrats.

6. Colin Powell with Joseph E. Persico, *My American Journey* (New York: Random House, 1995), p. 558.

7. The military's preference for overwhelming force is a tendency, not absolute. Exceptions include the Korean War and the Kosovo War. In both cases, the JCS opposed escalations favored by the field commanders, in part on grounds that maintaining readiness for a potential big war elsewhere took precedence over the small war that was actually going on. Richard K. Betts, *Soldiers, Statesmen, and Cold War Crises*, 2d ed. (New York: Columbia University Press, 1991), pp. 19–20, 254; General Wes-

ley K. Clark, USA (ret.), *Waging Modern War: Bosnia, Kosovo, and the Future of Combat* (New York: PublicAffairs, 2001), pp. 312–13.

8. Graham T. Allison, *Essence of Decision: Explaining the Cuban Missile Crisis* (Boston: Little, Brown, 1971); Barry R. Posen, *The Sources of Military Doctrine: France, Britain, and Germany between the World Wars* (Ithaca, NY: Cornell University Press, 1984); Eliot A. Cohen, *Supreme Command: Soldiers, Statesmen, and Leadership in Wartime* (New York: Free Press, 2002).

9. The second edition of Allison's book was more measured in its emphasis on errors due to organizational process and renamed the model "organizational behavior." Graham Allison and Philip Zelikow, *Essence of Decision*, 2d ed. (New York: Longman, 1999).

10. Cohen, *Supreme Command*, pp. 4–8, 174–75, 226–29.

11. H. R. McMaster, *Dereliction of Duty: Lyndon Johnson, Robert McNamara, the Joint Chiefs of Staff, and the Lies That Led to Vietnam* (New York: HarperCollins, 1997).

12. The members of the JCS in 1965 may have pulled punches more than they should have in telling civilian leaders they were wrong, but they did clearly recommend far more massive and speedy application of force in the air war and presented estimates within the Defense Department that victory would require a half-million men or more. They were not frank about their views in congressional testimony, as they should have been, because of a misguided notion that their responsibility to the commander in chief outweighed responsibility to the legislative branch of government. Their biggest mistake was in not forthrightly arguing in both arenas that withdrawal and acceptance of defeat were preferable to the weaker civilian strategy they opposed. They were complicit with the strategy because it was all they could get, and by 1965 the idea of giving up the fight was unthinkable to them, as it was to everyone of consequence in the American government except George Ball. Ibid., pp. 309–12, 328–31; Betts, *Soldiers, Statesmen, and Cold War Crises*, pp. 228–30; Leslie H. Gelb with Richard K. Betts, *The Irony of Vietnam: The System Worked* (Washington, DC: Brookings Institution, 1979), chap. 4. The mistake is clear only in hindsight, after the full calamitous costs of the venture came due. In the context of the time, none could realistically have expected soldiers to endorse defeat.

13. Introduction to Robert Higgs, ed., *Arms, Politics, and the Economy: Historical and Contemporary Perspectives* (New York: Holmes and Meier, 1990), p. xvii.

14. Morris Janowitz, *The Professional Soldier: A Social and Political Portrait*, 2d ed. (New York: Free Press, 1971), pp. 260–61.

15. See chapter 9 by Darrell W. Driver in this volume.

16. Previously they had been the link between the secretary of defense and the commanders in chief of the unified and specified commands.

17. Peter D. Feaver and Christopher Gelpi, *Choosing Your Battles: American Civil-Military Relations and the Use of Force* (Princeton, NJ: Princeton University Press, 2004), chap. 3.

18. Samuel P. Huntington, "The Defense Policy of the Reagan Administration,

1981–1982," in Fred I. Greenstein, ed., *The Reagan Presidency: An Early Assessment* (Baltimore: Johns Hopkins University Press, 1983), p. 85.

19. Glenn H. Snyder, "The 'New Look' of 1953," in Warner R. Schilling, Paul Y. Hammond, and Glenn H. Snyder, *Strategy, Politics, and Defense Budgets* (New York: Columbia University Press, 1962), pp. 440–43; Samuel P. Huntington, *The Common Defense* (New York: Columbia University Press, 1961), pp. 40, 42, 75, 221.

20. Arnold Kanter, *Defense Politics: A Budgetary Perspective* (Chicago: University of Chicago Press, 1979), pp. 24–28. See Huntington, *Common Defense*, chap. 6, on how interservice rivalry served civilian control.

21. See Huntington, *Common Defense*, pp. 146–51, 154, 157, 189–93, 369–78.

22. From the 1930s into the 1960s, Democrats "favored a higher level of military effort than did the Republicans. . . . In every year of the Eisenhower Administration except 1957, congressional Democrats attempted to increase the military budget." Ibid., pp. 252–53, 255, 261.

23. Lawrence J. Korb, "U.S. Defense Spending after the Cold War: Fact and Fiction," in Cindy Williams, ed., *Holding the Line: U.S. Defense Alternatives for the Early 21st Century* (Cambridge, MA: MIT Press, 2001), pp. 37, 43.

24. Richard K. Betts, "The Political Support System for American Primacy," *International Affairs* (London) 81, no. 1 (January 2005): 5–6, 12.

25. The lopsided identification of members of the academic profession with the Democratic Party—or groups further to the left—is no less objectionable. Whereas military officers are habituated to keeping their political preferences to themselves when acting in a professional capacity, many professors are far less scrupulous when it comes to teaching impressionable students.

26. By the time of the Vietnam War, social representativeness was reduced, as large portions of the highly educated escaped conscription. Lawrence M. Baskir and William A. Strauss, *Chance and Circumstance: The Draft, the War, and the Vietnam Generation* (New York: Knopf, 1978), pp. 5–11, 29–32.

27. See Peter D. Feaver and Richard H. Kohn, *Soldiers and Civilians: The Civil-Military Gap and American National Security* (Cambridge, MA: MIT Press, 2001).

28. For example, see Kathy Roth-Douquet and Frank Schaeffer, *AWOL: The Unexcused Absence of America's Upper Classes from Military Service—and How It Hurts Our Country* (New York: Collins, 2006).

29. In 1960 Janowitz reported that "the concentration of personnel with 'purely' military occupational specialties has fallen from 93.2 per cent in the Civil War to 28.8 per cent in the post–Korean Army and to even lower percentages in the Navy and Air Force." Janowitz, *Professional Soldier*, p. 9.

30. Allison, *Essence of Decision*, pp. 129–32; John D. Steinbruner, "An Assessment of Nuclear Crises," in Franklyn Griffiths and John C. Polanyi, eds., *The Dangers of Nuclear War* (Toronto: University of Toronto Press, 1979), p. 38.

31. Dan Caldwell, "A Research Note on the Quarantine of Cuba," *International Studies Quarterly* 22, no. 4 (December 1978): 625–33; Scott D. Sagan, "Rules of Engagement," *Security Studies* 1, no. 1 (Autumn 1991): 91–93; Sagan, "Nuclear Alerts and Cri-

sis Management," *International Security* 9, no. 4 (Spring 1985): 112–18; Joseph F. Bouchard, *Command in Crisis: Four Case Studies* (New York: Columbia University Press, 1991), pp. 111–12, 120–28; transcript of Cabinet Room meeting, October 22, 1962, in Ernest R. May and Philip D. Zelikow, eds., *The Kennedy Tapes: Inside the White House during the Cuban Missile Crisis* (Cambridge, MA: Harvard University Press, 1997), p. 212; Richard K. Betts, *Nuclear Blackmail and Nuclear Balance* (Washington, DC: Brookings Institution, 1987), pp. 118–19. The second edition of Allison's book omitted the stories in question and substituted a milder account of the notorious confrontation between McNamara and Anderson in the Navy Flag Plot; Allison and Zelikow, *Essence of Decision,* pp. 232–36.

32. In 1961 Senator J. W. Fulbright reported the 1958 NSC directive that led to these links. Daniel Bell, "The Dispossessed (1962)," in Daniel Bell, ed., *The Radical Right* (New York: Anchor, 1963), pp. 5–8.

33. Bob Woodward, *State of Denial: Bush at War, Part III* (New York: Simon and Schuster, 2006), p. 54.

34. John Newhouse, *Cold Dawn: The Story of SALT* (New York: Holt, Rinehart and Winston, 1973), pp. 124, 129.

35. Betts, *Soldiers, Statesmen, and Cold War Crises,* p. xii.

36. Huntington, *Soldier and the State,* pp. 158–59 and 158n.

37. This book goes to press before the 2008 general election. If McCain wins, the total of heroes elected will be three out of ten presidents, and the total of professional officers elected since Grant will be three.

38. Powell later commented, "I thought I would have an aneurysm." Powell, *My American Journey,* p. 576.

39. David Halberstam, *War in a Time of Peace: Bush, Clinton, and the Generals* (New York: Touchstone, 2002), pp. 246–47: "Powell did not believe that on those issues where the military power of the United States might be employed, Clinton's people had thought things out carefully. They were almost vague in their attitudes toward the use of force and its consequences. . . . They in turn, sensed his disdain for them. . . . 'You could feel it in the way he looked at us. We were doves, people who had sat out the war while he had fought it, people who had never really paid a price for what we had attained,' one senior member of the Clinton administration said."

40. David S. Broder, "No Veterans Preference in This Administration," *Washington Post,* December 26, 1993, p. C7. At the highest level, the symbolism actually got worse: during Clinton's first term, four of the five civilian members and statutory advisors of the National Security Council—all but the president himself—were veterans (Vice President Al Gore, Secretary of State Warren Christopher, Secretary of Defense Les Aspin, and Director of Central Intelligence James Woolsey); by the second Clinton term, only the Vice President was.

41. See, for example, chapter 12 by Christopher P. Gibson in this volume.

42. Powell, *My American Journey,* p. 559.

43. Just how Rumsfeld accomplished this—by persuasion, intimidation, co-optation,

side payments, or whatever means—is a story yet to be told. To a scholar looking in from outside, it is a fascinating mystery.

44. David S. Cloud and Steven Lee Myers, "Generals Differ on the Timing of Troop Cuts," *New York Times,* August 25, 2007, p. A1; David S. Cloud, "Why Well-Placed Officers Differ on Troop Reduction," *New York Times,* September 14, 2007, p. A11.

45. See the incidents reported in Kohn, "Out of Control," p. 3.

46. Betts, *Soldiers, Statesmen, and Cold War Crises,* pp. 262–63n30.

47. Huntington, *Common Defense,* pp. 135–46.

48. For the story of the reorganization, see Suzanne Christine Nielsen, "Preparing the Army for War: The Dynamics of Peacetime Military Reform" (Ph.D. dissertation, Harvard University, 2003), chap. 4.

49. Interview with Lewis Sorley, quoted in ibid., p. 224n185.

50. Quoted in Lewis Sorley, *Thunderbolt: General Creighton Abrams and the Army of His Times* (New York: Simon and Schuster, 1992), p. 364.

51. Michael R. Gordon and General Bernard E. Trainor, *Cobra II: The Inside Story of the Invasion and Occupation of Iraq* (New York: Pantheon, 2006), chap. 3 and pp. 96–100; Thomas E. Ricks, *Fiasco: The American Military Adventure in Iraq* (New York: Penguin, 2006), pp. 70–71, 75, 83–84. See the account in chapter 3 by Matthew Moten in this volume.

52. Huntington, *Soldier and the State,* p. 77.

53. Bouchard, *Command in Crisis,* pp. 96–97, 100.

54. Carl von Clausewitz, *On War,* ed. and trans. Michael Howard and Peter Paret (Princeton, NJ: Princeton University Press, 1976), p. 75. "If one side uses force without compunction, undeterred by the bloodshed it involves, while the other side refrains, the first will gain the upper hand. That side will force the other to follow suit; each will drive its opponent toward extremes, and the only limiting factors are the counterpoises inherent in war." Ibid., pp. 75–76.

55. Ibid., p. 598.

56. Cohen, *Supreme Command,* p. 177.

57. See Betts, *Soldiers, Statesmen, and Cold War Crises,* p. 211.

58. Janowitz, *Professional Soldier.*

59. Huntington, *Soldier and the State,* p. 253.

60. Cohen, *Supreme Command,* p. 229; Huntington, *Soldier and the State,* pp. 315–17.

61. As the editors clarify, "Clausewitz emphasizes the cabinet's participation in military decisions, not the soldier's participation in political decisions." Clausewitz, *On War,* , p. 608 and 608n1.

62. Huntington, *Common Defense,* p. 447.

CHAPTER THREE: A Broken Dialogue: Rumsfeld, Shinseki, and Civil-Military Tension

I would like to thank several colleagues for their learned criticism of this essay: Colonel Lance Betros, Dr. Conrad C. Crane, Major J. P. Clark, Lieutenant Colonel

Kevin Farrell, Lieutenant Colonel Gian Gentile, Colonel Chris Gibson, Professor Richard Kohn, Dr. Jarvis E. Miller, Lieutenant Colonel Suzanne Nielsen, Professor Cliff Rogers, and Professor Don Snider. I served with General Shinseki for three years during his tenure as chief of staff, first as his speechwriter and later as his legislative advisor; I am currently serving as general editor of his collected works.

1. "U.S. Senate Armed Services Committee Hearing on FY 2004 Defense Authorization," transcript, February 25, 2003, http://armed-services.senate.gov/e_witness .CFM?id=604; Michael R. Gordon and Bernard E. Trainor, *Cobra II: The Inside Story of the Invasion and Occupation of Iraq* (New York: Pantheon Books, 2006), p. 102nn 522–23; George Packer, *The Assassins' Gate: America in Iraq* (New York: Farrar, Straus and Giroux, 2005), p. 114; Thomas E. Ricks, *Fiasco: The American Military Adventure in Iraq* (New York: Penguin, 2006), pp. 96–97.

2. Eric Schmitt, "Pentagon Contradicts General on Iraq Occupation Force's Size," *New York Times*, February 28, 2003; Bob Woodward, *State of Denial: Bush at War, Part III* (New York: Simon and Schuster, 2006), p. 151; Gordon and Trainor, *Cobra II*, pp. 102–3, 486; Ricks, *Fiasco*, pp. 96–100; Packer, *Assassins' Gate*, p. 114.

3. Samuel P. Huntington, *The Soldier and the State: The Theory and Politics of Civil-Military Relations* (Cambridge, MA: Belknap Press of Harvard University Press, 1957), pp. 80–97, quotation, p. 84. For a discussion of the influence of this idea on the military profession, see Eliot Cohen, *Supreme Command: Soldiers, Statesmen, and Leadership in Wartime* (New York: Free Press, 2002), pp. 225–48.

4. It is worth noting, in fairness to Huntington, that he does not describe such a wall directly. Some may criticize my interpretation here as a caricature. Indeed, Huntington acknowledges that, because of our constitutional system, objective civilian control is difficult to achieve and that it has occurred in the United States only rarely, when the military was relatively weak and officers themselves reduced their political power and influence. Huntington, *The Soldier and the State*, pp. 189–92, 260–63. He also details moral, legal, and operational reasons why officers might disobey their civilian superiors. Ibid., 70–79. Yet he clearly prefers objective civilian control as an ideal type: "The antithesis of objective civilian control is military participation in politics. . . . The essence of objective civilian control is the recognition of an autonomous military professionalism." Ibid., p. 83.

5. Carl von Clausewitz, *On War*, ed. and trans. Michael Howard and Peter Paret (Princeton, NJ: Princeton University Press, 1976), pp. 87, 605–9 (emphasis in original).

6. For a contrary view of objective civilian control, see chapter 5 by Michael C. Desch in this volume.

7. Huntington, *The Soldier and the State*, pp. 80–85; quotation, p. 83. See also chapter 13 by Richard H. Kohn in this volume.

8. Huntington, *The Soldier and the State*, pp. 163–92.

9. The 1958 Defense Reorganization Act gave the secretary of defense "direction, authority, and control" over the Department of Defense and the armed services.

10. General Shinseki and Lieutenant General James L. Jones Jr. each answered such a question at their joint confirmation hearing in June 1999. U.S. Senate, Com-

mittee on Armed Services, Washington, DC, "Nominations of Gen. Eric K. Shinseki, USA, for Reappointment to the Grade of General and for Appointment as Chief of Staff United States Army and Lt. Gen. James L. Jones, Jr., USMC, to be General and for Appointment as Commandant of the Marine Corps, June 8, 1999," p. 111. In his confirmation hearings in 2007 to become commanding general of the Multi-National Force, Iraq, Lieutenant General David Petraeus, asked a similar question, pledged to give his "best professional military advice, and if people don't like it, then they can find someone else to give better professional military advice." Michael C. Desch, "Bush and the Generals," *Foreign Affairs* 86, no. 3 (May–June 2007): 108.

11. Mark R. Lewis, "Army Transformation and the Junior Officer Exodus," *Armed Forces and Society* 31, no. 1 (Fall 2004): 63–93.

12. Thomas E. Ricks, "For Today's Army, Suffering an Identity Crisis, Choice of New Chief Assumes Larger Significance," *Wall Street Journal,* March 3, 1999, p. A20.

13. Eric K. Shinseki, "Annual Address at the Dwight D. Eisenhower Luncheon," at the Association of the United States Army Annual Convention, Washington, DC, October 12, 1999. Shinseki coined the term "Transformation" in this speech, fifteen months before the Bush administration began. Eric K. Shinseki, "Remarks at Senate Army Caucus Breakfast," May 2, 2002.

14. Peter J. Boyer, "A Different War," *New Yorker,* July 1, 2002, pp. 60–62.

15. Gordon and Trainor, *Cobra II,* p. 8; Boyer, "A Different War," p. 54.

16. Eric K. Shinseki, "Address to the Eisenhower Luncheon," at the annual convention of the Association of the United States Army, Washington, DC, October 17, 2000; "U.S. House of Representatives Committee on Small Business, Hearing on Black Beret Procurement," transcript, May 2, 2001; Woodward, *State of Denial,* pp. 141–42; Boyer, "A Different War," pp. 62–63.

17. Rumsfeld outlined his thinking in several congressional committee appearances. See, for example, "Prepared Testimony of U.S. Secretary of Defense Donald H. Rumsfeld, Senate Armed Services Committee Hearing on Defense Strategy Review," June 21, 2001.

18. Thomas E. Ricks, "Rumsfeld on High Wire of Defense Reform: Military Brass, Conservative Lawmakers Are among Secretive Review's Unexpected Critics," *Washington Post,* May 20, 2001, p. A01. At an October 2001 briefing announcing the release of the QDR, a reporter asked, "Can you get more specific about sizing? . . . Since September 11th, has that all changed now?" The "senior defense official" replied: "Let me, at the risk of being contradicted—I don't know that there was ever a strong push to cut the force. What we had was—" Q: "There were some proposals, though, weren't there?" Senior Defense Official: "There were a thousand of them." Background Briefing on the QDR by "Senior Defense Official," Department of Defense News Briefing, October 1, 2001.

19. The author has found no evidence that Shinseki attempted to employ any leverage from outside the formal QDR process. In other words, he and his staff made their arguments within the closed-door sessions. He did not ask his friends in Congress or elsewhere to influence the internal Pentagon deliberations.

20. Boyer, "A Different War," pp. 63–65; Ricks, *Fiasco*, pp. 68–70.

21. Vernon Loeb and Thomas E. Ricks, "Rumsfeld's Style, Goals Strain Ties in Pentagon," *Washington Post*, October 16, 2002; Jeffrey M. Borns, "How Secretary of Defense Rumsfeld Sought to Assert Civilian Control over the Military," paper submitted to the National War College, Washington, DC, 2002. Borns quotes numerous sources expressing the idea that the Bush administration and Rumsfeld felt a need to reestablish civilian control of the military.

22. Dave Moniz and John Diamond, "Rumsfeld Is Perched at the 'Pinnacle of Power,' " *USA Today*, May 1, 2003, p. 10; Seth Stern, "Pentagon Iconoclasts," *Christian Science Monitor*, April 29, 2003, p. 1.

23. Ricks, "Rumsfeld on High Wire"; Department of Defense News Briefing, Secretary Rumsfeld and General Myers, January 29, 2003, www.defenselink.mil/transcripts/transcript.aspx?transcriptid=1349.

24. Ricks, "Rumsfeld on High Wire"; Loeb and Ricks, "Rumsfeld's Style, Goals Strain Ties in Pentagon"; Dave Moniz, "Rumsfeld's Abrasive Style Sparks Conflict," *USA Today*, December 10, 2002; Seymour M. Hersh, "Annals of National Security: Offense and Defense, the Battle between Rumsfeld and the Pentagon," *New Yorker*, April 7, 2003; Moniz and Diamond, "Rumsfeld Is Perched at 'Pinnacle of Power.' "

25. Peter Boyer, "The New War Machine," *New Yorker*, April 7, 2003; chapter 5 by Michael C. Desch in this volume.

26. Thomas E. Ricks, "Bush Backs Overhaul of Military's Top Ranks," *Washington Post*, April 11, 2002, p. A01; Shinseki, "Remarks at Senate Army Caucus Breakfast," May 2, 2002; Boyer, "A Different War," p. 65; Ricks, *Fiasco*, pp. 69–70.

27. The M109 howitzer was introduced into the Army inventory in the 1960s. It received several improvements, especially in its fire direction system, in the late 1970s.

28. The Army's Office of the Chief of Legislative Liaison, headed by a major general, reports directly to the secretary, but it supports all Army officials in their dealings with Congress. Both military officers and civil servants work in this office.

29. Boyer, "A Different War," p. 66.

30. "Secretary Rumsfeld Media Availability with Malaysian Defense Minister," The Pentagon, May 2, 2002; Michael Kilian, "Army Probes Lobbying to Save Crusader Gun," *Chicago Tribune*, May 4, 2002; James Dao, "Investigation Begun into Action by Army Secretary on a Weapon," *New York Times*, May 4, 2002; Greg Jaffe, "Army Probes Bid to Save Crusader after Pentagon Cancels Program," *Wall Street Journal*, May 6, 2002; Vernon Loeb, "Rumsfeld Untracks 'Crusader,' " *Washington Post*, May 9, 2002; Ellen Nakishima, "Crusader Claims Army Official," *Washington Post*, May 11, 2002; James Dao, "Army Liaison Who Lobbied Congress for Weapon Resigns," *New York Times*, May 11, 2002; Department of Defense Office of Public Affairs, "Pentagon Briefing: Voices on Crusader," May 13, 2002; Department of Defense Office of Public Affairs, "Voices on Crusader," May 16, 2002. Rumsfeld ordered the post of Army chief of legislative liaison downgraded to a one-star billet. Congress later reversed this decision in defense authorization legislation.

31. Greg Jaffe, David Rogers, and Anne Marie Squeo, "Rumsfeld Ends Crusader Program, Takes Weapons Debate to Capitol," *Wall Street Journal*, May 9, 2002; Dave Moniz, "Army Officials on Alert against Attacks from Above," *USA Today*, May 16, 2002; Ricks, *Fiasco*, p. 69.

32. Donald Rumsfeld, "A Choice to Transform the Military," *Washington Post*, May 16, 2002; Boyer, "A Different War," p. 66; Walter Pincus, "Rumsfeld Defends Decision to Recommend Killing Crusader," *Washington Post*, May 17, 2002; Tom Bowman, "Pentagon Defends Plans to Cancel Heavy Howitzer," *Washington Post*, May 17, 2002.

33. Eric K. Shinseki, "Statement for the Senate Armed Services Committee Hearing on the Crusader Self-Propelled Artillery Program," Washington, DC, May 16, 2002; Boyer, "A Different War," pp. 65–67; Pincus, "Rumsfeld Defends Decision to Recommend Killing Crusader"; Bowman, "Pentagon Defends Plans to Cancel Heavy Howitzer."

34. *Armed Forces Journal*, June 2002.

35. Gordon and Trainor, *Cobra II*, pp. 46–48, 51–52.

36. Ibid., pp. 24–54.

37. General (ret.) Richard B. Myers, former Chairman, Joint Chiefs of Staff, interview with author, November 13, 2007; Dr. Kori Schake, director for Defense Strategy and Requirements on the National Security Council during President Bush's first term, interview with author, February 15, 2007; Gordon and Trainor, *Cobra II*, pp. 24–54. General Myers noted that General Franks met the Joint Chiefs on several occasions, but did not seem to understand their roles other than as providers of forces to his operations.

38. Tommy Franks with Malcolm McConnell, *American Soldier* (New York: Regan Books, 2004), pp. 274–78.

39. Myers interview, November 13, 2007. General Myers noted that Rumsfeld paid close attention to the TPFDL, presiding over weekly meetings between CENTCOM and Transportation Command to resolve differences. Hersh, "Annals of National Security: Offense and Defense, The Battle between Rumsfeld and the Pentagon"; Gordon and Trainor, *Cobra II*, pp. 95–102; chapter 5 by Michael C. Desch in this volume.

40. James Fallows, "Blind into Baghdad," *Atlantic* 293, no. 1 (January–February 2004): 53–64; Gordon and Trainor, *Cobra II*, pp. 95–102; Ricks, *Fiasco*, pp. 71, 73–74; Myers interview, November 13, 2007; Schake interview, February 15, 2007. General Myers described this meeting as "positive" and not "contentious." Dr. Schake, the observer mentioned, was also present at the January 30, 2003, meeting in the Cabinet Room.

41. Gregory Fontenot, E. J. Degen, and David Tohn, *On Point: The United States Army in Operation Iraqi Freedom* (Fort Leavenworth, KS: Combat Studies Institute Press, 2004), pp. 141–50, 406–11.

42. Ricks, *Fiasco*, p. 145; Gordon and Trainor, *Cobra II*, pp. 304–26.

43. Jason Campbell, Michael O'Hanlon, and Amy Unikewicz, "Op-Chart: The State of Iraq: An Update," *New York Times*, March 9, 2008; Anne Flaherty, "Auditors Suggest Defense Contractors Disclose Financial Interests," Associated Press, March 11, 2008, Gov.Executive.com.

44. Eric K. Shinseki, "Remarks at Army Chief of Staff Retirement Ceremony," Fort Myer, Virginia, June 11, 2003. Shinseki routinely capitalized both words of the phrase "The Army"; I have maintained that convention in this rendering of his remarks.

45. Ibid.; Ricks, *Fiasco*, pp. 156–57.

46. Eric K. Shinseki, "Statement for the Senate Armed Services Committee Hearing on the Posture of the Army," Washington, DC, February 25, 2003.

47. Richard K. Betts argues in chapter 2 of this volume that the critique of civil-military relations, "popular among professional soldiers," found in H. R. McMaster's *Dereliction of Duty*, includes the notion that the service chiefs were wrong to go along with LBJ's misguided Vietnam strategy and to keep quiet about their reservations, "rather than resign or speak frankly to Congress." McMaster does fault the chiefs for their acquiescence and their silence, especially when that silence tacitly accepted administration lies, but he does not argue that they should have resigned. Moreover, I do not read in McMaster a refutation of objective control or any attempt to create a new norm for civil-military relations. Instead, he develops a narrative and argument about why the Vietnam War began so badly. H. R. McMaster, *Dereliction of Duty: Lyndon Johnson, Robert McNamara, the Joint Chiefs of Staff, and the Lies that Led to Vietnam* (New York: HarperCollins, 1997), especially pp. 323–34.

48. Secretary of State Colin Powell had been an Army general and chairman of the Joint Chiefs. His deputy, Richard Armitage, had been a naval officer as well as an assistant secretary of defense. Powell's chief of staff, Larry Wilkerson, was a retired Army colonel.

49. A former Air Force chief of staff, General Ronald R. Fogleman, retired early in 1997 in what was widely interpreted as a resignation or retirement in protest of certain decisions. However, Fogleman indicated at the time that he had no such intent, and later stated that he had requested relief because he thought that he had lost effectiveness as chief of staff and that the Air Force would be better served with another officer in the position. He specifically stated that his retirement was "consistent with historical practice and precedent." Richard H. Kohn, ed., "The Early Retirement of Gen. Ronald R. Fogleman, Chief of Staff, United States Air Force," *Aerospace Power Journal* 15, no. 1 (Spring 2001): 6–23. In March 2008 Admiral William "Fox" Fallon tendered his retirement request after an *Esquire* magazine article based upon an interview with him suggested that he had serious policy differences with the Bush administration. Both Fallon and Secretary of Defense Robert M. Gates, who accepted the request, denied such differences. Fallon retired, not in protest, but because, as he said, "Recent press reports suggesting a disconnect between my views and the president's policy objectives have become a distraction at a critical time and hamper efforts in the CENTCOM region. And although I don't believe there have ever been any differences about the objectives of our policy in the Central Command Area of Responsibility, the simple perception that there is makes it difficult for me to effectively serve America's interests there." Thomas P. M. Barnett, "The Man between War and Peace," *Esquire*, March 2008; Thomas E. Ricks, "Top U.S. Officer in Mideast Re-

signs," *Washington Post*, March 12, 2008, p. A01; Thom Shanker, "Mideast Commander Retires after Irking Bosses," *New York Times*, March 12, 2008.

50. Secretary Donald H. Rumsfeld and General Richard B. Myers, "Department of Defense News Briefing," April 1, 2003, www.defenselink.mil/transcripts/transcript.aspx?transcriptid=2229.

51. The Clinton administration relieved no senior flag officers, not even General Wesley Clark, whose actions in Bosnia and Kosovo as Supreme Allied Commander, Europe, clashed with administration policy. The Bush administration relieved no senior flag officers on Rumsfeld's watch, although some were allowed to retire quietly. For example, in the wake of Abu Ghraib, Lieutenant General Ricardo Sanchez, coalition commander in Iraq, retired after receiving no nomination for a fourth star. CENTCOM Commanding General John Abizaid retired and General George Casey was reassigned from his command in Iraq to become Army chief of staff when the administration changed its Iraq strategy in late 2006. In 2007, the Army surgeon general and the commanding general of Walter Reed Army Medical Center were relieved following revelations of poor administration and neglectful treatment of wounded soldiers. The services themselves have punished cases of indiscipline, but that is a separate category from sanctioning opposition to policy or operational failure.

52. Charles A. Stevenson, *SECDEF: The Nearly Impossible Job of Secretary of Defense* (Dulles, VA: Potomac Books, 2006).

53. My use of the male pronoun is simply for grammatical simplicity and is certainly not meant to suggest that the services may not have women as their chiefs of staff.

54. I have discussed these skills and their development at some length in Matthew Moten, "Root, Miles, and Carter: Political-Cultural Expertise and an Earlier Army Transformation," in Don M. Snider and Lloyd J. Matthews, eds., *The Future of the Army Profession*, 2d ed., rev. and exp. (New York: McGraw-Hill Primis, 2005), pp. 723–48. See also chaps. 1, 29, 30, 31, and 32 in the same volume.

55. Matthew B. Ridgway, *Soldier: The Memoirs of Matthew B. Ridgway* (New York: Harper and Brothers, 1956), pp. 286–89. Ridgway found it necessary to express his written concerns to Secretary of Defense Charles Wilson: "In that way they became a part of the historical record."

56. See the discussion of protected space for professional and moral autonomy in chapter 8 by James Burk in this volume.

57. Clausewitz, *On War*, pp. 607–8.

58. Cohen, *Supreme Command*, pp. 208–48.

59. My point is not that Eliot Cohen does not prescribe an ideal relationship, but that his prescription may easily be ignored by any of the parties at the civil-military nexus. See also chapter 2 by Richard K. Betts and chapter 5 by Michael C. Desch, both in this volume.

60. David S. Cloud, Eric Schmitt, and Thom Shanker, "Rumsfeld Faces Growing Revolt by Retired Generals," *New York Times*, April 13, 2006, www.nytimes.com/2006/04/13/washington/13cnd-military.html.

61. Michael E. O'Hanlon, "History Will Credit Shinseki," *Japan Times,* June 19, 2003; Thom Shanker, "New Strategy Vindicates Ex-Army Chief Shinseki," *New York Times,* January 12, 2007; "Senate Armed Services Committee Holds Hearing on Current Situation in Iraq and Afghanistan," transcript, November 15, 2006, http://armed-services.senate.gov/e_witnesslist.CFM?id=2427.

CHAPTER FOUR: Before and After Huntington: The Methodological Maturing of Civil-Military Studies

1. Gabriel A. Almond, "Who Lost the Chicago School of Political Science?" *Perspectives on Politics,* no. 2 (March 2004): 91–93.

2. Georg G. Iggers, *Historiography in the Twentieth Century: From Scientific Objectivity to the Postmodern Challenge* (Hanover, NH: Wesleyan University Press, 1997).

3. Pressing policy problems included assuring a high rate of production with a reduced labor force, and developing military training, recruitment, discharge, and civilian retransitioning strategies. Gabriel A. Almond, "Political Science: The History of the Discipline," in Robert E. Goodin and Hans-Dieter Klingemann, eds., *A New Handbook of Political Science* (New York: Oxford University Press, 1996), p. 69.

4. "The conditions which have brought our Association into existence are the corruption of politics by inhuman tyranny and total war which have brought and may again bring disastrous consequences to all sections of the world. The purpose which inspires our Association is to eliminate these corruptions by the universal application of scientific method in dealing with political problems." Quincy Wright, "The Significance of the International Political Science Association: Opening Address," *International Social Science Bulletin* 3, no. 2 (1951): 276.

5. Dorothy Ross, "Changing Contours of the Social Science Disciplines," in Theodore M. Porter and Dorothy Ross, eds., *The Cambridge History of Science,* vol. 7: *The Modern Social Sciences* (New York: Cambridge University Press, 2003), pp. 205–37.

6. See, for example, Jeffrey T. Bergner, *The Origin of Formalism in Social Science* (Chicago: University of Chicago Press, 1981); Alan F. Chalmers, *What Is This Thing Called Science?* 3d ed. (Indianapolis: Hackett, 1999); Jorgen Jorgensen, *The Development of Logical Empiricism* (Chicago: University of Chicago Press, 1951); and Otto Neurath, *Foundations of the Social Sciences: International Encyclopedia of Unified Science,* vol. 2, no. 1 (Chicago: University of Chicago Press, 1944).

7. Robert E. Goodin and Hans-Dieter Klingemann, "Political Science: The Discipline," in Goodin and Klingemann, *A New Handbook of Political Science,* pp. 3–49.

8. See, for example, Wilson Gee, *Social Science Research Methods* (New York: Appleton-Century-Crofts, 1950); Abraham Kaplan, *The Conduct of Inquiry: Methodology for Behavioral Science* (San Francisco: Chandler, 1964).

9. Thomas S. Kuhn, *The Structure of Scientific Revolutions* (Chicago: University of Chicago Press, 1962); on middle-range theories, see Robert K. Merton, *Social Theory and Social Structure* (New York: Free Press, 1967 [1957]).

10. Gary King, Robert O. Keohane, and Sidney Verba, *Designing Social Inquiry: Scientific Inference in Qualitative Research* (Princeton, NJ: Princeton University Press, 1994), pp. 3–31.

11. Modern civil-military research is generally dated from Lasswell and Vagts, though earlier work included Clausewitz's *On War*. Huntington himself included under the heading of civil-military studies the tradition of business pacifism—the notion that war interfered with commerce and so was "bad for business"—articulated by Herbert Spencer, John Fiske, William Graham Sumner, Andrew Carnegie, and others. Samuel P. Huntington, *The Soldier and the State: The Theory and Politics of Civil-Military Relations* (Cambridge, MA: Belknap Press of Harvard University Press, 1959 [1957]), pp. 222–26. See also Herbert Spencer, *The Principles of Sociology* (New York: Appleton, 1925); John Fiske, *Outlines of Cosmic Philosophy* (New York: Houghton, Mifflin, 1902); William Graham Sumner, *War and Other Essays* (New Haven, CT: Yale University Press, 1911); and Andrew Carnegie, *The Gospel of Wealth and Other Timely Essays* (Cambridge, MA: Harvard University Press, 1962). However, such statements never became systematized or developed enough to constitute a research program. James Burk, "Morris Janowitz and the Origins of Sociological Research on Armed Forces and Society," *Armed Forces and Society* 19, no. 2 (Winter 1993): 167–85.

12. Early U.S. works about postwar civil-military relations included Edward Mead Earle, "National Defense: A Program of Studies," *Journal of the American Military Institute* 4, no. 4 (1940): 199–208; and Joseph E. McLean, "Areas for Postwar Research," *American Political Science Review* 39, no. 4 (August 1945): 741–57.

13. Peter D. Feaver, "The Civil-Military Problematique: Huntington, Janowitz, and the Question of Civilian Control," *Armed Forces and Society* 23, no. 2 (Winter 1996): 149–78; Peter D. Feaver, "Civil-Military Relations," *Annual Review of Political Science*, no. 2 (1999): 211–41. Major early examples in this liberal-democratic tradition include Louis Smith, *American Democracy and Military Power* (Chicago: University of Chicago Press, 1951); John D. Millett, "National Security in American Public Affairs," *American Political Science Review* 43, no. 3 (June 1949): 524–25; Herman Miles Somers, "Civil-Military Relations in Mutual Security," *Annals of the American Academy of Political and Social Science* 288 (July 1953): 27–35; and Townsend W. Hoopes, "Civilian-Military Balance," *Yale Review* 43, no. 2 (1954): 218–34.

14. See James Burk, "Theories of Democratic Civil-Military Relations," *Armed Forces and Society* 29, no. 1 (September2002): 7–29.

15. Morris Janowitz, *The Professional Soldier: A Social and Political Portrait* (Glencoe, IL: Free Press, 1960).

16. Elias Huzar, *The Purse and the Sword* (Ithaca, NY: Cornell University Press, 1950).

17. Rowland T. Berthoff, "Taft and MacArthur, 1900–1901: A Study in Civil-Military Relations," *World Politics* 5, no. 2 (1953): 196–213; Warner R. Schilling, "Civil-Naval Politics in World War I," *World Politics* 7, no. 4 (1955): 572–91.

18. Burton M. Sapin and Richard C. Snyder, *The Role of the Military in American Foreign Policy* (Garden City, NY: Doubleday: 1954); William T. R. Fox, "Civilians, Soldiers, and American Military Policy," *World Politics* 7, no. 3 (1955): 402–18; Alfred

Vagts, *Defense and Diplomacy: The Soldier and the Conduct of Foreign Relations* (New York: King's Crown Press, 1956).

19. Paul P. Van Riper, "A Survey of Materials for the Study of Military Management," *American Political Science Review* 49, no. 3 (September 1955): 828–50; Alvin Brown, *The Armor of Organization* (New York: Hibbert Print, 1953); H. Struve Hensel, "Changes inside the Pentagon," *Harvard Business Review* 32, no. 1 (1954): 218–34.

20. Walter Millis, *Arms and Men* (New York: Putnam, 1956); and Arthur A. Ekirch, *The Civilian and the Military* (New York: Oxford University Press, 1956).

21. C. Wright Mills, *The Power Elite* (New York: Oxford University Press, 1956).

22. *Civil-Military Relations: An Annotated Bibliography, 1940–1952*, compiled by the Social Science Research Council Committee on Civil-Military Relations Research (New York: Columbia University Press, 1954).

23. In a series of publications between 1937 and 1952, Lasswell outlined his theory of the garrison state. Harold D. Lasswell, *Essays on the Garrison State*, ed. Jay Stanley (New Brunswick, NJ: Transaction, 1997); Alfred Vagts, *A History of Militarism* (New York: Norton, 1937). Lasswell's work was arguably the most theoretically rigorous of any before Huntington, although Vagts fully systematized his theory only after the war.

24. For example: R. Lindquist, *The Family Life of Officers and Airmen in a Bomb Wing* (Chapel Hill, NC: Institute for Research in Social Science, University of North Carolina at Chapel Hill, 1952); Albert J. Mayer and Thomas Ford Hoult, "Social Stratification and Combat Survival," *Social Forces* 34, no. 2 (1955): 155–59; Howard Brotz and Everett Wilson, "Characteristics of Military Society," *American Journal of Sociology* 51, no. 5 (1946): 371–75; Elizabeth G. French and Raymond R. Ernest, "The Relationship between Authoritarianism and Acceptance of Military Ideology," *Journal of Personality* 24, no. 2 (1955): 181–91; Robert K. Merton and Paul F. Lazarsfeld, eds., *Continuities in Social Research: Studies in the Scope and Method of the American Soldier* (Glencoe, IL: Free Press, 1950).

25. Samuel A. Stouffer, ed., *The American Soldier: Adjustment during Army Life* (Princeton, NJ: Princeton University Press, 1949); Samuel A. Stouffer, ed., *The American Soldier: Combat and Its Aftermath* (Princeton, NJ: Princeton University Press, 1949).

26. For example, Vagts, *A History of Militarism*, traced the development of militarism from the feudal era to modern totalitarian militarism. See also Frederic A. Ogg, "American Democracy—After War," *American Political Science Review* 36, no. 1 (February 1942): 1–15; Jerome G. Kerwin, ed., *Civil-Military Relationships in American Life* (Chicago: University of Chicago Press, 1948); and Bruce Catton, *The War Lords of Washington* (New York: Harcourt, Brace, 1948).

27. Smith, *American Democracy and Military Power.*

28. Ekirch, *The Civilian and the Military.*

29. Lasswell, *Essays on the Garrison State.*

30. For example, Hensel, "Changes inside the Pentagon"; and Hoopes, "Civilian-Military Balance."

31. See the critique of Lasswell in Huntington, *The Soldier and the State,* pp. 346–50.

32. See the critique of fusionism in ibid., pp. 350–54.

33. Feaver, "Civil-Military Relations."

34. Huntington, *The Soldier and the State,* p. vii.

35. Ibid., pp. 2–3.

36. Ibid.

37. Ibid., pp. 189–92, 260–63.

38. Ibid., pp. 155–57.

39. Ideology, however, was clearly treated as polychotomous or multinomial (though still categorical as opposed to continuous), taking one of four distinct values.

40. Huntington, *The Soldier and the State,* pp. 143–92.

41. Ibid., pp. 456–66.

42. See Samuel E. Finer, *The Man on Horseback: The Role of the Military in Politics* (London: Pall Mall, 1962). Although Huntington's specific formulation of military professionalism skirts the edge of this tautology, his broader notion of officership as profession has been productive for later work.

43. See, for example, Claude E. Welch, *Civilian Control of the Military: Myth and Reality* (Buffalo, NY: Council on International Studies, State University of New York at Buffalo, 1975); Alfred C. Stepan, *The Military in Politics: Changing Patterns in Brazil* (Princeton, NJ: Princeton University Press, 1971).

44. Feaver, "The Civil-Military Problematique," pp. 163.

45. Peter Feaver, *Armed Servants: Agency, Oversight, and Civil-Military Relations* (Cambridge, MA: Harvard University Press, 2003), pp. 16–53.

46. Burk, "Theories of Democratic Civil-Military Relations," p. 13.

47. Mattei Dogan, "Political Science and the Other Social Sciences," in Goodin and Klingemann, *A New Handbook of Political Science,* p. 108.

48. Huntington, *The Soldier and the State,* pp. 457–59. For more on Huntington's debt to Hartz, see chapter 5 by Michael C. Desch in this volume.

49. *The Soldier and the State* therefore anticipated—without the bureaucratic dimension—some of the two-level games and second-image-reversed debates of 1970s international relations theorizing; see, for example, Peter Gourevitch, "The Second Image Reversed: The International Sources of Domestic Politics," *International Organization* 32, no. 4 (1978): 881–912; Robert D. Putnam, "Diplomacy and Domestic Politics: The Logic of Two-Level Games," *International Organization* 42, no. 3 (1988): 427–60. Huntington also anticipated domestic-international aspects of later civil-military research. See, for example, Risa Brooks, *Political-Military Relations and the Stability of Arab Regimes* (New York: Oxford University Press for the International Institute of Strategic Studies, 1998); and Michael C. Desch, *Civilian Control of the Military: The Changing Security Environment* (Baltimore: Johns Hopkins University Press, 1999).

50. Historical facts and comparative case studies were the most appropriate sorts of evidence at Huntington's time, because relevant compilations of quantitative data did not exist and no compelling theory existed to be tested.

51. Dogan, "Political Science and the Other Social Sciences," p. 108.

52. Morris Janowitz, "Armed Forces and Society: An Interdisciplinary Journal," *Armed Forces and Society* 1, no. 1 (Fall 1974): 3–4.

53. Feaver, "Civil-Military Relations."

54. Burk, "Theories of Democratic Civil-Military Relations." While it is not entirely fair to judge the work of Morris Janowitz on the basis of the civil-military problematique because this was not his topical focus, the implications of his work for the problem of control still matter from a larger democratic framework of inquiry. His prescription—that professional ethics can supply civilian control—is only partially helpful, as it has the same tautological limitation as Huntington's work. Feaver, "The Civil-Military Problematique." Also like Huntington's, Janowitz's work suffered from a nation-state bias and incomplete democratic vision. Janowitz never explained how his citizen-soldier ideal could be realized without mass mobilization; his hope for embedding military service in a wider system of voluntary national service and political education was not realistic. Burk, "Theories of Democratic Civil-Military Relations," pp. 13–14.

55. See, for example, Charles Moskos, *The American Enlisted Man: The Rank and File in Today's Military* (New York: Russell Sage Foundation, 1970); Charles Moskos and Frank R. Wood, eds., *The Military: More Than Just a Job?* (Elmsford, NY: Pergamon-Brassey's International Defense Publishers, 1988); Charles Moskos, John Allen Williams, and David. R. Segal, *The Postmodern Military: Armed Forces after the Cold War* (New York: Oxford University Press, 2000); David Segal, *Recruiting for Uncle Sam: Citizenship and Military Manpower Policy* (Lawrence: University Press of Kansas, 1989); David Segal and H. Wallace Sinaiko, eds., *Life in the Rank and File: Enlisted Men and Women in the Armed Forces of the United States, Australia, Canada, and the United Kingdom* (Washington, DC: Pergamon-Brassey's International Defense Publishers, 1986); David Segal, Jerald G. Bachman, John D. Blair, and Davie R. Segal, *The All-Volunteer Force: A Study of Ideology in the Military* (Ann Arbor: University of Michigan Press, 1977).

56. See, for example, Samuel P. Huntington, *Political Order in Changing Societies* (New Haven, CT: Yale University Press, 1968).

57. Ibid., 194. For more on the limitations of this approach in comparative settings, see Robin Luckham, "A Comparative Typology of Civil-Military Relations," *Government and Opposition* 6, no. 1 (1971); and Robin Luckham, "Democratic Strategies for Security in Transition and Conflict," in Gavin Cawthra and Robin Luckham, eds., *Governing Insecurity: Democratic Control of Military and Security Establishments in Transitional Democracies* (New York: Zed Books, 2003).

58. Problems of democratic civil-military relations in comparative contexts and determining conditions of generalizability are still debated. Theorizing is still needed on how varied normative democratic concerns play out differently in different societal, historical, and cultural contexts. Some important insights have come from comparative work. For example, Bengt Abrahamsson's work on Sweden provided noteworthy evidence of countervailing features of professionalization: that there is always

latent political danger from the military, as there is from any cohesive and disciplined group that is well organized for action and influence. Bengt Abrahamsson, *Military Professionalization and Political Power* (Beverly Hills, CA: Sage, 1972).

59. Richard K. Betts, *Soldiers, Statesmen, and Cold War Crises* (Cambridge, MA: Harvard University Press, 1977); Bruce Russett and Alfred Stepan, *Military Force and American Society* (New York: Harper and Row, 1973); Bruce Russett, *Controlling the Sword* (Cambridge, MA: Harvard University Press, 1990); Eliot A. Cohen, *Citizens and Soldiers* (Ithaca, NY: Cornell University Press, 1985); Adam Yarmolinsky, ed., *The Military and American Society* (New York: Harper and Row, 1971).

60. For example, Russett and Stepan, *Military Force and American Society,* used surveys, event analysis, interviews, journal content analysis, and empirical evidence of stock market variations.

61. Betts argued that military leaders were neither more nor less inclined than civilians to suggest intervention; that once force had been chosen, the military was more aggressive on subsequent tactical decisions involving escalation; that the military's influence on civilian decision making was stronger when it opposed the use of force; and that service differences existed in attitudes toward the use of force. Betts, *Soldiers, Statesmen, and Cold War Crises.*

62. See, as an example, Don M. Snider and Miranda A. Carlton-Carew, eds., *U.S. Civil-Military Relations: In Crisis or Transition?* (Washington, DC: Center for Strategic and International Studies, 1995). See also Thomas E. Ricks, "The Widening Gap between the Military and Society," *Atlantic Monthly,* July 1997, pp. 67–78; Andrew J. Bacevich, "Civilian Control: A Useful Fiction?" *Joint Force Quarterly,* no. 6, (Autumn–Winter 1994–95); Steve Chapman, "When Soldiers Give Clinton a Different Salute," *Chicago Tribune,* October 25, 1998; Douglas Johnson and Steven Metz, "Civil-Military Relations in the United States: The State of the Debate," *Washington Quarterly,* no. 18 (Winter 1995): 197–213; Lawrence J. Korb, "The Military and Social Change," John M. Olin Institute for Strategic Studies Working Paper 5 for the Project on U.S. Post–Cold War Civil-Military Relations (Cambridge, MA, 1996); Mackubin T. Owens, "Civilian Control: A National Crisis?" *Joint Force Quarterly,* no. 6 (Autumn–Winter 1994–95): 80–83; Dana Priest, "Culture Gap: The Media and the Military," *Washington Post,* February 1, 1997; Kurt Campbell, "All Rise for Chairman Powell," *National Interest,* no. 23 (Spring 1991): 51–60; Admiral William J. Crowe Jr., *The Line of Fire: From Washington to the Gulf, the Politics and Battles of the New Military* (New York: Simon and Schuster, 1993); James R. Locher III, "Taking Stock of Goldwater-Nichols," *Joint Force Quarterly,* no. 13 (Autumn 1996): 10–16; Edward M. Luttwak, "Washington's Biggest Scandal," *Commentary* 97, no. 5 (May 1994): 29–33; Russell F. Weigley, "The American Military and the Principle of Civilian Control from McClellan to Powell," *Journal of Military History* 57, no. 5 (1993): 27–58; Charles J. Dunlap, "The Origins of the American Military Coup of 2012," *Parameters* 22, no. 4 (Winter 1992–93): 2–20; and Richard H. Kohn, "Out of Control: The Crisis in Civil-Military Relations," *National Interest,* no. 35 (Spring 1994): 3–17.

63. See especially Peter D. Feaver and Richard H. Kohn, eds., *Soldiers and Civil-*

ians: *The Civil-Military Gap and American National Security* (Cambridge, MA: MIT Press, 2001); Christopher Gelpi and Peter D. Feaver, "Speak Softly and Carry a Big Stick? Veterans in the Political Elite and the American Use of Force," *American Political Science Review* 96, no. 4 (December 2002): 779–93; Peter D. Feaver and Christopher Gelpi, *Choosing Your Battles: American Civil-Military Relations and the Use of Force* (Princeton, NJ: Princeton University Press, 2004); Ole R. Holsti, "A Widening Gap between the U.S. Military and Civilian Society? Some Evidence, 1976–96," *International Security* 23, no. 3 (Winter 1998–99): 5–42; Krista E. Wiegand and David L. Paletz, "The Elite Media and the Military-Civilian Culture Gap," *Armed Forces and Society* 27, no. 2 (Winter 2001): 183–204.

64. Deborah D. Avant and James Lebovic, "U.S. Military Attitudes towards Post–Cold War Missions," *Armed Forces and Society* 27, no. 1 (Fall 2000): 37–56.

65. Desch, *Civilian Control of the Military*.

66. Deborah Avant, *Political Institutions and Military Change: Lessons from Peripheral Wars* (Ithaca, NY: Cornell University Press, 1994); Deborah Avant, "Conflicting Indicators of 'Crisis' in American Civil-Military Relations," *Armed Forces and Society* 24, no. 3 (Spring 1998): 375–88, and Feaver, *Armed Servants*.

67. Risa Brooks, *Shaping Strategy: The Civil-Military Politics of Strategic Assessment* (Princeton, NJ: Princeton University Press, 2008). See also Risa Brooks and Elizabeth Stanley, *Creating Military Power: The Sources of Military Effectiveness* (Stanford: Stanford University Press, 2007).

68. Cori E. Dauber, "The Practice of Argument: Reading the Condition of Civil-Military Relations," *Armed Forces and Society* 24, no. 3 (Spring 1998): 435–46.

69. Douglas L. Bland, "A Unified Theory of Civil-Military Relations," *Armed Forces and Society* 26, no. 1 (Fall 1999): 7–25.

70. Don M. Snider and Lloyd J. Matthews, eds., *The Future of the Army Profession*, 2d ed., rev. and exp. (New York: McGraw-Hill Primis, 2005).

71. See James Burk, "The Logic of Crisis and Civil-Military Relations Theory: A Comment on Desch, Feaver, and Dauber," *Armed Forces and Society* 24, no. 3 (Spring 1998): 455–62. But see Thomas S. Sowers, "Beyond the Soldier and the State: Contemporary Operations and Variance in Principal-Agent Relations," *Armed Forces and Society* 31, no. 3 (Spring 2005): 385–409.

72. Moskos, Williams, and Segal, *The Postmodern Military*.

73. Rebecca L. Schiff, "Civil-Military Relations Reconsidered: A Theory of Concordance," *Armed Forces and Society* 22, no. 1 (Fall 1995): 7–24.

74. See Burk, "Theories of Democratic Civil-Military Relations."

75. See Goodin and Klingemann, "Political Science: The Discipline," p. 12.

CHAPTER FIVE: Hartz, Huntington, and the Liberal Tradition in America: The Clash with Military Realism

This chapter expands upon arguments the author made in "Bush and the Generals," *Foreign Affairs* 86, no. 2 (May–June 2007): 97–108.

1. A related phenomenon has been the increasing "Republicanization" of the officer corps of the U.S. Armed Forces. See Thomas E. Ricks, "A Widening Gap between the Military and Society," *Atlantic Monthly*, July 1977, pp. 66–78; Ole R. Holsti, "A Widening Gap between the U.S. Military and Civilian Society? Some Evidence, 1976–96," *International Security* 23, no. 3 (Winter 1998): 5–42; and essays in Peter D. Feaver and Richard H. Kohn, eds., *Soldiers and Civilians: The Civil-Military Gap and American National Security* (Cambridge, MA: MIT Press, 2001). But see chapter 9 by Darrell W. Driver in this volume.

2. I discuss this and other incidents in Michael C. Desch, *Civilian Control of the Military: The Changing Security Environment* (Baltimore: Johns Hopkins University Press, 1999), pp. 29–33. Also see, for example, reports of Major General Harold Campbell's punishment for speaking contemptuous words against President Clinton. Robert Burns, "General Who Maligned Clinton Agrees to Retire Early," *Associated Press*, June 19, 1993.

3. "George W. Bush Holds Campaign Rally in Grand Rapids, Michigan," November 3, 2000, transcripts.ccn.com/TRANSCRIPTS/022.03se.04.html.

4. Governor George W. Bush, "Acceptance Speech," First Union Center, Philadelphia, August 3, 2000, www.gwu.edu/~action/bush080300.html.

5. On Rumsfeld's early difficulties, see Thomas E. Ricks, "Rumsfeld on High Wire of Defense Reform: Military Brass, Conservative Lawmakers Are among Secretive Review's Unexpected Critics," *Washington Post*, May 20, 2001, p. 1; and Thomas E. Ricks, "Review Fractures Pentagon: Officials Predict Major Military Changes Far Off," *Washington Post*, July 14, 2001, p. 1.

6. On military reservations about the necessity for regime change in Iraq, see Thomas E. Ricks, "Some Top Military Brass Favor Status Quo in Iraq," *Washington Post*, July 28, 2002, p. 1; David Stout, "Former Military Leaders Urge Caution on War with Iraq," *New York Times*, September 23, 2002; Dale Eisman, "Two Retired Generals Voice Doubts over Bush's Plan to Attack Iraq," *Norfolk Virginian-Pilot*, October 17, 2002; and David Ignatius, "Doubt in the Ranks," *Washington Post*, November 1, 2002, p. 35. Military concerns about numbers of troops and strategy in Iraq are recounted in Thomas E. Ricks, *Fiasco: The American Military Adventure in Iraq* (New York: Penguin, 2006), pp. 40–43, 68–84; Michael R. Gordon and Bernard E. Trainor, *Cobra II: The Inside Story of the Invasion and Occupation of Iraq* (New York: Pantheon, 2006), pp. 24–54; Thom Shanker and John Tierney, "Top General Denounces Internal Dissent on Iraq," *New York Times*, April 2, 2003; Bill Keller, "Rumsfeld and the Generals," *New York Times*, April 5, 2003, p. A13; Seymour Hersh, "Offense and Defense: The Battle between Donald Rumsfeld and the Pentagon," *New Yorker*, April 7, 2003, www.newyorker.com/archive/2003/04/07/030407fa_fact1; Thomas DeFrank, "General Challenging Rumsfeld," *New York Daily News*, April 12, 2004; and Thomas E. Ricks, "Dissension Grows in Senior Ranks on War Strategy," *Washington Post*, May 9, 2004, p. 1.

7. See David Ignatius, "Rumsfeld and the Generals," *Washington Post*, March 30, 2005, p. 15; Fred Kaplan, "The Revolt against Rumsfeld: The Officer Corps Is Getting

Restless," *Slate*, April 12, 2006, www.slate.com/id/2139777/; David S. Cloud and Eric Schmitt, "More Retired Generals Call for Rumsfeld's Resignation," *New York Times*, April 14, 2006, p. A1; David Margolick, "The Night of the Generals," *Vanity Fair*, April 2007, www.vanityfair.com/politics/features/2007/04/iraqgenerals200704; James Kitfield, "The Generals' Case," *National Journal*, May 5, 2006, pp. 20–29; Major General Paul D. Eaton, "A Top-Down Review for the Pentagon," *New York Times*, March 19, 2006, sec. 4, p. 12; Lieutenant General Greg Newbold (ret.), "Why Iraq Was a Mistake," *Time*, April 9, 2006, www.time.com/time/magazine/article/0,9171,1181629-1,00 .html, pp. 42–43; Richard Whalen, "Revolt of the Generals," *Nation*, October 16, 2006, pp. 11–18; and Andrew Bacevich, "Warrior Politics," *Atlantic Monthly*, May 2007, pp. 25–26.

8. See James A. Baker III and Lee H. Hamilton, cochairs, "The Iraq Study Group Report," December 2006, Recommendation 46, http://bakerinstitute.org/files/pubs/ iragstudygroup_findings.pdf.

9. "Morale," Question no. 19, *Military Times* Poll, December 29, 2006, www .militarycity.com/polls/2006poll_morale.php.

10. Louis Hartz, *The Liberal Tradition in America* (San Diego, CA: Harcourt, Brace, Jovanovich, 1955).

11. See Samuel P. Huntington, *The Soldier and the State: The Theory and Politics of Civil-Military Relations* (Cambridge, MA: Belknap Press of Harvard University Press, 1957), pp. 2–3, 83–85. Hartz's influence upon Huntington has been profound, as the latter has acknowledged in personal conversations with author the over the years, most recently on Martha's Vineyard, Massachusetts, June 2006. See also Huntington, "Conservativism as an Ideology," *American Political Science Review* 51, no. 2 (June 1957): 454–73; and Huntington, *American Politics: The Promise of Disharmony* (Cambridge, MA: Belknap Press of Harvard University Press, 1981), pp. 221–62.

12. Desch, *Civilian Control of the Military*, pp. 13–17, 122–23.

13. The next two sections draw upon Michael C. Desch, "America's Liberal Illiberalism," *International Security* 32, no. 3 (Winter 2007–8): 7–43.

14. Stuart Gerry Brown, Review of *Freedom Limited: An Essay on Democracy, The Individual and the New World*, and *The Liberal Tradition in America*, *Ethics* 65, no. 4 (July 1955): 313.

15. Marvin Meyers, "Louis Hartz, *The Liberal Tradition in America*: An Appraisal," *Comparative Studies in Society and History* 5, no. 3 (April 1963): 263; and Michael W. Doyle, *Ways of War and Peace: Realism, Liberalism, and Socialism* (New York: W. W. Norton, 1997), pp. 206–7.

16. Arthur M. Schlesinger Jr., *The Vital Center: The Politics of Freedom* (Boston: Houghton Mifflin, 1949).

17. Hartz, *The Liberal Tradition in America*, pp. 176–77. Hartz here builds on the famous observation of Alexis de Tocqueville in *Democracy in America*, vol. 1 (New York: Vintage, 1945), p. 30.

18. Robert Packenham, *Liberal America and the Third World: Political Development Ideas in Foreign Aid and Social Science* (Princeton, NJ: Princeton University Press,

1973), chap. 3. These last two premises (opposition to revolution and radicalism and democracy being more crucial than stability) may seem contradictory, and they are in one sense, but they can be made consistent by arguing, as many Liberals do, that they are willing to accept short-term instability to achieve "perpetual peace" over the long run.

19. Hartz, *The Liberal Tradition in America*, pp. 12, 285.

20. Eric McKittrick, "Is There an American Political Philosophy?" *New Republic*, April 11, 1955, p. 23.

21. Packenham, *Liberal America and the Third World*, p. 173.

22. Ira Katznelson, "Review of Civic Ideals: Conflicting Visions of Citizenship in U.S. History," *Political Theory* 27, no. 4 (August 1999): 568. To be sure, there are many critics of Hartz's Liberal tradition thesis, including Rogers M. Smith, "Beyond Tocqueville, Myrdal, and Hartz: The Multiple Traditions in America," *American Political Science Review* 87, no. 3 (September 1993): 549–66; Daniel T. Rodgers, "Republicanism: The Career of a Concept," *Journal of American History* 79, no. 1 (June 1992): 11–38; Harry Jaffa, "Conflicts within the Idea of the Liberal Tradition," *Comparative Studies in Society and History* 5, no. 3 (April 1963): 274–78; Judith N. Shklar, "Redeeming American Political Theory," *American Political Science Review* 85, no. 1 (March 1991): 3–15; Daniel Boorstin, "American Liberalism," *Commentary* 20, no.7 (July 1955): 99–100; and chapter 13 by Richard H. Kohn in this volume. But Hartz's thesis has experienced something of a comeback . See, for example, Philip Abbott, "Still Louis Hartz after All These Years: A Defense of the Liberal Society Thesis," *Perspectives on Politics* 3, no. 1 (March 2005): 93–109. For a recent attempt at synthesizing the Liberal and multiple traditions in American political thought, see Stephen Skowronek, "The Reassociation of Ideas and Purposes: Racism, Liberalism, and the American Political Tradition," *American Political Science Review* 100, no. 3 (August 2006): 385–402.

23. There is a growing literature and concomitant wave of interest among scholars on this topic. See, for example, Uday Singh Mehta, *Liberalism and Empire: A Study in Nineteenth-Century British Liberal Thought* (Chicago: University of Chicago Press, 1999); Jennifer Pitts, *A Turn to Empire: The Rise of Imperial Liberalism in Britain and France* (Princeton, NJ: Princeton University Press, 2005); Bhiku Parekh, "Superior People," *Times Literary Supplement*, February 25, 1994, pp. 11–13; and David Glenn, "Liberalism: The Fuel of Empires?" *Chronicle of Higher Education*, September 2, 2005, chronicle.com/weeklyv51/i02a01901.htm.

24. For an excellent discussion of the role that putative altruism played in Liberal imperialism in nineteenth-century Britain, see Mehta, *Liberalism and Empire*, p. 81. The most vociferous advocates of "benign" or "benevolent hegemony" as the objective of contemporary United States foreign policy are neoconservatives such as Robert Kagan and William Kristol. See Kagan and Kristol, "The Present Danger," *National Interest*, no. 59 (Spring 2000): 58; and Kagan and Kristol, "Toward a Neo-Reaganite Foreign Policy," *Foreign Affairs* 75, no. 4 (July–August 1996): 20.

25. Moynihan and Glazer quoted in John Ehrman, *The Rise of Neoconservativism:*

Intellectuals and Foreign Affairs, 1945–1994 (New Haven, CT: Yale University Press, 1995), pp. 80, 108.

26. A contemporary example of this intolerance is how American Liberal intellectuals have dealt with non-Liberal thinkers, particularly Leo Strauss. Critics have not been content merely to prove him wrong; they often go well beyond that to try to demonize him as an elitist or a cryptofascist. On this point, see Peter Berkowitz, "Liberal Zealotry," *Yale Law Journal* 103, no. 5 (March 1994): 1363–82, reviewing Stephen Holmes, *The Anatomy of Antiliberalism* (Cambridge, MA: Harvard University Press, 1993). Also see Michael C. Desch, "What Would Strauss Do?" *American Conservative*, January 17, 2005, pp. 29–31, reviewing Anne Norton, *Leo Strauss and the Politics of the American Empire* (New Haven, CT: Yale University Press, 2004).

27. Hartz, *The Liberal Tradition in America*, p. 58.

28. H. L. Mencken, "A Blind Spot," in Alastair Cooke, ed., *The Vintage Mencken* (New York: Vintage, 1990), p. 77.

29. Louis Hartz, "Conflict within the Idea of the Liberal Tradition: Comment," *Comparative Studies in Society and History* 5, no. 3 (April 1963): 283.

30. Robert Kagan, "Power and Weakness," *Policy Review*, no. 113 (June 2002), www.policyreview.org/JUN02/kagan.html. He continues this theme in Robert Kagan, "Cowboy Nation," *New Republic*, October 23, 2006, pp. 20–23. Also see Packenham, *Liberal America and the Third World*, p. 7.

31. For more evidence of the links between neoconservativism and Liberalism, see Irving Kristol, "The Neoconservative Persuasion," *Weekly Standard*, August 25, 2003, www.weeklystandard.com/Content/Public/Articles/000/000/003/000tzmlw .asp; and Ehrman, *The Rise of Neoconservativism*, pp. viii, 40, 186. Many "Old Right" conservatives were suspicious of the Liberal tenets of neoconservativism. See Murray Friedman, *The Neoconservative Revolution: Jewish Intellectuals and the Shaping of Public Policy* (New York: Cambridge University Press, 2005), pp. 134–35. For a related discussion of the similarities between Liberalism and neoconservativism, see Jonathan Monten, "The Roots of the Bush Doctrine: Power, Nationalism, and Democracy Promotion in U.S. Strategy," *International Security* 29, no. 4 (Spring 2005): 116. Mehta, *Liberalism and Empire*, 214, points to clear parallels in the philosophies of Liberal imperialism and of neoconservativism.

32. Lawrence F. Kaplan, "Regime Change: Bush, Closet Liberal," *New Republic*, March 3, 2003, p. 21. Also see David Kennedy, "What 'W' Owes to 'WW,'" *Atlantic Monthly*, March 2005, pp. 36–40.

33. Hartz, *The Liberal Tradition in America*, p. 42.

34. Walter Russell Mead, "God's Country," *Foreign Affairs* 85, no. 5 (September–October 2006): 24–44. The continuity between Christianity and the Enlightenment is a central theme in John Gray, *Black Mass: Apocalyptic Religion and the Death of Utopia* (New York: Farrar, Straus and Giroux, 2007).

35. Ronald Steele, "The Missionary," *New York Review of Books* 50, no. 18 (November 20, 2003), www.nybooks.com/articles/16797.

36. This section draws upon Michael C. Desch, "Liberals, Neocons, and Real-cons," *Orbis* 45, no. 4 (Fall 2001): 520–22, 526–31.

37. But many Liberals still think U.S. hegemony is vital both for the establishment of multilateral institutions and to ensure that those institutions continue to provide necessary "public goods." See Robert O. Keohane, *After Hegemony: Cooperation and Discord in the World Political Economy* (Princeton, NJ: Princeton University Press, 1984); and Mancur Olson, *The Logic of Collective Action* (Cambridge, MA: Harvard University Press, 1965).

38. Friedman, *The Neoconservative Revolution*, p. 134.

39. Packenham, *Liberal America and the Third World*, pp. 62–63.

40. George W. Bush, *National Security Strategy of the United States* (Washington, DC: White House, September 2002), p. 17.

41. "President Bush Presses for Peace in the Middle East," May 9, 2003, www.whitehouse.gov/news/releases/2003/05/print/20030509-11.html.

42. "President Discusses Future of Iraq," February 26, 2003, www.whitehouse.gov/news/releases/2003/02/print/200030226-11.html.

43. "Interview of the Vice President by Wolf Blitzer, CNN," June 23, 2005, www.whitehouse.gov/news/releases/2005/06/print/20050623-8.html.

44. A powerful critique of this widely embraced assumption is Samuel P. Huntington, *Political Order in Changing Societies* (New Haven, CT: Yale University Press, 1965), p. 6.

45. "President Sworn in to Second Term," January 20, 2005, www.whitehouse.gov/news/releases/2005/01/20050120-1.html.

46. Quoted in Bob Woodward, *Plan of Attack* (New York: Simon and Schuster, 2004), p. 88.

47. "President Discusses Progress in Iraq," July 23, 2003, www.whitehouse.gov/news/releases/2003/07/print/20030723-1.html.

48. Wolfowitz quoted in Ricks, *Fiasco*, p. 17.

49. Quoted in Samuel Flagg Bemis, *The Latin American Policy of the United States: An Historical Interpretation* (New York: W. W. Norton, 1943), p. 175.

50. "President Bush Delivers Graduation Speech at West Point," June 1, 2002, www.whitehouse.gov.news/releases/2002/06/print20020601-3.html.

51. Bush, *National Security Strategy* (2002), p. 15.

52. Donald Rumsfeld, "Beyond Nation Building," February 14, 2003, www.dod.gov/speeches/2003/sp20030214-secdef0024.html.

53. This attitude was roundly and famously criticized in Jeane J. Kirkpatrick, "Dictatorships and Double Standards," *Commentary* 68, no. 5 (November 1979): 34–45.

54. Sean Loughlin, "Rumsfeld on Looting in Iraq: 'Stuff Happens,'" *CNN.com*, April 12, 2003, www.cnn.com/2003/US/04/11/sprj.irq.pentagon/.

55. "Council on Foreign Relations (Transcript)," May 27, 2003, www.dod.gov/speeches/2003/sp20030527-secdef0245.html.

56. Larry Diamond, "What Went Wrong in Iraq," *Foreign Affairs* 83, no. 5 (September–October 2004): 34–56.

57. Quoted in Ricks, *Fiasco*, p. 96.

58. "President Bush Calls for New Palestinian Leadership," June 24, 2002, www.whitehouse.gov/news/releases/2002/06/20020624-3.html.

59. "Interview with Arab Journalists," March 1, 2005, www.state.gov/secretary/rm/2005/42853.htm.

60. Steven R. Weisman, "Rice Admits U.S. Underestimated Hamas Strength," *New York Times*, January 30, 2006, p. A1.

61. "Special Briefing on Travel to the Middle East and Europe," Washington, DC, July 21, 2006, www.state.gov/secretary/rm/2006/69331.htm.

62. Ricks, *Fiasco*, p. 48.

63. Huntington, *The Soldier and the State*, p. 2.

64. Ibid., pp. 62–79. As chapter 9 by Darrell Driver in this volume suggests, Huntington's concept of a unified military mind-set characterized by "conservative Realism" is not without its critics. But there is substantial empirical data that does suggest that civilian and military attitudes diverge on a wide variety of issues and that "conservative Realism," as an ideal type, does capture the essence of the military mind-set. See Ole R. Holsti, "Of Chasms and Convergence: Attitudes and Beliefs of Civilians and Military Elites at the Start of the New Millennium," in Peter D. Feaver and Richard H. Kohn, eds., *Soldiers and Civilians: The Civil-Military Gap and American National Security* (Cambridge, MA: MIT Press, 2001), pp. 15–100.

65. Huntington, *The Soldier and the State*, pp. 148–62.

66. Ibid., p. 155.

67. John Mueller, "A False Sense of Insecurity?" *Regulation* 27, no. 3 (Fall 2004): 42–46.

68. On Clinton's preference for domestic politics, see David Halberstam, *War in a Time of Peace: Bush, Clinton, and the Generals* (New York: Scribner, 2001), pp. 167–68, 241.

69. Quoted in Bob Woodward, *State of Denial: Bush at War, Part III* (New York: Simon and Schuster, 2006), p. 3.

70. James Mann, *Rise of the Vulcans: The History of Bush's War Cabinet* (New York: Viking, 2004), pp. 255–60.

71. "A National Security Strategy of Engagement and Enlargement," Washington, DC, The White House, February 1996, www.fas.org/spp/military/docops/national/1996stra.htm#II.

72. "State of the Union Address," January 20, 2004, www.whitehouse.gov.news/releases/2004/01/print/20040120-7.html.

73. "National Security Advisor Dr. Condoleezza Rice Discusses War on Terror at McConnell Center for Political Leadership," March 8, 2004, www.whitehouse.gov/news/releases/2004/03/print/20040308-15.html.

74. Quoted in John J. Mearsheimer, *The Tragedy of Great Power Politics* (New York: W. W. Norton, 2001), p. 23.

75. Governor George W. Bush, "A Distinctly American Internationalism," Ronald Reagan Presidential Library, Simi Valley, California, November 19, 1999, www.mtholyoke.edu/acad/intrel/bush/wspeech.htm.

76. Franklin Foer and Spencer Ackerman, "The Radical: What Cheney Really Believes," *New Republic,* December 1, 2003, www.tnr.com/docprint.mhtml?i-20031201 &s-ackermanfoer120103.

77. On the significant increase in the U.S. military's operational tempo during the Clinton administration, see "United States Military Operations," fas.org/man/dod-101/ index.html.

78. Debate Transcript, "The Second Gore-Bush Presidential Debate," Commission on Presidential Debates, October 11, 2000, www.debates.org/pages/trans2000b _p.html.

79. Bob Woodward, *Bush at War* (New York: Simon and Schuster, 2002), p. 340.

80. Suggesting that military reluctance to go to war could be a source of civil-military conflict is Huntington, *The Soldier and the State,* pp. 69, 91. For evidence that this pattern of civil-military conflict characterized the Cold War, see Richard K. Betts, *Soldiers, Statesmen, and Cold War Crises* (New York: Columbia University Press, 1991), pp. 4–5.

81. For discussion of these two incidents, see Thomas L. Friedman, "Clinton Mends Fences at West Point," *New York Times,* May 30, 1993, p. A1.

82. See George Stephanopoulos, *All Too Human: A Political Education* (Boston: Little, Brown, 1999), pp. 69–77.

83. Margolick, "Night of the Generals."

84. Quoted in Jim Garamone, "For Churchill and Rumsfeld, 'The Best Will Do,'" *American Forces Information Service News Articles,* January 29, 2003, www.defenselink .mil/news/newsarticle.aspx?id=29513.

85. Stephanopoulos, *All Too Human,* pp. 123–29.

86. Gordon and Trainor, *Cobra II,* p. 3.

87. "Secretary Rumsfeld Interview with Associated Press," Friday, September 7, 2001, www.defenselink.mil/transcripts/2001/t09102001_t0907ap/html.

88. Videotaped interview with Thomas Ricks, "Rumsfeld's War," *Frontline,* October 3, 2005, www.pbs.org/wgbh/frontline/shows/pentagon/interviews/ricks.html.

89. Woodward, *Bush at War,* p. 61.

90. Newbold, "Why Iraq Was a Mistake," p. 43.

91. David S. Cloud and Eric Schmitt, "More Retired Generals Call for Rumsfeld's Resignation," *New York Times,* April 14, 2006, www.nytimes.com/2006/04/14/ washington/14military.html.

92. "Iraq, Afghanistan, and President Bush," *Military Times Poll,* December 29, 2006, Question no. 10, www.militarycity.com/polls/2006poll_iraq.php.

93. Videotaped interview with Thomas White for "Rumsfeld's War," *Frontline,* October 3, 2005, www.pbs.org/wgbh/frontline/shows/pentagon/interviews/white.html.

94. Gordon and Trainor, *Cobra II,* 499–500; Hersh, "Offense and Defense."

95. George W. Bush, "A Period of Consequences," speech delivered at the Citadel, South Carolina, September 23, 1999, www.citadel.edu/pao/addresses/pres_bush.html.

96. Joseph S. Nye Jr. and William A. Owens, "America's Information Edge," *Foreign Affairs* 75, no. 2 (March–April 1996): 20–36.

97. See "Is Rumsfeld Up to His Job?" *Milwaukee Journal Sentinel,* August 27 and 28, 2001, www.jsonline.com/; see also Ricks, "Rumsfeld on High Wire of Defense Reform"; Ricks, "Review Fractures Pentagon."

98. Gordon and Trainor, *Cobra II,* p. 53.

99. Kitfield, "The Generals' Case," p. 28. See Kenneth Adelman, "Cakewalk in Iraq," *Washington Post,* February 13, 2002.

100. Gordon and Trainor, *Cobra II,* pp. 210, 485.

101. White, *Frontline* interview.

102. Hersh, "Offense and Defense."

103. Ibid.

104. Kitfield, "The Generals' Case," p. 25; and Hersh, "Offense and Defense."

105. Huntington, *The Soldier and the State,* pp. 270–88, 457–60. I argue that this also explains the relatively harmonious civil-military relations of the Cold War period, which in some respects defied Huntington's expectations. See Desch, *Civilian Control of the Military,* p. 10 n14.

106. Huntington, *The Soldier and the State,* p. 155.

107. Ibid., pp. 80–85.

108. Mann, *Rise of the Vulcans,* p. 196. Also see Woodward, *State of Denial,* pp. xi, 34–35, 39; Gordon and Trainor, *Cobra II,* p. 3.

109. Donald Rumsfeld, "Rumsfeld's Rules," 1974, revised February 20, 2001, library.villanova.edu/vbl/bweb/rumsfeldsrules.pdf.

110. White, *Frontline* interview.

111. Eaton, "A Top-Down Review for the Pentagon."

112. Eliot A. Cohen, *Supreme Command: Soldiers, Statesmen, and Leadership in Wartime* (New York: Free Press, 2002).

113. On the influence of Cohen's book on the Bush administration, see Dana Milbank, "Bush's Summer Reading List Hints at Iraq," *Washington Post,* August 20, 2002, p. A11; Lawrence Freedman, "Rumsfeld's Legacy: The Iraq Syndrome," *Washington Post,* January 9, 2005, p. B04; and John Keegan, "Servant of a Theory," *Spectator,* November 16, 2002, www.spectator.co.uk/search/author/20316/servant-of-a-theory .thtml. Cohen served on the Defense Policy Board, a high-level advisory panel to Secretary of Defense Rumsfeld during the Bush administration, and no doubt had much influence on civil-military relations via that route too.

114. Cohen, *Supreme Command,* p. 84.

115. Ibid., p. 246.

116. Eliot A. Cohen, "Generals, Politicians and Iraq," *Wall Street Journal,* August 14, 2002, p. A12; Cohen, "Hunting 'Chicken Hawks,'" *Washington Post,* September 5, 2002, p. A31.

117. Stephen Goode, "The Character of Wartime Statesmen: Interview with Eliot Cohen," *Insight on the News,* May 30, 2003.

118. Quoted in ibid.; and Eliot Cohen, "Honor in Discretion," *Wall Street Journal,* April 22, 2006, p. 8.

119. Mann, *Rise of the Vulcans,* pp. 196–97.

120. Greg Jaffe, "The Two Star Rebel," *Wall Street Journal,* May 13, 2006, p. 1. For more detailed discussion of this incident, see chapter 3 by Matthew Moten in this volume.

121. White, *Frontline* interview.

CHAPTER SIX: Winning Wars, Not Just Battles: Expanding the Military Profession to Incorporate Stability Operations

1. Samuel P. Huntington, *The Soldier and the State* (Cambridge, MA: Belknap Press of Harvard University Press, 1957), p. 11.

2. Joint Publication (JP) 1-02, *Department of Defense Dictionary of Military and Associated Terms,* as amended through June 13, 2007, www.dtic.mil/doctrine/jel/new_pubs/jp1_02.pdf. DoD Directive 3000.05, "Military Support for Stability, Security, Transition, and Reconstruction (SSTR) Operations," defines stability operations as "Military and civilian activities conducted across the spectrum from peace to conflict to establish or maintain order in States and regions," November 28, 2005, www.dtic.mil/whs/directives/corres/pdf/300005p.pdf.

3. See especially Huntington, *The Soldier and the State,* pp. 7–18.

4. Quoted in "From My Bookshelf," *Military Review* 85, no. 1 (January–February 2005): 81; this comment about Huntington was included as part of a summary of the reading list recommended by the chief of staff of the U.S. Army.

5. Field Manual (FM) no. 1, *The Army,* Headquarters, Department of the Army, Washington, DC, June 14, 2005, chapter I, sections 1-3 and 1-4, www.army.mil/fm1/chapter1.html.

6. See Major Edwin C. Brouse, "The U.S. Army and Constabulary Operations," School of Advanced Military Studies, United States Army Command and General Staff College, Fort Leavenworth, Kansas, AY 05-06, available in the Combined Arms Research Library, Digital Library, cgsc.cdmhost.com/u?/p4013coll3,714. Also see Andrew Birtle, *U.S. Army Counterinsurgency and Contingency Operations Doctrine, 1860–1941* (Washington, DC: U.S. Government Printing Office, November 1997), chap. 1.

7. See, for example, Russell F. Weigley, *History of the United States State Army* (New York: Macmillan, 1967), pp. 395–420.

8. For a description of professional jurisdictions, see Andrew Abbott, *The System of Professions: An Essay on the Division of Expert Labor* (Chicago: University of Chicago Press, 1988).

9. Huntington, *The Soldier and the State,* p. 261.

10. Ibid.

11. Ibid., p. 324.

12. Ibid., p. 328.

13. See chapter 7 by Williamson Murray in this volume.

14. The best-known military histories of the Army tend to ignore this part of war, as detailed in Nadia Schadlow, "War and the Art of Governance," *Parameters* 33, no. 3 (Autumn 2003): 85–94.

15. See chapter 2 by Richard K. Betts in this volume.

16. See John L. Romjue, "The Evolution of the Airland Battle Concept," *Air University Review,* May–June 1984, www.airpower.maxwell.af.mil/airchronicles/aureview/1984/may-jun/romjue.htm.

17. The Weinberger Doctrine recommends: "1. Commit only if our or our allies' vital interests are at stake. 2. If we commit, do so with all the resources necessary to win. 3. Go in only with clear political and military objectives. 4. Be ready to change the commitment if the objectives change, since wars rarely stand still. 5. Only take on commitments that can gain the support of the American people and the Congress. 6. Commit U.S. forces only as a last resort." See Casper Weinberger, "Remarks to the National Press Club, November 28, 1984," *Defense,* no. 85 (January 1985), p. 9. It has also been widely associated with Colin Powell, who was Weinberger's military assistant at the time and who publicly embraced key elements of the doctrine in his tenure as chairman of the Joint Chiefs of Staff. See Colin Powell, "U.S. Forces: Challenges Ahead," *Foreign Affairs* 71, no. 5 (Winter 1992): 35–45.

18. On the military's preference for overwhelming force and its reflection in the Weinberger-Powell Doctrine, see also chapter 2 by Richard K. Betts in this volume.

19. Suzanne C. Nielsen, "The Rules of the Game? The Weinberger Doctrine and the American Use of Force," in Don M. Snider and Lloyd J. Matthews, eds., *The Future of the Army Profession,* 2d ed., rev. and exp. (New York: McGraw-Hill Primis, 2005), pp. 627–53.

20. See, in particular, Huntington, *The Soldier and the State,* chap. 12, pp. 315–44.

21. Antulio Echevarria II, "Transforming the Army's Way of Battle: Revising Our Abstract Knowledge," in Snider and Matthews, *The Future of the Army Profession,* p. 367.

22. This has been persuasively documented in Russell Weigley, *The American Way of War: A History of U.S. Military Strategy and Policy* (Bloomington: Indiana University Press, 1973), p. 475. The influence of Weigley's book is great; it is required reading at service and command schools and is on the Army chief of staff's list of recommended reading. Brian M. Linn, "The American Way of War Revisited," *Journal of Military History* 66, no. 2 (April 2002): 502.

23. For a description of the priority of combat expertise among a hierarchy of components of professional military expertise, see Richard Lacquement, *Army Professional Expertise and Jurisdictions* (Carlisle, PA: Strategic Studies Institute, 2003); and Lacquement, "Mapping Army Professional Expertise and Clarifying Jurisdictions of Practice," in Snider and Matthews, *The Future of the Army Profession,* pp. 213–35.

24. B. H. Liddell Hart, *Strategy* (New York: Praeger, 1954), p. 366 (emphasis added).

25. For an excellent summary of the laws of war and their applicability to postconflict governance, see David A. Wallace, "The Law of Occupation and Post-Armed-Conflict Governance: Considerations for Future Conflicts," *Military Review* 87, no. 6 (November–December 2007): 20–29.

26. Major James Gavrilis, "The Mayor of Ar Rutbah: Amid the Chaos in Iraq, One Company of U.S. Special Forces," *Foreign Policy,* no. 151 (November–December 2005): 30.

27. Nadia Schadlow, "Root's Rules: Lessons from America's Colonial Office," *American Interest* 2, no. 3 (January–February 2007): 95.

28. Ibid.

29. Edwin Dorn, Howard D. Graves, and Joseph J. Collins, *American Military Culture in the Twenty-First Century* (Washington, DC: Center for Strategic and International Studies, 2000); Thomas G. Mahnken and James R. Fitzsimonds, *The Limits of Transformation: Officer Attitudes toward the Revolution in Military Affairs* (Newport, RI: Naval War College Press, 2003).

30. For a detailed study of post–Cold War defense reform efforts, see Richard Lacquement, *Shaping American Military Capabilities after the Cold War* (Westport, CT: Praeger, 2003). The book describes and assesses American force structure and doctrinal responses to the changing strategic environment, including consideration of peace (stability) operations and the so-called revolution in military affairs, between the end of the Cold War and the immediate aftermath of 9/11.

31. Many of these tasks have been identified and spelled out in various recent reports. For example, see Center for Strategic and International Studies (CSIS) and the Association of the United States Army (AUSA), *Play to Win: Report of the Post-Conflict Reconstruction Commission* (2003), www.csis.org/media/csis/pubs/playtowin.pdf. In addition, some of these tasks are identified in James Dobbins et al., *America's Role in Nation-Building: From Germany to Iraq* (Santa Monica, CA: RAND, 2003), www.rand .org/publications/MR/MR1753/. Another prescient analysis of necessary stability operations tasks can be found in a report from the Army War College's Strategic Studies Institute before the invasion of Iraq in 2003. Conrad Crane and Andrew Terrill, *Reconstructing Iraq: Insights, Challenges, and Missions for Military Forces in a Post-Conflict Scenario* (Carlisle, PA: Strategic Studies Institute, February 2003), www.strategic studiesinstitute.army.mil/pdffiles/PUB182.pdf.

32. For one summary of this argument, see Nina M. Serafino, *Peacekeeping and Related Stability Operations: Issues of U.S. Military Involvement*, IB94040 (Washington, DC: Congressional Research Service, May 18, 2006), www.fas.org/sgp/crs/natsec/ IB94040.pdf. See also Katherine McIntire Peters, "The Price of Peace," *Government Executive*, March 1, 1997, www.govexec.com/features/0397s2.htm.

33. Defense Science Board, 2004 Summer Study, *Transition to and from Hostilities*, December 2004, www.acq.osd.mil/dsb/reports/2004-12-DSB_SS_Report_Final.pdf.

34. Report of the Defense Science Board Task Force, *Institutionalizing Stability Operations within DoD*, September 2005, www.acq.osd.mil/dsb/reports/2005-09-Stability _Final.pdf.

35. DoD Directive 3000.05, paragraph 4-1, p. 2. A DoD Directive is a powerful bureaucratic tool. A directive provides impetus in the form of high-level departmental leadership guidance to the civilian and military staffs, combatant commands, and armed services. It provides a strong signal for the focus of organizational effort and the allocation of resources.

36. Joint Publication (JP) 3-0, *Joint Operations*, September 17, 2006; and JP 5-0, *Joint Operation Planning*, December 26, 2006. The incorporation of stability opera-

tions is an important change to both documents and significantly is reflected in the restructuring of planning phases: the old four-phase construct was replaced by a new six-phase construct comprising "shape, deter, seize the initiative, dominate, stabilize, and enable civil authority." JP 3-0, p. iv. "Stabilize" and "enable civil authority" are new.

37. JP 3-0, *Joint Operations*, p. xxii: "To reach the national strategic end state and conclude the operation/campaign successfully, JFCs [joint forces commanders] must integrate and synchronize stability operations—missions, tasks, and activities to maintain or reestablish a safe and secure environment and provide essential governmental services, emergency infrastructure reconstruction, or humanitarian relief—with offensive and defensive operations within each major operation or campaign phase. Planning for stability operations should begin when joint operation planning is initiated." JP 3-0 also consolidates the previous version of JP 3-0, *Doctrine for Joint Operations*, and JP 3-07, *Joint Doctrine for Military Operations Other than War*. It discontinues the use of the term "military operations other than war."

38. See Major Stephanie Ahern, "Learning during War: Analyzing Organizational Change in the Army's Post 9/11 Environment," U.S. Military Academy, unpublished paper, pp. 16–17.

39. See Gavrilis, "The Mayor of Ar Rutbah."

40. Several examples of early successes and missteps by U.S. forces following the 2003 invasion of Iraq are described in Thomas E. Ricks, *Fiasco: The American Military Adventure in Iraq* (New York: Penguin, 2006); and George Packer, *The Assassins' Gate: America in Iraq* (New York: Farrar, Straus and Giroux, 2005).

41. See "Fact Sheet: Update on the New Iraq Strategy, Helping Iraq's Leaders Secure Their Population," April 20, 2007, www.whitehouse.gov/news/releases/2007/04/print/20070420-11.html.

42. See Andrew F. Krepinevich Jr., "How to Win in Iraq," *Foreign Affairs* 84, no. 5 (September–October 2005): 89.

43. For a more detailed argument about the relevance of stability operations to military professional expertise, see Richard Lacquement, "Mapping Army Professional Expertise and Clarifying Jurisdictions of Practice," in Snider and Matthews, *The Future of the Army Profession*, which focused explicitly on the U.S. Army. The present chapter extends that reasoning to the entire U.S. military, that is to say, to joint forces and their joint professional leadership.

44. Department of the Army, Field Manual (FM) 3-0, *Operations*, February 2008 (quotations are from the foreword by General William S. Wallace, Commander U.S. Army Training and Doctrine Command, and p. 3-1).

45. Ibid. The six "war-fighting functions" are movement and maneuver, intelligence, fires, sustainment, command and control, and protection.

46. Department of the Army, Field Manual (FM) 3-24/MCWP 3-33.5, *Counterinsurgency*, December 2006.

47. Leonard Wong, *Developing Adaptive Leaders: The Crucible Experience of Operation Iraqi Freedom* (Carlisle, PA: Strategic Studies Institute, July 2004).

48. Major Paul T. Stanton, U.S. Army, "Unit Immersion in Mosul: Establishing Stability in Transition," *Military Review* 86, no. 44 (July–August 2006): 63.

49. See Michael J. Meese and Sean M. Morgan, "New Requirements for Army Expert Knowledge," in Snider and Matthews, *The Future of the Army Profession,* pp. 353–59. See also CSIS and AUSA, *Play to Win;* and Post Conflict Reconstruction Project, forums.csis.org/pcrproject/.

50. Department of the Army, Field Manual (FM) 7-1, *Battle Focused Training,* September 2003, section 3-1, p. 47.

51. Dobbins et al., *America's Role in Nation-Building;* Richard B. Finn, *Winners in Peace: MacArthur, Yoshida, and Postwar Japan* (Berkeley: University of California Press, 1992); Robert Wolfe, ed., *Americans as Proconsuls: United States Military Government in Germany and Japan, 1944–1952* (Carbondale: Southern Illinois University Press, 1984).

52. For example, see Ross Coffey, "Revisiting CORDS: The Need for Unity of Effort to Secure Iraq," *Military Review* 86, no. 2 (March–April 2006): 24–34.

53. See also Lacquement, "Mapping Army Professional Expertise and Clarifying Jurisdictions of Practice Jurisdictions," in Snider and Matthews, *Future of the Army Profession,* pp. 213–36.

54. For example, see the Center for Strategic and International Studies project and associated reports on "Beyond Goldwater-Nichols," www.csis.org/isp/bgn/. A very thoughtful set of articles that prominently includes the theme of improving civilian capacity is U.S. Army Combined Arms Center, *Military Review* special edition, "Interagency Reader," June 2008, usacac.army.mil/CAC/milreview/English/IAReader/iareader.asp.

55. Briefing on Civilian Stabilization Initiative, Ambassador John E. Herbst, Coordinator for the Office of Reconstruction and Stabilization, Washington, DC, February 14, 2008, www.state.gov/s/crs/rls/rm/100913.htm.

56. For an excellent example of this challenge, see the statements and testimony by Representative Ike Skelton, Secretary of State Condoleezza Rice, and Secretary of Defense Robert Gates during a session of the House Armed Service Committee, "Hearing on Building Partnership Capacity and the Development of the Interagency Process," April 15, 2008, http://armedservices.house.gov/apps/list/speech/armedSVC_dem/skeltonopeningstatement041508.shtml, http://armedservices.house.gov/pdfs/FC041508/GatesTestimony041508.pdf, http://armedservices.house.gov/pdfs/FC041508/RiceTestimony041508.pdf.

57. For further discussion of the difference between ideal and realistic divisions of labor between armed forces and civilians, see FM 3-24, *Counterinsurgency,* especially chap. 2, "Unity of Effort." For a more detailed discussion of appropriate military and civilian roles in stability operations, see Richard Lacquement, "Building Peace in the Wake of War: Appropriate Roles for Armed Forces and Civilians," chap. 8 in Paul J. Bolt, Damon V. Coletta, and Collins G. Shackelford Jr., eds., *American Defense Policy,* 8th ed. (Baltimore: Johns Hopkins University Press, 2005), pp. 282–94.

58. Brian A. Jackson, "Counterinsurgency Intelligence in a Long War: The British Experience in Northern Ireland," *Military Review* 87, no. 1 (January–February 2007): 79.

59. Lacquement, "Building Peace in the Wake of War."

60. These ideas are developed and discussed in an unpublished briefing on Stability, Security, Transition, and Reconstruction Operations, by Andrew Krepinevich, Nadia Schadlow, and Marin Strmecki. See also John Nagl, *Institutionalizing Adaptation*, Center for New American Security, June 2007, www.newamericansecurity .org/publications/Nagl_AdvisoryCorp_June07.pdf. See also Charles L. Barry and Stuart E. Johnson, "Organizing for Stabilization and Reconstruction," chap. 4 in Hans Binnendijk and Stuart Johnson, eds., *Transforming for Stabilization and Reconstruction Operations* (Washington, DC: National Defense University, Center for Technology and National Security Policy, November 12, 2003), www.au.af.mil/au/awc/awcgate/ ndu/stab_rec_ops.pdf. The exact number of brigade-sized elements to support regional combatant commands should be determined by review of the national security challenges in each region. The development and allocation of at least two such brigade-sized elements, with one predominantly active-duty, appears appropriate for CENTCOM, PACOM, EUCOM, SOUTHCOM, and AFRICOM. An additional strategic reserve of one more expeditionary headquarters and two or three brigade-sized joint units would be appropriate.

61. These headquarters and units could also serve as tangible commitment to broader "whole of government" approaches to stability operations and are natural candidates to support the improvements in nonmilitary capability and capacity urgently advocated by many in the military in recent years.

62. FM 3-24, *Counterinsurgency*, pp. 2-13 to 2-14. For more information on civil-military operations centers, also see FM 3-05.401/CRP 3-33.1.A.

63. For a good overview of provincial reconstruction team (PRT) development, see Michael McNerney, "Stabilization and Reconstruction in Afghanistan: Are PRTs a Model or a Muddle?" *Parameters* 85, no. 4 (Winter 2005–6): 32–46. Also, with respect to Iraq, see the U.S. Embassy Iraq, "PRT Fact Sheet," March 2008, iraq .usembassy.gov/root/pdfs/factsheetapril2008.pdf.

64. For example, Stephen Peter Rosen, *Winning the Next War: Innovation and the Modern Military* (Ithaca, NY: Cornell University Press, 1991), offers evidence that successful military innovation requires institutional recognition and the creation of promotion pathways. Examples included the development of carrier aviation in the U.S. Navy, helicopter aviation in the U.S. Army, and U.S. Marine amphibious operations.

65. See ibid.; Williamson Murray and Allan R. Millett, *Military Innovation in the Interwar Period* (Cambridge: Cambridge University Press, 1996); and other literature on innovation in the military.

66. David Fastabend, "Adapt or Die: The Imperative for a Culture of Innovation in the United States Army," *Army*, February 1, 2004, www.ausa.org/webpub/Dept ArmyMagazine.nsf/byid/CCRN-6CCSBU.

67. Many of these humanitarian missions are, however, important for the mili-

tary. They can contribute directly to U.S. foreign policy aims by increasing goodwill toward the United States, provide valuable training opportunities in tough regions of the world, and provide important insights into local cultures in regions of the world much less familiar to the United States.

CHAPTER SEVEN: Professionalism and Professional Military Education in the Twenty-first Century

1. Samuel P. Huntington, *The Soldier and the State: The Theory and Politics of Civil-Military Relations* (Cambridge, MA: Belknap Press of Harvard University Press, 1957).

2. In this respect, one should consult Sir Michael Howard's brilliant examination of this issue in Michael E. Howard, *War and the Liberal Conscience,* George Treveleyan Lectures in the University of Cambridge, 1977 (New Brunswick, NJ: Rutgers University Press, 1978).

3. Huntington's book is not as relevant outside of the United States, where the historical, cultural, and political contexts are very different.

4. A 1948 letter from General Leo Geyer von Schweppenburg, a graduate of the Kriegsakademie shortly before World War I, to B. H. Liddell Hart suggests the lack of real intellectual understanding of military professionalism among senior German officers of the Wehrmacht: "I have never read Clausewitz or Delbrück or Haushofer. The opinion on Clausewitz in our general staff was that of a theoretician to be read by professors." Letter, 3,8.49, Liddell Hart Papers, September 24, 1961, King's College Library, London. Huntington's examination of the German military in World War II is, not surprisingly, flawed, given that he was unaware of what scholars have unearthed since then about the Wehrmacht's enthusiastic cooperation in the Third Reich's crimes against humanity. For the new view of the German military, one might consult Gerhard Weinberg, *A World at Arms: A Global History of World War II* (Cambridge: Cambridge University Press, 2005); or the various volumes on *Das Deutsche Reich und der Zweite Weltkrieg* published by the Militärgeschichtliche Forschungsamt, the German military's military history institute.

5. A recent article by U.S. Army Lieutenant Colonel Paul Yingling spells out the basic problem, thus far, in Iraq: a lack of professionalism at the top. Yingling quotes Frederick the Great to his officers: "You officers amuse yourself with God knows what buffooneries and never dream in the least of serious service. This is a source of stupidity which would become most dangerous in case of a serious conflict." Paul Yingling, "A Failure in Generalship," *Armed Forces Journal,* May 2007, http://www.armedforcesjournal.com/2007/05/2635198.

6. See particularly Michael Howard, "The Use and Abuse of Military History," in Howard, *The Causes of Wars* (Cambridge, MA: Harvard University Press, 1984).

7. Carl von Clausewitz, *On War,* trans. and ed. by Michael Howard and Peter Paret (Princeton, NJ: Princeton University Press, 1976), p. 579 (emphasis added).

8. In this regard, James Lacey of the Institute for Defense Analyses and I ran a conference on "The Making of Peace," Carlisle Barracks, PA, December 2006, to con-

tribute to the historical understanding of how politicians, diplomats, and generals have made peace.

9. For this evolution, see Howard, *War and the Liberal Conscience*.

10. Thomas Hobbes, *The Leviathan* (Chicago: Gateway Editions, 1956), chap. 8.

11. Michael Howard, *The Invention of Peace: Reflections on War and International Order* (New Haven, CT: Yale University Press, 2000).

12. Beginning in the nineteenth century, this aspect of the contest between Islam and the West as a continuous war disappeared almost entirely from Western minds, mostly because the contest seemed to have become so unequal.

13. Part of the cause of reason for the slaughter lay in the desperate resistance of the citizens of Magdeburg against the imperial army. See Geoffrey Parker, ed., *The Thirty Years' War* (London: Routledge, 1984), p. 125.

14. During the campaign that eventually resulted in the great victory at Crécy, the English army heard mass in the morning and then advanced to take Caen during the day, raping nearly every woman they came across, including nuns. (The Japanese "rape of Nanking" was not so different from wartime behavior of previous centuries.) For the behavior of Edward III's army, see Jean Froissart, *Chronicles,* trans. and ed. Geoffrey Brereton (London: Penguin, 1968).

15. To a certain extent, the first achievement resulted from the refusal of the papal legate to participate in the negotiations with the Protestant Swedes and Germans. As two historians of the conference have noted, "The concessions that the Catholics eventually made to the Protestants in the Empire were so offensive to the papacy that Pope Innocent X . . . formally condemned the Peace of Westphalia and refused to recognize its legitimacy. Whereas the negotiations had begun under the auspices of the papacy, they ended with a peace that the papacy would not accept." Derek Croxton and Geoffrey Parker, " 'A Swift and Sure Peace,' The Congress of Westphalia, 1643–1648," paper presented to the conference on "The Making of Peace," Carlisle Barracks, PA, December 2006, p. 3. Quoted with permission of the authors.

16. The partisan war in Yugoslavia during World War II, and perhaps insurgencies in Algeria and elsewhere, may not have fit the definition. But in those cases and similar ones, the insurgents sought legitimacy in terms of recognition as a state.

17. Croxton and Parker, "'A Swift and Sure Peace," p. 33.

18. For the crucial influence of the Romans on the creation of modern military organizations in the seventeenth century, see William H. McNeil, *The Pursuit of Power: Technology, Armed Force, and Society since A.D. 1000* (Chicago: University of Chicago, 1982), pp. 126–33.

19. Clausewitz, *On War,* p. 583.

20. Ibid., p. 592.

21. For a modern examination of the theoretical basis of German military professionalism, see Azar Gat, *A History of Military Thought: From the Enlightenment to the Cold War* (Oxford: Oxford University Press, 2001), chaps. 6–8.

22. "Not until statesmen had at last perceived the nature of the forces that had emerged in France, and had grasped that new political conditions now obtained in

Europe, could they foresee the broad effect all this would have on war; and only in that way could they appreciate the scale of the means that would have to be employed, and how best to apply them." Clausewitz, *On War,* p. 609.

23. For the Congress of Vienna and its efforts to establish a lasting peace, see the excellent work by Harold Nicholson, *The Congress of Vienna: A Study in Allied Unity, 1812–1822* (repr., New York: Grove Press, 2001). See also Richard Hart Sinnreich, "In Search of Military Repose: The Congress of Vienna and the Making of Peace," in Williamson Murray, ed., *The Making of Peace: Rulers, States, and the Aftermath of War* (Cambridge: Cambridge University Press, 2008).

24. It was clearly useful to bring German nationalism to bear in Bismarck's efforts to overwhelm the particularism of the smaller German states.

25. For a discussion of military revolutions and revolutions in military affairs, see Williamson Murray and MacGregor Knox, "Thinking about Revolutions in Warfare," in MacGregor Knox and Williamson Murray, eds., *The Dynamics of Military Revolution, 1300–2050* (Cambridge: Cambridge University Press, 2001).

26. I am indebted to Professor MacGregor Knox of the Department of International History, London School of Economics, for suggesting this point.

27. For a recent examination of the professionalism of the Prussian army during the Franco-Prussian War, see Geoffrey Wawro, *The Franco-Prussian War: The German Conquest of France in 1870–1871* (Cambridge: Cambridge University Press, 2003).

28. For how the German professional military educational system functioned at the height of its influence, see David N. Spires, *Image and Reality: The Making of the German Officer, 1921–1933* (Westport, CT: Praeger, 1984).

29. For the processes of German tactical adaptation, see Timothy T. Lupfer, *The Dynamics of Doctrine: The Changes in German Tactical Doctrine during the First World War* (Leavenworth, KS: Combat Studies Institute, U.S. Army Command and General Staff College, 1981); and Bruce I. Gudmundsson, *Stormtroop Tactics: Innovation in the German Army, 1914–1918* (Westport, CT: Praeger, 1989).

30. One of the myths perpetrated by all too many historians is that because military organizations study the last war, they do badly in the next conflict. In fact, an examination of the post-1919 period suggests that most military organizations failed to study with any honesty what had happened in the last war, a major reason for their troubles in the next conflict. For the German experience in the years immediately following the First World War, see James S. Corum, *The Roots of Blitzkrieg: Hans von Seeckt and German Military Reform* (Lawrence: University of Kansas Press, 1992). For the failure of the British army to adapt successfully, see Harold R. Winton, *To Change an Army: General Sir John Burnett-Stuart and British Armored Doctrine, 1927–1939* (Lawrence: University of Kansas Press, 1988).

31. Huntington, *The Soldier and the State,* pp. 230–36.

32. What most of the military reformers of the 1980s entirely missed was that the emphasis given by America's military forces to logistics had a great deal to do with the demands imposed by the geographic position of the United States on the North American continent with two great oceans on each side.

33. Dwight Eisenhower's successful efforts to graduate first in his class at Leavenworth underline the fact that, at this time, intellectual performance was seen by many officers as an important attribute of professionalism.

34. The Industrial College of the Armed Forces, the successor to the Army's earlier effort, has recently put all of the college's lectures and student papers on its Web site; see www.ndu.edu/library/ic3/icaflectures1.html. They show that the captains of industry came in to address the students and that some of the most important leaders of the American war effort, such as Dwight Eisenhower, attended the college as students. Eisenhower's paper was on the legal and administrative issues that would confront the army in the case of a national mobilization, a task that he would face in the last months of peace and the first months of America's participation in the Second World War.

35. Captain Walter Warlimont, "The Procurement Activities of the German Army Prior to and during the World War," The Army Industrial College, Washington, DC, Course 1929–1930, January 20, 1930 (emphasis added); available at www.ndu.edu/library/ic3/icaflectures1.htm.

36. For the failures of the German war economy, see the brilliant new study by Adam Tooze, *The Wages of Destruction: The Making and Breaking of the Nazi War Economy* (New York: Penguin, 2007).

37. See "Joseph Lawton Collins," Arlington National Cemetery Web site, www.arlingtoncemetery.net/josephla.htm, and "William Hood Simpson," Arlington National Cemetery Web site, www.arlingtoncemetery.net/whsimpson.htm.

38. See particularly the brilliant biography of the military career of Marine General Gerald Thomas from the First World War to Korea by Allan R. Millett, *In Many a Strife: General Gerald C. Thomas and the U.S. Marine Corps* (Annapolis, MD: Naval Institute Press, 1993).

39. See particularly Thomas C. Hone, Norman Friedman, and Mark D. Mandeles, *American and British Aircraft Carrier Development, 1919–1941* (Annapolis, MD: Naval Institute Press, 1999); and Stephen Peter Rosen, *Winning the Next War: Innovation and the Modern Military* (Ithaca, NY: Cornell University Press, 1994).

40. Hone, Friedman, and Mandeles, *British and American Carrier Development*, pp. 34–36.

41. Quoted in Michael Vlahos, *The Blue Sword: The Naval War College and the American Mission, 1919–1941* (Newport, RI: Naval War College Press, 1980), p. 119.

42. See Allan R. Millett, "Assault from the Sea: The Development of Amphibious Warfare between the Wars—the American, British, and Japanese Experiences," in Williamson Murray and Allan R. Millett, eds., *Military Innovation in the Interwar Period* (Cambridge: Cambridge University Press, 1996).

43. See Williamson Murray, "The Army's Advanced Strategic Art Program," *Parameters* 30, no. 4 (Winter 2000–1), www.carlisle.army.mil/usawc/PARAMETERS/00winter/murray.htm.

44. An indicator of the collapse of serious study of the military profession was the fact that virtually all the serious thinking about the implication of nuclear weapons was done not by the military but by civilian think tanks.

45. Admiral Raymond A. Spruance returned as a four-star admiral from conducting the campaigns in the Pacific to become the president of the Naval War College. During the interwar period he had served two tours on the faculty of that institution. One tour is today believed by many naval officers to be sufficient to end prospects for promotion.

46. General William C. Westmoreland, *A Soldier Reports* (Garden City, NJ: Doubleday, 1976).

47. Ibid., p. 364 (emphasis added). General Westmoreland was indeed a man of his word: only the first chapter of Jean Larteguy's novel, *The Centurions*, is about the French battle with the Viet Minh. The remainder deals with the French struggle against the FLN in Algeria.

48. "Hearings before the Panel on Military Education of the Committee on Armed Services," House of Representatives, 100th Congress, 1st and 2d sess., 1987–88.

49. Eliot Cohen, Stephen Peter Rosen, John Lewis Gaddis, Holger Herwig, John Gooch, Arthur Waldron, William Fuller, Brad Lee, and George Baer, among others, taught in the Strategy and Policy course at the Naval War College during, and subsequent to, Admiral Turner's reforms.

50. The one war college that rises above this mediocre standard is the Advanced Strategic Arts Program founded in 2000 at the Army War College by Major General Robert Scales, then commandant.

51. On the intellectual state of the war colleges in the mid-1980s, see Williamson Murray, "Grading the War Colleges," *National Interest*, no. 6 (Winter 1986–87): 12–19.

52. The Joint Staff College in Norfolk still employs a high school curriculum and is as marked by a lack of serious education as it was in the late 1980s. There has been no significant effort since the Skelton subcommittee to study professional military education across the board.

53. There was a suggestion in the Army Staff in 2004 that perhaps the army should close down its professional military education schools, given the challenges of Iraq and Afghanistan.

54. "Wicked" problems are those that yield to no unambiguous or definitive solutions, but are always unique and susceptible only partially, at best, to a number of potential solutions, few of which are truly satisfactory because they inevitably alter the framework of the original problem. For the original statement of this crucial nonlinear phenomenon, see among others Horst Rittel and Melvin Webber, "Dilemmas in a General Theory of Planning," *Policy Sciences* 4 (1973): 155–69. See also Peter DeGrace and Leslie Hulet Stahl, *Wicked Problems, Righteous Solutions* (New York: Prentice Hall, 1990).

55. One of the more bizarre theories to emerge in this era of globalization is that states are going to disappear, a theory that rests entirely on a general ignorance of what might happen when the restraints of a political framework are removed. The results speak for themselves, as in Somalia and Iraq.

56. This chapter would be remiss not to mention Huntington's other major contribution to our understanding of fundamental political issues, Samuel P. Hunting-

ton, *The Clash of Civilizations and the Remaking of the World Order* (New York: Simon and Schuster, 1998).

57. Joseph Wheelan, *Jefferson's War: America's First War on Terror, 1801–1805* (New York: PublicAffairs, 2003).

58. General Charles E. Wilhelm, USMC (ret.), Chairman, Lieutenant General Wallace C. Gregson Jr., USMC (Ret), Lieutenant Bruce B. Knutson Jr., USMC (ret.), Lieutenant General Paul K. Van Riper, USMC (ret.), Dr. Andrew F. Krepinevich Jr., and Dr. Williamson Murray, "U.S. Marine Corps Officer Professional Military Education, 2006 Study and Finding," Quantico, VA, 2006.

59. Mark Bowden, *Black Hawk Down* (New York: New American Library, 2002). Saddam Hussein found the U.S. retreat from Somalia astonishing. On how entirely differently the Ba'athist regime saw the world, compared to the American view, see particularly Kevin Woods et al., *Iraqi Perspectives Project: A View of Operation Iraqi Freedom from Saddam's Senior Leadership* (Norfolk, VA: U.S. Joint Forces Command, Joint Center for Operational Analysis, 2006).

60. See Williamson Murray and Robert Scales Jr., *The Iraq War: A Military History* (Cambridge, MA: Cambridge University Press, 2003); and Michael R. Gordon and General Bernard E. Trainor, *Cobra II: The Inside Story of the Invasion and Occupation of Iraq* (New York: Pantheon Books, 2006).

61. For evidence that this is true, see Murray and Scales, *The Iraq War;* and Gordon and Trainor, *Cobra II.*

62. Here the preparations at places such as the School of Advanced Military Studies, as well as the creation of training facilities such as the National Training Center, have played major roles.

63. For accounts of the trials and failures of postconflict operations, along with the rise of the Iraqi insurgencies, see, among others, James Fallows, *Blind into Baghdad: America's War in Iraq* (New York: Vintage, 2006); Bob Woodward, *State of Denial: Bush at War, Part III* (New York: Simon and Schuster, 2006); Rajiv Chandrasekaran, *Imperial Life in the Emerald City: Inside Iraq's Green Zone* (New York: Vintage, 2006); and L. Paul Bremer III, *My Year in Iraq: The Struggle to Build a Future of Hope* (New York: Simon and Schuster, 2006).

64. How little Americans and their government understood the Iraqis is suggested by Woods et al., *Iraqi Perspectives Project.* See also the article based on the study by Kevin Woods, James Lacey, and Williamson Murray, "Saddam's Delusions: The View from Inside," *Foreign Affairs* 85, no. 3 (May–June 2006): 2–26.

65. In this regard, see particularly Thomas E. Ricks, *Fiasco: The American Military Adventure in Iraq* (New York: Penguin, 2006).

66. One of the few depressing aspects of the two years that this author has spent in teaching midshipmen at the U.S. Naval Academy at Annapolis has been to discover the appallingly bad job that so many American high schools have done in educating their smartest students in the simplest of historical concepts such as when the American Civil War occurred. These are young people with high SAT scores (1200 to 1600), so clearly the blame lies with bad courses and poor teaching in their high schools.

67. The U.S. invasion of Panama in "Operation Just Cause" led to the overthrow of Manuel Noriega's regime, his military, and his police forces in a matter of hours in December 1989. That huge operational military success was followed immediately by massive looting that wrecked the Panamanian economy, and a sustained period during which the American military government and military had to devote substantial resources to restore a modicum of government and control.

68. This is not to suggest, as some have, that other Western militaries could have done any better. Only in a few specialized circumstances, such as Malaya, have Western militaries managed to defeat a local insurgency.

69. In this regard, the reader is urged to see the 2004 documentary film, *Voices from Iraq.*

70. Huntington, *The Soldier and the State,* p. 31.

71. Wilhelm et al., "U.S. Marine Corps Officer Professional Military Education," p. 16.

72. A paraphrase of an e-mail sent by General James Mattis, USMC, to the authors of the Wilhelm study.

73. Much of the thinking in the following suggestions is contained in Murray, "Grading the War Colleges"; and Leonard D. Holder Jr. (Lieutenant General, U.S. Army) and Williamson Murray, "Prospects for Military Education," *Joint Force Quarterly,* no. 18 (Spring 1998): 81–90.

74. This observation comes from one of the brigade commanders at the time.

75. A young American Marine lieutenant asks, at the end of the documentary film *No End in Sight:* "Are you telling me that that's the best America can do? Don't tell me that." See also Charles H. Ferguson, *No End in Sight: Iraq's Descent into Chaos* (New York: PublicAffairs, 2008).

76. See particularly Richard Haass, "U.S. Foreign Policy in a Nonpolar World," *Foreign Affairs* 87, no. 3 (May–June 2008): 44–56.

CHAPTER EIGHT: Responsible Obedience by Military Professionals: The Discretion to Do What Is Wrong

Thanks to Andrew Bacevich, Ted Burk, Martin Cook, Ronald Krebs, Steven Lee, and David Perry for detailed and helpful comments on an earlier version of this paper. I benefited also from discussions with participants in the Senior Conference on American Civil-Military Relations held at the United States Military Academy, West Point, NY, May 31–June 2, 2007, and with Don Snider and Suzanne C. Nielsen, who organized the conference. Not least, I am indebted to Teresa J. Lawson and an anonymous reviewer for pushing me to clarify my arguments even when evasion seemed a safer course.

1. See also the arguments made by Michael C. Desch in chapter 5 and by Nadia Schadlow and Richard A. Lacquement Jr. in chapter 6, both in this volume.

2. Samuel P. Huntington, *The Soldier and the State* (Cambridge, MA: Belknap Press of Harvard University Press, 1957), p. 73.

3. Alfred Thayer Mahan, *Retrospect and Prospect* (Boston: Little, Brown, 1903), pp. 279–80.

4. Max Weber, "The Meaning of Discipline," in Hans Gerth and C. Wright Mills, eds., *From Max Weber* (New York: Oxford University Press, 1958), pp. 251–64. For instance, Weber notes, "Gun powder and all the war techniques associated with it became significant only with the existence of discipline—and to the full extent only with the use of war machinery, which presupposes discipline." Ibid., p. 257.

5. Huntington, *The Soldier and the State*, p. 73.

6. Ulysses S. Grant, *Memoirs and Selected Letters* (New York: Library of America, 1990), p. 1043. On blueprints as an "order" to be "obeyed" by electricians, see Arthur L. Stinchcombe, *When Formality Works: Authority and Abstraction in Law and Organizations* (Chicago: University of Chicago Press, 2001).

7. See the discussion of professions by David R. Segal and Karin De Angelis in chapter 10 of this volume.

8. There is at least one other possibility that deserves consideration, namely, that private military companies may have corporate clients or many states as clients. Dealing with this possibility is worthwhile but beyond the scope of this chapter. Attention here is confined to militaries created by states to ensure their own security. On the matter of private military companies, see Deborah D. Avant, *The Market for Force* (Cambridge: Cambridge University Press, 2005).

9. The phrase is found in Huntington, *The Soldier and the State*, p. 70. My discussion of the domains of the military and the state is taken from ibid., pp. 70–72. See also discussion of this issue elsewhere in this volume.

10. A domain may be defined as the legitimate site of institutional activity. See James D. Thompson, *Organizations in Action* (New York: McGraw-Hill, 1967). The term domain is broader than and encompasses Abbott's idea of "professional jurisdictions." See Andrew Abbott, *The System of the Professions* (Chicago: University of Chicago Press, 1988). I prefer the broader term domain for this discussion. After all, the state is more than a professional occupation with a jurisdiction, yet it clearly has a domain of legitimate action.

11. Thus, the statesman is constrained: within the domain of military expertise, the statesman "must accept the judgments of the military professional." Huntington, *The Soldier and the State*, p. 71.

12. Ibid., p. 73.

13. Ibid., p. 351.

14. For an argument that the military and political domains are always intermingled, see Hew Strachan, *The Politics of the British Army* (New York: Oxford University Press, 1997). As Suzanne C. Nielsen makes clear, Clausewitz also believed it was theoretically and practically futile to separate any use of military force from the political domain. See Suzanne C. Nielsen, *Political Control over the Use of Force: A Clausewitzian Perspective* (Carlisle, PA: Strategic Studies Institute, 2001), www.strategicstudies institue.army.mil/pdfiles/PUB349.pdf.

15. Arthur Isak Applbaum, *Ethics for Adversaries* (Princeton, NJ: Princeton University Press, 1999), chap. 4, esp. pp. 73–74.

16. Hannah Arendt, *Eichmann in Jerusalem* (New York: Penguin, 1977 [1963]), p. 25.

17. Ibid., p. 114.

18. It is common that organizations punish those who would act on moral principle when doing so is not part of the plan that organizational leaders hope to pursue. See Robert Jackall, *Moral Mazes* (New York: Oxford University Press, 1988), pp. 101–33.

19. Hannah Arendt, *Eichmann and the Holocaust* (New York: Penguin, 2006 [1963]), p. 20.

20. Ibid., p. 115. Eichmann was an officer in the Nazi SS, not a member of the regular—the professional—German army, the Wehrmacht, but he stands nonetheless as a clear example of where blind obedience leads.

21. Martin Cook, *The Moral Warrior* (Albany: State University of New York Press, 2004), p. 61.

22. Quoted by Huntington, *The Soldier and the State*, p. 73. Quoted for the same purpose in Paul Christopher, "Unjust War and Moral Obligation," *Parameters* 25, no. 3 (Autumn 1995): 4–8; and in Michael Walzer, *Just and Unjust Wars* (New York: Basic Books, 1992), p. 39.

23. Lynn Marshall and Sam Howe Verhovek, "Prosecutor Says Officer Caused Shame," *Los Angeles Times*, February 7, 2007, p. A10. The case against Watada was still pending as of mid-2008.

24. Vitoria quoted in Walzer, *Just and Unjust Wars*, p. 39.

25. This general point was made by Applbaum, *Ethics for Adversaries*, pp. 220–21.

26. Here is an important difference between the military and (say) medical professionals. While the state can command the military to go to war even when doing so is unnecessary, patients cannot command their doctors to perform unnecessary surgery on them. Doctors would have a professional right to withhold treatments; military professionals do not have a parallel right.

27. Huntington, *The Soldier and the State*, p. 72.

28. Cook, *Moral Warrior*, p. 62.

29. Ibid., pp. 65–66.

30. For a description of this contentious process using a principal-agent model, see Peter Feaver, *Armed Servants: Agency, Oversight, and Civil Military Relations* (Cambridge, MA: Harvard University Press, 2003). A related but less conflictual version of the process can be found in Peter Roman and David W. Tarr, "Military Professionalism and Policymaking," in Peter Feaver and Richard H. Kohn, eds., *Soldiers and Civilians: The Civil-Military Gap and American National Security* (Cambridge, MA: MIT Press, 2001), pp. 403–28.

31. H. R. McMaster, *Dereliction of Duty: Johnson, McNamara, the Joint Chiefs of Staff, and the Lies that Led to Vietnam* (New York: HarperCollins, 1997), pp. 309–12, quoted at p. 312.

32. Ibid., pp. 318–20.

33. Ibid., p. 330.

34. Ibid., p. 331.

35. One might think my description of blind obedience is too negative, neglecting a positive example like Abraham, whose blind faith God counted as a virtue. Yet Abraham is not such a simple case. Abraham was crafty and resourceful in his social relations to advance his interests, including his willingness to father a child with Hagar, servant of Sarah, as a way of making God's promise that he would have many descendants come true. The one time he seems to have been blindly obedient was in response to God's command that he sacrifice his son Isaac. That would have been a tragedy and difficult to count as just, if God had allowed it to go on. Whatever the theological significance of the story, it reminds us that blind obedience can have awful consequences.

36. Huntington, *The Soldier and the State,* p. 74.

37. Ibid.

38. Ibid., p. 75.

39. Ibid.

40. Ibid., pp. 76–78.

41. Ibid., p. 78.

42. Arnold Wolfers, "Statesmanship and Moral Choice," *World Politics* 1, no. 2 (January 1949): 175–95. To be clear, Wolfers argues that the choice to do what is least destructive of values is a moral choice that is not in principle very different from many moral choices made by everyone.

43. Huntington, *The Soldier and the State,* p. 78.

44. This argument is sadly incomplete because it provides no realistic guidance to those we ask to maintain and someday perhaps to launch weapons of mass destruction, which would clearly be an act of genocide.

45. For a brief review of recent social science accounts of autonomy, see Diana T. Meyers, *Self, Society, and Personal Choice* (New York: Columbia University Press, 1989), pp. 25–41. For a comprehensive intellectual history of the meaning and roots of the concept of autonomy, see J. B. Schneewind, *The Invention of Autonomy* (Cambridge: Cambridge University Press, 1997).

46. This distinction attempts to specify what is the military's legitimate domain of action, without incorporating Huntington's assumption that the domain is defined solely in terms of professional military competence.

47. The Posse Comitatus act is found in 18 U.S.C. § 1385. The text provides for the punishment of anyone who uses the Army or Air Force "as a posse comitatus or otherwise to execute the laws" unless "expressly authorized" to do so by the Constitution or an act of Congress.

48. This argument embraces moral realism and rejects moral skepticism, including societal relativism, which assumes that moral judgments are simply the judgments of public opinion influenced by those with power. For brief arguments defending the moral realist position, see Michael Smith, "Realism," in Peter Singer, ed., *A Companion to Ethics* (Oxford: Blackwell, 1991), pp. 399–410; and Russ Shafer-Landau,

Whatever Happened to Good and Evil? (Oxford: Oxford University Press, 2004). Also see Russ Shafer-Landau, *Moral Realism: A Defence* (Oxford: Oxford University Press, 2003). The moral realist argument assumes that moral principles exist, like the rules of arithmetic, independent of any mind. Whether we recognize a moral principle and act on it is another matter. Only after the revelations of abuses at Abu Ghraib did most Americans begin to reflect on and debate what constitutes torture. The debate is not yet resolved. See Sanford Levinson, ed., *Torture: A Collection* (Oxford; Oxford University Press, 2004); and Karen J. Greenberg, ed., *The Torture Debate in America* (Cambridge: Cambridge University Press, 2006). Nevertheless, military professionals may be judged on the basis of their conformity with our best knowledge of the moral principles in play. Whether or to what degree they should be held legally liable and punished for acting in violation of these principles depends on how egregious was the act, that is, on how plain it was at the time that the act violated a fundamental moral principle.

49. William A. Edmundson, *An Introduction to Rights* (Cambridge: Cambridge University Press, 2004), p. 136 (emphasis in original).

50. My discussion of conscientious objection and conscientious refusal is drawn from Paul Graham, *Rawls* (Oxford: Oneworld, 2007), pp. 107–19.

51. All details for this case study come from W. "Rick" Rubel and George R. Lucas, eds., *Case Studies in Military Ethics* (Boston: Pearson Education, 2004), pp. 77–80, 185.

52. I am grateful to Suzanne Nielsen for citing a particular military regulation that provides a basis for justifying Thompson's exercise of discretion to intervene in defense of larger values, despite the lack of explicit authorization—a direct command—to intervene. Title 10 of the U.S. Code, Section 3583, says that all commanding officers and others with authority in the Army must "guard against and suppress all dissolute and immoral practices, and to correct, according to the laws and regulations of the Army, all persons who are guilty of them."

53. Rubel and Lucas, *Case Studies in Military Ethics,* pp. 81–82, 187–89.

54. CNN.com, "U.S. Officer Fined for Harsh Interrogation Tactics," December 13, 2003, www.cnn.com/2003/US/12/12/sprj.nirq.west.ruling. The CNN report claims that the interrogation yielded useful information to thwart an ambush. But no similar claim is made in the account by Thomas E. Ricks, *Fiasco: The American Military Adventure in Iraq* (New York: Penguin, 2007), pp. 280–81.

55. Discussing this passage in an earlier version of this chapter presented at a conference, Thomas E. Ricks observed that West could be accused of acting imprudently. Because West had reason to believe that he was the particular object of the ambush, his reasons for wanting quick intelligence about the plan and his willingness to employ questionable methods to get it may have been self-interested. It can be argued that self-interest, however understandable, may have clouded his professional judgment. To avoid such a possibility, the norm is that one may not interrogate about matters concerning oneself. Marine Major General James Mattis, reflecting on this case, observed that West had lost his "moral balance." See Ricks, *Fiasco*, p. 318.

56. The reporter was Seymour Hersh. The empirical facts in this discussion are

drawn from Seymour Hersh, "Last Stand," *New Yorker*, July 10, 2006, www.newyorker
.com/printables/fact/060710fa_fact.

57. See Timothy L. Challans, *Awakening Warrior: Revolution in the Ethics of Warfare*
(Albany: State University of New York Press, 2007), p. 11. He describes an approach
he calls "the warrior ethos." I believe that Huntington's argument provides an example of that approach: "The warrior ethos," writes Challan, "is really about a special
kind of work ethic, one that centers on mission accomplishment and potential self-
sacrifice, not on moral restraints and law-abidingness." Ibid.

58. See Ronald Dworkin, *Taking Rights Seriously* (Cambridge, MA: Harvard University Press, 1978), pp. 31–39. "The concept of discretion is at home in only one sort
of context; when someone is in general charged with making decisions subject to
standards set by a particular authority. Discretion, like the hole in a doughnut, does
not exist except as an area left open by a surrounding belt of restriction. It is therefore a relative concept. It always makes sense to ask, 'Discretion under which standards?' or 'Discretion as to which authority?'" Ibid., p. 31.

59. My discussion of this matter draws on recently published work by Don Snider
and his team of scholars in Don M. Snider and Lloyd J. Matthews, eds., *Forging the
Warrior's Character*, 2d ed. (New York: McGraw-Hill Primis, 2008); and by Challans,
Awakening Warrior. Any program of moral education is bound to be (and perhaps
ought to be) controversial. Challans, for instance, is highly critical of the military's
approach to this subject matter.

60. See Paul Lewis, George B. Forsthe, Pattrick Sweeney, Paul Bartone, Craig
Bullis, and Scott Snook, "Identity Development during the College Years," *Journal of
College Student Development* 46, no. 4 (July–August 2005): 357–73.

61. Paul Yingling, "A Failure of Generalship," *Armed Forces Journal,* May 2007,
www.armedforcesjournal.com/2007/05/2635198.

62. Reporting on all four issues has been extensive. On Tillman, see, for example,
Mary Tillman with Narda Zacchino, *Boots on the Ground: My Tribute to Pat Tillman*
(New York: Modern Times, 2008); and Robert Collier, "Family Demands the Truth,"
SFGate.com, September 25, 2005, http://sfgate.com/cgi-bin/article.cgi?file=c/a/2005/
09/25/MNGD7ETMNM1.DTL. On Abu Ghraib, see the executive summary of the
August 2004 Fay-Jones Report: "[Lieutenant General Anthony] Jones found that
while senior level officers did not commit the abuse at Abu Ghraib they did bear responsibility for lack of oversight of the facility, failing to respond in a timely manner
to the reports from the International Committee of the Red Cross and for issuing policy memos that failed to provide clear, consistent guidance for execution at the tactical level." The report is reprinted in Karen J. Greenberg and Joshua L. Dratel, eds., *The
Torture Papers* (Cambridge: Cambridge University Press, 2005), p. 989. Also available
at www.defenselink.mil/news/Aug2004/d20040825fay.pdf. On Haditha, see Thomas E.
Ricks, "In Haditha Killings, Details Came Slowly," *Washington Post*, June 4, 2006, p.
A01. On soldiers' mental-health care, see Dan Frosch, "Fighting the Terror of Battles
That Rage in Soldiers' Heads," *New York Times*, May 13, 2007, at www.nytimes.com/
2007/05/13/us/13carson.htm?ref=pagewanted=print; and Kristen Roberts, "Penta-

gon Says More Funds Needed for Mental Health," *Washington Post,* June 15, 2007, www.washingtonpost.com/up-dyn/content/article/2007/06/15/AR200706150138_pf .html.

63. Anthony E. Hartle, "Moral Principles and Moral Reasoning in the Ethics of the Military Profession," in Snider and Matthews, *Forging the Warrior's Character,* 223. Hartle quotes U.S. Department of the Army, Field Manual (FM) 27-10, *The Law of Land Warfare* (Washington DC: U.S. Government Printing Office, 1956), p. 182.

64. The quoted words are those Plato attributed to Socrates as he argues with Glaucon about the need for an army, in Plato, *The Republic,* trans. R. E. Allen (New Haven, CT: Yale University Press, 2006), p. 56 (book II, 373d). Huntington's attribution of this Hobbesian view of the world as central to the military mind is found in Huntington, *The Soldier and the State,* p. 63: "The man of the military ethic is essentially the man of Hobbes," whom no one—certainly not Hobbes—supposes to be driven by moral concerns.

CHAPTER NINE: The Military Mind: A Reassessment of the Ideological Roots of American Military Professionalism

1. Craig Reinarman, *American States of Mind: Political Beliefs and Behavior among Private and Public Workers* (New Haven, CT: Yale University Press, 1987), pp. 15–18.

2. Peter Feaver has summarized this dilemma as the basic civil-military problematique. Peter Feaver, "The Civil-Military Problematique: Huntington, Janowitz, and the Question of Civilian Control," *Armed Forces and Society* 23, no. 2 (Winter 1996): 149–78. See also chapter 4 by Peter D. Feaver and Erika Seeler in this volume.

3. Samuel Finer, *The Man on Horseback: The Role of the Military in Politics* (New Brunswick, NJ: Transaction, 2003), pp. 24–26.

4. Feaver argues that more useful and independent measures of effective civilian control can be found through the mechanism of principal-agent theory, whereby civilian political control is measured by the degree of responsiveness (lack of shirking) of the military agents to their civilian superiors. Peter Feaver, *Armed Servants: Agency, Oversight, and Civil-Military Relations* (Cambridge, MA: Harvard University Press, 2003). For similar criticisms of Huntington's model, see Finer, *The Man on Horseback,* p. 25.

5. In the twentieth century, Louis Hartz was the most influential advocate of the idea that liberalism has been the dominant American ideology; in Hartz's estimation, it has been the only American ideology. In his later writings, Huntington, too, would take up the liberal lens as a means of understanding the American experience. Largely agreeing with Hartz, Huntington would find in periods of American political and social disharmony the course corrections of a nation trying to get back to its more liberal roots after a period of drift. Louis Hartz, *The Liberal Tradition in America* (New York: Harcourt Brace Jovanovich, 1955); Samuel P. Huntington, *American Politics: The Promise of Disharmony* (Cambridge, MA: Harvard University Press, 1981). See also chapter 5 by Michael C. Desch in this volume.

6. Samuel Huntington, *The Soldier and the State* (Cambridge, MA: Belknap Press of Harvard University Press, 1957), p. 93.

7. By 1957 this brand of conservatism was experiencing a bit of an awakening in the United States. As reflected in Russell Kirk, *Conservative Mind* (Washington, DC: Regnery, 1953), and William F. Buckley's biweekly conservative news magazine, *National Review*, starting in 1955, much of American conservatism was attempting to define itself according to the writings of the British parliamentarian Edmund Burke. For an early critique of the argument that the American military was classically conservative, see Allen Guttman, *The Conservative Tradition in America* (New York: Oxford University Press, 1967), pp. 100–122.

8. It should be noted that neither Huntington's military-mind thesis nor the present investigation of its ideological component addresses the role of various extrinsic rewards in maintaining effective civilian control over the military. Factors such as adequate pay, retirement and other benefits, and job security likely play important roles in ensuring that military service members remain committed to a life of satisfied service without meddling in political affairs. Because these variables are outside of the scope of Huntington's thesis, they are not addressed here.

9. Angus Campbell et al., *The American Voter* (New York: John Wiley and Sons, 1960); Philip E. Converse, "The Nature of Belief Systems in Mass Publics," in David E. Apter, ed., *Ideology and Discontent* (New York: Free Press, 1964); Herbert McClosky, "Consensus and Ideology in American Politics," *American Political Science Review* 58, no. 2 (June 1964): 361–82.

10. Converse, "The Nature of Belief Systems in Mass Publics," p. 207.

11. Robert E. Lane, *Political Ideology: Why the American Common Man Believes What He Does* (Glencoe, IL: Free Press, 1962); Robert E. Lane, *Political Man* (New York: Free Press, 1972).

12. Jennifer Hochschild, *What's Fair? American Beliefs about Distributive Justice* (Cambridge, MA: Harvard University Press, 1981); Karl Lamb, *As Orange Goes: Twelve California Families and the Future of American Politics* (New York: Norton, 1974); Karl Lamb, *The Guardians: Leadership Values and the American Tradition* (New York: Norton, 1981); Lane, *Political Man;* Grant Reeher, *Narratives of Justice: Legislative Beliefs about Distributive Fairness* (Ann Arbor: University of Michigan Press, 1996); Reinarman, *American States of Mind.*

13. Reeher, *Narratives of Justice;* Reinarman, *American States of Mind*, pp. 30–35; Jerome Bruner, "Life as Narrative," *Social Research* 71, no. 3 (Fall 2004): 691–710.

14. According to Huntington, "Conservatism, as used here and hereafter . . . refers to the philosophy of [Edmund] Burke, and not to the meaning given this term in popular political parlance in the United States to refer to the laissez-faire, property-rights form of liberalism as exemplified, for instance, by Herbert Hoover." Huntington, *The Soldier and the State*, p. 93n.

15. For discussions of liberalism as an organizing principle for society, see, for instance, John Rawls, *Political Liberalism* (New York: Columbia University Press, 1993); and Michael Sandel, *Liberalism and the Limits of Justice* (Cambridge: Cambridge Uni-

versity Press, 1982). With respect to the American case specifically, see J. David Greenstone, "Political Culture and Political Development," *Studies in American Political Development* 1 (1986): 1–49; and Hartz, *The Liberal Tradition in America.* On Huntington's description of conservatism, see also Samuel Huntington, "Conservatism as an Ideology," *American Political Science Review* 51, no. 2 (June 1957): 454–73.

16. Steven R. Brown, "Consistency and Persistence of Ideology: Some Experimental Results," *Public Opinion Quarterly* 34, no. 1 (Spring 1970): 60–68.

17. Bengt Abrahamsson, *Military Professionalization and Political Power* (London: Sage, 1972); Terry Busch, "A Comparative Cross Service 'Operational Code' Analysis of the 'Military Mind' Concept: The Post World War II American Military Profession" (Ph.D. dissertation, Miami University, 1975); Huntington, *The Soldier and the State,* pp. 62–64, 79; Drew Middleton, "The Enigma Called the Military Mind," *New York Times Magazine,* April 18, 1948.

18. Q-method is a technique developed specifically to test the connections between beliefs and to measure the degree to which an individual's set of beliefs and attitude priorities conform to those of others. Steven R. Brown, "Bibliography on Q-Technique and Its Methodology," *Perceptual and Motor Skills* 26, no. 2 (1968): 587–613; Steven R. Brown, *Political Subjectivity* (New Haven, CT: Yale University Press, 1980); Bruce McKeown and Dan Thomas, *Q-Methodology,* Sage University Paper (London: Sage, 1988).

19. The military sample was drawn exclusively from U.S. Army officers in order to allow the maximum opportunity for single-service socialization to create the homogeneity of public beliefs the military-mind thesis predicts. One may surmise that adding enlisted military personnel or officers of other armed services to the sample would create the potential of even greater variability in the ideological categories than observed in this exploration. This proposition is not addressed here; it could be tested with further research.

20. Huntington, *The Soldier and the State,* p. 373.

21. In total, the Army sample included five female officers (11 percent) and forty male officers, approximating a current Army active officer corps that is 15 percent women. It included nine self-identified ethnic and racial minorities (20 percent), compared to 23 percent in the active officer corps. Department of the Army, *Army Demographics: FY03 Army Profile* (Department of the Army: Deputy Chief of Staff for Personnel, G-1, 2003), www.armyg1.army.mil/hr/demographics/fy03armyprofileweb Vs.pdf; Mady Wechsler Segal and Chris Bong, "Professional Leadership and Diversity in the Army," in Don Snider and Lloyd Matthews, eds., *The Future of the Army Profession,* 2d ed., rev. and exp. (New York: McGraw-Hill Primis, 2005), pp. 505–20. The civilian comparison group similarly approximated gender and ethnic minority representation in the broader corporate and New York area small-business communities: women constituted 12.5 percent of corporate officers in Fortune 500 companies in 2004, and 11 percent in Fortune 1,000 companies; ethnic minority representation on corporate boards for the Fortune 100 companies was reported at 14.9 percent. Joint 2005 report by Catalyst, The Prout Group, The Executive Leadership Council, and the

Hispanic Association on Corporate Responsibility. A more extensive survey in 2003 of minority representation on Fortune 1,000 corporate boards put ethnic minority representation at 21 percent, up from 19 percent in 2001. A 1997 census by the Department of Commerce places minority business ownership in the sampled locale, Orange County, New York, at 9 percent, and business ownership among women there at 26 percent. U.S. Census Bureau, "Economic Census Surveys of Minority- and Women-Owned Business Enterprises," Department of Commerce, 1997, www.census .gov/csd/mwb/; Cora Daniels, "50 Best Companies for Minorities," *Fortune Magazine,* June 28, 2004; Alliance for Board Diversity, *Women and Minorities on Corporate 100 Boards* (New York: Catalyst, The Prout Group, The Executive Leadership Council, and the Hispanic Association on Corporate Responsibility, 2005).

22. James Davison Hunter and Carl Bowman, *The State of Disunion: 1996 Survey of American Political Culture* (Ivy, VA: Post-Modernity Project, University of Virginia, 1996); Aaron Wildavsky, "A World of Difference—the Public Philosophies and Political Cultures of Rival American Cultures," in Anthony King, ed., *The New American Political System,* 2d ed. (Washington, DC: American Enterprise Institute for Public Policy Research, 1990); Pew Research Center for the People and the Press, *The 2005 Political Typology: Beyond Red vs. Blue* (Washington DC: Pew Research Center, 2005).

23. The appendix shows the fifty statements provided to the respondents to sort in accordance with their value priorities. The text provides a short synopsis of each group's most favorable statements. For a more in-depth discussion of methodology, supporting data, and explanatory detail, see Darrell Driver, "Sparta in Babylon: Case Studies in the Public Philosophies of Citizens and Soldiers" (Ph.D. dissertation, Maxwell School, Syracuse University, 2006).

24. Nine respondents failed to offer statement orderings statistically similar enough to the two broadest ideological groupings to warrant their inclusion in either.

25. Robert Grafstein, "A Realist Foundation for Essentially Contested Political Concepts," *Western Political Quarterly* 41, no. 1 (1988): 9–28.

26. Walter B. Gallie, "Essentially Contested Concepts," in Max Black, ed., *The Importance of Language* (Englewood Cliffs, NJ: Prentice-Hall, 1962), p. 123.

27. For more on deeply contestable concepts and the prospect of enduring debate, see Alasdair MacIntyre, *After Virtue* (Notre Dame, IN: University of Notre Dame Press, 1981), pp. 6–22.

28. For a variety of criticisms of American liberal consensus claims, see Joyce Appleby, "Republicanism and Ideology," *American Quarterly* 37, no. 4 (Autumn 1985): 461–73; Bernard Bailyn, *The Ideological Origins of the American Revolution* (Cambridge, MA: Harvard University Press, 1967); J. G. A. Pocock, *The Machiavellian Moment: Florentine Political Thought and the Atlantic Republican Tradition* (Princeton, NJ: Princeton University Press, 1975); Rogers Smith, *Civic Ideals* (New Haven, CT: Yale University Press, 1997); and James A. Morone, *Hellfire Nation: The Politics of Sin in American History* (New Haven, CT: Yale University Press, 2003).

29. Smith, *Civic Ideals.*

30. J. David Greenstone, *The Lincoln Persuasion: Remaking American Liberalism*

(Princeton, NJ: Princeton University Press, 1993); Greenstone, "Political Culture and Political Development."

31. Clinton Rossiter, *Conservatism in America* (New York: Vintage Books, 1962), p. 5.

32. Ole R. Holsti, "Of Chasms and Convergences: Attitudes and Beliefs of Civilians and Military Elites at the Start of a New Millennium," in Peter Feaver and Richard Kohn, eds., *Soldiers and Civilians: The Civil-Military Gap and American National Security* (Cambridge, MA: MIT Press, 2001), pp. 15–99; Ole R. Holsti, "A Widening Gap between the U.S. Military and Civilian Society? Some Evidence, 1976–1996," *International Security* 23, no. 3 (Winter 1998–99): 5–42.

33. Indeed, in one of Huntington's more provocative passages, he entreats American liberals to embrace more readily the brand of conservatism he attributes to the military mind. A broad embrace of conservative values would, Huntington suggests, be important to defeating the Soviet threat. Huntington, *The Soldier and the State*, pp. 465–66.

34. Rawls, *Political Liberalism*; Michael Walzer, *Spheres of Justice: A Defense of Pluralism and Equality* (New York: Basic Books, 1983).

35. Robert Dahl, *Democracy and Its Critics* (New Haven, CT: Yale University Press, 1989); Robert Dahl, *Who Governs? Democracy and Power in an American City* (New Haven, CT: Yale University Press, 1961); McClosky, "Consensus and Ideology in American Politics," pp. 361–82.

36. Marybeth Peterson Ulrich, "Infusing Civil-Military Relations in the Officer Corps," in Don Snider, Gayle L. Watkins, and Lloyd J. Matthews, eds., *The Future of the Army Profession* (New York: McGraw-Hill Primis, 2002), p. 249.

37. Statement was nonsignificant at $p < .01$, obtained according to the following algorithm. "For every statement: if any pair of the $k(k-1)$ pairs of factor scores differs at $p < .01$, drop statement. For the remainder: provisionally flag statement; if any of the $k(k-1)$ pairs of factor scores differ at $p < .05$, drop flag." Thus, nonsignificance at $p < .01$ indicates that, with the most discrepant factors, factor scores do not differ at $p < .01$. Peter Schmolck, e-mail, May 30, 2005. No statements, even in the "military only" subsample, had factor scores that did not differ at $p < .05$ across the two most discrepant factors.

38. This is what Morris Janowitz hints at, in contending that three professional military ethics, not just one, are emerging from the demands of modern military service: the heroic leader, from the demands of traditional combat; a management ethos, from the bureaucratic institutionalization of the defense establishments; and the military technologist, extending from an increase in engineering-centered problems and rapidly expanding technology. Morris Janowitz, *The Professional Soldier: A Social and Political Portrait*, 2d ed. (New York: Free Press, 1971).

39. Charles Moskos, John Williams, and David Segal, eds., *The Postmodern Military: Armed Forces after the Cold War* (New York: Oxford University Press, 2000).

40. Indeed, a primary purpose of *The Soldier and the State* was to call civil-military relations back to the functional fount, where separation and a conservative ideology would ensure force effectiveness in war. Huntington, *The Soldier and the State*, p. 3.

41. Robert Reich, *Tales of a New America: The Anxious Liberal's Guide to the Future* (New York: Vintage Books, 1988), pp. 10–11; Barry Shain, *The Myth of American Individualism: The Protestant Origins of American Political Thought* (Princeton, N.J.: Princeton University Press, 1994); Robert Bellah et al., *Habits of the Heart: Individualism and Commitment in American Life,* updated ed. (Berkeley: University of California Press, 1996).

42. Appleby, "Republicanism and Ideology," pp. 461–73; Michael Sandel, *Democracy's Discontent: America in Search of a Public Philosophy* (Cambridge, MA: Belknap Press of Harvard University Press), 1996.

43. Sources of the statements in the appendix were Lane, *Political Ideology;* Feaver and Kohn, *Soldiers and Civilians;* Reeher, *Narratives of Justice;* Hochschild, *What's Fair?* For descriptions of the ideology of the military mind, see Abrahamsson, *Military Professionalization and Political Power;* Busch, "A Comparative Cross Service 'Operational Code' Analysis of the 'Military Mind' Concept"; Huntington, *The Soldier and the State;* Alfred Vagts, *A History of Militarism: Civilian and Military* (New York: Greenwich Editions, Meridian Books, 1959).

CHAPTER TEN: Changing Conceptions of the Military as a Profession

The writing of this chapter was supported by the U.S. Army Research Institute for the Behavioral and Social Sciences under Contract W74V8H-05-K-0007. The views expressed in this chapter are those of the authors and not necessarily of the Army Research Institute, the Department of the Army, or the Department of Defense. We are grateful to Lieutenant Colonel Suzanne Nielsen for comments on an earlier draft and to Kirby Bowling for research assistance.

1. Samuel P. Huntington, *The Soldier and the State* (Cambridge MA: Belknap Press of Harvard University Press, 1957); Morris Janowitz, *The Professional Soldier* (Glencoe, IL: Free Press, 1960).

2. For a historical perspective on the military's changing demographics, see David R. Segal and Mady Wechsler Segal, "America's Military Population," *Population Bulletin* 59, no. 4 (December 2004): 3–5.

3. Bernard Boene, "Social Science Research, War, and the Military in the United States," in Gerhard Kummel and Andreas Prufert, eds., *Military Sociology in the United States: The Richness of a Discipline* (Baden-Baden: Nomos, 2000), pp. 149–251.

4. An example of current interdisciplinary social science research is David R. Segal, "Current Developments and Trends in Social Research on the Military," in Giuseppe Caforio, ed., *Social Sciences and the Military: An Interdisciplinary Overview* (London: Routledge, Taylor and Francis, 2007), pp. 46–66.

5. See Robert M. Yerkes, ed., *Psychological Examining in the U.S. Army,* Official Report of the Division of Psychology (Washington, DC: Surgeon General's Office, 1921). Group performance is examined in Edward L. Munson, *The Management of Men* (New York: Henry Holt, 1921).

6. Quincy Wright, *A Study of War* (Chicago: University of Chicago Press, 1942).

7. For example, Eli Ginzburg et al., *The Ineffective Soldier: Lessons for Management and the Nation* (New York: Columbia University Press, 1959).

8. Samuel A. Stouffer, ed., *The American Soldier: Adjustment during Army Life* (Princeton, NJ: Princeton University Press, 1949); Samuel A. Stouffer, ed., *The American Soldier: Combat and Its Aftermath* (Princeton, NJ: Princeton University Press, 1949).

9. For a more detailed discussion of the impact of these changes on political science, see chapter 4 by Peter D. Feaver and Erika Seeler in this volume.

10. C. Wright Mills, *The Power Elite* (New York: Oxford University Press, 1956), pp. 198–225; Harold D. Lasswell, "The Garrison State," *American Journal of Sociology* 46, no. 4 (January 1941): 455–68.

11. Herbert Spencer, *Principles of Sociology* (New York: Appleton, 1896).

12. Everett C. Hughes, "The Sociological Study of Work," in Everett C. Hughes, *The Sociological Eye: Selected Papers* (Chicago: Aldine, 1971), pp. 298–303.

13. William J. Goode, "Encroachment, Charlatanism, and the Emerging Profession," *American Sociological Review* 25, no. 6 (December 1960): 903. This list is paraphrased except where indicated. All italics and the numbers in parentheses have been added by the authors.

14. Occupations other than the professions are increasingly practiced in formalized work settings—bureaucracies—under the supervision of management. By contrast, members of the professions are frequently able to practice independently, controlled only by fellow professionals and professional associations. Physicians or attorneys, for example, can hang out a shingle and open a professional practice if they have been certified by a bar association or a medical board. Over time, however, the traditionally autonomous professions have themselves increasingly been practiced in bureaucratic settings—the physician in a hospital or clinic, the attorney in a corporation or large law firm—under increasing managerial control, and subject to the same legal constraints as other occupations. Physicians, for example, find their activities increasingly affected by hospital administrators and insurance company managers who do not have medical degrees. Eliot Friedson, "The Changing Nature of Professional Control," *Annual Review of Sociology* 10 (1984): 1–20.

15. Regarding political neutrality as a common characteristic of professions, see Suzanne Keller, *Beyond the Ruling Class* (New York: Random House, 1968).

16. The general process of rationalization of society, of which professionalization is one facet, is characterized by increasing specialization. Within a profession, this can be manifested by the development of specialized subcommunities: physicians, surgeons, neurosurgeons. In the environment of the profession, it can be manifested by the development of other occupations that intrude on the jurisdiction of the profession.

17. Bengt Abrahamsson, *Military Professionalization and Political Power* (Beverly Hills, CA: Sage, 1972).

18. A. M. Carr-Saunders and P. A. Wilson, *The Professions* (Oxford: Clarendon Press, 1933).

19. For example, see Ernest Greenwood, "Attributes of a Profession," in Sigmund

Nosow and William H. Form, eds., *Man, Work, and Society: A Reader in the Sociology of Occupations* (New York: Basic Books, 1962), pp. 207–18.

20. Albert J. Reiss, "Occupational Mobility of Professional Workers," *American Sociological Review* 20, no. 6 (December 1955): 693–700.

21. See, for example, David R. Segal and Meyer Kestnbaum, "Professional Closure in the Military Labor Market: A Critique of Pure Cohesion," in Don M. Snider, Gayle L. Watkins, and Lloyd J. Matthews, eds., *The Future of the Army Profession* (New York: McGraw-Hill Primis, 2002), pp. 439–58.

22. Mills, *The Power Elite*; David R. Segal and John D. Blair, "Public Confidence in the U.S. Military," *Armed Forces and Society* 3, no. 1 (Fall 1976): 3–11.

23. It is notable that some countries, such as Japan, do not have independent systems of military justice or courts-martial and that in the European community military service has been ruled to be a form of employment: civilian employment discrimination laws are applicable, and civilian courts have jurisdiction.

24. Reiss, "Occupational Mobility of Professional Workers," pp. 693–700.

25. Segal and Segal, "America's Military Population," p. 10.

26. For example, see Thomas Jager and Gerhard Kummel, eds., *Private Military and Security Companies: Chances, Problems, Pitfalls and Prospects* (Weisbaden: VS Verlag für Sozialwissenschaften, 2007).

27. Huntington, *The Soldier and the State*; Janowitz, *The Professional Soldier*.

28. European sociologists had earlier begun analyzing the military as a profession; however, Norbert Elias's insightful analysis of the genesis of the naval profession was never completed during his lifetime and has only recently been reconstructed and published, while Demeter's study of the military profession in Europe was not regarded as social science. Norbert Elias, *The Genesis of the Naval Profession* (Dublin: University College Dublin Press, 2007); Karl Demeter, *Das Deutsche Heer und Seine Offiziere* (Berlin: Verlag von Reimer Hobbing, 1935).

29. Charles C. Moskos, *The American Enlisted Man* (New York: Russell Sage Foundation, 1970).

30. David Easton, *The Political System: An Inquiry into the State of Political Science* (New York: Alfred A. Knopf, 1953); David Easton, "Traditional and Behavioral Research in American Political Science," *Administrative Science Quarterly* 2, no. 1 (June 1957): 110–15; David Easton, *A Framework for Political Analysis* (Englewood Cliffs, NJ: Prentice-Hall, 1965).

31. Samuel P. Huntington, "The Election Tactics of the Nonpartisan League," *Mississippi Valley Historical Review* 36, no. 4 (March 1950): 613–32.

32. Harold L. Wilensky, "The Professionalization of Everyone?" *American Journal of Sociology* 70, no. 2 (September 1964): 137–58.

33. Huntington, *The Soldier and the State*, p. 11.

34. Morris Janowitz, "Civic Consciousness and Military Performance," in Morris Janowitz and Stephen D. Wesbrook, eds., *The Political Education of Soldiers* (Beverly Hills, CA: Sage, 1983), pp. 55–80.

35. Paul L. Savage and Richard A. Gabriel, "Cohesion and Disintegration in the

American Army," *Armed Forces and Society* 2, no. 3 (Spring 1976): 340–76; John Helmer, *Bringing the War Home* (New York: Free Press, 1974); G. David Curry, *Sunshine Patriots* (South Bend, IN: Notre Dame University Press, 1984).

36. David R. Segal, *Recruiting for Uncle Sam: Citizenship and Military Manpower Policy* (Lawrence: University Press of Kansas, 1989); Bernard Rostker, *I Want You: The Evolution of the All-Volunteer Force* (Santa Monica, CA: RAND, 2007).

37. The Total Force includes active-duty personnel, the reserve component, and Department of Defense civilian employees and contractors.

38. Charles C. Moskos, "The All-Volunteer Military: Calling, Profession, or Occupation?" *Parameters* 7, no. 1 (1977): 2–9.

39. Charles C. Moskos, "From Institution to Occupation: Trends in Military Organization," *Armed Forces and Society* 4, no. 1 (October 1977): 43.

40. David R. Segal, "Measurement of the Institutional/Occupational Change Thesis," *Armed Forces and Society* 12, no. 3 (Spring 1986): 351–75.

41. Morris Janowitz, "From Institutional to Occupational: The Need for Conceptual Clarity," *Armed Forces and Society* 4, no. 1 (October 1977): 51–54.

42. George Kourvetaris and Betty Dobratz, "The Present State and Development of Sociology of the Military," in George Kourvetaris and Betty Dobratz, eds., *World Perspectives in the Sociology of the Military* (New Brunswick, NJ: Transaction Books, 1977), p. 12.

43. Zeb B. Bradford and Frederick J. Brown, *The United States Army in Transition* (Beverly Hills, CA.: Sage, 1973).

44. Charles C. Moskos, "The Emergent Military: Civil, Traditional, Plural?" *Pacific Sociological Review* 16, no. 2 (April 1973): 255–80.

45. Ibid., p. 275.

46. Huntington, *The Soldier and the State*, pp. 17–18.

47. U.S. Army, Sergeant Major of the Army, "The NCO Creed," www.army.mil/leaders/sma/creed.htm.

48. Congressional Budget Office, *Educational Attainment and Compensation of Enlisted Personnel* (Washington, DC, 2004), p. 1.

49. Ibid., p. 11.

50. The approximately 8 percent of new officers who lack college degrees are predominantly prior enlisted personnel. The advanced degrees are held largely by officers entering into professions within the military profession: doctors, lawyers, and chaplains. See Office of the Under Secretary of Defense, Personnel and Readiness, *Population Representation in the Military Services, FY 2004*, p. vi, www.defenselink.mil/prhome/poprep2004/download/2004report.pdf.

51. Half of the respondents in 2005 expressed "very favorable views." The proportion of "very favorable" dropped to 29 percent in 2007. Jodie Allen, Nilanthi Samaranayake, and James Albrittain Jr., *Iraq and Vietnam: A Crucial Difference in Opinion* (Washington, DC: Pew Research Center), pewresearch.org/pubs/432/iraq-and-vietnam-a-crucial-difference-in-opinion.

52. Huntington, *The Soldier and the State*, p. 12.

53. Moskos, "The All-Volunteer Military," pp. 5–6.

54. U.S. Army, "The NCO Creed."

55. Reserve forces were used, despite the Korean War's classification as a limited war. Reservists accounted for more than one-third of personnel during the first year of mobilization. David R. Segal and Mady Wechsler Segal, "U.S. Military's Reliance on the Reserves," *Population Reference Bureau Bulletin* (2005), www.prb.org/Articles/2005/USMilitarysRelianceontheReserves.aspx.

56. Christine E. Wormuth, Michele A. Flournoy, Patrick T. Henry, and Clark A. Murdock, *The Future of the National Guard and Reserves* (Washington, DC: Center for Strategic and International Studies, 2006), p. 1.

57. Ibid.

58. Segal and Segal, "U.S. Military's Reliance on the Reserves."

59. Ruth H. Phelps and Beatrice J. Farr, eds., *Reserve Component Soldiers as Peace-keepers* (Alexandria, VA: U.S. Army Research Institute for the Behavioral and Social Sciences, 1996).

60. The reserve component served 1 million duty-days per year, on average, during the 1990s. This number increased to 12 million duty-days annually between 1996 and 2000. See Wormuth et al., *The Future of the National Guard and Reserves*, p. 2.

61. David R. Segal, "Military Sociology," in Clifton D. Bryant and Dennis L. Peck, eds., *21st Century Sociology: A Reference Handbook* (Thousand Oaks, CA: Sage, 2006), p. 358.

62. Ibid.

63. Joseph E. Whitlock, LTC, *How to Make Army Force Generation Work for the Army's Reserve Components* (Carlisle, PA: Strategic Studies Institute of the Army War College, 2006), p. v.

64. For example, the active-component Army will provide fourteen brigade combat teams, the reserve component four. These brigades are designed to be interchangeable and will require cyclical deployments from both active-duty and reserve soldiers. See Wormuth et al., *The Future of the National Guard and Reserves*.

65. Ibid., p. 7.

66. See Questions and Answers with Lieutenant General Jack C. Stultz, Chief, Army Reserve and Commanding General, U.S. Army Reserve Command, www.armyreserve.army.mil/ARWEB/NEWS/20060908.htm.

67. Reiss, "Occupational Mobility of Professional Workers," p. 693.

68. Charles C. Moskos, "From Institution to Occupation: Trends in Military Organization," *Armed Forces and Society* 4, no. 1 (October 1977): 41–50.

69. See, for example, Ryan Kelty and David R. Segal, "The Civilianization of the U.S. Military," in Jager and Kummel, *Private Military and Security Companies*, pp. 213–39.

70. Albert D. Biderman, "What Is Military?" in Sol Tax, ed., *The Draft: A Handbook of Facts and Alternatives* (Chicago: University of Chicago Press, 1967), pp. 122–37; Bernard Boene, "How 'Unique' Should the Military Be?" *European Journal of Sociology* 31, no. 1 (1990): 3–59.

71. See Christian Schaller, "Private Security and Military Companies under the International Law of Armed Conflict," in Jager and Kummel, *Private Military and Security Companies*, pp. 324–360.

72. See U.S. Department of Defense. *Report of the Defense Science Task Force on Human Resources Strategy* (Washington, DC: Office of the Under Secretary of Defense for Acquisitions, Technology, and Logistics, 2000).

CHAPTER ELEVEN: Militaries and Political Activity in Democracies

1. See, for example, Samuel Finer, *The Man on Horseback* (Middlesex: Penguin, 1962). For the idea that military power varies on a continuum, also see R. Hrair Dekmejian, "Egypt and Turkey: The Military in the Background," in Roman Kolkowicz and Andrzej Korbonski, eds., *Soldiers, Peasants and Bureaucrats* (London: George Allen and Unwin, 1982); Yehuda Ben Meir, *Civil-Military Relations in Israel* (New York: Columbia University Press, 1995).

2. Samuel P. Huntington, *The Soldier and the State* (Cambridge, MA: Belknap Press of Harvard University Press, 1957).

3. See chapter 12 by Christopher P. Gibson in this volume.

4. Huntington's normative influence may also have had a perverse effect by discouraging self-conscious debate among military officers about their own and peers' potential political activities. Officers may conceive of themselves as professionals in such a way that, when they engage in political behavior, they may not recognize it is as such, because doing so, could challenge the underlying identity they have developed as "professional" officers. In contrast, if we understood political behavior to be more "natural" and even perhaps inevitable, and recognize that it may coincide with some aspects of professionalism, we might encourage more self-reflection by officers about the issues.

5. Thom Shanker, "Mideast Commander Retires after Irking Bosses," *New York Times,* March 12, 2008, www.nytimes.com/2008/03/12/washington/12military.html.

6. David S. Cloud and Eric Schmitt, "More Retired Generals Call for Rumsfeld's Resignation," *New York Times,* April 13, 2006, www.nytimes.com/2006/04/14/washington/14military.html.

7. See Thom Shanker, "Mideast Commander Retires after Irking Bosses," *New York Times,* March 12, 2008; Michael C. Desch, "Bush and the Generals," *Foreign Affairs* 86, no. 3 (May–June 2007): 97–108; chapter 3 by Matthew Moten in this volume.

8. Huntington, *The Soldier and the State,* p. 84.

9. Finer, *The Man on Horseback.*

10. Alfred Hurley, *Billy Mitchell* (Bloomington: Indiana University Press, 1975 [1964]), pp. 60–62, 92. Also see Burke Davis, *The Billy Mitchell Affair* (New York: Random House, 1967).

11. Hurley, *Billy Mitchell,* pp. 68–69, 95.

12. David H. Petraeus, "Military Influence and the Post-Vietnam Use of Force,"

Armed Forces and Society 15, no. 4 (Summer 1989): 494. That Petraeus would author an article speaking to themes of political behavior may strike some as ironic, given accusations that he behaved "politically" in supporting Bush administration strategy in congressional testimony, or that the Bush administration attempted to politicize him by making him the spokesperson for its policies in Iraq.

13. Mike Allen and Roberto Suro, "Vieques Closing Angers Military, Hill GOP," *Washington Post*, June 15, 2001.

14. See Michael R. Gordon, "Powell Delivers a Resounding No on Using Limited Force in Bosnia," *New York Times*, September 28, 1992; Colin L. Powell, "Why Generals Get Nervous," Op-Ed, *New York Times*, October 9, 1992, p. A-35; Colin Powell, "U.S. Forces: Challenges Ahead," *Foreign Affairs* 71, no. 5 (Winter 1992–93): 32–45.

15. His actions were frequently cited as evidence of an imminent crisis in U.S. civil-military relations. For an overview, see the introduction in Don M. Snider and Miranda A. Carlton-Carew, eds., *U.S. Civil-Military Relations: In Crisis or Transition* (Washington, DC: Center for Strategic and International Studies, 1995).

16. This is noted in Peter Feaver and Richard Kohn, "The Gap," *National Interest,* no. 61 (Fall 2000): 29–37.

17. See H. R. McMaster, *Dereliction of Duty: Lyndon Johnson, Robert McNamara, the Joint Chiefs of Staff, and the Lies That led to Vietnam* (New York: HarperCollins, 1997).

18. See Eliot Cohen, "Enough Blame to Go Around," *National Interest, no.* 51 (Spring 1998): 103–9; see also Feaver and Kohn, "The Gap."

19. Feaver and Kohn, "The Gap."

20. See chapter 13 by Richard H. Kohn in this volume; and Desch, "Bush and the Generals."

21. See DoD Directive 1344.10, dated August 2, 2004, Enclosure 3 (superseding DoD Regulation 5500); the rules in this directive are quoted at length in the notes to chapter 12 by Christopher P. Gibson in this volume.

22. For example, see reports of Major General Harold Campbell's punishment for speaking contemptuous words against President Clinton. Robert Burns, "General Who Maligned Clinton Agrees to Retire Early," Associated Press, June 19, 1993.

23. James Burk refers to this as the military's "institutional salience." James Burk, "The Military's Presence in American Society, 1950–2000," in Peter Feaver and Richard Kohn, eds., *Soldiers and Civilians: The Civil-Military Gap and American National Security* (Cambridge, MA: MIT Press, 2001), pp. 247–74.

24. Matthew B. Stannard, "Military Voters Increasingly Vocal with Their Opinions," *San Francisco Chronicle*, October 12, 2004, p. A1.

25. See Robert Burns, "Officers Endorsing Clinton Say His Military History Shouldn't Matter," Associated Press, October 14, 1992.

26. See Steven Lee Myers, "The 2000 Campaign: Support of the Military; Military Backs Ex Guard Pilot over Private Gore," *New York Times*, September 21, 2000.

27. See "Military Endorsements," *PBS NewsHour with Jim Lehrer* transcript, September 25, 2000, www.pbs.org/newshour/bb/military/july-dec00/military_9-25 .html.

28. Douglas Turner, "Enlisting Aid of Generals," *Buffalo News* (New York), August 1, 2004, p. A1; "Military Endorsements Seen as Increasing Kerry's National Security Credibility," *Frontrunner*, July 30, 2004; Stannard, "Military Voters Increasingly Vocal with Their Opinions."

29. There were other indications of this growing political activity. After military absentee votes played a central role in securing a recount of Florida votes in 2002, the Pentagon designated October 11–15, 2004, as "Absentee Voting Week," even designating "voting assistance officers." Discussion and debate at bases and military facilities were reportedly much more heated and open than in previous elections. This might not have been so significant without the partisan bias in the military. In an unscientific survey of 2,754 active-duty and 1,411 reserve and Guard members (federal law prohibits active polling of military personnel), individuals reported supporting Bush over Kerry by a margin of 4–1. By mobilizing absentee votes, the Pentagon voting assistance efforts, deliberately or not, bolstered Republicans in the election. See Stannard, "Military Voters Increasingly Vocal with Their Opinions."

30. Turner, "Enlisting Aid of Generals."

31. Steven Lee Myers, "The Nation; When the Military (ret.) Marches to Its Own Drummer," *New York Times*, October 1, 2000.

32. This point is made in ibid.

33. See "Military Endorsements," *PBS NewsHour with Jim Lehrer* transcript.

34. Rear Admiral Craig Quigley, Vice Admiral (ret.) John Shanahan, and defense reporter and author George Wilson on the *NewsHour with Jim Lehrer*, "Civilians on Board," March 5, 2001, http://www.pbs.org/newshour/bb/military/jan-june01/sub_3-5.html.

35. See John Kifner, "Despite Sub Inquiry, Navy Still Sees Need for Guests on Ships," *New York Times*, April 22, 2001.

36. See Edward Walsh, "A Longtime Military PR Practice," *Washington Post*, February 15, 2001. This practice drew public scrutiny when a Navy submarine, the USS *Greeneville*, collided with a Japanese shipping vessel in February 2001. Sixteen civilians were on board the submarine at the time, among them donors to the *Missouri* restoration fund, as well as influential business executives. Christopher Drew, "Civilian Says Submarine Took Precautions," *New York Times*, February 17, 2001.

37. The U.S. Air Force's activities in relation to the F-22 Raptor offer examples of these tactics. See Greg Schneider, "Red-Hot Fighter, Trail of Deception," *Baltimore Sun*, July 18, 1999.

38. See, for example, Gordon Adams, *The Politics of Defense Contracting* (New Brunswick, NJ: Transaction, 1981).

39. For a useful study of these "liaising" activities, see Stephen Scroggs, *Army Relations with Congress* (Westport, CT: Praeger, 2000). I discuss lobbying-like activities throughout the text, but the most overt and explicit lobbying tactics are prohibited by law and regulation. For example, the Army's rules for the administration of legislative liaisons prohibit Army officials from asking members of Congress to support funding requests not supported by the president's budget or to enact legislation inconsistent

with Department of Defense or administration policy or position. These regulations can be found at the Army's OCLL (Office, Chief of Legislative Liaison) Web site, www .hqda.army.mil/ocll/AR120/AR%201-20.pdf.

40. Art Pine, "Issue Explodes into All-out Lobbying War," *Los Angeles Times*, January 28, 1993. In addition, military sources reported that enlisted personnel on military bases were carrying out organized call-ins to senators and house members to register their opposition to the policy change. In January 1993 Senator Bob Dole met with the leaders of twenty-four different veterans groups opposed to ending the ban. Internally, the services also communicated their opposition to changing the policy. In an article in the *Marine Corps Gazette,* an active-duty Marine officer at the Naval War College suggested that the Marine Corps should be disbanded rather than openly accept homosexuals. Discussed in Eric Schmitt, "Military Cites Wide Range of Reasons for Its Gay Ban," *New York Times*, January 27, 1993. Also see David M. Rayside, "The Perils of Congressional Politics," in Craig A. Rimmerman, ed., *Gay Rights, Military Wrongs: Political Perspectives of Lesbians and Gays in the Military* (New York: Garland, 1996), pp. 151, 152, 155, 169; esp. p. 190n81.

41. "Integration" is one component of military effectiveness; it involves the capacity to ensure consistency in all military arenas, create synergies within and across different levels, and avoid counterproductive actions. See Risa Brooks and Elizabeth Stanley, eds., *Creating Military Power: The Sources of Military Effectiveness* (Stanford: Stanford University Press, 2007). Also see Barry R. Posen, *The Sources of Military Doctrine: France, Britain, and Germany between the World Wars* (Ithaca, NY: Cornell University Press, 1984). The concept is also implicit in Allan R. Millett and Williamson Murray, eds., *Military Effectiveness*, vol. 1: *The First World War* (Boston: Allen and Unwin, 1988).

42. Some might respond that it is not up to military leaders to compensate for the failings of the civilian population or Congress. This is somewhat persuasive: better civic education and debate about military-related issues would help alleviate deficiencies in knowledge and expertise. But this argument neglects the exceptional position of military leaders: they are in a unique position to gain access to information and have skills and training that allow them to interpret it in ways that very few civilian analysts or members of society would be capable of doing.

43. The generals who publicly expressed their opposition included Army Major General Paul D. Eaton, who commanded the training of Iraqi security forces until 2004; Marine Lieutenant General Gregory Newbold, director of operations, Joint Chiefs of Staff, 2000–2002; and Army Major General John Batiste, who commanded an army division in Iraq before retiring. See Cloud and Schmitt, "More Retired Generals Call for Rumsfeld's Resignation."

44. Lieutenant General Greg Newbold (ret.), "Why Iraq Was a Mistake," *Time*, April 9, 2006, www.time.com/time/magazine/article/0,9171,1181629,00.html.

45. Ralph Peters, "Hawks for Dissent: A Pro–Iraq War Ex-soldier Defends the Generals Who Took on Rumsfeld," *Washington Monthly*, June 2006.

46. See Kevin Drum, "Political Animal," *Washington Monthly*, April 18, 2006, www

.washingtonmonthly.com/archives/monthly/2006_04.php. Quotations from other blog participants can be found at www2.washingtonmonthly.com/mt/mt-comments .cgi?entry_id=8641.

47. For the term *fire alarm,* see Matthew McCubbins and Thomas Schwartz, "Congressional Oversight Overlooked: Police Patrols versus Fire Alarms," *American Journal of Political Science* 27, no. 4 (February 1984): 165–79.

48. For a review of these approaches to innovation, and Rosen's own argument, see Stephen P. Rosen, *Winning the Next War: Innovation and the Modern Military* (Ithaca, NY: Cornell University Press, 1991).

49. See Roy K. Flint, "The Truman-MacArthur Conflict: Dilemmas of Civil-Military Relations in the Nuclear Age," in Richard Kohn, ed., *The United States Military under the Constitution of the United States, 1789–1989* (New York: New York University Press, 1991), p. 258.

50. See Michael R. Gordon, "Powell Delivers a Resounding No on Using Limited Force in Bosnia," *New York Times,* September 28, 1992; Powell, "Why Generals Get Nervous"; and Powell, "U.S. Forces: Challenges Ahead"; Snider and Carlton-Carew, *U.S. Civil-military Relations;* Richard Kohn, "Out of Control: The Crisis in Civil-Military Relations," *National Interest,* no. 35 (Spring 1993): 3–17.

51. See Pine, "Issue Explodes into All-Out Lobbying War"; Schmitt, "Military Cites Wide Range of Reasons for Its Gay Ban"; Rayside, "The Perils of Congressional Politics," pp. 151, 152, 155, 169; especially p. 190n81.

52. For example, one might distinguish appropriate from inappropriate behavior by specifying issue areas. Thus, some might accept military leaders using these tactics in the realm of budgets and procurement—the typical fare of bureaucratic politics—but not in national dialogue about security goals or strategy. A counterargument is that outcomes in both spheres can have substantial influence on how resources are allocated and how the United States is oriented toward security threats and ambitions, and therefore dividing them by issue area may be too arbitrary.

53. Leon V. Sigal, *The Changing Dynamics of U.S. Defense Spending* (Westport, CT: Praeger, 1999), p. 40.

54. See Alfred Stepan, *Re-thinking Military Politics* (Princeton, NJ: Princeton University Press, 1988), p. 84.

55. Americans consistently rate the military high on Gallup surveys that measure confidence in public and private institutions, www.gallup.com/poll/specialReports/pollSummaries/aoa_index.asp. Also see figures cited in Paul Gronke and Peter D. Feaver, "Uncertain Confidence: Civilian and Military Attitudes about Civil-military Relations," in Feaver and Kohn, *Soldiers and Civilians,* p. 134.

56. Andrew Bacevich, "Grand Army of the Republicans: Has the U.S. Military Become a Partisan Force?" *New Republic* 217, no. 23 (December 8, 1997): 22–25.

57. Holsti finds that in 1976 a solid majority of officers queried identified themselves as independent. By 1996 the proportion had dwindled to 22 percent. At the same time the number of officers identifying themselves as Republicans grew from 33 percent to roughly 64 percent. See Ole R. Holsti, "A Widening Gap between the U.S.

Military and Civilian Society?" *International Security* 23, no. 3 (Winter 1998–99): 5–42. Also see the studies by the Triangle Institute for Security Studies (TISS) reported in Feaver and Kohn, *Soldiers and Civilians.*

58. Comparable figures for civilians are 29 percent Republican; 35 percent Democratic; 31 percent independent; and 5 percent no preference. See Feaver and Kohn, *Soldiers and Civilians,* p. 106.

59. Feaver and Kohn, "The Gap," p. 6.

60. Bacevich, "Grand Army of the Republicans." On the notion of the Republican Party becoming the military's party, see Donald Zillman, "Maintaining the Political Neutrality of the Military," Op-Ed, *Inter-University Seminar Newsletter,* Spring 2001, p. 17; Feaver and Kohn, *Soldiers and Civilians.*

61. For an excellent analysis of the nature of military profession, see Don M. Snider and Lloyd J. Matthews, eds., *The Future of the Army Profession,* 2d ed., rev. and exp. (New York: McGraw-Hill Primis, 2005).

CHAPTER TWELVE: Enhancing National Security and Civilian Control of the Military: A Madisonian Approach

The views expressed in this paper are mine alone and are not those of the National Defense University, Army War College, Department of the Army, Department of Defense, or any other governmental agency. This chapter is derived from my War College Fellowship manuscript entitled *Securing the State: Reforming the National Security Decisionmaking Process at the Civil-Military Nexus* (London: Ashgate Press, 2007). In that manuscript, completed during my time as a Hoover Institution National Security Affairs Fellow, I thank many individuals for their helpful comments and suggestions reviewing earlier drafts. I reaffirm that gratitude here.

1. The Iraq war was the most important issue to voters in the 2006 U.S. election, according to exit polling data. See, for example, CNN exit polling at www.cnn.com/ELECTION/2006/special/issues/.

2. See especially Michael R. Gordon and General Bernard E. Trainor, *COBRA II: The Inside Story of the Invasion and Occupation of Iraq* (New York: Pantheon Books, 2006); Thomas E. Ricks, *Fiasco: The American Military Adventure in Iraq* (New York: Penguin, 2006); and Bob Woodward, *State of Denial: Bush at War, Part III* (New York: Simon and Schuster, 2006).

3. The Iraq Study Group, comprising ten prominent former members of government of both parties, also came to this conclusion. Recommendation no. 46 of its report states: "The new Secretary of Defense should make every effort to build healthy civil-military relations, by creating an environment in which the senior military feel free to offer independent advice not only to the civilian leadership in the Pentagon but also to the President and the National Security Council, as envisioned in the Goldwater-Nichols legislation." *Report of the Iraq Study Group, Authorized Edition* (New York: Vintage Books, 2006), p. 77.

4. Rumsfeld dominated not just General Myers but others, including CENTCOM

Commander General Tommy Franks. This conclusion is shared in a number of books critical of the administration's handling of the Iraq war, including those sources cited in note 2. Rumsfeld's actions—putting the military in its place and superimposing his views on the war-planning process and transformation efforts at the Pentagon—are also the central theme of Rowan Scarborough, *Rumsfeld's War* (Washington, DC: Regnery Books, 2004), which Scarborough explicitly intended to be read as an endorsement of the defense secretary's tenure.

5. H. R. McMaster, *Dereliction of Duty: Lyndon Johnson, Robert McNamara, the Joint Chiefs of Staff, and the Lies That Led to Vietnam* (New York: HarperCollins Publishers, 1997), pp. 300–322.

6. For another view, see chapter 13 by Richard H. Kohn in this volume, asserting that the military should take responsibility for shaping the civil-military dynamic.

7. Samuel P. Huntington, *The Soldier and the State: The Theory and Politics of Civil-Military Relations* (Cambridge, MA: Belknap Press of Harvard University Press, 1957); Morris Janowitz, *The Professional Soldier: A Social and Political Portrait*, 2d ed. (New York: Free Press, 1971). Post–Cold War reprises of these approaches were, respectively, Richard H. Kohn, "The Erosion of Civilian Control of the Military in the United States Today," *Naval War College Review* 55, no. 3 (Summer 2002): 9–59; and Eliot Cohen, *Supreme Command: Soldiers, Statesmen, and Leadership in Wartime* (New York: Free Press, 2002).

8. Some presidents have worked effectively with the military, even without a conscious or established normative framework. The Madisonian approach incorporates "best practices" from some of these positive examples. While any relationship should be flexible enough to deal with unexpected developments, a model agreement or framework helps establish clear expectations to guide the relationship, especially in times of crisis, with accountability, efficiency, and effectiveness.

9. Richard H. Kohn, "Out of Control: The Crisis in Civil-Military Relations," *National Interest*, no. 35 (Spring 1994): 3–31.

10. Chapter 11 by Risa Brooks in this volume raises the question of what constitutes appropriate behavior for military officers at the civil-military nexus and points out reasons why the objective control model cannot provide compelling answers.

11. Huntington, *The Soldier and the State*.

12. A prominent example was Harold D. Lasswell, *National Security and Individual Freedom* (New York: McGraw-Hill, 1950). See chapter 5 by Michael C. Desch in this volume for more on the impact of the liberal tradition on American civil-military relations.

13. Huntington, *The Soldier and the State*, p. 80.

14. Ibid., pp. 83–85.

15. Huntington's philosophy and logic underpin the treatment of civil-military relations in U.S. Army, Field Manual (FM) 100-1, *The Army*, June 14, 1994.

16. Huntington, *The Soldier and the State*, p. 8.

17. To be fair, Huntington recognized that there would be times when roles for civilian and military leaders would overlap, but he believed that there was enough division of labor on which to base a theory.

18. One can get an appreciation for this point by reading the memoirs of any four-star general. See, for example, Colin Powell, *My American Journey* (New York: Random House, 1996); and H. Norman Schwarzkopf, *It Doesn't Take a Hero* (written with Peter Petre) (New York: Bantam Books, 1992).

19. Here I essentially agree with the argument made in Janowitz, *The Professional Soldier*, pp. 417–40.

20. Such assumptions resulted in civil-military conflicts over budgets and budget shares, prompting General Maxwell Taylor to take early retirement and publish his book critical of the Eisenhower administration. Maxwell D. Taylor, *Uncertain Trumpet* (New York: Harper, 1960).

21. In National Security Action Memorandum (NSAM 55), President to Chairman of the Joint Chiefs of Staff (CJCS), 28 June 1961, Kennedy demanded that his service chiefs frame their politically sensitive military advice as if they were the decision maker, not the advisor. Willard J. Webb and Ronald H. Cole, *The Chairmen of the Joint Chiefs of Staff* (Washington, DC: Historical Division, Joint Chiefs of Staff, 1989), p. 60. Document is available at www.jfklibrary.org/Historical + Resources/Archives/ Reference + Desk/NSAMs.htm.

22. See also Gibson, *Securing the State;* chapter 4 treats Huntington's variant of objective control, and chapter 5 covers Richard Kohn's reprise of it.

23. Huntington, *The Soldier and the State*, p. 155.

24. Janowitz, *The Professional Soldier*.

25. Ibid.

26. Ibid., p. 418.

27. Ibid., p. 440.

28. Ibid., chap. 17.

29. Ibid., p. 436.

30. For more on civil-military relations in the former Soviet Union, see Timothy Colton, *Commissars, Commanders and Civilian Authority: The Structure of Soviet Military Politics* (Cambridge, MA: Harvard University Press, 1979); and Timothy Colton, *Soldiers and the Soviet State: Civil-Military Relations from Brezhnev to Gorbachev* (Princeton, NJ: Princeton University Press, 1990).

31. Huntington, *The Soldier and the State*, pp. 154–57.

32. I am specifically referring to the Center for Military Readiness led by Elaine Donnelly; see cmrlink.org.

33. See J. D. Lynch, "All Volunteer Force is in Crisis," *USNI* 123, no. 9 (September 1997): 30–34; John Hillen, "The Civilian-Military Gap: Keep It, Defend It, Manage It," *USNI* 1124, no. 10 (October 1998): 2–4; John Hillen, "Must U.S. Military Culture Reform?" *Orbis* 43, no. 1 (Winter 1999): 43–57; James Webb, "The War on Military Culture," *Weekly Standard* 2, no. 18 (January 20, 1997): 17–22.

34. In fact, Sergeant Leigh Ann Hester of the 617th Military Police Company, a National Guard unit out of Richmond, Kentucky, received the Silver Star for heroism in battle on March 20, 2005. See the Army news, www.defenselink.mil/news/ Jun2005/20050616_1745.html. More recently, medic Private First Class Monica

Brown was also awarded the Silver Star for service in Afghanistan; Ann Scott Tyson, "Woman Gains Silver Star—and Removal from Combat: Case Shows Contradictions of Army Rules," *Washington Post,* May 1, 2008, www.washingtonpost.com/wp-dyn/content/article/2008/04/30/AR2008043003415.html?sid=ST2008043003513.

35. Huntington, *The Soldier and the State,* pp. 2–3.

36. See also Eliot Cohen's arguments on this score. Cohen cites ideological armies that were highly successful on the battlefield, specifically Waffen SS forces and the People's Liberation Army of China. Thus, one cannot claim that subjectively controlled armies will always be ineffectual. See Cohen, *Supreme Command,* pp. 243–44.

37. Janowitz, *The Professional Soldier,* pp. 417–40. See also Gibson, *Securing the State,* chap. 3.

38. See Federalist Papers, no. 10 and no. 51, in Isaac Kramnick, ed., *James Madison, Alexander Hamilton, and John Jay: The Federalist Papers* (New York: Penguin, 1987), pp. 122–28, 318–22.

39. Contrast the relationships of Washington and of Marshall with the dysfunctional and ineffective relationships between General Earle Wheeler and Defense Secretary Robert McNamara, when dominating structures led to flawed policies, and between General Richard Myers and Defense Secretary Donald Rumsfeld, when they led to failed and struggling outcomes. See Gibson, *Securing the State,* chap. 3.

40. The best source on the nature and essence of the Stimson-Marshall relationship is Forrest C. Pogue, "Marshall on Civil-Military Relationships," in Richard Kohn, ed., *The United States Military under the Constitution of the United States, 1789–1989* (New York: New York University Press, 1991), esp. pp. 200–202. Other excellent sources include the closest thing we have to a memoir by General C. Marshall, *George C. Marshall Interviews and Reminiscences for Forrest C. Pogue,* ed. Larry I. Bland and Joellen K. Bland, with an introduction by Forrest C. Pogue, rev. ed. (Lexington, VA: George C. Marshall Research Foundation, 1991); and Henry L. Stimson and Mc-George Bundy, *On Active Service in Peace and War* (New York: Harper, 1948).

41. Another good partnership at the Pentagon was the 1989–92 relationship between Joint Chiefs of Staff Chairman General Colin Powell and Defense Secretary Richard Cheney during their interactions overseeing the Panama Invasion, the Persian Gulf War, and shaping the post–Cold War military. I see this as exemplary civil-military interaction, but my approval does not extend to Powell's actions during 1992 presidential election, when he published an op-ed in the *New York Times* with a partisan flavor or to these individuals' contributions in government service subsequent to the George H. W. Bush administration. The Cheney-Powell Pentagon of 1989–92 is a good example of how professionally prepared civilian and military leaders can partner to help elected leaders appreciate the strategic landscape and sort through weighty decisions. Another example was the effective partnership of Defense Secretary William Perry with Joint Chiefs of Staff Chairman General John Shalikashvili during the Clinton administration. See Charles Stevenson, *Warriors and Politicians: U.S. Civil-Military Relations under Stress* (New York: Routledge, 2006).

42. Schwarzkopf, *It Doesn't Take a Hero,* pp. 368–70.

43. On professional preparation, see Christopher P. Gibson and Don M. Snider, "Civil-Military Relations and the Potential to Influence: A Look at the National Security Decisionmaking Process," *Armed Forces and Society* 25, no. 2 (Winter 1999): 193–218.

44. Peter D. Feaver, *Armed Servants: Agency, Oversight, and Civil-Military Relations* (Cambridge, MA: Harvard University Press, 2003).

45. Ibid., pp. 54–95.

46. The secretary of defense is thus an "auxiliary" as described by Plato in the *Republic*, which provides extensive treatment of what today is classified as civil-military relations. In book II, the term "Guardian" describes the responsibilities of elites who govern society and who influence group norm development. Book III presents variants of the principal-agent model. Plato divides Guardians into two classes: "rulers" and "auxiliaries." In Republican forms of government that empower elected representatives to make the laws and govern society, Plato's "rulers" are the elected leaders. All those who assist rulers are auxiliaries. Hence, politically appointed officials at the Pentagon, as well as military professionals, are auxiliaries. See Plato, *Republic*, books II and III, in John Cooper, ed., *Plato: Complete Works* (Indianapolis: Hackett, 1997), pp. 998–1052.

47. Feaver, *Armed Servants*, p. 3.

48. Huntington, *The Soldier and the State*, pp. 8–9.

49. A must-read on military professionalism is Don M. Snider and Lloyd J. Matthews, eds., *The Future of the Army Profession*, 2d ed., rev. and exp. (New York: McGraw-Hill Primis, 2005).

50. See Michael J. Meese and Sean M. Morgan, "New Requirements for Army Expert Knowledge: Afghanistan and Iraq," in Snider and Matthews, *The Future of the Army Profession*, pp. 349–66.

51. Two of the best accounts are David McCullough, *1776* (New York: Simon and Schuster, 2005); and Marshall, *George C. Marshall Interviews and Reminiscences*.

52. As Richard Kohn has argued, partisanship causes civilian mistrust of the officer corps. See chapter 13 by Richard H. Kohn in this volume.

53. Janowitz, *The Professional Soldier*, pp. 422–23.

54. For a detailed history of the Goldwater-Nichols Act, see James Locher, *Victory on the Potomac* (College Station: Texas A&M University Press, 2002).

55. See James Lyons, "The Missing Voice," *Washington Times*, September 20, 2006, p. 19; and comments by General James Jones, former commandant of the USMC and JCS member, in Woodward, *State of Denial*, p. 404.

56. Because flag officers in the Navy are admirals, during those times when a naval officer holds the position, he or she would be the commander, U.S. Armed Forces, rather than commanding general (CG). This officer should hold the title "Commanding General" rather than "Commander" in order to mark the contrast between that officer and the president, who is "commander in chief." The top military officer is a general or admiral, and emphasizing that status in the title reinforces civilian control of the military.

57. See Stephen Skowronek, *Building a New American State: The Expansion of National Administrative Capacities, 1877–1920* (Cambridge: Cambridge University Press, 1982), pp. 219–21; and Matthew Moten, "Root, Miles, and Carter: Political-Cultural Expertise and an Earlier Army Transformation," in Snider and Matthews, *The Future of the Army Profession*, pp. 723–48. Given that, under this proposal, the CG would have authority over the Joint Staff and be able to coordinate the services' efforts, the Madisonian approach should avoid the problems of the earlier period when the position of CG existed. The CG under the Madisonian approach should have ample authority to harness the potential of the Pentagon and Washington, D.C., policy community to support the field army.

58. Bruce Palmer, introduction to Lloyd J. Matthews and Dale E. Brown, eds., *Assessing the Vietnam War* (New York: Pergamon-Brassey's International Defense Publishers, 1987), p. ix.

59. As Steven Brint has persuasively argued, despite the significant expansion of the size of professions after World War II, professional advice has, somewhat counterintuitively, increasingly given way to political control and direction by political appointees within the various departments of the U.S. government during policy debates. Political appointees now have access to so many "experts" that even a minority or radical viewpoint is able to find "expert" support; these voices may carry the day against mainstream professional judgment and advice. As a consequence, political appointees have come to dominate professionals within many departments and policy debates. Brint's findings and analysis provide substantial weight and support for my recommendation to create the position of commanding general, in order to ensure that professional military judgment and advice is available to the elected leaders of the United States. Political appointees might find other general officers within the Department of Defense to support their analysis and recommendations, but only the commanding general would speaks for the profession: his or her advice would represent "best military judgment." The professionally informed opinion of the defense secretary is "best national security professional judgment," not "best military judgment," and the distinction is worth preserving. See Steven Brint, *In an Age of Experts: The Changing Role of Professionals in Politics and Public Life* (Princeton, NJ: Princeton University Press, 1994), pp. 135–37.

60. The Joint Chiefs of Staff previously had this kind of authority, although it was not vested in a commanding general. Under the 1948 Key West Agreement (which defined the post–World War II roles and missions for each of the three services, including the new U.S. Air Force), until 1953 the service chiefs were designated as executive agents for unified and specified commands. See *Joint Staff Officer's Guide, 2000* (Norfolk, VA: Joint Forces Staff College, 2000), pp. 1–21.

61. Marshall described his relationship with Stimson as indispensable and could not imagine doing his job well without him. For more, see Marshall, *George C. Marshall Interviews and Reminiscences*, p. 621.

62. General Eric Shinseki, remarks at the occasion of his retirement, June 11, 2003, www.army.mil/features/ShinsekiFarewell/farewellremarks.htm. Secretary of

the Army White was forced out of office by Secretary of Defense Rumsfeld in 2002 as a result of the controversy over canceling the Crusader program; see chapter 3 by Matthew Moten in this volume.

63. Gibson and Snider, "Civil-Military Relations and the Potential to Influence."

64. For this reason, the under secretary for personnel should give consideration to the levels of professional preparation among top-level civilian and military officers when making top-tier assignments.

65. The "Beyond Goldwater-Nichols" project at the Center for Strategic and International Studies (CSIS) has made a similar recommendation. See Clark A. Murdock et al., *Beyond Goldwater Nichols Phase II Report: U.S. Government and Defense Reform for a New Strategic Era* (Washington, DC: CSIS, July 2005), p. 7, www.csis.org/component/option,com_csis_pubs/task,view/id,1849/type,1/. See also "White House Planning Major Overhaul of National Security Education," *Inside the Pentagon,* February 22, 2007, asserting that the president was preparing to issue an executive order enacting sweeping changes in education programs and career development for those federal workers in the national security arena, primarily within the Department of Defense.

66. Edward J. Shanahan, "Military Alone Can't Deliver Us Peace," *Hartford Courant,* September 11, 2006.

67. See cisac.stanford.edu/docs/about_cisac; www.sais-jhu.edu/; www.wcfia.harvard.edu/olin/; www.rand.org/ard/.

68. See Marybeth Ulrich, "Infusing Normative Civil-Military Relations Principles in the Officer Corps," in Snider and Matthews, *The Future of the Army Profession,* pp. 655–82. See also Marybeth Ulrich and Martin Cook, "U.S. Civil Military Relations since 9/11: Issues in Ethics and Policy Development," *Journal of Military Ethics* 5, no. 3 (November 2006): 161–82.

69. Don M. Snider, "The Shared Identity and Professional Practice of Army Officers," in Snider and Matthews, *The Future of the Army Profession,* pp. 143–45. See also Moten, "Root, Miles, and Carter."

70. See, in particular, Meese and Morgan, "New Requirements for Army Expert Knowledge."

71. An excellent treatment of desired competencies for flag officers is Leonard Wong and Don M. Snider, "Strategic Leadership of the Army Profession," in Snider and Matthews, *The Future of the Army Profession,* pp. 601–24; see also the *Strategic Leadership Primer,* 2d ed., Department of Command, Leadership, and Management, United States Army War College (Carlisle, PA, 2004).

72. The purpose of removing oneself from the situation (as by retirement or resignation) is to allow for new professional representation in the civil-military nexus. When the officer in the advisory role has failed to persuade principals of his or her best military judgment, despite strong views, it is time for new voices to enter the process with fresh perspectives. Officers should not make a spectacle of their departure. The retirement or resignation is not "in protest": officers possess no such entitlement, because decision-making authority rests solely with elected leaders. For a

somewhat different perspective on this issue, see chapter 13 by Richard H. Kohn in this volume.

73. Colin Powell, "Why Generals Get Nervous," *New York Times*, October 8, 1992, p. A8.

74. *DoD Regulation 5500 Joint Ethics*, chap. 6.

75. DoD Directive 1344.10, dated August 2, 2004, Enclosure 3 (superseding DoD Regulation 5500):

> Active duty members of the armed services *may:* 1) Register, vote, express a personal opinion on political candidates and issues, but not as a representative of the Armed Forces. 2) Promote and encourage other military members to exercise their voting franchise, if such promotion does not constitute an attempt to influence or interfere with the outcome of an election. 3) Join a political club and attend its meetings when not in uniform. 4) Serve as an election official, if such service is not as a representative of a partisan political party, does not interfere with military duties, is performed when not in uniform, and has the prior approval of the Secretary concerned or the Secretary's designee. 5) Sign a petition for specific legislative action or a petition to place a candidate's name on an official election ballet, if the signing does not obligate the member to engage in partisan political activity and is done as a private citizen and not as a representative of the Armed Forces. 6) Write a letter to the editor of a newspaper expressing the member's personal views on public issues or political candidates, if such action is not part of an organized letter-writing campaign or a solicitation of votes for or against a political party or partisan cause or candidate. 7) Make monetary contributions to a political organization, party, or committee favoring a particular candidate or slate of candidates. 8) Display a political sticker on the member's private vehicle. 9) Attend partisan and nonpartisan political meetings or rallies as a spectator when not in uniform.
>
> Active duty members of the armed services *may not:* 1) Use official authority or influence to: interfere with an election, affect the course or outcome of an election, solicit votes for a particular candidate or issue, or require or solicit political contributions from others. 2) Be a candidate for civil office in Federal, State, or local government (with some exceptions, see regulations) or engage in public or organized soliciting of others to become partisan candidates for nomination or election to civil office. 3) Participate in partisan political management, campaigns, or conventions (except as a spectator when not in uniform) or make public speeches in the course thereof. 4) Make a contribution to another member of the Armed Forces or a civilian officer or employee of the US for the purpose of promoting a political objective or cause, including a political campaign. 5) Solicit or receive a contribution from another member of the Armed Forces or a civilian officer or employee of the US for the purpose of promoting a political objective or cause, including a political campaign. 6) Allow or cause to be published partisan political articles signed or written

by the member that solicits votes for or against a partisan political party, candidate, or cause. 7) Serve in any official capacity or be listed as a sponsor of a partisan political club. 8) Speak before a partisan political gathering, including any gathering that promotes a partisan political party, candidate or cause. 9) Participate in any radio, television, or other program or group discussion as an advocate for or against a partisan political party, candidate, or cause. 10) Conduct a political opinion survey under the auspices of a partisan political group or distribute partisan political literature. 11) Use contemptuous words against the officeholders described in 10 USC. 12) Perform clerical or other duties for a partisan political committee during a campaign or on an election day. 13) Solicit or otherwise engage in fundraising activities in Federal offices or facilities, including military reservations, for a partisan political cause or candidate. 14) March or ride in a partisan political parade. 15) Display a large political sign, banner, or poster (as distinguished from a bumper sticker) on the top or side of a private vehicle. 16) Participate in any organized effort to provide voters with transportation to the polls if the effort is organized by, or associated with, a partisan political party or candidate. 17) Sell tickets for, or otherwise actively promote, political dinners and similar fundraising events. 18) Attend partisan political events as an official representative of the Armed Forces.

76. I expand treatment of this topic in Gibson, *Securing the State*; see especially chap. 3, which relies on multiple sources, including General Tommy R. Franks, *American Soldier* (New York: HarperCollins, 2004); Gordon and Trainor, *COBRA II*; Ricks, *Fiasco*; Woodward, *State of Denial*; and the pro-Rumsfeld work, *Rumsfeld's War*, by Rowan Scarborough. All of these sources corroborate the recollections of my professional colleagues who participated in the planning process.

77. See Gibson, *Securing the State*, chap. 3. See also chapter 8 by James Burk in this volume, suggesting that there should be a professionally and morally protected space in which the military operates as it pursues national security policies and operations. Burk makes a solid contribution to the debate, but his illustrative cases are mostly on the extremes, such as accountability of Nazi officers and U.S. Army officer actions at My Lai. More analysis is needed to give meaning to these concepts.

78. Two leading scholars in the field, Richard Kohn and Eliot Cohen, with the best of intentions and most impressive command of history and theory, advanced normative models that, although markedly different, both contributed to a dominating dynamic at the Pentagon, to such a degree that elected leaders have not had access to professional military advice at the level, frequency, and quality they need. See Kohn, "The Erosion of Civilian Control of the Military in the United States Today"; Eliot Cohen, "Generals, Politicians and Iraq," *Wall Street Journal*, August 18, 2002; Eliot Cohen, "Hunting Chicken Hawks," *Washington Post*, September 5, 2002, p. A31; and Cohen, *Supreme Command*.

79. On the status of the officer corps relative to its responsibilities to elected leaders and the nation, see Fred Kaplan, "After Rumsfeld: What Robert Gates Can Achieve

in the Next Two Years," *Slate,* November 14, 2006, www.slate.com: "Kick some gumption into the active-duty officer corps. It is pathetic to see so many three- and four-star generals reduced to quivering yes-men by the dismissive vindictiveness of the sitting secretary of defense. Their kowtowing may be motivated by respect for civilian authority, but obeying lawful orders is different from abrogating professional responsibility. The master-servant relationship that Rumsfeld has established with his officers—and which his officers have too obsequiously accepted—is a terrible thing for morale; it sets an intimidating example to career officers of lower rank; and, most of all, it's bad for national security. A defense secretary shouldn't feel he has to take an officer's advice—quite often, he shouldn't—but he should at least hear it in unvarnished form. If Gates' tenure is to be a period of restoration, one of the most useful things he could do is to persuade senior officers that they can speak their minds again without fear of demotion or reprisal." I believe Kaplan has a point, but the military does not need Secretary Gates to "kick some gumption into the officer corps." The officer corps should be capable of renewing its own ethic, even if it will need some assistance from civilian leaders for other reforms related to the civil-military nexus.

80. A special edition of *Military Review,* March–April 1999, was dedicated to the role of the U.S. Congress in the U.S. national security establishment, including the armed forces; see also Matthew Moten and Christopher P. Gibson, "The Soldier and Congress," *Military Review* 79, no. 1 (March–April 1999): 65–68.

81. Robert Gates stated this as one of his chief goals during his confirmation hearing before the Senate Armed Services Committee on December 5, 2006. See also Peter Grier, "A New Chief at the Pentagon," *Christian Science Monitor,* December 8, 2006, p.1.

82. Richard H. Kohn, chapter 13 in this volume, argues that the military should take responsibility for shaping the civil-military dynamic. There are at least a couple of problems with this approach. First, because it is a relationship, by definition, at least two parties will have responsibilities for shaping the dynamic. Second, because elected leaders enjoy a superior standing in the relationship, they and not military officers will dominate the dynamic, whether conscious of that or not. See chapter 3 by Matthew Moten in this volume for illustration. He concludes that there was little more that General Shinseki could have done to render the Rumsfeld-Shinseki relationship functional. Indeed, the evidence in Moten's piece undermines Kohn's position that the military should be responsible for shaping the civil-military dynamic. What is needed instead is a clear set of expectations and guidelines expounded by the president, early on in a new administration, so that all parties at the civil-military nexus understand their roles, individually and collectively. Scholars could play a helpful role by offering competing frameworks for how to organize the relationship from which the president could choose. It would be helpful as well if the chairs of the House and Senate Armed Services Committees also produced a document outlining their expectations.

CHAPTER THIRTEEN: Building Trust: Civil-Military Behaviors for Effective National Security

Portions of this chapter were delivered as lectures to the Program for Senior Executives in National Security and the National Security Fellows, Kennedy School of Government, Harvard University; Industrial College of the Armed Forces, National Defense University; U.S. Army Military History Institute; National Defense Intelligence College; and as the Dr. James J. Whalen Memorial Lecture, U.S. Army War College. For reading earlier versions of this chapter and offering comments, the author thanks Charles D. Allen, Andrew Bacevich, Tami Davis Biddle, Dennis Blair, Alexander Cochran, Eliot Cohen, Raymond Dawson, Charles J. Dunlap Jr., Peter Feaver, Zane Finkelstein, H. R. McMaster, Lloyd Matthews, Richard B. Myers, Alex Roland, John Salapatas, Charles Stevenson, Matthew Turpin, Walter Ulmer, Marybeth Ulrich, and colleagues in the Dickinson College Political Science and History Departments, in the Department of Command, Leadership, and Management at the U.S. Army War College, and the students in the Civilian Control of the Military elective there during the 2006–7 academic year. Suzanne Nielsen and Don Snider provided cogent advice and criticism, as did other authors in this volume.

1. Other scholars had investigated this cultural clash, but as part of the larger concern about military displacement of civilian government. See Alfred Vagts, *A History of Militarism: Civilian and Military* (London: Hollis and Carter, 1959 [1937]); Harold D. Lasswell, "Sino-Japanese Crisis: The Garrison State versus the Civilian State," *China Quarterly* 11 (Fall 1937): 643–49; Harold D. Lasswell, "The Garrison State," *American Journal of Sociology* 46, no. 4 (January 1941): 455–68, both reprinted in Harold Lasswell, *Essays on the Garrison State*, ed. Jay Stanley (New Brunswick, NJ: Transaction Publishers, 1997), pp. 43–78. The best recent scholarly reviews of Huntington's work are by Huntington students Eliot A. Cohen, *Supreme Command: Soldiers, Statesmen, and Leadership in Wartime* (New York: Free Press, 2002); and Peter Feaver, *Armed Servants: Agency, Oversight, and Civil-Military Relations* (Cambridge, MA: Harvard University Press, 2003). See also the other chapters in this volume.

2. Samuel P. Huntington, *The Soldier and the State: The Theory and Politics of Civil-Military Relations* (Cambridge: Belknap Press of Harvard University Press, 1957), p. 80.

3. Huntington's key admission was: "The military mind, in this sense, consists of the values, attitudes, and perspectives which inhere in the performance of the professional military function and which are deducible from the nature of that function." Ibid., p. 61.

4. Allen Guttmann, *The Conservative Tradition in America* (New York: Oxford University Press, 1967), pp. 109, 110, 115. Cohen, *Supreme Command*, pp. 225–32, reprises Guttman's critique more fully. See also the famous essay published in 1952, before Huntington's book, by T. Harry Williams, "The Macs and the Ikes: America's Two Military Traditions," in *The Selected Essays of T. Harry Williams, with a Biographical Intro-*

duction by Estelle Williams (Baton Rouge: Louisiana State University Press, 1983), pp. 173–81. Significantly, writing just before Huntington, C. Wright Mills, *The Power Elite* (New York: Oxford University Press, 1956), chap. 9, put the military squarely within the American elite: "Historically the warlords have been only uneasy, poor relations within the American elite; now they are first cousins; soon they may become elder brothers." Ibid., p. 198.

5. Ellen Fitzpatrick, *History's Memory: Writing America's Past, 1880–1980* (Cambridge, MA: Harvard University Press, 2002), chap. 5, "The Myth of Consensus History." See also Howard Zinn, *The Politics of History,* 2d ed. (Urbana: University of Illinois Press, 1990), p. 239; Peter Charles Hoffer, *Past Imperfect: Facts, Fictions, Fraud—American History from Bancroft and Parkman to Ambrose, Bellesiles, Ellis, and Goodwin* (New York: Public Affairs, 2004), pp. 13–72 but particularly 44–61; Ian Tyrrell, *Historians in Public: The Practice of American History, 1890–1970* (Chicago: University of Chicago Press, 2005), pp. 237–38, 245–46; Leon F. Litwack, "Troubled in Mind: The Education of a Historian," *Proceedings of the American Antiquarian Society,* no. 116 (2006): 40–42; Sean Wilentz, "American Political Histories," *Magazine of History* 21, no. 2 (April 2007): 24–25. As Fitzpatrick demonstrates, Huntington's generalizations about liberalism would have generated heated disagreement among historians even in the mid-1950s. Today these statements would be rejected emphatically by an overwhelming majority of historians of the United States. "The American knows only liberalism. . . . The political ideology of Woodrow Wilson was essentially the same as that of Elbridge Gerry. Liberalism in the United States has been unchanging, monotonous, and all-embracing. . . . Steady economic growth diluted class conflict. There were few struggles over the distribution of the pie because the pie was always growing larger. No nascent group ever developed a radical ideology challenging the established order: it was always too quickly assimilated into that order. . . . Radicalism and conservatism were equally superfluous. . . . In the absence of European feudalism, European classes, and a European proletariat, political struggle in America was restricted to squabbles for limited objectives among interest groups all of whom shared the same basic values. . . . Not only did every group in American society normally feel economically secure but also American society as a whole normally felt politically secure. American awareness of the role of power in domestic politics was dulled by the absence of class conflict. American awareness of the role of power in foreign politics was dulled by the absence of external threats." Huntington, *The Soldier and the State,* pp. 144–45.

6. John M. Gates, "The Alleged Isolation of U.S. Army Officers in the Late-19th Century," *Parameters* 10, no. 3 (September1980): 32–45. Robert P. Wettemann Jr., "A Part or Apart: The Alleged Isolation of Antebellum U.S. Army Officers," *American Nineteenth Century History* 7, no. 2 (June 2006): 193–217, suggests that isolation increased in the 1840s but notes considerable interaction before then.

7. William B. Skelton, *An American Profession of Arms: The Army Officer Corps, 1784–1861* (Lawrence: University Press of Kansas, 1992).

8. Christopher McKee, *A Gentlemanly and Honorable Profession: The Creation of the U.S. Naval Officer Corps, 1795–1815* (Annapolis, MD: Naval Institute Press, 1991).

9. Huntington, *The Soldier and the State*, pp. 2–3. See Woodward's 1960 essay in the *American Historical Review*, subsequently revised, "The Age of Reinterpretation," in C. Vann Woodward, *The Future of the Past* (New York: Oxford University Press, 1989), pp. 75–99.

10. See Richard H. Kohn, "The Constitution and National Security: The Intent of the Framers," in Richard H. Kohn, ed., *The United States Military under the Constitution of the United States, 1789–1989* (New York: New York University Press, 1991), pp. 61–94.

11. Huntington, *The Soldier and the State*, p. 7.

12. David C. King and Zachary Karabell, *The Generation of Trust: Public Confidence in the U. S. Military since Vietnam* (Washington, DC: AEI Press, 2003). For the recent rise of the military and its role in American society, see Andrew J. Bacevich, *American Empire: The Realities and Consequences of U. S. Diplomacy* (Cambridge, MA: Harvard University Press, 2002), especially chaps. 5–7; Andrew J. Bacevich, *The New American Militarism How Americans Are Seduced by War* (New York: Oxford University Press, 2005), especially chap. 2; Dale R. Herspring, *The Pentagon and the Presidency: Civil-Military Relations from FDR to George W. Bush* (Lawrence: University Press of Kansas, 2005); Charles A. Stevenson, *Warriors and Politicians: U.S. Civil-Military Relations under Stress* (New York: Routledge, Taylor and Francis Group, 2006).

13. Lawrence S. Kaplan, Ronald D. Landa, and Edward J. Drea, *The McNamara Ascendancy, 1961–1965*, vol. 5: *History of the Office of the Secretary of Defense* (Washington, DC: Historical Office, Office of the Secretary of Defense, 2006). I am indebted to Dr. Alfred Goldberg, Office of the Secretary of Defense historian, for alerting me to the publication of the volume and permitting me to review the next volume on McNamara in draft in his office.

14. See Theodore H. White, "An Inside Report on Robert McNamara's Revolution in the Pentagon," *Look*, April 23, 1963; David S. Cloud, "Rumsfeld Also Plays Hardball on Squash Courts," *New York Times*, September 24, 2006; "The Rumsfeld War: Squash as Metaphor (2 Letters)," ibid., letters to the editor, September 26, 2006.

15. A comparison of McNamara and Rumsfeld is presented in Caitlin Talmadge, "Transforming the Pentagon: McNamara, Rumsfeld and the Politics of Change," *Breakthroughs* (MIT Security Studies Program), no. 15 (Spring 2006): 12–20. McNamara's first four years in office are described overall in Kaplan, Landa, and Drea, *McNamara Ascendancy*, chaps. 1, 2, 20. See also Deborah Shapley, *Promise and Power: The Life and Times of Robert McNamara* (Boston: Little, Brown, 1993). Defenses of and attacks on Rumsfeld include Midge Decter, *Rumsfeld: A Personal Portrait* (New York: ReganBooks, 2003); Rowan Scarborough, *Rumsfeld's War: The Untold Story of America's Anti-Terrorist Commander* (Washington, DC: Regnery Publishing, 2004); Andrew Cockburn, *Rumsfeld: His Rise, Fall, and Catastrophic Legacy* (New York: Scribner, 2007); and Dale R. Herspring, *Rumsfeld's Wars: The Arrogance of Power* (Lawrence:

University Press of Kansas, 2008). For his emphasis on civilian control, see, "Rumsfeld's Rules," rev. ed., January 17, 2001, www.defenselink.mil/news/jan2001/rumsfeldsrules.pdf, or February 1, 2007, pp. 8–9, library.villanova.edu/vbl/bweb/rumsfeldsrules.pdf. An attempt at a balanced portrait is Robert D. Kaplan, "What Rumsfeld Got Right: How Donald Rumsfeld Remade the U.S. Military for a More Uncertain World," *Atlantic Monthly*, July–August 2008, www.theatlantic.com/doc/200807/rumsfeld. For the diminution of civilian control after 1945, see D. W. Brogan, "The United States: Civilian and Military Power," in Michael Howard, ed., *Soldiers and Governments: Nine Studies in Civil-Military Relations* (London: Eyre and Spottiswoode, 1957), pp. 167–85; Richard H. Kohn, "Out of Control: The Crisis in Civil-Military Relations," *National Interest*, no. 35 (Spring 1994): 3–17; Richard H. Kohn, "The Erosion of Civilian Control of the Military in the United States Today," *Naval War College Review* 55, no. 3 (Summer 2002): 8–59; and Andrew J. Bacevich, "Elusive Bargain: The Pattern of U.S. Civil-Military Relations since World War II," in Andrew J. Bacevich, ed., *The Long War: A New History of U.S. National Security Policy since World War II* (New York: Columbia University Press, 2007), pp. 207–64.

16. James A. Baker III and Lee H. Hamilton, co-chairs, et al., *The Iraq Study Group Report* (New York: Vintage Books, 2006), 77. Robert Gates promised a more consultative relationship: "As the President has asked for my unvarnished advice, I expect the same of you. . . . The key to successful leadership, in my view, is to involve in the decision making process, early and often, those who ultimately must carry out the decisions." Gates, Message to Department of Defense Personnel, December 18, 2006, www.defenselink.mil/speeches/speech.aspx?speechid=1081. The consensus, echoed by the *New York Times*, was that the senior military had refused "to stand up to the bullying and ideological blindness of . . . Rumsfeld." Editorial, "Good Choice for the Chiefs," *New York Times*, June 13, 2007, p. A22. See also Michael Desch, "Bush and the Generals," *Foreign Affairs* 86, no. 3 (May–June 2007): 97–108; Richard B. Myers and Richard H. Kohn, "The Military's Place," *Foreign Affairs* 86, no. 5 (September–October 2007): 147–49.

17. Cohen, *Supreme Command*, chap. 7.

18. "Exercise of Power in the U.S. Government," enclosure in Lt. General V. P. Mock, DCSOPS, "Memorandum For: Chief of Staff, U. S. Army," n.d. (circa March 1966), Harold K. Johnson Papers, U.S. Army Military History Institute, Carlisle, PA. I am indebted to Dr. Edward Drea of the Historical Office, Office of the Secretary of Defense, for bringing this document and another, also from the Harold K. Johnson Papers, and a third from the Lyndon Baines Johnson Library, cited later, to my attention and for sharing copies.

19. "Extract of Remarks by General J. P. McConnell, Chief of Staff, USAF, New General Officer Orientation, Headquarters, USAF, Tuesday, 2 May 1967," enclosed in W. W. Rostow to the President, May 11, 1967, folder Walt Rostow, May 1–15, 1967, box 16, NSF memos to President, Walt Rostow, item no. 44, Lyndon Baines Johnson Library, Austin.

20. Woodring had adhered to the "principle . . . that military men, not civilian leaders, should make decisions on matters that were primarily military in nature"; he "wrote five years after leaving office that: 'leaving the military decisions to the General Staff' was justified because civilians did not know more than professional military strategists who made it a life study and profession." Keith D. McFarland, *Harry H. Woodring: A Political Biography of FDR's Controversial Secretary of War* (Lawrence: University Press of Kansas, 1975), pp. 139, 114, 115.

21. Keith D. McFarland and David L. Roll, *Louis Johnson and the Arming of America: The Roosevelt and Truman Years* (Bloomington: Indiana University Press, 2005), pp. 360–61.

22. The most complete analysis of the event is Jeffrey G. Barlow, *Revolt of the Admirals: The Fight for Naval Aviation, 1945–1950* (Washington, DC: Naval Historical Center, 1994).

23. Douglas MacArthur, *Reminiscences* (New York: McGraw-Hill, 1964), p. 101.

24. Marriner Eccles, *Beckoning Frontiers: Public and Personal Recollections*, ed. Sidney Hyman (New York: Knopf, 1951), p. 336.

25. Robert J. Watson, *History of the Office of the Secretary of Defense*, vol. 4: *Into the Missile Age, 1956–1960* (Washington, DC: Historical Office, Office of the Secretary of Defense, 1997), p. 775. See also A. J. Bacevich, "The Paradox of Professionalism: Eisenhower, Ridgway, and the Challenge to Civilian Control, 1953–1955," *Journal of Military History* 61, no. 2 (April 1997): 303–33; Donald Alan Carter, "Eisenhower versus the Generals," *Journal of Military History* 71, no. 4 (October 2007): 1169–99.

26. Lieutenant General Charles G. Cooper, U.S. Marine Corps (ret.), with Richard E. Goodspeed, *Cheers and Tears: A Marine's Story of Combat in Peace and War* (Victoria, BC: Trafford Publishing, 2002), pp. 4–5.

27. "Exercise of Power in the U.S. Government," p. 25.

28. An excellent analysis of the differences and their implications is "The Soldier and the Statesman," in Cohen, *Supreme Command*, chap. 1.

29. For a good example of how such issues regularly caused conflict, see John D. Mini, "Conflict, Cooperation, and Congressional End-Runs: The Defense Budget and Civil Military Relations in the Carter Administration, 1977–1978" (M.A. thesis, University of North Carolina at Chapel Hill, 2007).

30. See Kohn, "The Erosion of Civilian Control," p. 51n75.

31. For the standing of the military with the public, see King and Karabell, *Generation of Trust*.

32. Christopher P. Gibson and Don M. Snider, "Civil-Military Relations and the Potential to Influence: A Look at the National Security Decision-Making Process," *Armed Forces and Society* 25, no. 2 (Winter 1999): 193–218.

33. This argument is in Kohn, "The Erosion of Civilian Control."

34. Memorandum, Charles Bonesteel to Harold K. Johnson, "Increasing Centralization in the Office of the Secretary of Defense," Harold K. Johnson Papers. Bonesteel, a Rhodes Scholar, was a highly respected soldier shortly thereafter pro-

moted to full general. See the eulogy by Dean Rusk in *Assembly,* no. 36 (March 1978): 18, 110.

35. A recent survey of secretaries of defense is Charles A. Stevenson, *SECDEF: The Nearly Impossible Job of Secretary of Defense* (Washington, DC: Potomac, 2006).

36. Former chairman of the Joint Chiefs General Richard B. Myers emphasized the primacy of trust in the relationship in an interview on National Public Radio with reporter Tom Bowman, September 26, 2007, www.npr.org/templates/story/story.php ?storyId=14707004.

37. Colonel Lloyd J. Matthews, *The Political-Military Rivalry for Operational Control in U.S. Military Actions: A Soldier's Perspective* (Carlisle, PA: Strategic Studies Institute, U.S. Army War College, June 22, 1998), pp. 20–26, 30–32, 34–35 (emphasis in original).

38. Robert Gates, "Evening Lecture at West Point," April 21, 2008, www.defense link.mil/speeches/speech.aspx?speechid-1232.

39. A thoughtful discussion of public statements by serving senior officers is Major General Charles J. Dunlap Jr., USAF, "Voices from the Stars? America's Generals and Public Debates," *American Bar Association National Security Law Report,* no. 28 (November 2006): 8–11. General Dunlap is deputy judge advocate general of the U.S. Air Force and a prominent civil-military relations scholar.

40. The statutory language pertaining to the Joint Chiefs of Staff reads: "(f) Recommendations to Congress.—After first informing the Secretary of Defense, a member of the Joint Chiefs of Staff may make such recommendations to Congress relating to the Department of Defense as he considers appropriate." Title 10, U.S. Code, Chapter 5, Section 151 (f), frwebgate.access.gpo.gov/cgi-bin/getdoc.cgi?dbname=browse_ usc&docid=Cite:+10USC151. The point about forthright testimony to Congress is made in Marybeth P. Ulrich and Martin L. Cook, "U.S. Civil Military Relations since 9/11: Issues in Ethics and Policy Development," *Journal of Military Ethics* 5, no. 3 (November 2006): 161–82.

41. See, for example, "Lawmakers Concerned Generals Are Silenced on End Strength Topic," *Inside the Army,* July 18, 2005, p. 1; Damon Coletta, "Courage in the Service of Virtue: The Case of General Shinseki's Testimony before the Iraq War," *Armed Forces and Society* 34, no. 1 (October 2007): 109–21, argues that General Shinseki should have avoided public disagreement with his superiors on troop requirements for the occupation of Iraq when testifying before Congress in early 2003. I find his reasoning weak. See chapter 3 by Matthew Moten in this volume.

42. Paul Gronke and Peter D. Feaver, "Uncertain Confidence: Civilian and Military Attitudes about Civil-Military Relations," in Peter Feaver and Richard H. Kohn, eds., *Soldiers and Civilians: The Civil Military Gap and American National Security* (Cambridge, MA: MIT Press, 2001), pp. 154–57. For the survey question (number 49), see p. 490. The dataset is archived and publicly available at the Odum Institute at the University of North Carolina, Chapel Hill. For information, see 152.2.32.107/odum/jsp/ content_node.jsp?nodeid'7.

43. Ole R. Holsti, "Of Chasms and Convergences: Attitudes and Beliefs of Civilians

and Military Elites at the Start of a New Millennium," in Feaver and Kohn, *Soldiers and Civilians*, pp. 27–32, 96–99; and James A. Davis, "Attitudes and Opinions among Senior Military Officers and a U.S. Cross-Section, 1998–1999," ibid., pp. 104–7.

44. "United States Naval Academy Commencement: As Delivered by Secretary of Defense Robert M. Gates, Annapolis, Maryland, Friday, May 25, 2007," www .defenselink.mil/speeches/speech.aspx?speechid=1154; "Remarks as Delivered by Secretary of Defense Robert M. Gates, Colorado Springs, Colorado, Wednesday, May 30, 2007," www.defenselink.mil/speeches/speech.aspx?speechid=1157.

45. Michael S. Mullen, "CJCS Guidance for 2007–2008," October 1, 2007, www.jcs.mil/CJCS_GUIDANCE.pdf. See also Mullen's plea to the military to be non-political: "From the Chairman: Military Must Stay Apolitical," *Joint Force Quarterly*, no. 50 (Summer 2008): 2–3.

46. Conversation between the author and a three-star general, Washington, DC, January 1995.

47. On February 28, 2003, I moderated an evening seminar of the Triangle Institute for Security Studies in Chapel Hill, North Carolina, when General Myers said that the terrorist threat was the most dangerous the United States faced since the Civil War; I discussed that statement with him the next morning. In the first Defense Department Town Meeting, June 29, 2005, beamed worldwide on the Pentagon's cable channel, Myers called terrorism "perhaps the most serious threat we've ever faced to our way of life and our—freedoms that we hold dear," www.defenselink.mil/ transcripts/transcript.aspx?transcriptid=3248. See also Sergeant Sara Wood, "Pentagon Holds First Worldwide Town Hall Meeting," June 29, 2005, www.defenselink .mil/news/newsarticle.aspx?id=16261.

48. George C. Herring, *America's Longest War: The United States and Vietnam, 1950–1975*, 3d ed. (New York: McGraw-Hill, 1996), p. 199; and Robert Dallek, *Flawed Giant: Lyndon Johnson and His Times, 1961–1973* (New York: Oxford University Press, 1998), pp. 468, 491, 498, 504.

49. Colin L. Powell, "Why Generals Get Nervous," *New York Times*, October 8, 1992, query.nytimes.com/gst/fullpage.html?res=9E0CEFD8163BF93BA35753C1A96 4958260&sec. David Petraeus, "Battling for Iraq," *Washington Post*, September 26, 2004, p. B07. For an analysis critical of Powell, see Russell F. Weigley, "The American Military and the Principle of Civilian Control from McClellan to Powell," *Journal of Military History* 57, no. 5 (October 1993): 28–30.

50. Thomas E. Ricks, "Exchanges: Leave Politics to Us, Warner Tells General," *Washington Post*, January 24, 2007; p. A21, and subsequent public comments www .washingtonpost.com/ac2/wp-dyn/comments/display?contentID=AR2007012301306.

51. General Peter Pace et al. to Philip Bennett, January 31, 2006, Pace to Reggie B. Walton, May 21, 2007, copy attached in e-mail to the author, July 27, 2007. The documents, available on the Internet, animated the blogosphere to accuse General Pace of being partisan.

52. Quotations are from Peter Baker, "Daily Politics Discussion," June 19, 2007, www.washingtonpost.com/wp-dyn/content/discussion/2007/06/15/DI20070615018

23.html; Paul Krugman, "All the President's Enablers," *New York Times*, July 20, 2007, p. A23; Christopher Gelpi, "Let's End the Charade," *News and Observer* (Raleigh, NC), September 17, 2007, p. 17A; Andrew J. Bacevich, "Sycophant Savior: General Petraeus Wins a Battle in Washington—if Not in Baghdad," *American Conservative*, October 8, 2007, www.amconmag.com/2007/2007_10_08/print/coverprint.html; and Julian E. Barnes, "Military wants more view on Iraq reports: September's assessment put too much focus on Gen. Petraeus, say officials concerned about war's effect on public support," *Los Angeles Times*, November 26, 2007, www.latimes.com/news/printedition/front/la-na-trust26nov26,1,7684143.story. Also see Congressman John Murtha on MSNBC *Hardball*, May 1, 2007, www.youtube.com/watch?v=SZJOsWXVnSQ; Thomas E. Ricks, "Bush Leans on Petraeus as War Dissent Deepens; General Set Up as Scapegoat, Some Say," July 15, 2007, *Washington Post*, p. A7; Frank Rich, "Who Really Took Over during that Colonoscopy," *New York Times*, July 29, 2007, p. 10wk; Andrew J. Bacevich, "The Overhyping of David Petraeus: Army of One," *New Republic* 237, no. 3 (August 6, 2007): 18–19; Lawrence J. Korb, "Political General," *Foreign Affairs* 86, no. 5 (September–October 2007): 152–53. A balanced analysis is John F. Burns, "For Top General in Iraq, Role Is a Mixed Blessing," *New York Times*, August 14, 2007, p. A6. For statements by Petraeus and subordinate commanders, see "Petraeus: Increased U.S. Troops Yielding Results," *All Things Considered*, July 19, 2007, National Public Radio, www.npr.org/templates/story/story.php?storyId=12099511; John Burns, "U.S. General in Iraq Speaks Strongly against Troop Pullout," and Thom Shanker and David S. Cloud, "U.S. Generals Request Delay in Judging Iraq: But Lawmakers Reject Waiting to November," *New York Times*, July 16, 20, 2007, pp. A6, A1; Robert Burns and Lolita C. Baldor, "Generals Want No Cuts in Iraq until at Least 2008," *Arizona Daily Star* (Tucson), July 21, 2007, p. 1.

53. "A Letter from General Ridgway to the Secretary of Defense," June 27, 1955, in General Matthew B. Ridgway, USA (ret.), as told to Harold H. Martin, *Soldier: The Memoirs of Matthew B. Ridgway* (New York: Harper and Brothers, 1956), pp. 330–31.

54. See David Margolick, "The Military: The Night of the Generals," *Vanity Fair*, April 2007, www.vanityfair.com/politics/features/2007/04/iraqgenerals200704; Lieutenant General Greg Newbold (ret.), "Why Iraq Was a Mistake: A Military Insider Sounds Off against the War and the 'Zealots' Who Pushed It," *Time*, April 9, 2006; Richard J. Whalen, "Revolt of the Generals," *Nation*, October 16, 2006, www.thenation.com/doc/20061016/whalen.

55. The author attended that lecture and asked the general those questions.

56. Lieutenant General John H. Cushman, U.S. Army (ret.), "Planning and Early Execution of the War in Iraq: An Assessment of Military Participation," Program on Information Resources Policy, Harvard University, January 14, 2007, pp. 19–20, pirp.harvard.edu/pubs_pdf/cushman%5Ccushman-p07-1.pdf.

57. James H. Baker, "Military Professionalism: A Normative Code for the Long War," *Joint Force Quarterly*, no. 44 (Winter 2007): 72–73.

58. Among the scholars endorsing or encouraging the idea of "resignation" are Desch, "Bush and the Generals," 11; Leonard Wong and Douglas Lovelace, "Knowing

When to Salute," *Orbis* 52, no. 2 (Spring 2008): 278–88; Don M. Snider, *Dissent and Strategic Leadership of the Military Professions* (Carlisle, PA: Strategic Studies Institute, February 2008); Martin L. Cook, "Revolt of the Generals: A Case Study in Professional Ethics," *Parameters* 38, no. 1 (Spring 2008): 4–15; and Herspring, *Rumsfeld's Wars*, pp. 205–7.

59. Admiral Mike Mullen, Commencement Address, U.S. Naval Academy, Annapolis MD, May 23, 2008, www.jcs.mil/chairman/speeches/USNACommencement Address2008.html. Mullen expressed the same thought at the Army's Command and General Staff College. In response to a question about the state of civil-military relations, Mullen answered "that the civil/military relationship wherein the elective leaders of our country essentially make the policy decisions and from a security standpoint we carry them out, is bedrock solid. I believe those, particularly those of us on active duty need to carry out our orders and that if we are unable to belong to an organization that is carrying out those orders, then the proper response is to vote with our feet and leave." Address to Command and General Staff College Students, Fort Leavenworth, Kansas, October 23, 2007, www.jcs.mil/chairman/speeches/071023 Address_QA_CGSC.html.

60. George C. Marshall, *George C. Marshall Interviews and Reminiscences for Forrest C. Pogue*, ed. Larry I. Bland and Joellen K. Bland, with an introduction by Forrest C. Pogue, rev. ed. (Lexington, VA: George C. Marshall Research Foundation, 1991), p. 416.

61. General Ronald Fogleman retired a year early and left in silence; he did not resign but asked to be replaced because he believed he had lost his effectiveness. The decision was complicated and difficult for him. See Richard H. Kohn, ed., "The Early Retirement of General Ronald R. Fogleman, Chief of Staff, United States Air Force," *Aerospace Power Journal* 15, no. 1 (Spring 2001): 6–23. For a thoughtful discussion of resignation as well as other civil-military behaviors, see Mackubin Thomas Owens, "Rumsfeld, the Generals, and the State of U.S. Civil-Military Relations," *Naval War College Review* 59, no. 4 (Autumn 2006): 68–80.

62. See the argument and questions of Richard Swain, "Reflection on an Ethic of Officership," *Parameters* 37, no. 1 (Spring 2007): 18–20.

63. See the remarks by General Charles G. Boyd, USAF (ret.), Air University Graduation Address, May 25, 2006, www.airwarcollegealumni.org/8455.html; Whalen, "Revolt of the Generals"; Margolick, "Night of the Generals"; advertisements by retired army Major Generals Paul Eaton and John Batiste (directed toward Senators Susan Collins and John Sununu), VoteVets.Org, www.votevets.org/index .php?option=com_content&task=view&id=289&Itemid=102; Thom Shanker, "Army Career behind Him, General Speaks Out on Iraq," *New York Times*, May 13, 2007, p. 16.

64. "Transcript: Democratic Response to President Bush's Radio Address," November 25, 2007, www.foxnews.com/story/0,2933,312735,00.html. For the address by Lieutenant General Ricardo Sanchez to military reporters and editors, October 12, 2007, see www.militaryreporters.org/sanchez_101207.html. Sanchez has also published a memoir before the Bush administration left office.

65. E-mail, Colonel Zane Finkelstein, USA (ret.) to author, November 15, 2006. Colonel Finkelstein, who served as General Vessey's staff judge advocate when the general headed Combined Forces Command Korea in the late 1970s and advised him occasionally during his later assignments, has confirmed the incident with the general.

66. Neil King Jr., "The Courting of General Jones: Candidates from Both Parties Woo Policy-Savvy Ex-Marine," *Wall Street Journal,* April 23, 2007, p. 6.

67. "Walter Scott's Personality Parade," *Parade: The Sunday Newspaper Magazine,* April 8, 2007, p. 4. For the involvement of four-star officers in recent presidential campaigns, see Erik Riker-Coleman, "Breaking with Marshall? The Apolitical Ideal and the Reality of Increased Partisanship among the Senior Military Elite, 1968–Present," paper presented at the Society for Military History Annual Meeting, Ogden, Utah, April 19, 2008.

68. John Barry, Richard Wolffe, and Evan Thomas, "Stealth Warrior," *Newsweek,* March 19, 2007, www.msnbc.msn.com/id/17554602/site/newsweek/page/0/; Thom Shanker and Mark Mazzetti, "New Defense Chief Eases Relations Rumsfeld Bruised," *New York Times,* March 12, 2007, p. 6.

69. This is the argument of Cohen, *Supreme Command.*

70. Fred Kaplan, "The Professional: Defense Secretary Robert Gates Is the Anti-Rumsfeld," *New York Times Magazine,* February 10, 2008, p. 92.

71. On the issue of whether military officers have the broad political picture in mind, see "Transcript: Confirmation Hearing of Robert Gates to Be Secretary of Defense," *Washington Post,* media.washingtonpost.com/wp-srv/politics/documents/rgates_hearing_120506.html; Cohen, *Supreme Command,* pp. 8–10. Desch, "Bush and the Generals," pp. 106, 108, recommends a kind of reflexive deference by civilians to the military, although he denies this in "Desch Replies," *Foreign Affairs* 86, no. 5 (September–October 2007): 156.

72. *Greer v. Spock,* 424 U. S. 828 (March 24, 1976).

73. Ridgway to Secretary of Defense, June 27, 1955, in Ridgway, *Soldier,* p. 331.

74. Barry, "Stealth Warrior"; Gordon Lubold, "The Un-Rumsfeld: Robert Gates's Way at Defense," *Christian Science Monitor,* March 19, 2007, p. 1.

75. CBS News, "Face the Nation," March 18, 2007, www.cbsnews.com/htdocs/pdf/face_031807.pdf; "Gates Mum on Call for Pace Apology," *USA Today,* March 19, 2007, p. 5; Josh White and Thomas E. Ricks, "Joint Chiefs Chairman Will Bow Out," *Washington Post,* June 9, 2007, p. A1; Mark Perry, "Gates' Way Forward, Part 1: After Rumsfeld, a New Dawn?" *Asia Times,* June 19, 2007, www.atimes.com/atime/Middle_East/IF2-Ak07.html; "Gates' Way Forward, Part 2: A Clean Sweep?" ibid., June 20, 2007, www.atimes.com/atime/Middle_East/IF2-Ak02.html; Gates News Briefing, June 5, 2008, www.defenselink.mil/transcripts/transcript.aspx?transcriptid=4236; Gates, "Remarks to Airmen and Women (Langley, VA)," June 9, 2008, www.defenselink.mil/speeches/speech.aspx?speechid=1256; Rowan Scarborough, "Air Force Firings Followed Budget Battle: Spending, Future Capabilities Split Gates, Top Brass," *Washington Times,* June 15, 2008, p. 1.

76. Feaver, *Armed Servants.*

77. Marshall, *George C. Marshall Interviews and Reminiscences*, p. 297. Marshall pointed out that his staff, at the time (1940), "spent their time trying to force me to take open action contrary to the administration, which I declined to do." Ibid., p. 304.

78. Quoted in Stewart W. Husted, *George C. Marshall: The Rubrics of Leadership* (n.p. [Carlisle, PA]: n.p. [U.S. Army War College Foundation], 2006), pp. 187, 215.

79. Quoted in Stevenson, *Warriors and Politicians*, p. 98.

80. Forrest C. Pogue, "George C. Marshall on Civil Military Relationships," in Kohn, *U.S. Military under the Constitution*, p. 205. Secretary of Defense Gates discussed Marshall at length, endorsing him "as a textbook model of the way military officers should handle disagreements with superiors and in particular with the civilians vested with control of the armed forces under our Constitution." See Gates, "Evening Lecture at West Point."

81. Quoted in Eric Larrabee, *Commander in Chief: Franklin Delano Roosevelt, His Lieutenants, and Their War* (New York: HarperCollins, 1987), p. 644.

82. See the summary in Stevenson, *Warriors and Politicians*, pp. 106–13.

83. Conversation with the author, February 2007, Carlisle, Pennsylvania.

84. Robert D. Kaplan, "Looking the World in the Eye," *Atlantic Monthly*, December 2008, p. 70.

85. Telford Taylor, "Review of *The Soldier and the State*," *Yale Law Journal* 67 (1957): 164, 167.

CHAPTER FOURTEEN: Conclusions

1. Samuel P. Huntington, *The Soldier and the State: The Theory and Politics of Civil-Military Relations* (Cambridge, MA: Belknap Press of Harvard University Press, 1957), p. 2.

2. Carl von Clausewitz, *On War*, trans. and ed. Michael Howard and Peter Paret (Princeton, NJ: Princeton University Press, 1976), p. 111.

3. See Eliot A. Cohen, *Supreme Command: Soldiers, Statesmen, and Leadership in Wartime* (New York: Free Press, 2002).

4. See Richard K. Betts, *Soldiers, Statesmen, and Cold War Crises* (New York: Columbia University Press, 1991).

5. Huntington, *The Soldier and the State*, p. 11.

6. Ibid., p. 56.

7. Clausewitz, *On War*, p. 177.

8. Ibid., p. 87.

9. Huntington, *The Soldier and the State*, p. 2.

10. Ibid., p. 36.

11. Ibid., pp. 56–57.

12. Ibid., pp. 83–84.

13. The best scholarly treatment of this subject, an ambitious project in which several of the authors in the present volume also participated, is Peter D. Feaver and Richard H. Kohn, eds., *Soldiers and Civilians: The Civil-Military Gap and American Na-*

tional Security (Cambridge MA: BCSIA Studies in International Security, MIT Press, 2001).

14. See, for example, Don M. Snider, "An Uninformed Debate on Military Culture," *Orbis* 43, no. 1 (Winter 1999): 11–26.

15. Huntington, *The Soldier and the State*, p. 84.

16. Don M. Snider, "The Army as Profession," in Don M. Snider and Lloyd J. Matthews, eds., *The Future of the Army Profession*, 2d ed., rev. and exp. (New York: McGraw-Hill Primis, 2005), pp. 11–12.

17. Christopher Gibson and Don M. Snider, "Civil-Military Relations and the Potential to Influence: A Look at the National-Security Decision Making Process," *Armed Forces and Society* 25, no. 2 (Winter 1999): 193–218.

18. Of course, members of Congress might push a military witness to embrace an administration's policy on grounds that extend beyond the military officer's particular responsibilities. This would constitute another form of politicization.

Contributors

Richard K. Betts is the Arnold A. Saltzman Professor and Director of the Saltzman Institute of War and Peace Studies at Columbia University. He has taught at Harvard University and the Nitze School of Advanced International Studies at Johns Hopkins University and was a Senior Fellow at the Brookings Institution. He has been Director of National Security Studies at the Council on Foreign Relations and served long ago on the staffs of the original Senate Select Committee on Intelligence (the Church Committee), the National Security Council, and the Mondale presidential campaign. For six years in the 1990s he was a member of the National Security Advisory Panel of the Director of Central Intelligence and in 1999–2000 he was a member of the National Commission on Terrorism (the Bremer Commission). Betts has published numerous articles on U.S. foreign policy, military strategy, intelligence operations, security issues in Asia and Europe, terrorism, and other subjects, and is the author of five books—*Soldiers, Statesmen, and Cold War Crises; Surprise Attack; Nuclear Blackmail and Nuclear Balance; Military Readiness;* and *Enemies of Intelligence*—and coauthor or editor of *The Irony of Vietnam; Cruise Missiles: Technology, Strategy, and Politics; Conflict After the Cold War;* and *Paradoxes of Strategic Intelligence.*

Risa A. Brooks is assistant professor of political science at Northwestern University. She specializes in issues related to civil-military relations, military effectiveness, Middle East politics, and terrorist organizations. She is author of *Shaping Strategy: The Civil-Military Politics of Strategic Assessment* (2008) and editor (with Elizabeth Stanley) of *Creating Military Power: The Sources of Military Effectiveness* (2007). Her prior professional experiences include serving as a postdoctoral fellow at Stanford University's Center for International Security and Cooperation; research associate at the International Institute for Strategic Studies, London; and affiliation with Harvard University's Olin Institute for Strategic Studies.

James Burk is professor of sociology at Texas A&M University where he studies and teaches courses in social theory and civil-military relations. He received his B.S. from Towson University, and his M.A. and Ph.D. from the University of Chicago. Before joining Texas A&M in 1983, he taught for two years at Mc-Gill University. He is on the editorial board and has served as editor of the journal *Armed Forces and Society,* has been a consulting editor for the *American Journal of Sociology,* and has chaired the Peace, War, and Social Conflict Section of the American Sociological Association. His most recent publication is "The Changing Moral Contract for Military Service," in Andrew Bacevich, ed., *The Long War: America's Quest for Security since World War II* (forthcoming).

Karin De Angelis is a graduate student at the University of Maryland, College Park, specializing in military sociology. She served as a personnel officer in the United States Air Force from 2000–2006 with assignments in the Washington, D.C., area, northern Italy, and Qatar. She holds a Bachelor of Arts in sociology from the University of Chicago. Her current research includes a qualitative analysis of the U.S. Air Force Academy's response to past sexual assault complaints and the impact of this response on the organization's culture.

Michael C. Desch is the founding Director of the Scowcroft Institute of International Affairs and the first holder of the Robert M. Gates Chair in Intelligence and National Security Decision-Making at the George Bush School of Government and Public Service at Texas A&M University. He has also been Professor and Director of the Patterson School of Diplomacy and International Commerce at the University of Kentucky; Assistant Director and Senior Research Associate at the Olin Institute; a John M. Olin Postdoctoral Fellow in National Security at Harvard University's Olin Institute for Strategic Studies; a member of the political science faculty at the University of California, Riverside; and a visiting scholar at the Center for International Studies at the University of Southern California. He received his B.A. with honors in political science from Marquette University and his A.M. in international relations and Ph.D. in political science from the University of Chicago. He is the author, most recently, of *Power and Military Effectiveness: The Fallacy of Democratic Triumphalism;* as well as *When the Third World Matters: Latin America and U.S. Grand Strategy;* and *Civilian Control of the Military: The Changing Security Environment;* coeditor of *From Pirates to Drug Lords: The Post-Cold War Caribbean Security Environment,* and editor of *Soldiers in Cities: Military Operations on Urban Terrain.* He has published widely in scholarly journals such as *Foreign Affairs, International Organization, International Security,* and *Ethics.* He has served on the editorial boards of *International Security* and *Security Studies.* He is a frequent commentator in the press and on radio and television. His other experience includes work on the staff of a U.S. senator, in the Bureau of Intelligence and Research at the Department of State, and in the Foreign Affairs and National Defense Division of the Congressional Research Service.

Darrell W. Driver is a major and strategic plans and policy officer in the U.S. Army. He is currently serving as the Director of Plans and Strategy for the George C. Marshall European Center for Security Studies in Garmisch, Germany. His previous assignment was as an assistant professor of political science at the United States Military Academy at West Point, New York. At the Marshall Center and West Point, Major Driver has taught courses in National Security Strategy, American politics, and public policy. His publications include articles and book chapters in the areas of political science education, civil-military relations, and defense policy. He holds a Bachelor of Arts degree from the University of Notre Dame in South Bend, Indiana, and a Masters degree and Ph.D. in political science from Syracuse University. Major Driver's early Army assignments were as an Infantry officer, serving in the Army's 25th Infantry Division in Schofield Barracks, Hawaii, and in the 101st Airborne Division in Fort Campbell, Kentucky.

Peter D. Feaver is the Alexander F. Hehmeyer Professor of Political Science and Public Policy at Duke University and Director of the Triangle Institute for Security Studies (TISS). He received his Ph.D. from Harvard University and is the author of *Armed Servants: Agency, Oversight, and Civil-Military Relations* (2003) and of *Guarding the Guardians: Civilian Control of Nuclear Weapons in the United States* (1992). He is coauthor with Christopher Gelpi of *Choosing Your Battles: American Civil-Military Relations and the Use of Force* (2004), and with Christopher Gelpi and Jason Reifler of *Paying the Human Costs of War* (forthcoming). With Richard H. Kohn, he coedited *Soldiers and Civilians: The Civil-Military Gap and American National Security* (2001). He has published widely on American foreign policy, public opinion, nuclear proliferation, civil-military relations, information warfare, and U.S. national security. From June 2005 to July 2007, Feaver was on leave from Duke to serve as Special Advisor for Strategic Planning and Institutional Reform on the National Security Council Staff at the White House.

Christopher P. Gibson, a colonel in the U.S. Army, commands one of the Army's Brigade Combat Teams in Iraq. He recently served as a War College Fellow with the Hoover Institution at Stanford University. Prior to that he commanded 2nd Battalion, 325th Airborne of the 82nd Airborne, an assignment that included two tours to Iraq in support of three national elections there. Earlier he fought in the Persian Gulf War, served in the NATO peace enforcement operation to Kosovo, taught American politics at West Point, and served two liaison tours with the U.S. Congress, one as a Congressional Fellow. His M.P.A., M.A., and Ph.D. in government were awarded by Cornell University, and he was the Distinguished Honor Graduate of the U.S. Army Command and General Staff College. His awards and decorations include the Legion of Merit, three Bronze Star Medals, a Purple Heart, the Combat Infantryman's Badge with Star, and the Ranger Tab.

Richard H. Kohn is Professor of History and of Peace, War, and Defense at the University of North Carolina at Chapel Hill. He was Omar N. Bradley Professor of Strategic Leadership at the U.S. Army War College and Dickinson College, Carlisle, Pennsylvania, during the 2006–7 academic year. A specialist in American military history and civil-military relations, Kohn has written and edited, usually with colleagues, numerous books. His 1997 coauthored book, *The Exclusion of Black Soldiers from the Medal of Honor in World War II*, resulted in the retroactive award of seven Medals of Honor. His most recent book, coedited with Peter D. Feaver, *Soldiers and Civilians: The Civil-Military Gap and American National Security* (2001), was the result of a three-year investigation of differences between military and civilian attitudes and perspectives. His recent writings have focused on civilian control of the military, including "The Erosion of Civilian Control of the Military in the United States Today," which won the 2002 Edward S. Miller History Prize of the *Naval War College Review*. He is working on a study of presidential war leadership in American history and continuing his interest in civil-military relations.

Richard A. Lacquement Jr., U.S. Army, is currently assigned to the Army War College. Previously he served as a strategist in the Office of the Deputy Assistant Secretary of Defense for Stability Operations, where his duties focused on implementation of DoD Directive 3000.05, "Military Support to Stability, Security, Transition and Reconstruction Operations." He is an Army strategist and field artillery officer whose assignments have included U.S. Forces Korea, the 82nd Airborne Division, 1st Armored Division (including Desert Storm), 3rd

Infantry Division, and the 101st Airborne Division (Air Assault). He participated in Operation Iraqi Freedom as a strategist in the Army War Plans Division and in the 101st Airborne Division during operations in Northern Iraq.
He has also served as an assistant professor of social sciences at the United
States Military Academy and as Professor of Strategy and Policy at the U.S.
Naval War College. He is a graduate of the United States Military Academy,
has a Ph.D. in international relations from Princeton University, and a Masters
of Arts in national security and strategic studies from the Naval War College.
His areas of expertise include stability operations, counterinsurgency, interagency operations, professional military education, and doctrine. He is the author of *Shaping American Military Capabilities After the Cold War* (2003) and was
the lead author for the "Unity of Effort" chapter in the U.S. Army and Marine
Corps Field Manual 3-24, *Counterinsurgency.* He has also published widely on
defense transformation and stability operations.

Matthew Moten has been professor and deputy head of the Department of History
at the United States Military Academy, West Point, New York, since March
2006. He spent much of his previous career in armor and cavalry assignments.
In April 1999 he became speechwriter to the Chief of Staff, Army, General Eric
K. Shinseki, for whom he later served as legislative advisor. In 2002 Colonel
Moten was selected as an Academy Professor in the U.S. Military Academy De-
partment of History and was assigned as Chief, Military History Division.
From January to June of 2005, he served as deputy commanding officer, Dragon
Brigade, XVIII Airborne Corps and Task Force Dragon, Multi-National Corps,
Iraq. He holds a doctorate in history from Rice University and is author of *The
Delafield Commission and the American Military Profession.*

Williamson Murray is professor emeritus at The Ohio State University, Senior
Fellow at the Institute of Defense Analyses, and Class of 1957 Distinguished
Professor at the United States Naval Academy. He graduated from Yale University and earned his doctorate from Yale after serving in the United States
Air Force, including a tour in Southeast Asia. He has taught at Yale University and at The Ohio State University, as well as at the United States Military
Academy, the Air War College, the Naval War College, the Army War College,
and Marine Corps University. He has also been the Centennial Visiting Professor at the London School of Economics; a Secretary of the Navy Fellow at
the Naval War College; and the Horner Professor of Military Theory at the
Marine Corps University.

Suzanne C. Nielsen is the Director of the International Relations and National Security Studies program in the Department of Social Sciences at West Point. During the first half of 2008, Lieutenant Colonel Nielsen served in Iraq as the deputy director of the Commanding General's Initiatives Group. In academic year 2008–9 she was the U.S. Military Academy Fellow at the National War College in Washington, D.C. She has also served in the Republic of Korea, Germany, Bosnia, and on the staff of the director of the National Security Agency. A graduate of the U.S. Military Academy, she holds an M.A. and a Ph.D. in political science from Harvard University. Her dissertation, "Preparing for War: The Dynamics of Peacetime Military Reform," won the American Political Science Association's Lasswell Award for the best dissertation completed in the field of public policy in 2002–3. Her research interests also include civil-military relations and strategy. She has published a monograph, *Political Control over the Use of Force: A Clausewitzian Perspective*, as well as several chapters in *The Future of the Army Profession*, and articles in *Defence Studies*, *International Studies Perspective*, *Public Administration and Management*, and *Military Review*. She is also a coauthor of the sixth edition of *American National Security* to be published by Johns Hopkins University Press in 2009. She is a member of the Council on Foreign Relations.

Nadia Schadlow is a senior program officer in the International Security and Foreign Policy Program of the Smith Richardson Foundation, with responsibility for identifying strategic issues warranting further attention from the U.S. policy community and developing and managing programs and projects related to these issues. She was previously a Presidential Management Fellow at the Department of Defense and then a career civil servant in the Office of the Secretary of Defense. She received a B.A. in government and Soviet studies from Cornell University and M.A. and Ph.D. degrees from the John Hopkins Nitze School of Advanced International Studies. Her dissertation, "War and the Art of Governance: The U.S. Army's Role in Military Government from the Mexican War to Operation Just Cause," examines the U.S. Army's experiences with the reconstruction of states in times of war. Dr. Schadlow also serves as a consultant to the Department of Defense on a project related to the implementation of the Army's new stability operations doctrine. Her articles have appeared in *Parameters*, *American Interest*, the *Wall Street Journal*, and edited volumes.

Erika Seeler is a Ph.D. candidate in political science at Duke University. She received her M.A. with distinction in political science from Duke University and a B.A. from The Ohio State University with honors and distinction in political science and Japanese. Her dissertation examines the relationship between religion and regime type in world politics. Other research projects examine evangelical attitudes towards foreign policy; religion and violent extremism in world politics; and the role of reputation concerns in nuclear management.

David R. Segal is Distinguished Scholar-Teacher, Professor of Sociology, and Director of the Center for Research on Military Organization at the University of Maryland. He received his Ph.D. from the University of Chicago, and served on the faculty of the University of Michigan, and as a division chief at the Army Research Institute for the Behavioral and Social Sciences, before joining the Maryland faculty. His research has dealt with military organization, operations, manpower, and personnel.

Don M. Snider is Emeritus Professor of Political Science at West Point, from which he retired in 2008, and is a visiting research professor at the Army War College. He holds a doctorate in public policy from the University of Maryland and master's degrees in economics and in public policy from the University of Wisconsin. In addition to three combat tours in Vietnam as an infantryman followed by battalion command, he served as Chief of Plans for Theater Army in Europe, Joint Planner for the Army Chief of Staff, in the Office of the Chairman of the Joint Chiefs of Staff, and in the White House on the staff of the National Security Council; he retired from the Army in 1990 as a colonel. He has been the director of political-military research at the Center for Strategic and International Studies and was for three years the Olin Distinguished Professor of National Security Studies at West Point. His current research examines military innovation and adaptation, American civil-military relations, the identities and development of the American Army officer, and military professions. He was research director for and coeditor of *The Future of the Army Profession*, 2d ed. (2005), now a textbook at the Army War College and West Point. Recent publications include "Dissent and Strategic Leadership of Military Professions" (*Orbis*), and "Officership: The Professional Practice" (*Military Review*). The second edition of his book (with Lloyd J. Matthews), *Forging the Warrior's Character*, appeared in 2008. He is a member of the Council on Foreign Relations and serves on the Executive Committee of the Inter-University Seminar on Armed Forces and Society.

Index